Decentering Rushdie

Decentering Rushdie

Cosmopolitanism and the Indian Novel in English

Pranav Jani

THE OHIO STATE UNIVERSITY PRESS * COLUMBUS

Library of Congress Cataloging-in-Publication Data

Jani, Pranav, 1972–
    Decentering Rushdie : cosmopolitanism and the Indian novel in English / Pranav Jani.
        p. cm.
    Includes bibliographical references and index.
    ISBN 978-0-8142-1133-5 (cloth : alk. paper)—ISBN 978-0-8142-9232-7 (cd-rom)
    1. Indic fiction (English)—20th century—History and criticism. 2. Postcolonialism—
India. 3. Postcolonialism in literature. 4. Cosmopolitanism—India. 5. Cosmopolitanism
in literature. 6. Sahgal, Nayantara, 1927—Criticism and interpretation. 7. Markandaya,
Kamala, 1924—Criticism and interpretation. 8. Desai, Anita, 1937—Criticism and interpretation. 9. Rushdie, Salman—Criticism and interpretation. 10. Roy, Arundhati—Criticism and interpretation. I. Title.
    PR9492.6.P67J36 2010
    823'.91409954—dc22
                                            2010006109

This book is available in the following editions:
Cloth (ISBN 978-0-8142-1133-5)
CD-ROM (ISBN 978-0-8142-9232-7)

Cover design by Laurence J. Nozik
Text design by Juliet Williams
Type set in Adobe Sabon
Printed by Thomson-Shore, Inc.

♾ The paper used in this publication meets the minimum requirements of the American
National Standard for Information Sciences—Permanence of Paper for Printed Library
Materials. ANSI Z39.48-1992.

9 8 7 6 5 4 3 2 1

To my family and friends, forging homes across worlds

To Howard Zinn, who redefined home

contents

Acknowledgments   ix

Introduction   Looking Back   1

Chapter 1   The Multiple Cosmopolitanisms of the Indian Novel
in English   14

Chapter 2   Dawn of Freedom: *Namak-Halaal* Cosmopolitanisms in
A Time to Be Happy and *The Coffer Dams*   54

Chapter 3   Twilight Years: Women, Nation, and Interiority in
The Day in Shadow and *Clear Light of Day*   98

Chapter 4   After Midnight: Class and Nation in *Midnight's Children*
and *Rich Like Us*   141

Chapter 5   "*Naaley.* Tomorrow." Suffering and Redemption in
The God of Small Things   191

Conclusion   Looking Ahead   233

Notes   245

Works Cited   256

Index   268

acknowledgments

"To understand me," says the protagonist of *Midnight's Children* rather pompously, "you'll have to swallow a world." And so it is with books.

Neil Lazarus, Bill Keach, and Phil Rosen guided this manuscript through its first avatar as a dissertation at Brown University. Neil's scholarship in Postcolonial Studies has influenced every page. Bill's constant presence as an advisor and comrade has been tremendous.

Many colleagues at Ohio State gave careful and attentive feedback on the manuscript in various contexts, including Lékè Adéèkò, Frederick Aldama, Chad Allen, Jim Phelan, Mytheli Sreenivas, and Joel Wainwright. Special thanks to Chad and Jim for their extended engagements with the manuscript, their mentorship, and their friendship.

Helen Scott and Nagesh Rao, dear friends and comrades each, have tolerated my long phone calls and emails on everything from the manuscript to pedagogy to local and global politics. Their fresh perspectives never fail to make visible new horizons.

Ohio State's Assistant Faculty Research Fund and the Diversity Enhancement Program, projects of the College of Humanities, provided critical institutional support for my work. I thank those who brought such programs into being.

Chapter 5 is an extended version of an article that appeared in *Globalizing Dissent: Essays on Arundhati Roy*. Ranjan Ghosh and Antonia Navarro-Tejero, the editors of the collection, have graciously allowed me to publish it here in a new form.

Sandy Crooms, Maggie Diehl, and Malcolm Litchfield of The Ohio State University Press have made the publishing process as smooth as can be. Thanks also to the anonymous reviewers for their excellent guidance.

It is a privilege to finally acknowledge the individuals and communities that have supported me over the course of writing *Decentering Rushdie:*

~ More English department colleagues than I can name have influenced my research, writing, and teaching. Their generosity of spirit directly reflects the democratic and collaborative ethos of the department I joined in 2004—then led by Valerie Lee, for whom all things are possible. In particular, the US Ethnic and Postcolonial Studies Group (USEP) in English has been a blessing, and I laud the efforts of faculty and graduate students within these related fields who have helped to form and sustain it. Joe Ponce's camaraderie and his dedication to creating USEP and similar entities have been irreplaceable.

~ I cherish the collegiality and friendship of the dozens of colleagues in English, Women's Studies, History, Asian American Studies, Comparative Studies, the Kirwan Institute, and the South Asian Studies committee who—along with their partners and kids—have helped make Columbus home. The hospitality of Joe Ponce and Ricky Haberstroh, Judy Wu and Mark Walter, Jared Gardner and Beth Hewitt, Guisela Latorre, Ryan and Ruth Friedman, and Robin Judd and Kenny Steinman has passed into legend in our house.

~ I've benefited a great deal from the generous collaboration of scholars in a variety of contexts, including Shahzad Bashir, Purnima Bose, Patrick Brantlinger, Brian Caton, Piya Chatterjee, Daniel Dadras, Priyamvada Gopal, Ghazala Hashmi, Anupama Jain, Gautam Kundu, David Lelyveld, Anita Mannur, Sunaina Maira, Rohit Negi, Gautam Premnath, Shazia Rahman, Pallavi Rastogi, Dan Seward, Prakashbhai Shah, Snehal Shingavi, Amritjit Singh, and Rashmi Varma. Likewise, former colleagues at Wagner College inspired me by always creating spaces for intellectual exchange, especially Susan Bernardo, Mark Farag, Anne Hurley, Marilyn Kiss, Laura Morowitz, Felicia Ruff, Margarita Sánchez, Anne Schotter, Peter Sharpe, Mark Wagner, and Lori Weintrob.

~ Activism has decisively shaped my worldview over the past fifteen years. I salute all of those individuals and groups I've worked with—locally and nationally—to organize forums and actions around war and empire, racial and global justice, workers' and immigrants' rights, LGBT equality, and reproductive rights.

This book is dedicated to those whose support for me goes beyond words:

~ To friends far away yet always present: Manish Ajvalia, Sandhya Purohit Caton, Ammu Kirtane, Yesha Naik, Jyotiben Shah, Nilesh and Apexa Shukla, and their families.

~ To my grandparents, just a memory away. To my extended family: from the Jersey homeland to all corners of the United States, from Ahmedabad and Vadodara to Bangalore and beyond.

~ To my parents, Mahendra Jani and Vandana Jani, who have always taught by example that "it's better to wear out than to rust out"—that we have a responsibility to better the world we inhabit. To my second set of parents, V. Sreenivas and Nagarathna Sreenivas, for their constant affection and support.

~ To Mytheli, whose companionship—personal, scholarly, political—brings such deep joy. I've learned so much from your cutting-edge research, dedicated teaching, and remarkable ability to steer steadily through life. To Meenakshi and Savita, who make our world turn. Your peals of laughter, your loving natures, your *tofaan*—thinking about it brings a smile to my lips. And guess what, Ihskaneem and Ativas? I now have an answer to your question: "Is the book done yet?"

Finally, I also dedicate this book to the memory of Howard Zinn. He transformed so many of us through his conviction, demonstrated in *A People's History of the United States,* that it is the struggle of ordinary people that makes possible extraordinary change.

introduction

Looking Back

o jaane-vaale, jaao naa ghar apnaa chhod ke
maataa bulaa rahi hai tumhen haath jod ke
nagari tumhaari galiyaan tumhaari ye bastiyaan
in sabko chhodkar jaarahe hain tum kahaan?

O *jaane-vaale!* Don't go, leaving your home behind
Your mother is calling you back, with folded palms
These towns are yours, these streets and settlements are all yours
Where are you going, leaving all of these behind?

—Radha in Mehboob Khan's *Mother India* (1957)

It may be that writers in my position, exiles or emigrants or expatriates, are haunted by some sense of loss, some urge to reclaim, to look back, even at the risk of being mutated into pillars of salt. But if we do look back, we must do so in the knowledge—which gives rise to profound uncertainties—that our physical alienation from India almost inevitably means that we will not be capable of reclaiming precisely the thing that was lost; that we will, in short, create fictions, not actual cities or villages, but invisible ones, imaginary homelands, Indias of the mind.

—Salman Rushdie, "Imaginary Homelands" (1982)

Postcolonial Indian literary and cinematic texts, like many others around the world, have often concerned themselves with the question of "looking back." The processes of postcolonial capitalist modernity—urbanization, industrialization, globalization—have pushed and pulled Indians from villages to cities, from the nation to the wider world (and back), creating a wide spectrum of experiences ranging from forced expulsion to voluntary emigration. In this light, many different kinds of texts, whether produced from within India or by artists linked to India through various cultural and ethnic ties, have sought to represent and define postcolonial subjects in relation to what they and many of those in their audiences have left behind. Of course, postcolonial migrations have only continued the move-

1

ment and dispersion of South Asians already underway for centuries; the negotiation between "the home" and "the world," as Rabindranath Tagore famously described it, has been in full swing all along.[1] But political independence from Britain in 1947 added a crucial element: Indian artists and intellectuals since then have imagined "home" in a changed material context, one shaped by the policies, institutions, and ideological maneuvers of a nation-state claiming to be run by the people for the people. Postcolonial intellectuals and artists, within the nation or in the diaspora, have been shaped and constituted by these historical and ideological contexts. Postcolonial narratives of looking back, likewise, have often referred explicitly to the nation in the process of telling their stories about individuals, communities, and the prospects of freedom.

It goes without saying that different texts look back in various ways and for divergent purposes. Consider the two quotations cited above. There is a world of difference between the "home" that is imagined by Mehboob Khan's *Mother India* (1957), the classic Bollywood production that ties home to land and nation through the figure of a hardworking peasant mother/goddess (Radha), and the "imaginary homelands" of Salman Rushdie, the writer of magical-realist novels, whose fictional depictions of India are hardly concerned with rural life or beholden to "national progress." *Mother India,* a nationalist text par excellence, devotes all of its narrative energies—structure, characterization, voice, plot, music, symbolism—to persuading its viewers that the path to rural uplift runs through the policies of industrial development being pursued by Jawaharlal Nehru, Prime Minister of India from 1947 until his death in 1964. At the heart of the movie is Radha's song *"O Jaane-vaale,"* illustrating her attempts to persuade her in-text audience—peasants fleeing famine and poverty—to return to their land/mother/nation. The close-up shots of Radha's dirt- and sweat-stained face aim to deliver the message directly to the various members of its real audience, too—whether they are peasants, urbanites, or NRIs ("Non-Resident Indians"), whether they are *jaane-vaale* ("those who are going") or those who have already left.

The quotation from Rushdie, in contrast, is from a 1982 essay that argues for the *productive* potential of those who have left, whether "exiles or emigrants or expatriates." In Rushdie's fiction and nonfiction, the inbetweenness that produces "imaginary homelands" has a positive value, for it is precisely the space from which the (emigrant) novelist does her/his work. The essay anticipates Rushdie's oft-cited comment on his novel *The Satanic Verses* (1988), prescribing a vision for (postcolonial) literature: it "celebrates hybridity, impurity, intermingling, the transformation that comes of new and unexpected combinations of human beings, cultures, ideas, politics, movies, songs. It rejoices in mongrelization and fears the absolutism of the Pure" ("In Good Faith" 394). The difference between *Mother India* and Rushdie's work, then, appears to be that the one is nationalist, privileges linearity and didacticism, and is oriented toward fixed notions of home, while the other, valuing border-crossing and indeterminacy on all levels, demonstrates a "new cosmopolitanism" that, as Timothy Brennan puts it, is "at home in the world."[2] Rushdie's lampooning of *Mother India* in his novel *The Moor's Last Sigh* (1995) underlines, as it were, the differences between these two modes of relating to the nation, between nationalism and cosmopolitanism.[3]

Let's pause for a moment to recognize the larger significance of juxtaposing these different orientations toward the nation. By and large, a "cosmopolitan" position such as Rushdie's is commonly recognized as "postcolonial," a term that has become associated with postnational and postmodern ways of seeing. However, like much else that is not produced for English-language audiences, and like much else from the early decades of the Indian nation-state, the representations of Indian life in nation-oriented texts such as *Mother India* have not been worked into contemporary theories of postcoloniality.[4] The "hybridity" and cosmopolitanism of a director such as Mehboob Khan—a Gujarati Muslim who left his village for Bombay to become a pioneer in late colonial and early postcolonial Indian cinema—are scarcely considered. Indeed, literary texts and criticism in the vernacular languages are given no real status in Anglo-American Postcolonial Studies; preposterously, we can become scholars of non-Western literature without knowing or studying non-Western languages. These are the sorts of critical aporias that resonate beneath Harish Trivedi's claim, made in 1996 but still poignant today, that "[p]ost-colonial discourse as at present globally constituted hardly begins to address either the post-colonial situation in India or its post-colonial literature except perhaps in some incidental and tangential ways" (243). How would our concepts of postcoloniality change if we included a larger group of post-independence works in our considerations? What are the consequences of implicitly excluding texts that may not be immediately accessible to Western readers?

Decentering Rushdie draws out the limitations of postcolonial discourse by examining alternative representations of postcolonial society. However, I remain as interested in points of convergence and continuity between celebrated and marginalized texts as in their points of divergence. For the inclusion of the latter group of texts illuminates the former in new ways; hidden aspects of "Imaginary Homelands" emerge when we read it against "O *Jaane-vaale*." Despite Rushdie's overall project in the essay to establish migrancy as an Archimedean site from which to view the nation, the cited passage exudes a nostalgia for India that is distinctly modernist and mournful rather than postmodernist and celebratory. As in a palimpsest, to use one of Rushdie's favorite metaphors, the nation both constitutes and emerges from beneath Rushdie's postnational scripts.[5] Creativity and imagination are grounded upon a fundamental loss that cannot be overcome: "we will not be capable of reclaiming precisely the thing that was lost [. . .] we will, in short, create fictions, not actual cities or villages, but invisible ones, imaginary homelands, Indias of the mind." "Looking back" is thus heroic and necessary—writers must do it "even at the risk of being mutated into pillars of salt." But "profound uncertainties" are triggered by the recognition of alienation.

Indeed, the passage problematizes efforts to interpret it strictly within the paradigms of postmodernist epistemology. First, Rushdie's allusion to the Abrahamic tale of Lot's wife—who is turned into a pillar of salt for looking back, against God's orders, to her home, the burning city of Sodom—challenges the notion that "looking back" is inherently reactionary or conservative, and that only "rootlessness" leads to greater understanding.[6] Rather, by placing the writer in the position of Lot's wife, Rushdie associates looking back with three of his favorite tropes: the writer's courage in defying authority, the risky but necessary processes of mutation and metamorphosis, and, in terms of the allusion itself, the need to reinterpret and rethink the injunctions of (scriptural) tradition. The modernist sense of a lost wholeness is further generated, second, when Rushdie uncharacteristically asserts the materiality of the body over artistic volition, emphasizing that even heroic acts of "looking back" are insufficient given the emigrant writer's "physical alienation" from the nation. By emphasizing the expatriate writer's *inability* to reclaim the "actual" India and by counterposing this real, tangible India to "Indias of the mind," Rushdie implies not only that reclamation and representation may be possible for writers situated within India but also that perhaps the "fictions" created by displaced writers are, in the last instance, derivative and inferior. The postmodernist notion that there are no originals but only copies appears very strongly in much of Rushdie's work but is not apparent here.[7] This mourning for India's "actual cities and villages" acknowledges, at a deep symbolic level, the logic of Radha's argument about the home/nation and the need to return: "These towns are yours, these streets and settlements are all yours / Where are you going, leaving all of these behind?" The geographies of home in "O *Jaane-vaale*" and in the passage from "Imaginary Homelands" are thus strikingly similar—though they are admittedly articulated from different times, in different languages and genres, and, ultimately, with different orientations toward the nation.[8]

Reading texts from across the postindependence period together in this way opens up new ways of considering postcolonial literature and culture. On the one hand, we find that even known quantities such as Rushdie exceed "Rushdie"—the sign that functions as shorthand for the idea that the postcolonial and the postmodern are one and the same. On the other hand, paying attention to marginalized texts—often realist, nation-oriented texts from before the 1980s—reveals that they are also more complex than they may appear at first glance. *Mother India,* for instance, diligently strives to corral within the framework of the nation Radha's narrative of steadfastness in the face of poverty. The core story is told in flashback through the memories of an aged Radha, asked to preside over the ceremonial opening of a dam in the town that sprouted up after the *jaane-vaale* heeded her call and came back. But the brief return to the narrative present at the end of the film is insufficient to eradicate the overwhelming sense of tragedy that constitutes the bulk of the plot, which ends with Radha deliberately shooting her eldest son dead after he abducts a young woman from the village. Whereas Radha is depicted as heroic for choosing to be the mother and protector of the village/nation at the expense of her own son's life, the camera does not allow us to look away from her pain, dwelling on her face before returning us to the postcolonial present of tractors and dams and electrification. From Radha's perspective, the water that gushes forth from the dam is full of blood: there is no easy closure here.

Plan of the Book

Informed by an understanding of the complexities of postcolonial (Indian) literature and film as they have developed over time, *Decentering Rushdie* aims to illuminate the multiplicity of postcolonial representations of Indian society and identity as they are expressed within a specific genre of writing: the Indian novel in English. I am particularly interested in drawing out the genre's "multiple cosmopolitanisms"—its various articulations of elite/middle-class subjectivity and cosmopolitan identity.[9] On one level, Indian English novels across the board often foreground cosmopolitan-elite characters and voices in their depictions of postcolonial life, meditating on their relationship to the postcolonial nation and its people. On another, since the very use of English by Indian novelists is embedded with their middle-class status, the production and consumption of the Indian English novel generate cosmopolitan spaces, in which authors who are linked to both India and the West communicate with other English speakers, whether they are Indian elites or foreign readers. The novels themselves can be read as manifestations of cosmopolitan practice: their diverse and multiple explorations of Indian life from an elite standpoint are at once self-representations and communiqués, demanding that their English-educated readers also reflect on their own identities and relationships to the nation (especially if they are Indian, too) and consider the difficulties and complexities of "looking back" to the nation from a cosmopolitan-elite perch.

But the cosmopolitan identities forged by Indian English novels across the postcolonial period are far from unitary. *Decentering Rushdie* demonstrates that the genre is much more heterogeneous in terms of its narrative strategies, its orientation toward the nation, and its ideological positions than is usually allowed for by the critical paradigms that dominate the field. I read seven Indian novels in English published from across the first five decades after decolonization—including three texts by Nayantara Sahgal, a prolific writer whose virtual invisibility in Anglo-American Postcolonial Studies exemplifies the limited nature of our literary canon. Juxtaposing well-known and little-read novels and/or novelists, I take up Sahgal's *A Time to Be Happy* (1958), Kamala Markandaya's *The Coffer Dams* (1969), Sahgal's *The Day in Shadow* (1971), Anita Desai's *Clear Light of Day* (1980), Rushdie's *Midnight's Children* (1980),[10] Sahgal's *Rich Like Us* (1985), and Arundhati Roy's *The God of Small Things* (1997). All of these novels are attentive to questions of class position and identity formation, especially as produced by categories of nation, gender, class, and/or sexuality. However, they take up different orientations toward the nation, make use of different aesthetics and narrative strategies, and/or articulate different ideological positions in identifying postcolonial problems and resolutions (if any). The fact that all but one of these texts are by women—a direct consequence, in fact, of highlighting early postcolonial novels—allows us to extend observations about the ideological and aesthetic diversity of the Indian English novel to postcolonial women's writing as well.

In reading such texts together, enabled by a historicist method, my analysis interrogates theoretical assumptions about postcoloniality and cosmopolitanism that associate these terms with postnational perspectives, magical realism, and postmodernist epistemology—that reduce "postcolonial (Indian) literature," in short, to "Rushdie." Drawing out the multiple cosmopolitanisms of the postcolonial Indian English novel and explaining their conditions of emergence serves to decenter "Rushdie" by 1) revealing the specific contexts in which Anglophone, postmodern, postnational novels have come to define the category of "Postcolonial Literature"; 2) recovering the nation-oriented texts and authors from the early decades of postcolonial India that have been effectively set aside; and then 3) rereading contemporary writing through the lens of this earlier literature and bringing it back into a larger literary history. In the process, *Decentering Rushdie* offers a methodology of reading that is attentive to broad shifts in the Indian English novel over time even as it draws attention to the limits of periodization and categorization.

On one level, thus, I describe a general movement from novels that associate themselves with the national project, however critically, to those that explicitly turn away from it—and I suggest that this shift occurs in the aftermath of Indira Gandhi's Emergency (1975–77). In the early decades of independence, Indian English novels often exhibited and encouraged in their audiences what I call "*namak-halaal* cosmopolitanism," a cosmopolitanism that remained "true to its salt" in that it was oriented toward and committed to the nation as a potentially emancipatory space. In the context of a an intellectual environment, from the 1930s to the 1960s, that was charged by the cultural and political radicalism of the All-India Progressive Writers' Association and the Indian Peoples' Theater Association, this "*namak-halaal* cosmopolitanism" expressed a worldliness and rejection of parochialism that was, at the same time, "salt of the earth."[11] It is only after the Emergency and the crackdown on democracy and popular struggle conducted by Nehru's daughter, under the aegis of "secularism" and "socialism" no less, that we see English-novelists look away from the nation as a potential site for fulfilling the promises of decolonization. The ongoing inequalities in postcolonial India since then, brought about by the neoliberal strategies of development, communalist politics, and heightened militarism that were engendered in the early 1980s, have only served to deepen the postnational turn among Indian novelists working in English.

The transition from *namak-halaal* to postnational orientations that I describe corresponds to Neil Lazarus's characterization of postcolonial Anglophone fiction from sub-Saharan Africa as it moved from the time of "great expectations" of the early independence years to "the mourning after" from the 1970s on (*Resistance* 1–26). It is from observing these same trends that K. Anthony Appiah calls postcolonial Anglophone novels of the 1970s and 1980s the "novels of delegitimation"—rejecting "not only the Western imperium but the nationalist project of the national bourgeoisie" ("Is the Post" 353). While I show that most early postcolonial Indian English novels are less naïve about the problems of mainstream nationalism than Appiah suggests, he describes accurately the turn away from the nation that becomes prominent in Anglophone postcolonial fiction in later decades. Indeed, what Appiah depicts as a corresponding turn away from realism also fits with my discussion about the emergence of psychological realism and metafictional texts in the Indian English novel—although, once again, my readings problematize such strict pairings of aesthetics, ideology, and orientation.

Rather than directly assigning "realism" to early, *namak-halaal* texts and "magical realism" to postnational ones, I find it more useful to think about how changing orientations toward the nation relate to broad shifts in the narrative projects of the Indian English novel. *Namak-halaal* novels are marked by "concordant" relations between the implied author, the narrator, and the implied audience, aiming to produce in the reader a sense of ethical and activist commitment to the nation as a site of potential emancipation, to the *truth* of oppression and resistance. Postnational works, however, tend to turn away from coherence and the *telos* of the nation through narrative strategies that produce discordant relationships and disrupt processes of knowing.[12] Both strategies seek to develop a critical consciousness, but *namak-halaal* texts point to the need for solidarity, whereas postnational ones question its possibility. In the former, agency (for characters and for the readers) emerges out of the ability to identify the processes of hegemony and dominance, and then to manipulate subject positions effectively in order to forge spaces for change. In the latter, subjectification and the processes of hegemony are confronted through a paradoxical move: History and Power are portrayed as so overwhelming and transcendent that only the solitary, migrant, protagonist/storyteller/writer can have agency. As *namak-halaal* texts are far less recognized in Postcolonial Studies, most of the book is devoted to drawing out the presence of this alternative articulation of cosmopolitanism, one that pursues "the empowering effects of constructing a coherent identity" (Parry 42–43). I do not simply valorize such texts but bring them more clearly into discussions about postcoloniality and cosmopolitanism.

Chapter 1 builds the case for this diachronic narrative, establishing the historical and ideological contexts that influenced middle-class intellectuals and writers, and tracing shifts from *namak-halaal* to postnational orientations and strategies. The chronological organization of chapters 2 through 5 duly supports this narrative. However, I am not simply interested in plotting literary developments on the map of history or in reading Anglophone novels as mere mouthpieces for expressing the ideology of a globalized elite. Rather, I operate through a Marxist critical methodology that refrains from overdetermining the relationship between cosmopolitan-elite location, political ideology, and narrative strategies. I track the dynamic and dialectical interplay between historical contexts and literary forms, between class position and cosmopolitan identity, between general orientations and specific ideologies as they develop over time. Therefore, my close readings of the novels themselves complicate the diachronic narrative and produce a more synchronic narrative of the genre—revealing both sharp differences between texts sharing a common orientation to the nation and commonalities between texts published across the divide of the Emergency. Each chapter explores the specific and relatively unique narrative strategies by which Indian English novelists have represented postcolonial life, mapping out the various configurations of nation, cosmopolitan location, ideology, and narrative. In the process, I sequentially take up pertinent theoretical questions around modernity, identity, gender, class, and political criticism, revealing that a broader and more inclusive understanding of the field of postcolonial cultural production forces us to develop more nuanced categories of analysis than those currently on offer.

In chapters 2, 3, and 4, I juxtapose a more celebrated novelist and/or novel with a text by Sahgal, whose *namak-halaal* and nationalist visions provide a backdrop against which we can gauge developments in the genre—not to speak of those within Sahgal's own writing. Let me take a moment to explain the prominence of Sahgal in this book. I am certainly interested in foregrounding Sahgal's work for the way that she has attempted to negotiate, for over five decades now, the relationship between historical and political questions and those of gender, sexuality, and family. Methodologically, furthermore, the steady presence of Sahgal throughout the book is valuable because it allows me to develop more precisely the diachronic and synchronic narratives. First, her novels provide a counternarrative to the one implicit in limiting the postcolonial to "Rushdie." The early texts of Sahgal, one of Nehru's nieces, show the prominence of *namak-halaal* writing—and her consistent commitment to the nation even after the Emergency confirms that the turn towards magical realism and the postnational was not absolute. Second, the aesthetic and ideological shifts that *do* occur in Sahgal over time reveal that changes in historical and intellectual contexts leave their mark in differentiated ways. The map we draw of the Indian English novel, then, cannot simply show the dominant trajectories but must account for detours, countermovements, and literary innovations other than magical realism.

Chapter 2 explores the sharp ideological differences around Nehruvian modernity and notions of elite responsibility in Sahgal's *A Time to Be Happy* and Markandaya's *The Coffer Dams*—even though I mark the texts as sharing a *namak-halaal* orientation toward the nation and being concerned with similar problems of postcolonial, middle-class subjectivity. I differentiate, thus, the "orientation" that emerges in a given historical moment, analogous to Raymond Williams's "structures of feeling," from the more directed term "ideology," the worldview that can be derived from the way that a text organizes its themes, dramatic tensions, and resolutions. The euphoria of decolonization in Sahgal is contested and tempered by the sober critique of postcolonial capitalism in Markandaya. Furthermore, their very different representations of cross-cultural identity formation question the usefulness of the category of "hybridity" except as a very general description of the complexity that haunts all identities.

Chapter 3 interrogates the intersections of gender, nation, and narration in two *namak-halaal* texts emerging from the tumultuous 1970s. I juxtapose Sahgal's social-realist *The Day in Shadow* with Desai's psychological-realist *Clear Light of Day,* examining how these women-centered texts experiment with interiority and voice. Contesting narrow, gendered oppositions between "political novels" and "psychological novels" as well as theories that automatically counterpose nationalism and feminism, I describe how each text offers "feminist resolutions to the national question," interrogating their female protagonists' experiences of oppression in postcolonial society even while seeking to reconstruct gender-egalitarian models of nation and family.[13]

Chapter 4 seeks to complicate our understanding of the post-Emergency novel in a number of ways. Evaluating the class politics of *Midnight's Children* and Sahgal's *Rich Like Us,* I demonstrate that these novels converge in elite-centered representations of Indian postcoloniality despite crucial differences in terms of national orientation and narrative form. In fact, not only does this chapter question the radical oppositionality of postmodern, postnational novels, but it shows how more recent *namak-halaal* texts also engage with metafictional forms. On the flip side, the clear presence of a national longing in *Midnight's Children* suggests its organic links with *namak-halaal* novels, past and present. The newness of *Midnight's Children* can be better particularized, I contend, when its commonalities with very different novels are not ignored. Even as we can trace, through these three chapters, the broad movement toward metacritical narratives, the development of interior voices, and the shift away from the nation and the subaltern, we can also see that neither historical location nor class position nor cosmopolitan cultural identity overdetermines these narratives in any linear or simple way.

My study of Roy's *The God of Small Things* in chapter 5, in a sense, ties together many of the aspects of the book in its attempt to pursue an antideterministic strategy of Marxist literary criticism. Against leftist critics who have denigrated the novel as "bourgeois" and "romantic anti-capitalist," I suggest that its narrative strategies, its representations of elites and subalterns, its dialectic of suffering and redemption, and its fierce commitments to concepts such as truth and justice in the age of neoliberal globalization hearken back to early postcolonial texts' *namak-halaal* orientation. Marking the novel as "anti-Communist" takes us away from recognizing that Roy's postmodern aesthetics and cosmopolitan-elite subject position do not translate into a postmodernist epistemology and elitist politics. By reading this magical-realist, post-Emergency novel as *namak-halaal,* even though it is penned by a fierce critic of postcolonial modernity and mainstream nationalism, I challenge not only deterministic tendencies in Postcolonial Studies but also the temptation, in analyses such as mine, to interpret form as a sign of ideology or epistemology, to make middle-class subjectivity itself the final arbiter of literary interpretation, to judge the politics of a text by its reception, or to produce a periodizing narrative that is inattentive to detours from the larger trajectory. All in all, *Decentering Rushdie* seeks new ways of conceptualizing postcoloniality and cosmopolitanism so that we can better speak to the complex and uneven relations of orientation, ideology, and aesthetics in postcolonial literature and culture.[14]

"Rushdie" Versus Rushdie

Decentering Rushdie comes neither to bury Rushdie nor to praise him. Paradoxically, indeed, I have developed a greater appreciation for Rushdie's fiction, especially the novels from *Midnight's Children* to *The Moor's Last Sigh,* over the same period in which his explicit political positions have moved away from my own. Since early 2001, when I completed the dissertation that became the basis for this book, Rushdie's political trajectory has been decidedly rightwards. His defense of the U.S. war in Afghanistan in 2001, his support for the Iraq war in 2003, his inability and/or unwillingness to separate, in the public sphere, his secular-liberal ideas from the right wing's open Islamophobia—all of these have alienated me from Rushdie's opinions as a commentator on public affairs.[15] Rushdie's quiet acceptance of knighthood from Queen Elizabeth II in 2007 evoked feelings of both betrayal and amusement: could this really be the author whose early fiction brilliantly mocked the figure of the *chamcha,* the syco-phantic Indian? And yet, each revision of *Decentering Rushdie* has moved toward what I consider to be a more nuanced approach to Rushdie, one that is more firmly aware of the Anglo-American academic and pedagogi-cal contexts in which I find myself.

In a word, I have found it important to integrate my scholarly assess-ments of Rushdie with my pedagogical practice, for teaching Rushdie's fiction to undergraduates in the United States has been an overwhelmingly positive experience. Since the terrorist attacks of September 11, 2001, I have faced a set of difficult questions as a South Asian American profes-sor, openly socialist and antiwar, teaching about postcolonial and world literature in Staten Island and central Ohio. How do I negotiate the fact that I physically embody the Other of the "war on terror" with the need to do right by my students, regardless of their knowledge of the themes being covered or their political positions on them? How do I maintain a demo-cratic classroom environment while teaching critical thinking—especially when dealing with texts and approaches that put forward very different worldviews from the ones inundating the mainstream media? In both pri-vate and public institutions, I have found that even the basic forms of mul-ticulturalism and international awareness, for all their limitations, have had a transformative potential on students open to learning more about the world. Rushdie's fiction has proved to be incredibly valuable in this regard, as a tool for opening up critical and democratic discussions—for conveying something important about the value of art, about the politics of narrative, and about the importance of speaking truth to power.

And so I have attempted to convey in this book the sense that Rush-die's move away from his resolute anti-imperialism of the 1980s has been a great loss for those opposed to war and empire—and that this is a phe-nomenon to be thought through carefully for what it teaches us about history, politics, and literature. For whatever Rushdie's current ideas and however problematic his canonization, his novels, especially the early ones, remain crucial contributions to the political and pedagogical projects of Postcolonial Studies as we enter the second decade of the twenty-first century. This applies just as well to the postmodernist standpoints that I have critiqued in this book, not to speak of my debates with Marxists and other critics of empire. As my inbox continues to log case after case of colleges and universities unfairly denying tenure to or refusing to extend the contracts of professors in Postcolonial Studies, Middle Eastern Studies, and related areas, it seems more important than ever to keep a clear understanding of our basic commonalities even in the midst of healthy and rigorous debates about literature, culture, theory, and politics. *Decentering Rushdie* operates, therefore, with due respect for what Rushdie has achieved and for the progressive visions and desires that motivate various theories of cosmopolitanism, postnationalism, and postcoloniality—even as I argue that there is much more to postcolonial literature and thought, especially around the question of the nation, than what has been presented to us under the sign "Rushdie."

1

The Multiple Cosmopolitanisms
of the Indian Novel in English

> Major work is being done in India in many languages other than English [but] outside India there is just about no interest in any of this work. The Indo-Anglians seize all the limelight. Very little is translated; very few of the best writers—Premchand, Anantha Moorthy—or the best novels are known, even by name.
>
> —Salman Rushdie, "'Commonwealth Literature' Does Not Exist" (1983)

> The prose writing—both fiction and non-fiction—created in this [post-independence] period by Indian writers *working in English,* is proving to be a stronger and more important body of work than most of what has been produced in the 16 "official languages" of India, the so-called "vernacular languages," during the same time.
>
> —Salman Rushdie, introduction to *Mirrorwork* (1997)

In 1981 the India-born, England-residing Salman Rushdie exploded onto the global literary stage when *Midnight's Children,* a magical-realist novel about postcolonial India, was awarded the prestigious Booker Prize for Fiction. In terms of literary innovation, as Makarand Paranjape writes, *Midnight's Children*'s "energy, its self-indulgence, irresponsibility, disorder, and cockiness really shocked the daylights out of the staid form of the Indian English novel"; subsequently, "heaps of novels" have been shaped by "Rushdie's liberating touch [. . .]" ("Inside and Outside the Whale" 220). Novelist Anita Desai said, indeed, that Rushdie showed Indian English novelists "a way to be 'post-colonial'" (qtd. in Dingwaney 317). Besides such contributions to Indian and global literature, however, the aura of radicalism that continues to surround Rushdie's novel points to its achievements on a much broader level. Critics regard the 1981 Booker as the moment of arrival for the entire field of postcolonial literatures in

English—literatures whose narrative strategies and cultural-political imaginaries are grounded in contexts shaped by British colonization and subsequent decolonization. While other postcolonial texts had already captured the Booker by 1981, including novels by V. S. Naipaul and J. M. Coetzee, *Midnight's Children* and its author have gained iconic status as English literary studies has truly gone global. As if to underline the point, *Midnight's Children* won awards for the Booker of Bookers in 1993 and the Best of the Booker award in 2008—securing, in the latter case, the support of thousands of readers in a worldwide vote.[1]

Midnight's Children stands out, in hindsight, for its ideological and stylistic affiliation with and contribution to new tendencies that were already transforming the Western intellectual landscape by the late 1970s and early 1980s. The rise of French poststructuralist and postmodernist thought out of the crucible of the 1960s has been well documented, weaving together and working against the ideas of earlier European philosophers from Friedrich Nietzsche and Ferdinand de Saussure to Søren Kierkegaard and Jean-Paul Sartre. Developing in more or less tension with these ideas were various articulations of Marxian thought, including the work of Frantz Fanon around colonialism and racial oppression, E. P. Thompson in historiography, Theodor Adorno and the Frankfurt School in cultural studies, and Louis Althusser in philosophy. *Midnight's Children* can be read in light of Anglophone works that emerged slightly later, as the radical moment of the 1960s and early 1970s came to a close. Along with texts as different as Gayatri Spivak's English translation of Jacques Derrida's *Of Grammatology* (1976), Edward Said's *Orientalism* (1978), Ranajit Guha's *Subaltern Studies, Volume 1* (1982), and Benedict Anderson's *Imagined Communities* (1983), Rushdie's novel was part of a self-consciously avant-gardist network of writings that specifically sought to challenge the Eurocentrism and violence underpinning the dominant structures of thought about history, politics, language, and aesthetics.[2] The novel fictionalized and popularized the "linguistic turn" in the humanities and allowed for a more joyous and intimate experience of the liminal and fractured subjectivities described in the heavy theoretical and philosophical works of its time. It is precisely within this intellectual milieu that the category of "the postcolonial" first emerged in Western disciplines as a way to describe cultures and societies from decolonized spaces—a term distinct from "the postmodern" yet closely linked to it insofar as postcolonial texts also seemed to target the Enlightenment through their critique of both colonial and nationalist discourse. Standing at the intersection where the postcolonial and the postmodern met, as it were, *Midnight's Children* contributed to their development and convergence, helping to open up the postmodern globally and pushing postcolonial writing in new directions.

These days, the newness of that moment in the early 1980s might be difficult to imagine. Postcolonial Studies and postmodernism are now bulwarks of many a humanities department and academic journal in the West—making some non-Western scholars ask whether Postcolonial Studies and its theoretical apparatus itself constitutes a form of cultural imperialism.[3] Rushdie's legacy in the Western literary establishment is immensely secure and, in the United States, his voice emerges from *New York Times* opinions pages and interviews with Charlie Rose with the ring of authority. But Rushdie's writing from the 1980s reveals that the Booker victory appeared in the midst of a much larger debate about the place of the non-Western world in Anglo-American and global discussions about culture, ideas, and politics. Reaganism and Thatcherism had risen up from the ashes of the anti-establishment and anti-imperialist movements of the 1960s and 1970s, the euphoria of decolonization in Asia and Africa was giving way to despair as authoritarian regimes came into power, and "actually-existing socialism" in the Soviet Union and China was proving to be, let's just say, a disappointment. To the left-leaning intellectual and artist in the West, especially one with links to the Third World, raising provocative questions about imperialism and culture must have seemed like a necessary act of self-preservation. This radical edge is apparent in Rushdie's "'Commonwealth Literature' Does Not Exist" (1983), conducted in the discourse of "crashing the party." I revisit this piece in order to read the Rushdie of the early 1980s as being on the cusp of the old and new, well positioned to make demands of English literary studies and yet marginalized by it.

The premise of the essay is simple and direct: Rushdie rails against the very notion of "Commonwealth Literature," "this very oddest of beasts" that throws together writers whose "differences were much more significant than their similarities," simply because of their national and racial identities ("'Commonwealth Literature'" 61, 63). He contends that the category, one of the predecessors of today's "Postcolonial Literature," gives second-class status to non-Western/nonwhite writing in English— and, as the first epigraph above suggests, no status at all to postcolonial writing in the vernacular languages. With a keen awareness about the conditions shaping his own rise in the world of letters, Rushdie deplores the fact that the global dominance of English and the lack of interest in or resources for widespread translation has led to a situation in which "Indo-Anglians seize all the limelight" even though "[m]ajor work" is being done in non-English writing (69). "Commonwealth Literature," then, not only "has the effect of creating a ghetto" for writers on the basis of nationality and race, but an "exclusive ghetto" that keeps out, ironically enough, non-English texts from Asia, Africa, and elsewhere (63). With rebellious flair Rushdie seeks to dismantle the category of Commonwealth Literature that implicitly placed "Eng. Lit. at the center and the rest of the world at the periphery" (66).

The essay's critique of "Commonwealth Literature" as a segregationist category, then, is grounded on its defense of postcolonial writing in the vernacular languages. In particular, his narrative and understanding of the *aesthetic* devaluation of non-English Indian writing is historicist and political. English became the dominant world language, first, because of the "physical colonization of a quarter of the globe" by the British and then as a result of the "primacy of the United States of America in the affairs of the world" ("'Commonwealth Literature'" 64). The lack of Western interest in vernacular writing, then, rests not on the "worthiness" of the writing itself but on the political underpinnings of categories such as "Commonwealth Literature." The cosmopolitan compatriot must bring these texts to light by constructing a transnational space that escapes both the Anglocentrism that constructs ghettoes based on nationality and race, and the "ghetto mentality" of a nativist response that mirrors it (63). By requesting a seat at the table not only for the elite, English-educated writer such as himself but for also the entire, polylingual spectrum of postcolonial authors, Rushdie conceptualizes a comparative and horizontal model of global cultural production. The presence of literature from the ex-colonies—both English and vernacular—would not only force a decentering of England from "English Literature" but would encourage the rewriting of literary studies itself, demanding the construction of an non-Anglocentric category that was much more radically comparative. Though the language was not available to Rushdie in 1983, he is effectively demanding that the category of postcoloniality be expanded to include a much broader range of cultural production and experience from the formerly colonized world. Implicit in this gesture is a certain ethical sensibility: the cosmopolitan-elite writer of English-language texts has a responsibility to employ her/his voice in the service of those that are being ignored.

"'Commonwealth Literature'" ends with a grand, anti-imperialist flourish: "The English language ceased to be the sole possession of the English some time ago. Perhaps 'Commonwealth Literature' was intended to delay the day when we rough beasts actually slouch into Bethlehem. In which case, it's time to admit that the centre cannot hold" (70).

Rushdie's invocation of W. B. Yeats's "The Second Coming" does an incredible amount of discursive work in the interests of rewriting the Western "metropole" from the vantage point of the non-Western "periphery." First, it cleverly uses a classic metaphor from a high modernist poem in order to describe and enact the dismantling of the literary canon, both heralding the arrival of the "rough beasts" (who know their classic Yeats poetry very well, thank you very much) and fulfilling the anarchistic scenario imagined by the poem. Second, the content of Rushdie's argument—confirming the value of literature in English from the colonized world—reminds us of the double anticolonial resonances already linked to Yeats's poem when we recall it today: the Irish context of the poem itself, and Nigerian writer Chinua Achebe's groundbreaking novel, *Things Fall Apart* (1958), whose title is derived from the lines to which Rushdie alludes. Ultimately, the passage suggests that the issue at hand is not simply one of inclusion but the very transformation of the center-periphery paradigm and our understanding of it. In reminding us of the earlier entry of Irish writers into the English literary universe under processes of colonialism and (cultural) resistance to it, the passage inscribes the arrival of the postcolonial "rough beasts" within a larger narrative of the perpetual cross-pollination of languages and literatures, dismantling the notion of a pure English canon at the center.

So far, so good. But as the reader undoubtedly suspects from the second epigraph above, the Rushdie of the 1983 essay undergoes a major shift. What explains the narrowing of Rushdie's vision in his now infamous denunciation, in the introduction to his edited anthology, *Mirrorwork* (1997), of Indian writing that is *not* in English? Why would Rushdie, only fourteen years after lamenting that there was "just about no interest" in Indian writing in the indigenous languages, exemplify that lack of interest by including only one non-English story in a collection that supposedly commemorates the best *Indian* writing of the past half-century? How does one judge the sweeping aesthetic claim that English-language texts are unequivocally "stronger" and "more important" than "most of what has been produced in the 16 'official languages' of India" ("Introduction" viii) in light of the earlier piece—which suggested that comparative aesthetic judgments are problematic when political and socioeconomic factors so limit the availability of non-English texts that "very few of the best writers [. . .] or the best novels are known, even by name" ("'Commonwealth'" 69)? What happens to a marginalized literature when a select few of its practitioners make what Said calls "the voyage in" (*Culture and Imperialism* 295), and are then allowed to define the whole?

Apparently the center *can* hold. The long-awaited "second coming," represented by the "rough beasts" of the postcolonial world taking their place in literary studies, has turned out to be merely a changing of the guard—not the beginning of a new order. As with the decolonized nations so with postcolonial literature: the displacement of white European figures by Brown or Black ones, while quite significant in many ways, has not sufficiently challenged the basic paradigms of power. Understanding the difference between Rushdie's pronouncements in 1983 and 1997—understanding, in other words, the shifts that have occurred in postcolonial cosmopolitan writing and thinking about the nation over time—is crucial to the argument I make in this book about the Indian novel in English, its permutations over the postcolonial period, and the critical lens through which we study the genre.

The Postcolonial Indian English Novel
A Different Lens

The starting point for *Decentering Rushdie* is the recognition of a significant problem in the current critical understanding of postcolonial literature: since Rushdie's Booker in 1981, Anglo-American Postcolonial Studies has effectively restricted the category of postcolonial literature to texts that value postmodern epistemologies and narrative forms. As the postcolonial has become conflated with the postmodern—as the postcolonial, in other words, has been dehistoricized—the political and aesthetic diversity of postcolonial Indian writing in English has also been erased. Indian novels in English since independence have negotiated cosmopolitanism and the nation in multiple and divergent ways, but the genre—and postcolonial cosmopolitanism itself—is narrowly equated with a celebration of rootlessness and "hybridity," a cynicism toward nation-oriented politics and identities, and a magical-realist narrative mode. In short, today's postmodernized postcolonial theory has reconstructed postcolonial literature in its own image, with dire consequences to literary criticism. The theoretical dismissal of nation-oriented thinking as inherently reactionary is reflected, in the study of Indian literature, with the limiting of the publication and circulating of postcolonial texts by period (few texts before 1980), by ideology (few nation- or subaltern oriented texts), by form (overemphasis on magical-realist texts), and by language (mainly English-language texts). In fact, "Rushdie" has developed into a lens for viewing and defining the entire field. As Neil Lazarus writes, deliberately overstating the case, "there is in the strict sense only one author in the postcolonial literary canon [. . .] Salman Rushdie," whose novels "are endlessly cited in the critical literature as testifying to the imaginedness [. . .] of nationhood, the ungeneralizable subjectivism of memory and experience, the instability of social identity, the volatility of truth, [and] the narratorial constructedness of history" ("Politics" 424).

Decentering Rushdie constructs an alternative lens for viewing the postcolonial Indian English novel, allowing for a greater appreciation of its nuances and a rethinking of prior accounts of postcoloniality and cosmopolitanism. Expanding my purview to texts from across the postcolonial period, I historicize Rushdie's achievement and draw attention to the multiple cosmopolitanisms produced within the genre over the last sixty years. Each of the novels I have selected is penned by cosmopolitan writers, addresses cosmopolitan audiences, and features cosmopolitan protagonists. But given the variety of formal techniques and range of ideological positions available in these novels, they produce no unitary, homogenous definition of "cosmopolitanism." In my reading, cosmopolitanism emerges as a category of cultural identity, one that describes the way that certain elites and intellectuals view themselves and experience the world. However, although cosmopolitan identities are always linked to middle-class subject positions, this should not overdetermine our understanding of either a novelist's ideology or artistic practice. My study thus recovers significant voices from the early postcolonial period, allows new ways of thinking about the contemporary Indian English novel, and reshapes current theoretical concepts of postcoloniality and cosmopolitanism.

I construct this new lens in three ways, decentering "Rushdie" as the pre-eminent sign of "the" postcolonial. First, I employ a historicist methodology to show that there have been different phases in the Indian English novel, revealing a multiplicity of cosmopolitan practices. Since the late 1940s, a broad shift has developed in the genre from nation-oriented/social-realist modes to postnational/magical-realist ones. Before the early 1980s, I contend, the Indian English novel was dominated by *"namakhalaal* cosmopolitanism"—a cosmopolitanism that, though not necessarily nationalist, was "true to its salt" in imagining national and local spaces as sites for combating postcolonial inequalities.[4] But the authoritarianism and brutality of Indira Gandhi's Emergency (1975–77), the Indian ruling class's response to the global economic decline of the early 1970s and the domestic upheavals that had accelerated since the mid-1960s, sharply called into question the emancipatory claims of the Indian nation-state. *Midnight's Children* signified the emergence in this literature of a new postnational attitude among many artists and the intelligentsia, one that has remained interested in the nation and its history but regards nationalisms and nation-states as being always already reactionary and suspect, the product of failed visions. By historicizing the postcolonial and recovering early postcolonial texts, I show that the contemporary Indian English novel represents a crucial development in the genre but not its entirety.

Through such a resituating of the Indian English novel, second, *Decentering Rushdie* challenges existing theories about postcoloniality and cosmopolitanism. The rigid binary opposition often drawn between cosmopolitanism (marked as progressive) and nationalism (marked as reactionary) fails to explain the various nation-oriented cosmopolitanisms that have proliferated in colonial and postcolonial texts and contexts. Certainly, both pre- and post-Emergency texts tend to be fairly critical of Indian postcoloniality, to expose continuing social inequalities, and to highlight the liminal identities of elite, Westernized Indians. But the early, *namak-halaal* texts I read here—no less postcolonial or cosmopolitan than their contemporary counterparts—maintain an activist orientation toward the nation and deploy narrative strategies that make ethical demands of their audiences of English-speaking elites, challenging them to confront postcolonial problems in the world outside the text. Acknowledging the presence of such *namak-halaal* texts when speaking of the genre as a whole requires the development of concepts and categories to better explain its heterogeneity.

The third component of my alternative lens is a Marxist critical methodology that refrains from deterministically relating cosmopolitan-elite location, political ideology, and narrative strategies. While conducting discussions about the sociohistorical determinants of literature, my readings also emphasize the power of literature to "imagine a world other than this" (Scott 21).[5] Ultimately, therefore, I base my critical assessments of the literature on the narrative strategies that drive each text forward and not on assumptions one might make from the authors' elite subject positions. *Decentering Rushdie* does not simply champion pre-Emergency writing and/or vernacular texts over contemporary Anglophone writing in order to correct current attitudes. Rather, I have selected novels that allow me to map the complexity of the field, both the larger patterns and the smaller movements and tensions, investigating the complex and dialectical interaction of history and literature, of class position and cultural identity. The chronological organization of my chapters gives evidence for the broad trajectory, over time, from *namak-halaal* to postnational cosmopolitanisms—but the close readings that constitute those chapters also demonstrate that literature does not march in lockstep with history, that

ideological and aesthetic diversity exists even between texts from similar periods and with similar orientations toward the nation. Through the
course of the book, thus, I contrast the ideological paradigms and narrative strategies of different *namak-halaal* novels, draw out similarities
between pre- and post-Emergency texts, trace some early novels' relevance
to contemporary debates about subjectivity and identity, and even note the
presence of *namak-halaal* attitudes in later, metafictional works.

I am attempting, therefore, not only to clear space for less prominent
texts and authors but also to recover, in the process, the more popular
texts on a new basis. As my title suggests, the critical focus around the
work of Rushdie as being paradigmatically "postcolonial" has deterred
a truly historicized understanding of postcoloniality and cosmopolitanism. However, I am recovering marginalized voices not to create a new
center around Nayantara Sahgal or another writer, but to draw out the
organic links between them all. Just as Sahgal's novels can be seen to have
shifted over time within the overall framework of her Nehruvian politics,
Rushdie, too, has not been a static figurehead for the postnational and the
postmodern. Mapping Rushdie's own shifts allows us to glimpse the kinds
of historical and cultural forces that have instigated a broader movement
in the Indian English novel as a whole.

From the vantage point of the first decade of the twenty-first century,
as Rushdie has openly supported the U.S. "war on terror" and blamed the
global Muslim community for the rise of Islamic fundamentalism, we can
read his critical work of the 1980s as a veritable transition point between
the *namak-halaal* and postnational moments.[6] Rushdie's trajectory from
rebellious outsider to establishment insider instigates queries about the status of Anglophone postcolonial writing in the age of neoliberal globalization, a process still dominated by the West but one that allows strategically
placed postcolonial states such as India to make their mark on the world.
"Decentering Rushdie" by historicizing and particularizing him, then,
renders problematic assumptions about universality and political oppositionality made on behalf of his novels. His work, in fact, represents the
worldview of a specific, elite constituency of Indians after the experience
of the Emergency period—liberal yet individualist; eager to speak for India
but oriented toward the West; interested in the nation and its history but
more as a site of endless narrative possibilities than as a material reality;
skeptical of religious traditions but also of the political lessons of mass
struggle drawn from the heydays of the anticolonial period. This orientation emerges not as a consequence of cosmopolitan-elite subjectivity in and
of itself but in response to a specific historical juncture.

Let's return to the contrast between the 1983 and 1997 pieces with this argument in mind. Rushdie's statements in his introduction to *Mirrorwork* caused a huge furor, as they were probably meant to, when he claimed that only one non-English excerpt deserved to be anthologized after the editors reviewed "most of what has been produced in the 16 'official languages' of India," "both fiction and non-fiction" (viii). Prominent Indian writers such as the Malayali poet K. Satchidanandan, writing as the secretary of India's Sahitya Akademi, justifiably countered Rushdie's claims by arguing for the continuing strength of Indian writing in the vernacular languages and drawing our attention to significant texts and authors (Maramkal and Rajadhyaksha). In this vein, though not in response to Rushdie, several scholars have articulated the need to broaden the field to "native voices."[7] Recent work by scholars in Anglo-American institutions, such as Priyamvada Gopal and Revathi Krishnaswamy, has added a new richness to our conceptions of postcolonial literature.[8] Such studies reveal the injustice and narrow-mindedness of Rushdie's 1997 conclusions about Indian literatures; I'd like to interrogate, further, the different yardstick by which he's measured them, one that has everything to do with his new centrality as the field has moved from "Commonwealth Literature" to "Postcolonial Literature."

For the *Mirrorwork* introduction refutes precisely what was at the heart of the radicalism in "'Commonwealth Literature' Does Not Exist": the idea that aesthetic criticism, especially when comparing literature across languages and critical traditions, is not a science but a practice whose very enactment exposes the subjective and contingent dimension of aesthetic evaluation itself. By Rushdie's earlier criteria, his *Mirrorwork* assessments are suspect: a seismic, socioeconomic shift would have had to occur between 1983 and 1997 that would *reduce* the global hegemony of English and create even the possibility of a fair and equal comparison between English and non-English writing from India (not to speak of comparisons between vernacular literatures). In fact, the opposite occurred: the value of English as a lingua franca for global-elite communication and class mobility intensified by the late 1990s, under the aegis of a United States that continued its "primacy [. . .] in the affairs of the world."

What Rushdie's 1997 piece misses is that the valuing of postnational, postmodern Indian English writing in Western publishing houses, bookstores, and college curricula cannot simply be seen as "proof" of the superiority of its literary achievement. Clearly, the rise of India in the post–Cold War hierarchy of nation-states between the early 1980s and the late 1990s has everything to do with the global proliferation of the Indian

English novel and Anglophone Indian writing in general. As the Oscar success of *Slumdog Millionaire* (2008) and the Booker victory of Aravind Adiga's *The White Tiger* (2008) indicate, India sells in the West as never before. On the home front, publishers such as Ravi Dayal and Penguin India, along with new presses like Rupa Paperback and IndiaInk, "have provided a marketing network able to deliver more affordable English-language fiction to the expanding urban middle class" (Mee 319). While the recent crop of Anglophone novels are certainly not uniform—see, for instance, the determined realism of Mukunda Rao's *Chinnamani's World* (2003)—the authors best known in the West often follow the "Rushdie" template of uncritically celebrating a cosmopolitan-elite identity that turns away from the nation as an ongoing site of struggle. This postnational turn is paradoxical in at least two ways. First, its emergence within India and its popularity in the West are intimately tied to the growth of the Indian nation-state itself. Second, though writers associated with this turn are often critical of the exoticization of India and of ongoing inequalities due to globalization today, their renderings of a radical cosmopolitan identity are quite compatible with the hybrid identities encouraged by those same processes of globalization. At issue is not Anglophone writing or cosmo-politanism in and of themselves but explaining the particularities of their recent emergence.

Undoubtedly, the need for a radical critique of the sort Rushdie made in 1983 still exists. "Postcolonial Literature" has turned out to be not a solution to the problems of hierarchy and ghettoization described by Rushdie with regard to "Commonwealth Literature" but only the latter's most recent avatar. In the field of Postcolonial Studies, now often under the management of intellectuals with filial ties to the Third World, writers' and critics' passports and pigmentation still go quite far in determining their value.[9] Like its predecessor, Postcolonial Literature rarely shows much interest in non-English writing, and the "Indo-Anglians" continue to "seize all the limelight" ("'Commonwealth'" 69). Rather than challenging the Anglocentric paradigms implicit in such developments, however, Rushdie in 1997 presides over their construction. Earlier, a Eurocentric "Commonwealth Literature" did the seizing of the limelight for writers in English; under "Postcolonial Literature," apparently, they do it for themselves. We might summarize the shifts thus: in 1983 the dismissal of indigenous literature by the academy was explained as a material consequence of imperialism and the blindness produced by the category of "Commonwealth Literature" itself. But in 1997 it is just a matter of stating the obvious aesthetic reality, as it were, that these texts are simply inferior. Whereas the 1983 essay was self-conscious about the rise of the Indian English writer, the 1997 piece unabashedly underscores his dominance, securing credibility for Rushdie's utterly subjective statements on little more than his celebrity.

It is important to assert, though, that Rushdie's discursive shift from gate-crashing to gatekeeping does not emerge solely from the unique circumstances of his personal life: from the heights of the 1981 Booker to the vicious attacks against him after Ayatollah Khomeini's 1989 fatwa, from his underground life under protection of the British state to his current place among the glitterati. Whatever we make of the new era that Rushdie ushered in, "it has to be acknowledged that he was more of a sign of the times than their creator" (Mee 319). Specifically, the turn toward the postnational marks the orientation of a specific section of the cosmopolitan intelligentsia whose changed subject positions and left-leaning ideological stances translated, after the Emergency period, into aesthetic practices and political stances that were in vogue in the West. I outline the Marxist methodology that I bring to this project in the next section before moving toward a more detailed discussion of the historical and ideological contexts that have shaped the Indian English novel and its reception.

History, Politics, Literature

In *Caribbean Women Writers and Globalization,* Helen Scott offers a succinct and useful discussion of Marxist methods for analyzing intellectual and artistic work. Taking up the centrality of the terms "totality," "contradiction," "mediation," and "change" in Georg Lukacs's *History and Class Consciousness,* Scott expresses the Marxist problematic thus: "Capitalism is a totality, yet is immediately experienced as disconnected parts; the parts are in a relationship of mutual conditioning, or mediation, and this relationship is not static but contradictory and fluid" (14). Marxist (literary) analysis, therefore, is driven toward explaining this totality in opposition to bourgeois theories of knowledge which, according to Lukacs, are engaged in making "of every historical object a variable monad which is denied any interaction with other—similarly viewed—monads and which possess characteristics that appear to be absolutely immutable essences" (qtd. in Scott 12). In other words, as Scott emphasizes, historical-materialist analyses of literary and cultural texts operate not by being "linear, rigid, reductive" and discovering simplified unities (14), but by developing an understanding of the dialectical interplay between historical contexts, class positions, ideologies, and artistic forms in a way that *challenges* the linearity, rigidity, reductivity, and simple universalisms that constitute bourgeois thought.

Moving toward an understanding of the whole, thus, also means recognizing the relative separation between and even autonomy of the different parts as they move in relation to one another; their unevenness and tension, indeed, produces newness and change. In terms of individuals and authors in particular, as Raymond Williams writes, recognizing this layered series of relations leads to "the reciprocal discovery of the truly social in the individual, and the truly individual in the social" (qtd. in Scott 18). Indeed, as Williams puts it, tracing the historical and political contexts of novels and the "structures of feeling" that are shared by many different authors goes hand-in-hand with the recognition that individual authors may break the mold. The interaction between the individual and the social "may include radical tension and disturbance, even actual and irresolvable contradictions of a conscious kind, as often as they include integration" (qtd. in Scott 18). As Scott argues in relation to Caribbean literature, then, "despite the class character of the novel—strongly associated with the rise of the bourgeoisie—we are often also able to see beyond this limited perspective and to grasp broader truths about postindependence Caribbean societies. The writer is neither simply a representative of their class position and social environment nor the autonomous subject of bourgeois ideology: the two exist dialectically" (17).

Decentering Rushdie is motivated by this method of examining the postcolonial Indian English novel in terms of its historical contexts, its politics, and its literary forms. Without engaging with the Indian nation-state and its fortunes in a changing world, the shift in ideas that has accompanied the fizzling-out of the national liberation struggles, and the specific impact of these on the middle-class, English-speaking author, we cannot grapple with postcoloniality, its literature, and its production of multiple cosmopolitan identities in any meaningful way. Theorizations of the postcolonial that delimit the field to contemporary and/or postmodern fiction, and then construct generalizations about postcolonial society from these novels alone, participate precisely in the sorts of simplified, antimaterialist approaches that Lukacs and Scott describe—even if they are politically and theoretically opposed to bourgeois methods of analysis. At the same time, to reduce literature to the status of either a sociological artifact or a political tract—and this tendency is especially prevalent with regard to critiques

of Anglophone postcolonial texts—is also to go against the very principles of the Marxist critique of bourgeois thought. Therefore, as John Mee
argues, "any assumption that [the Indian English novel of the 1980s and
1990s] is simply doing the work of the globalized middle classes"—though
offering "a useful corrective to [critiques that] celebrate postcolonial literature as a subversive rewriting of the authority of the colonial center"—is
not considering the complexities of culture and class with regard to, for
instance, the continuing role of English in India today as a mediator both
within and beyond the nation (335).

A rigid determinism between class position, cosmopolitan identity, and
politics very much describes the ways in which postmodernism's euphoric
embrace of contemporary postcolonial writing has been critiqued. Take,
for instance, K. Anthony Appiah's famous argument that "Post-coloniality
is the condition of what we might ungenerously call a comprador intelligentsia: of a relatively small, Western-style, Western-trained, group of writers and thinkers who mediate the trade in cultural commodities of Western
capitalism at the periphery" ("Is the Post" 348). To a degree, Appiah is
concerned about the Western institutions' labeling of non-Western culture:
he wants to separate the writing that happens in formerly colonized spaces
from the terms "postcolonial" and "postcoloniality." This concern is quite
understandable, and articulated frequently by scholars who actually live
and work in postcolonial nations. But very close to the surface of such
remarks is the assumption that class position is simply to be equated with
ideology and politics, giving us no way to analyze, for instance, the left/
progressive politics of contemporary Indian English writers, the nation-
oriented and anticolonial stances of earlier ones, and/or the ways in which
all postcolonial writers and critics work in contexts shaped by Western
institutions and markets.

This is not to back away from the realities of class and nation that, in
fact, enable cosmopolitan experiences and identities. It is absolutely essential to recognize how small a fraction of the postcolonial world we are
discussing when we speak of postcolonial novelists and their audiences,
Anglophone or not. Timothy Brennan suggests, for instance, that

> under the conditions of illiteracy and shortages, and given simply the
> leisure-time necessary for reading one, the novel has been an elitist and
> minority form in developing countries when compared to poem, song,
> television, and film. Almost inevitably, it has been a form through which
> a thin, foreign-educated stratum (however sensitive or committed to
> domestic political interests) has communicated to metropolitan reading

publics, often in translation. It has been, in short, a naturally cosmopolitan form that empire has allowed to play a national role, as it were, only in an international arena. (*Salman Rushdie* 17–18)

As Tabish Khair writes in relation to India, there has certainly been a large increase in levels of literacy, wealth, and leisure time—growing over the course of the twentieth century and accelerating after 1947. General literacy has increased from 6 percent (in 1911) to about 15 percent (in the early 1940s) to about 50 percent in the 1990s; life expectancy has gone from 32.1 years in 1951 to 60.8 in 1992; GNP has risen from Rs. 180,000 crores in 1984 to Rs. 530,000 in 1992, and so forth (Khair 58–59). Nevertheless, though millions of Indians today can afford to "indulge in commoditized leisure activities and . . . have the exposure and education [. . .] to include the reading of novels and stories" within this, "*it is a small percentage of this privileged class which actually reads fiction in English*" (Khair 59; original italics). So the Indian (English) novel seems to mainly look abroad for its readers, partly because it appeals only to elites and partly because even in the context of a growing middle class there is only a small audience.

Now, what shall we do with this knowledge? We can interrogate Indian English writers' claims to speak for all Indians or problematize the assumptions made about the writers by foreign audiences. We can use it to trace, as Khair does, why the genre seems to produce so little that speaks about ordinary Indians' lives, that describes their spaces, that crosses the lines of class and caste. But if we merely isolate these empirical facts and allow them to carry the weight of a de facto ideological critique or literary analysis, we will not be able to grasp, for instance, how new literary forms have emerged out of the same social milieu, how middle-class intellectuals have expressed a range of political positions, or how artists, intellectuals, and novelists both reflect and participate in shaping the world around them. As I show in the next section, Indian English novelists have been linked to the societies they inhabit in complicated ways, engaged in the formation of new movements and ideological currents on multiple levels.

With regard to questions of art and political criticism, Leon Trotsky's reflections of the 1920s and 1930s, written against both the emerging Russian Formalists, on the one hand, and Stalinist socialist realism, on the other, have helped me negotiate a path between today's variants of the same: dehistoricized formalism and deterministic political criticism. In *Literature and Revolution* (1923), for example, Trotsky writes:

It is unquestionably true that the need for art is not created by economic conditions. But neither is the need for food created by economics. On the contrary, the need for food and warmth creates economics. It is very true that one cannot always go by the principles of Marxism in deciding whether to reject or accept a work of art. A work of art should, in the first place, be judged by its own law, that is, by the laws of art. But Marxism alone can explain why and how a given tendency in art has originated in a given period of history; in other words, who it was who made a demand for such an artistic form and not another, and why. (207)

Trotsky presents a dynamic picture of Marxist methodology in response to the Formalists' caricature of Marxism as economic determinism. First, he establishes the dominance of material reality (the need for food, warmth, and art) over the theoretical understanding of that reality (economics, Marxism, criticism) by arguing, in fact, that the very existence of the former is what "creates" the conditions of possibility for the latter. The familiar base-superstructure paradigm is in operation here, but in ways that complicate notions of the "base": the "need for art," indeed, joins "the need for food and warmth" as an essential aspect of human life. Further, now narrowly focusing on the question of art, Trotsky asserts the primacy of criticism ("the law of art") in judging any work of art over Marxism per se, though the latter is essential to analyzing the historical conditions of that art and, we might add, of artistic criticism as well. The methodological point being made is that the question of artistic judgment achieves a certain autonomy from the fields of politics and economics even as, following Marxism's holistic approach, the different fields remain dialectically connected. Given the drab history of the Proletkult and the doctrine of socialist realism, it is worth emphasizing that Trotsky does not draw an opposition between form (to be analyzed by "the law of art") and content (to be analyzed by Marxism). Indeed, he argues that Marxist analysis is required for an adequate understanding of "artistic form," which itself has a history. Refusing to simply merge the elements of the base-superstructure paradigm actually has the effect, in this methodology, of emphasizing both their distinctiveness and their dialectical relationship. Art and artistic form need to be related to economic, ideological, and historical analysis but cannot be reduced to it.

As Marx writes in *The Eighteenth Brumaire of Louis Bonaparte*, human beings "make their own history. But they do not make it [. . .] under circumstances chosen by themselves, but under circumstances directly encountered, given, and transmitted from the past" (595). Eschewing the mechanical determinism that flows from both vulgar formalism and vulgar political criticism, Marxist literary criticism, when at its best, aims to both ground and allow for the expansiveness of the artistic imagination—not only when texts set the discovery of their material circumstances as their own task, but also when their claims to radical indeterminacy aim to make us believe that the search for determinacy and causality is itself a fiction.

Literature in a Whirlwind of Change

Three related contexts can help explain the postnational turn: 1) the transformation brought about by the global economic crisis of the 1970s and the ideological shifts corresponding to it, 2) the relationship of the crisis to India and the Emergency period, and 3) the middle-class subject positions constructed in these contexts, and—as a specific subgroup of this—the left-leaning intellectual's tendency to turn away from the legacies of anti-colonial struggle in constructing a new cosmopolitan identity. In a succinct discussion of the economic and political contexts in which many postcolonial societies found themselves after World War II, Lazarus suggests that we can roughly divide the era into two phases: "a quarter-century or so of explosive growth, marked by significant gains and the [unprecedented and] wide dispersal of social, economic, and political benefits to the population at large," and a period of decline as, leading up to and following the steep hike of oil prices in 1973, "the world system stumbled into economic recession and attendant political crisis" ("Global" 21). While capitalist accumulation over both phases was undoubtedly marked by exploitation, social hierarchies, and unevenness, movements of marginalized and oppressed peoples had had the scope to demand a bit more from their rulers before the economic downturn. The first phase (1945–73) was marked by the rise of welfare states and movements for civil rights and equality in the West, with Europe now subordinated to the United States, the development of state capitalism in the Soviet Bloc, and the growth of democratization and modernization, however selective and limited, in the newly decolonized spaces of the "Third World," joining Latin America. The second phase (since 1973) saw the reversal of these trends with capitalist classes everywhere, in the context of a falling rate of profit, embarking on a full-scale redistribution of the wealth toward the wealthy. Neoliberalism and privatization—though challenged everywhere and far

from inevitable—become the order of the day, translating into the dismantling of welfare states in the West, the outright collapse of Soviet-style state
capitalism, and the end of state-protected capitalist growth and development in the global South.[10]

As can be expected, the poorer economies of the world faced the greatest consequences, as "structural adjustment programs" under the World
Bank and International Monetary Fund prioritized profits over social services and subordinated national sovereignty to global markets dominated
by the West. This strengthened the hands of national capitalists for whom
governments, both elected and dictatorial, paved the way by beating down
unionizing efforts, movements by indigenous peoples and national minorities, and struggles to expand democracy. After independence, the "cross-
class alliance disintegrated as the different poles of the national liberation
movements pursued their antagonistic class interests" (Scott 16).[11] While
internal struggles to move from political freedom to true emancipation
continued, in other words, they did so in a wretched global context. The
newly independent nation-states, already impoverished and exploited by
a period of colonial looting of natural and human resources, were forced
to take their place "in an inegalitarian, unevenly integrated, and highly
polarized world-system of nation-states" (Lazarus, "Global" 19) whose
inequalities and polarizations only accelerated over the course of the twentieth century.

On the level of ideas and aspirations, to speak in very broad terms,
the two phases were linked to a general shift from the notion that revolution and change were possible and immanent to the notion that "there
is no alternative" to capitalism, as Prime Minister Margaret Thatcher of
Britain famously phrased it.[12] It is in these various contexts that we can
read Krishnaswamy's observation that the first generation of Anglophone
novels from Asia and Africa "largely reflected the belief [. . .] that new
literatures in new nations should be anti-colonial and nationalistic," while
novels from the 1970s and the 1980s "aimed to expose corrupt national
bourgeoisies that had championed the causes of rationalization, industrialization, and bureaucratization in the name of nationalism and nativism" and "repudiated the realist novel because it naturalized a failed
nationalism" ("Mythologies" 125–26). This shift in ways of representing
the nation has a firm basis in material relations. In India, while popular
struggles continued in various arenas—combining leftist, nationalist, and/
or "traditionalist" discourses in their demands for local rights, for sus-
tainable development, for education, and so forth—the growing class
divide by the 1970s and 1980s meant that unlike during the years of the

31

anticolonial movement and the building of the new nation-state, middle-class writers were often cut off from the dynamic possibilities of change emerging within the nation itself. Their left/progressive orientation drew them toward investigating the breakdown of the liberation project, but the nation increasingly became little more than an abstraction in their writing. It is not only that writers (in all languages) have made a *thematic* shift from forging unity with the nation to questioning "the nature of that unity" (Mee 318–19) but also that—as Scott writes about post-1970s Caribbean writers—we see a "cavernous" gap between the world of the writer and of most Indians (Scott 17), one to which metafictional texts often pointed with various degrees of concern.

Let me focus for a moment on the enormous sense of possibility that was spawned by the anticolonial struggles—the petering-out of which explains the depth of the contemporary turn away from the nation among many left/progressive writers and theorists. The earlier Indian English texts were generally oriented toward the nation, then, primarily because it was not seen as antithetical to their cosmopolitan identities and self-perceptions as progressive, democratic, and antiparochial. The period that historians have described as being one of "hope and achievement" (Chandra, Mukherjee, and Mukherjee) also extended to leftist activists and the critical intelligentsia in that the specific conditions of the new India, for all of its problems, expanded the basis on which deeper and more comprehensive versions of democracy and social justice could be enacted. The Constitution of 1950 established, for the first time, universal adult franchise, the basis for civil liberties and an independent press, new opportunities for education and social welfare, and explicit mandates against caste discrimination. It is for this reason that the many who opposed the ongoing inequalities, whether under Nehru or his daughter, often did so in the name of *returning* to the original principles of the anticolonial movement and the early postcolonial period, regarded as genuinely radical and independent. As Basil Davidson puts it in *The Black Man's Burden*, a book whose subtitle (*Africa and the Curse of the Nation-State*) leaves little doubt about its recognition of the crises following decolonization, the hopefulness of the aftermath of independence was based on the real changes that independence brought: "The social freedoms that had been the magnet for nationalism were making themselves increasingly felt; and the grim silence of the colonial years was already shattered by a hubbub of plans and schemes for a more favorable future" (195–96).

This is not only about charting a simple movement from faith to disillusionment. Among most postcolonial writers, the support for the new nation-state was hardly ever uncritical. Precisely *because of* their links to the populist elements of the anticolonial struggle, many Indian writers and intellectuals recognized that Nehruvian India, like other nation-states decolonized after World War II, was always engaged in the decidedly nonrevolutionary work of developing a modern, capitalist nation-state—with all of its attending class divisions and compromises with urban and rural elites, its border disputes and wars, and its internal conflicts between regional, linguistic, and religious groups. For radical writers such as Faiz Ahmad Faiz, for instance, who were critical of the Partition of British India and the contradictions of postcolonial development, the projects of "India" and "Pakistan" were to be challenged from the very start. While such intellectuals and artists supported the anticolonial struggle fully, they were conscious of the class contradictions that it could not resolve and, in that light, refused to "pain[t] the bourgeois-led national liberation movements in revolutionary socialist colors" (Lewis).

The tenor of the following lines from the Sudanese writer Tayeb Salih's *Season of Migration to the North* (1969) is unremarkably common in the literature of the time, mixing the anticipation of self-determination (material, cultural, and otherwise) with a clear recognition of challenges: "Sooner or later they'll leave our country, just as many people throughout history left many countries. The railways, ships, hospitals, factories, and schools will be ours and we'll speak their language without either a sense of guilt or a sense of gratitude. Once again we shall be as were—ordinary people—and if we are lies we shall be lies of our own making" (qtd. in Sivanandan 49). The radical desire for sheer ordinariness reminds us of the ending of Langston Hughes's "The Negro Artist and the Racial Mountain" (1926): "We younger Negro artists who create now intend to express our individual dark-skinned selves without fear or shame. [. . .] We know we are beautiful. And ugly too." The nation-oriented, realist writings of the early postcolonial period, whether in English or in other Indian languages, were not "legitimations of nationalism" (Appiah, "Is the Post" 353) in the sense of being uncritical celebrations of the present but were engaged in the process of formulating what that nation was and would become. Even in the naïvely titled novel *A Time to Be Happy*, Sahgal has her protagonist describe the hope and anticipation of the postindependence moment as being ambiguous and amorphous, "the kind of dim reality which exists in a theater before the curtain rises for the next scene of the performance" (182).

In these early postcolonial Indian (English) writers, we see the continuing articulation of what Priyamvada Gopal, in *Literary Radicalism in*

India, calls the "critical spirit" of those associated with the All-India Progressive Writers Association (PWA)—a national organization that, like its partner group the Indian People's Theater Association (IPTA), provided venues for an entire generation of artists and intellectuals "who shared the conviction that art, literature, and film could help share and transform the nascent nation-state in progressive directions" (2). In their manifesto of 1936, drafted by the Indian English writer Mulk Raj Anand in conjunction with those who wrote primarily in vernacular languages, the PWA attested to the "[r]adical changes [. . .] taking place in Indian society" and set the goal of constructing an Indian literature focused on "the problems of hunger and poverty, social backwardness, and political subjection" (qtd. in P. Gopal, *Literary* 13). In the process, though, they reminded themselves and others that there not all elements of the anticolonial movement were progressive: "All that drags us down to passivity, inaction and unreason we regard as re-actionary [*sic*]. All that arouses in us the critical spirit, which examines institutions and customs in the light of reason, which helps us to act, to organize ourselves, to transform, we accept as progressive" (13–14). PWA writers such as Khwaja Ahmad Abbas, Ahmad Ali, Rajinder Singh Bedi, Ismat Chughtai, Rashid Jahan, Saadat Hasan Manto, and Sajjat Zaheer took up a wide variety of themes and social issues, contesting colonialism, communalism, sexism, caste hierarchy, and traditional notions about sexuality, and always seeking to push the limits of social consciousness. Realism dominated aesthetically, but rather than simply offering a cover for mainstream nationalism, it engaged in the process of constructing the nation through an independent lens.[13]

The PWA's critical orientation toward anticolonial nationalism demonstrates the claims that many historians and theorists have made since. Although decolonization and its aftermath had many failures, anticolonial nationalism was not a unitary or homogenous enterprise; it was made of up an incredible amalgam of elite and subaltern interests, and "the nation" was a site of struggle that could be shaped in any number of ways. We are not speaking of theory or ideology here but of history. As Ranajit Guha articulates in an early critique of Benedict Anderson's *Imagined Communities:* "By conceptualizing nationalism exclusively in terms of interaction between the indigenous elite and the colonizers, it fails to acknowledge and explain the sturdy nationalism of the mass of the people, especially in the Indian peasantry [. . .] As recent work on Indian history [. . .] has established without a doubt, much of this movement originated in popular initiatives independently of elite leadership" ("Nationalism" 104). Living in the moment itself, many Indian writers realized that "there was a range of radical *possibilities* that were thrown up by the very nature of the anti-colonial struggle and the process of decolonization; what happens after independence does not negate these possibilities even as it may eliminate, co-opt, or reshape them" (P. Gopal, *Literary Radicalism* 23).[14] Whether or not early postcolonial Indian English novelists explicitly agreed with the agenda of the PWA, its critical support for the nationalist project motivated writers across the board.

Though it has been relatively understudied and even minimized, the Emergency period and its aftermath represented India's break from the early phase of decolonization, in terms of both socioeconomic and ideological trajectories.[15] The Emergency was a "critical event" in the sense that Veena Das and Emma Tarlo use the term: in the context of the deterioration of the project of decolonization, it produced an environment in which relations between ordinary Indians, bureaucrats, politicians, and the state were reorganized and produced anew.[16] Whereas India's turn to neoliberal expansion of the economy is usually linked to the regimes of Rajiv Gandhi (1984–89) and P. V. Narasimha Rao (1991–96), the rejection of Nehruvian state capitalism and the accelerated transfer of wealth toward private capital originated earlier, in Indira Gandhi's second term (1980–84), and even in policies enacted during the Emergency. Gandhi's militarism and foreign policy, including the suppression of Leftist radicals during the 1971 war for Bangladeshi liberation and the first nuclear explosion in 1976, laid the groundwork for India's rise, today, as a subimperialist power. The crushing of labor struggles, as in the Railway Workers strike of 1974 and the Bombay textile strike of 1982–83, the suppression of civil liberties, the overt abuse of executive power over the legislative and judicial branches, atrocities such as slum demolition and forced vasectomies and hysterectomies—all of these cleared the way for the new phase in capitalism. It is in this context that, as host of the Non-Aligned Movement conference in 1983, Indira Gandhi effectively sided with those who wanted to turn the "Third World" from being a political project that stood for anti-imperialism and economic sovereignty into a doormat for neoliberal ideology and corporate globalization (Prashad 207–23). Ironically, "socialism" remained the mantra for a whole host of Third World nation-states like India that, after the 1970s, increased the rate of exploitation of their own people by intensifying their integration with Western capital.

As Nagesh Rao writes in relation to Amitav Ghosh's *The Shadow Lines* (1988), therefore, the postnational turn and "the discourse of diaspora, hybridity, and migrancy [have] not been conjured up by [Indian

English novelists] out of thin air" but have "a material and historical referent" in these ideological and socioeconomic contexts ("Cosmopolitanism" 112). It is worth remembering that many in the same class of people,
after all, had radicalized in periods of mass struggle and given support to
anticolonial nationalism, often through an internationalist lens—and the
afterglow of this association continued into the 1970s. But the postcolonial intellectuals faced a host of contradictions in the 1980s and 1990s.
The socioeconomic forces of transnational capitalism that made the labor
of mobile, English-educated writers and scholars incredibly marketable—
along with everyone from white-collar workers in software, professionals
from the technical-managerial ranks, and members of the Indian bourgeoisie—also enabled the demise of the great movements of the twentieth
century (national liberation, nonalignment, socialism) and of left visions
more generally.

Certainly, most of these elites have embraced liberalization and privatization enthusiastically and celebrated the end of the obstacles that Nehruvian protectionism placed on their advancement. The period after the
Emergency period meant, for them, the opening up of vast horizons.
But while Indian English novelists have certainly benefited from the new
dynamics, they have also been critical of "the pernicious globalism sur-
facing in dispersed local contexts" (B. Ghosh 5). As such, they have consistently "looked back" to the Emergency in order to launch a left and
progressive critique of the nation. An explicit referent in many post-1980
novels, including *The Great Indian Novel, Midnight's Children, Rich Like
Us,* and Rohinton Mistry's *A Fine Balance* (1995), the Emergency appears
as both a historical marker of and a symbol for the demise of the nation—
engendering, in Rushdie, Tharoor, and Mistry, a historiographical argument that forges direct links between Indira Gandhi's policies and those of
her father. For many left/progressive intellectuals and artists—or, at least,
the ones who dominate Postcolonial Studies—their class status has linked
them to the cosmopolitan middle and upper classes benefiting from neoliberal globalization while their politics has led them to adopt, amidst the
general demise of secularism and the Left, a postnational stance, postmodern aesthetics, and/or postmodernist epistemologies.

These are the historical, political, and ideological contexts that can
help explain not only Rushdie's shifting perspectives on Indian writing
between the early 1980s and the late 1990s but the general movement of
Indian English writers from *namak-halaal* to postnational views on the
nation. In the following sections, I turn specifically to the category of cosmopolitanism and how it can be used to understand the Indian English

novel if we recognize its malleability in relation to the nation and its histories. In particular, I offer a clearer discussion of what I mean by *"namak-halaal cosmopolitanism."*

Indian (English) Cosmopolitanisms

Cosmopolitanism in Indian English writing is nothing new. A cosmopolitan perspective has been implicit in the genre since it came into its own in the early nineteenth century when, for instance, Raja Ram Mohun Roy agitated for English education to replace Orientalist-supported Sanskrit and Arabic seminaries that would only "load the minds of youth with grammatical necessities and metaphysical distinctions with little or no particular use to the possessor or to society" (qtd. in Viswanathan 138). As Nehru said of himself, he was "a queer mixture of East and West, out of place everywhere, at home nowhere" (L. Gandhi 171). While such examples hint at the pervasiveness of cosmopolitan attitudes and questions in the colonial period, they also show that cosmopolitan identity, especially for colonized/postcolonial subjects, is always specific and contingent, shaped by class, nation, race, and gender. In this study of English-educated elites, then, I define cosmopolitanism in the following way: it describes the experience of sections of the (urban) bourgeoisie and middle-class intelligentsia, who because of their class location, upbringing, and national location (and often their gender) can engage with and inhabit European cultures (languages, foods, dress, music, art, mythologies, social customs)—with a degree of comfort and even "competence."[17]

My restriction of the term is not meant to exclude or devalue the innumerably diverse array of cross-cultural experiences that make up the fabric of every individual and community. Rather, I'm being specific in order to cut "cosmopolitanism" down to size. Tragically, therefore, cosmopolitanism can never be as universal and all-encompassing as it desires, countering Paul Rabinow's claim that "We are all cosmopolitans" (qtd. in Brennan, *At Home* 4). We can define a few limits right away. First, cosmopolitanism does not include all types of cross-cultural contact throughout history because it is embedded within the period of capitalist modernity and the economic and political processes through which nation-states have emerged throughout the world. It is on the basis of the (unequal) historical relations between these nation-states that this modern cosmopolitanism is even made possible. As a consequence, second, the cosmopolitanism of colonized/postcolonial elites in particular is always directed toward developing a comfort with *the West,* looking toward it from a position of inferiority deriving from the contexts from which the very desire emerges. Finally, my definition excludes a specifically working-class "comfort" with different national cultures because "cosmopolitanism" has historically been associated with classes that have a more direct relation to the ownership of economic and cultural capital. There is a tremendous volition, a veritable "will to cosmopolitanism," that is the calling card of cosmopolitan identity—apparent even in Rabinow's characterization of cosmopolitanism as a universal state of being. The term applies easily to Roy and Nehru, as well as the novelists being studied here, because they explicitly interrogate their relationships to Englishness and the West.

Nevertheless, as we have seen, the fact that cosmopolitan identity is always tied to class and national identity does not mean that cosmopolitanism automatically implies certain ideological positions. Over time, for instance, Indian English writing has contained many different ideological currents—from loyalism to anticolonial nationalism, from parochialism of all kinds to liberal and socialist versions of internationalism. The construction of cosmopolitan identity and perspective in a given historical moment—and not simply the fact of a writer's access to English education (i.e., of class position)—becomes important, then. While the Indian English novel has always been located in elite centers of production and consumption, its contradictory position, simultaneously tied to structures of British colonialism and literary tradition on the one hand and the imperatives of anticolonial and/or cultural nationalism on the other, has allowed different possibilities for the ideological perspectives and representational strategies emerging from that location. In reading the Indian English novel, we can recover the progressive, antiparochial thrust that lies behind the term even as we gauge the ways in which the class position and historical contexts of such cosmopolitans shape their political views—and representations of postcolonial life. By grounding postcolonial cosmopolitanism thus—but without necessarily linking this to any specific ideology or perspective—we can account for its different articulations over time. My readings show that cosmopolitanism's (literary) identities are multiple and uneven; the Indian English novels I have selected display a variety of perspectives on and approaches to the nation—"looking back" in the process of "looking away."

Intellectuals, incessantly reflecting on themselves as a group, have often taken up the movement between "home" and "world" in a number of ways, but there has been a tendency in Postcolonial Studies and other fields to emphasize the importance of "looking away" much more than "looking back." Liberation and freedom in thought seem to be linked much more to discourses of rootlessness than rootedness. One example is the category of "cosmopolitics" that has been put forward by critics and theorists in different disciplines, asserting that cosmopolitan location is inherently associated with radical and democratic ideologies.[18] This is true even of intellectuals such as Edward Said, whose writings are quite supportive of radical nationalist movements and whose celebratory comments about "exile" are often qualified by the recognition that it is a condition constituted by loss and pain. In *The World, the Text, and the Critic* (1983), for example, Said points to the dynamic by which the intellectual 1) learns how to identify her/his "filiative" and "natural" moorings, 2) develops a critical consciousness and moves outside of the native space through "affiliative" links and associations, and then 3) moves toward either a reappropriation and restructuring of filial spaces or a radical break from them (16–30). For Said, indeed, this movement describes not only the work of intellectuals but human consciousness in general. But although Said, unlike many more explicitly postmodernist critics, often leaves room for the multiple possibilities inherent in the process of filiation/affiliation, he clearly values "looking away," seeing it as fundamentally more radical and necessary than "looking back."[19] In order to grapple with the fact that intellectuals have often defended and played a role within anticolonial and progressive nationalist movements—a task that Said himself both encouraged and embodied—we need to be able to describe the multiple formations of cosmopolitan (literary) identity and production in ways that are not proscriptive. Rather than rejecting nation-oriented cosmopolitanisms out of hand, we need categories that bear witness to its presence—regardless of our own positions on the national question.

The category of "*namak-halaal* cosmopolitanism" allows me to group together one such set of cosmopolitan perspectives and strategies that dominated Indian English novels from the late 1940s to the Emergency period but appears only fitfully after this time. It's worth emphasizing that in India, as elsewhere, the development of the novel was itself linked to the emergence of the nation. The novel form became prominent among Indian English writers only in the 1930s and 1940s, at the height of the nationalist movement (L. Gandhi 173). These *namak-halaal* texts value a mode of cosmopolitan-elite identity that 1) remains committed to the project of popular emancipation from oppression and poverty; 2) envisions a national and/or local space, as opposed to a Western or transnational one, as a potential vehicle for that emancipation; and 3) educates its cosmopolitan-elite readers about their role in constructing such a national space. I call this cosmopolitanism *"namak-halaal"* rather than "nationalist" in order to emphasize the difference between orientation and ideology, and, thus, to group together texts that continue to align themselves with the nation whether or not they are also sympathetic to the Indian government and leaders sanctioned by nationalist historiography. While some novels of this period do subscribe to a mainstream nationalist ideology, many others, such as Khushwant Singh's *Train to Pakistan* (1956) or Bhabani Bhattacharya's *Shadow from Ladakh* (1966), are fiercely skeptical of official India even while remaining optimistic about the possibility of transforming the nation into a fit vehicle for popular progress. *Namak-halaal* novels are "true to their salt," therefore, not because they engage in flag-waving or naïvely swallow the populist rhetoric of politicians, but because they continue to privilege "India" as the reference point for emancipation and progress.

Indeed, many novels of the early postcolonial period positioned themselves as critical supporters of the legacies of the national liberation struggle as part of their general desire to transform society anew. Through characterization, voice, plot, and theme, *namak-halaal* texts foreground the explicit criticism of British-colonial racism; the victimization of Indian subjects, especially oppressed groups, under Western modernity; the growing national and subaltern-centered consciousness of Westernized elite protagonists; and the betrayal of cosmopolitan-elites who either turn away from Indian languages and culture or romanticize India in ways that mask existing inequalities. "*Namak-halaal* cosmopolitanism" describes both the lens through which these novels are structured and the identities that they construct. The classic tale of the transformation of the cosmopolitan-elite protagonist, marked by his/her development of a nationalist and/or activist consciousness, is offered here in a didactic mode. The characters become models for training and molding the cosmopolitan-elite readers in the novels' real and implied audiences.

When noting the influence of the anticolonial movement on Indian writers in English, it is important not to divorce their cosmopolitan experience too sharply from that of Indian (elite) writers in all languages. On the structural level, British colonialism not only brought English to India but decisively shaped Indian modernity and the production of the indigenous petit bourgeoisie and bourgeoisie. Further, as several commentators have noted, through its educational institutions and the introduction of print capitalism, colonialism shaped the very development and spread of the modern Indian languages and literatures (e.g., Iyengar 30). It would have been impossible for any Indian intellectual, not to speak of an Indian English writer, to produce writing without having the structures and themes of colonialism penetrate into their work. As Susie Tharu and K. Lalitha suggest, "What was to become modern Indian literature was largely produced by an English-educated urban middle class" (9); many of the early writers in the various Indian languages were bilingual and also published in English. On the individual level, both late colonial and early postcolonial writers in English influenced and were influenced by literary and artistic movements that inevitably involved them in the political questions all around them.[20] "We are all instinctively bilingual," says Indian English novelist Raja Rao in the foreword to *Kanthapura* (1938).

As an illustration of this "bilingualism," let's look again at the role of Mulk Raj Anand in the PWA, alluded to in the last section. The PWA writers' links to English, English-influenced institutions, and England itself are multiple and varied, but they seem to associate with "Englishness" without—as Tayeb Salih phrases it—"either a sense of guilt or a sense of gratitude" (qtd. in Sivanandan 49). While many of Anand's PWA associates wrote in vernacular languages, many also published in English on occasion, and critical discussions of literature often occurred in English (P. Gopal, *Literary* 25). All were open to inspirations wherever they found them; Chughtai, for instance, primarily wrote in Urdu but received a B.A. in English and the Arts from Isabella Thoburn College and claimed to be stimulated by everything from the Bible to Darwin, Freud, and nineteenth-century European novels (P. Gopal, *Literary* 68). Indeed, the nucleus for what became the PWA was initially formed by a group of Indian expatriate writers in London, at a meeting in the Nanking Restaurant in 1935.

We see, in Anand's reminiscences, an interesting tension between the pull toward and away from English and England. Anand's attraction to the PWA and its unquestioning anti-imperialism emerged from his disillusionment with the Bloomsbury group, its "undeclared ban on political talk," and its acceptance and even endorsement of British imperialism in India (P. Gopal, *Literary* 23; Ranasinha 33). The concerns that dominate Rushdie's "'Commonwealth Literature' Does Not Exist" reverberate here; Anand and fellow-founders of the PWA such as Sajjat Zaheer felt that unless an organization was formed in India, in proximity to the struggle of "the ugly face of Fascism in our country" as Anand called it, the group would just end up representing India to the West and the West to India in simplistic ways (P. Gopal, *Literary* 25). For intellectuals such as Anand, this turn to the nation was completely in conjunction with their cosmopolitan identity and (in his case) internationalist politics—not only theoretically but practically, as Anand was jailed briefly during the Non-Cooperation movement of the early 1920s, participated in conferences on fascism and racism across Europe in the 1930s, and joined the International Brigade during the Spanish Civil War in 1936 (L. Gandhi 174–75).

Perhaps Anand's famous discussion with M. K. Gandhi about his novel *Untouchable* (1935), one of the earliest and most important Indian English novels, exemplifies the fluidity with which cosmopolitan subjects moved across borders of language and ideology. The novel itself was inspired by Gandhi's account in his (English-language) newspaper *Young India* about the story of Uka, an ordinary Dalit sweeper-boy. Moving "from Bloomsbury to Sabarmati," Anand lived in Gandhi's Sabarmati Ashram, received comments from him on the initial draft of *Untouchable* (Gandhi recommended revision on the grounds that the protagonist, Bakha, was too much like a "Bloomsbury intellectual"), and took Gandhi's counsel on writing in English on Indian themes (L. Gandhi 175). Gandhi's response to Anand on the politics of English—"The purpose of language is to communicate, isn't it? If so, say your say in any language that comes to hand" (qtd. in Mehrotra 13)—privileges language's use-value over any perceived political stigma engrained within it.[21] The Anand-Gandhi exchange can serve as an example of the openness of English-educated cosmopolitanisms toward the nation, the openness of nationalists toward English, and the ways in which Indian English writers were part of the same terrain as other nation-oriented cosmopolitans, both writers and political leaders. Indeed, English was structurally tied into the very working of the postcolonial state as the only all-India language: at Nehru's insistence, the Constitution of 1950 decreed that English would "continue to be used for all the official purposes of the Union" as an all-India language was necessary (Mehrotra 13).

Consider, in contrast to my definitions and methods of discussing the dynamics between class position, cosmopolitan identity, and ideology, Makarand Paranjape's and Adil Jussawalla's criticisms of Indian (English) literature. In "Inside and Outside the Whale," Paranjape argues: "During the mass movement for independence the bourgeois Indian English novelists had identified themselves with the aspirations of the proletariat, but after independence, they retreated back to their traditional class positions of elitism and aloofness" (214). Since no Indian English writer "was jailed or tortured for his or her beliefs as in some other Third World countries" and all "remained insulated and secure from most of the major shocks of post-independence India" (216), the Indian English novel remained a thoroughly bourgeois novel.[22] While Paranjape does imply that writing from India in the vernacular languages has been politically committed, Jussawalla, in *New Writing in India* (1974), gives no quarter to any Indian literature. He writes that the metaphors of dismemberment, obsession with death, and sociopolitical paralysis in Indian literature are reflections of

> the Indian petty bourgeoisie's present inability to find a dynamic role for itself in a society which is slowly transforming itself from the semi-feudal [to the capitalist]. Wedged between the class that employs it and the broad masses of peasants and the growing urban proletariat, it can only torment itself with its own contradictions or turn on itself in a fury of self-destruction. This is the writing of a bourgeoisie at a dead end. (qtd. in Dharwadker, "Indian" 237)

Jussawalla's attempt to relate literary metaphors, the class positions of the writers, and the broader context of postcolonial India mirrors the type of integrated analysis that my book conducts, simultaneously considering the relationship between history, class position, ideology, and aesthetics. However, there seems to be a deterministic relationship between the different elements that is centered on an assumption about the cosmopolitan, middle-class intellectual, namely that s/he always turns toward the paradigms established by the bourgeoisie.

I sympathize with the observation that the postcolonial Indian English consistently turns inwards decisively and remains remarkably "untouched by mass movements and mass aspirations" (Paranjape, "Inside and Outside" 215). Compared with the postcolonial African novel in English, for example, the genre appears to be far less willing to construct narratives through the voices of oppressed and marginalized subjects. Nevertheless, the deterministic paradigms of causality at play here lead Paranjape and Jussawalla to lump together all Indian English writing and to misread important shifts that do develop—including political shifts. For instance, Paranjape's comment that Anita Desai's "psychological studies of half-mad women" and Kamala Markandaya's "clumsy and unconvincing naturalism of course, do not show any political commitment" (215) is not only blind to the deep political concern with which these novelists address the failed project of national liberation, but also depends on and constructs a masculinist category of the political that excludes issues concerning women, especially middle-class women, from its purview. In actuality, we find that at key historical moments—decolonization, the Emergency, recent globalization—Indian cosmopolitan writers, especially those concerned with women's oppression, have often turned *against* the postcolonial bourgeoisie, such that their writing cannot be called "the writing of a bourgeoisie" in any useful way. Ideology, form, and content do not follow from a particular class position or cultural identity—*especially* when that class is the petit bourgeoisie, whose definition, in classical Marxism, is precisely that it moves back and forth between classes in ways that are sometimes unpredictable. A more fluid definition of cosmopolitanism allows us to see, rather, when and how the cosmopolitan-elite artist breaks with the project of national liberation, and to investigate aspects of the political whose relationship to the nation may be tangential precisely because of the masculinist and elitist limitations of mainstream nationalist consciousness and the inequities of postcolonial reality.

Theories of cosmopolitanism create strange bedfellows. What Paranjape and Jussawalla negatively describe as cosmopolitan-elite aloofness from the nation and its struggles is supported by writers such as K. Anthony Appiah, Richard Rorty, and Robert Reich who have questioned cosmopolitanisms for opposing and/or lacking patriotism and national feeling. From a diametrically opposed view, in terms of content but not form, those who celebrate cosmopolitan rejections of the nation, such as Martha Nussbaum, Bruce Robbins, and Carol Breckenridge, to take a few examples, root their support for cosmopolitanisms of various kinds in their implicit criticism of nationalisms as being always already reactionary. The cosmopolitanism/nationalism opposition holds in each case (though Appiah has a category called "cosmopolitan patriotism"). Only a few theorists, such as Tim Brennan, Pheng Cheah, and Hamid Dabashi—coming from a variety of positions themselves—have developed notions of cosmopolitanism that are more thoroughly historicized and open to the fact that the nation, especially in anticolonial contexts, has often been central to cosmopolitan and/or internationalist visions of change.[23] Indeed, Brennan interrogates the ways in which certain antinationalist cosmopolitanisms actually end up defending the existing hierarchies of nation-states by seeking to delegitimize "legacies of decolonization" and minimizing the self-determination won by communities terrorized by imperialism now and in the past (*At Home* 25–26). In terms of literature, the rejection of nation-oriented thinking as unitary and simplistic has meant, for the most part, disregarding the postcoloniality and cosmopolitanism of early postcolonial literature: texts whose defining feature—like that of their contemporary counterparts—is the reimagining of the possibilities following the end of colonial occupation.

Why "*Namak-Halaal*"?

My choice of the word "*namak-halaal*" to describe cosmopolitan orientations toward the nation might initially seem odd to readers already familiar with the Urdu term, whether through regular usage or scholarly knowledge. In common parlance, *namak-halaal* signifies loyalty to a superior, describing someone who will not "bite the hand that feeds." Indeed, it is possible that the term's meaning may be hopelessly overdetermined by the classic Bollywood *masala* movie *Namak-Halaal* (1982), in which Amitabh Bachchan plays Arjun, the son of a security guard who is killed while unsuccessfully trying to defend his boss from murderous and appropriately mustachioed ruffians. Ignorant of his family history, Arjun grows up with his grandfather in a village and comes to the city to become "a man"—only to miraculously end up becoming a servant for Raja, the boss's son, who has returned from his European exile to take his place among the wealthy, post-Emergency elite. By celebrating Arjun's faithfulness to Raja, the film underlines the conservative and even feudal connotation to "*namak-halaal*": servants will quietly serve their masters, happily locked in that relationship from generation to generation. Coming to South Asian usage via Persian and Arabic, "*namak-halaal*" has consistently been used to mark fealty and loyalty.[24] How can the term stand for anything critical and oppositional, then, when its contemporary and historical usage seems to denote a fundamental unwillingness to critique those in power? Indeed, the preeminent Sayyid Ahmad Khan used its antonym, "*namak-haraam*," to describe the Indian soldiers in the British army who mutinied in 1857: "To be faithless to one's salt is to disregard the first principles of our religion" (Khan).[25] Scholars familiar with this deliberately political usage of the concept may be inclined to associate "*namak-halaal*" with a pro-colonial loyalism, not a national orientation.

I find the term useful, however, when I translate it not as "loyal" or "traditionalist" but, more literally, as "true to one's salt." First of all, this works ideally as a translation in a double way: the idiomatic expression in English not only conveys the sense of the Urdu phrase but also alludes to a common metaphorical usage of "salt" as a positive signifier of value (*namak* means "salt"). The common use of the metaphor in Urdu and English and other languages is not a coincidence, given the world-historical value of salt to human life. Second, the use of the self-reflexive pronoun ("one's own") allows me to construct "*namak-halaal* cosmopolitanism" as an open, descriptive category: it describes an ethics of commitment to and engagement with the nation without overdetermining *how* that orientation is constructed. From its etymology, then, the word "*namak-halaal*" works by associating loyalty with the fulfillment of material needs; it highlights a social relationship (to be loyal to "the giver of salt") and not necessarily a particular individual or entity as such (the boss, the nation, the family). Defining the term in this way opens up a space for describing how allegiances shift and change over time—for examining the critical assessments occurring during times of historical and/or personal crises when individuals and communities think through where their loyalties really lie and who really "butters their bread." In terms of the subject at hand, as I will explain, the phrase "*namak-halaal* cosmopolitanism" does much more to describe the complexity of nation-oriented, early postcolonial literature than a term such as "nationalist cosmopolitanism" because it better allows the separation of orientation from ideology, avoids the difficulty of using a term ("nationalism") that is *seen* as being unitary and elite-oriented, and allows for an explanation of how elite and subaltern loyalties often converged around the nation in the midst of the anticolonial struggle. Just as "salt" has become a symbol of value historically because of its material importance as a commodity and a staple of human health, "nation" in an anticolonial context gained credibility among different classes and groups because it linked itself to various material and political needs such as land, food, cultural freedom, and self-determination.

As Michael Kuransky's *Salt: A World History* reminds us, salt has always been crucial to human existence. Within the body itself, the form of salt we like best, NaCl, is necessary for transporting nutrients and oxygen, transmitting nerve impulses, and moving muscles (sodium), and for digestion and respiration (chloride) (6). Salt also preserves food—making it one of "the most sought-after commodities in human history" until about a century ago (6). Cities were built around places where salt was formed naturally; "salt roads" were built for distribution; salt taxes were central to state revenues; and the control of salt was often central to clashes between peoples. For example, a monopolized control of the price of salt was crucial to the government of ancient Rome which would raise and drop prices based on political necessity. The English language has certainly recorded this history; the word "salary" comes from the Latin *salarium,* referring to the fact that Roman soldiers were either paid in salt (Latin, *sal*) or paid so that they could purchase salt.[26] The 1882 Salt Tax in colonial India, similarly, enabled the British monopolization of salt production and distribution—smashing indigenous centers of salt manufacture, criminalizing the making of salt (which was also available naturally on the seashore), and taxing its usage. This control of salt yielded "a large part of the revenue" of the colonial government, according to a contemporary source (Balfour 504). The destruction of these established industries, especially in Orissa, led to impoverishment and even famine as the livelihood of so many was linked to such networks (Kuransky 336–38).

Because of its high value both in material terms and in the realm of social power, salt gained a broad positive significance as a metaphor and symbol, and has been linked to God's will, to good luck, to love and sexuality, and to moral substance and character. As such, Kuransky details, parables and idioms around salt have been recorded in languages and cultural practices all over the world. In particular, as a brief survey of friends and family familiar with South Asian languages quickly revealed, salt has been used as a signifier for relations between people in a variety of ways— not necessarily for the purpose of maintaining the status quo. A proverb in Kannada, for instance, advises that "*uppitavana muppina tanaka nene*" ("The giver of salt should be remembered until one has reached a ripe old age").[27] Here, appealing to "salt" is neither an inherently conservative nor radical gesture; as with all language and symbolism, usage and context matters immensely.

Indeed, one can discern different threads within proverbs and idioms around salt that identify its value but not necessarily in order to cement hierarchies. In English, the idea that someone is "worth his salt" *can* signify a relationship of power and exchange ("he's worth our investment") but can also be an evaluation of character and moral "fiber" in a more general sense. Another Kannada saying, "*uppunda manege droha bagayabaradu*" ("One should never think of harming a house where salt has been eaten"), can thus be used to describe horizontal relationships (between neighbors and equals), not just vertical ones (between, say, bosses and workers). Even further away from explicit political and social hierarchies is the English phrase "salt of the earth," describing worthiness in a more organic way that rests on characteristics and ethical behavior. This is in line with the Gujarati idiom that expresses the same idea negatively in describing a person who has no depth or backbone: "*e mitthaa vagarno maanas cche*" ("He is a man without any salt").[28] One might say, then, that there is a spectrum of possibilities here between ethical guidelines and compulsory responsibilities, between salt as a signifier of moral substance and as a signifier of power relationships. But even when proverbs allude to the exchange of salt as a metaphor for describing social hierarchies, it is crucial to note that many expressions configure the taking of salt as a volitional act and, giving agency to the person being advised, emphasize that s/he ought to be aware of the consequences. A third saying in Kannada, for example, warns *"uppu thindava neeru kudiyale-beku"* ("One who has consumed salt has to drink water"), while a Santal custom apparently forbids the taking of salt in food offered by someone from an out-group, symbolically rejecting any implication of subservience or social obligation.[29] There is a recognition, here, that hierarchical relations can be bent and resisted.

Clearly, the symbol of salt has been used in a variety of ways, whether to fix existing relations of power or even to foment rebellion. Kuransky's chapters on the role of salt in the American and French Revolutions are eye-opening, but it is when he discusses the anticolonial Salt Satyagraha in British India that it all comes together, for salt is invoked both as a material need and as a metaphor on many levels simultaneously. The grassroots manufacturing of salt initiated by the Salt March of 1930 provided self-sufficiency on the immediate, day-to-day level and moved forward the fight for political and economic self-determination. The very process through which this lawbreaking happened—a 240-mile trek through Gujarat, from Gandhi's Sabarmati Ashram in Ahmedabad to the seashore in Dandi—constructed a broad, rebellious anticolonial space, physically connecting together thousands and thousands of people in marches, speeches, organizing meetings, and cultural festivals as it passed through many villages and towns (see Hardiman, *Peasant Nationalists* 194, 198–99). The illegal production of salt spread through the country, quickly snowballing into a mass, all-India satyagraha that included the defiance of forest laws (Maharashtra, Karnataka), the withholding of various taxes (Bengal, Gujarat), and the general boycott of British goods (Habib 57). Though the British government initially scoffed at the enterprise, the Salt Satyagraha became an explosive site for mass rebellion and repression: a global media event that made Gandhi a household name after tens of thousands were beaten and arrested.

Crucially, for our purposes, the Salt Satyagraha became a site at which the historic, cross-class alliance against colonialism was forged, bringing together those whose opposition to the British was based on questions of law and democracy and/or those for whom the high price of salt was literally impoverishing. The radical possibilities engendered by this event ought not to be minimized. Indeed, the Salt Satyagraha famously engendered the activism of women in large numbers (see Hardiman, *Gandhi* 113), and the bullets that Gaffar Khan and the Khudai Khidmatgar faced in Peshawar gave a concrete manifestation to hopes for communal harmony in the nation-to-be. It is crucial to remember, further, that the tens of thousands who joined the Salt March were not only responding to a call from the Congress Party; salt had been part of anticolonial agitations of various sorts since the late nineteenth century, especially in Orissa (Kuransky 342–43).

It is more than appropriate, therefore, to speak of *"namak-halaal"* in a late colonial and postcolonial context as commitment to the nation and its people even when—during the colonial context and earlier—it may have been used to justify colonialism, feudal relationships, and other hierarchies. On the level of ideas and consciousness, the anticolonial movement had to enact a reversal of signs, demanding that Indians' allegiance to their own welfare (their land, their salt, their home) be linked not to the British Raj but to a new entity, the nation. The movement sought to define what it meant to be loyal, to be *"namak-halaal"*—even though it did not and could not dissolve the many different positions and ideas from which people arrived at that common ground. In effect, this signified not a real discursive break from previous uses of *namak-halaal* but a struggle to redefine the idea through displaying the contradiction between British claims and material realities—expressed concretely through laws like the Salt Tax. Whatever theoretical position on nationalism we hold, we must explain why movements such as the Salt Satyagraha worked: why they resonated with people who required and/or desired far more radical changes than those promised by the official nationalist organizations. We need to make room for the ideological debate and complexity engendered by the emergence of the nation in anticolonial struggle, a series of tensions and contradictions whose trace can be found in literature and elsewhere.[30]

Namak-halaal cosmopolitanism, then, signifies the cultural identity of middle-class intellectuals and writers whose ways of looking toward "the world" are explicitly centered on "the home," constructing the nation as their space of engagement. "Postnational cosmopolitanism" is also complex in its negotiations of home and the world—but its explicit orientation is the "look away" from the nation as an emancipatory space. I do not call this *"namak-haraam* cosmopolitanism," however, because the connotations of *that* term ("disloyal, ungrateful") would skew the perception of my project and fail to describe the progressive and even radical tendencies that generally motivate the turn away from the nation after the Emergency. Such a category might imply a wholesale rejection of English-language texts as such, regarding Anglophone writers as "anti-national," and would be unable to account for postnational writers' explicit critiques of colonialism, of racism, and of the violence that the modern nation-state has inflicted on ordinary people. *"Namak-halaal"* and "postnational" cosmopolitanisms are labels, in this book, both for demarcating the broad shift that has occurred within the Indian English novel and its representations of the nation and for mapping the organic links between pre- and post-Emergency texts.

I identify the majority of Indian English novels from the 1980s and after as expressing postnational orientations because their narratives tend to construct nations and nationalisms in dehistoricized ways, as little more than barriers to emancipation and progress. It is not that interest in the nation, in politics, or in history disappears with the postnational turn, and it is unquestionable that the narrative and linguistic innovations with which contemporary writers are involved have shed a powerful light on new Indian realities. Novels such as Amitav Ghosh's *The Shadow Lines* (1988), Upamanyu Chatterjee's *English, August* (1988), Shashi Tharoor's *The Great Indian Novel* (1989), Vikram Chandra's *Red Earth and Pouring Rain* (1995), and Rohinton Mistry's *A Fine Balance* (1995), for instance, are profoundly shaped by an interest in India—its history, its institutions, its cultural and social identities. Furthermore, for all of the epistemological and methodological differences between them, such texts powerfully highlight questions of power, especially the ongoing impact of colonialism, political repression, class and caste divisions, and communalism. Indeed, like many *namak-halaal* texts, postnational ones also implicate elite Indians in these processes precisely for their turn away from Indianness; Rushdie's hilarious employment of the term *chamcha* (sycophant) in *The Satanic Verses,* for example, stands out in this regard. On the thematic level, then, there is much overlap between these novels and earlier ones—and part of the argument of *Decentering Rushdie,* indeed, is to show that such "postcolonial" and "cosmopolitan" concerns do not begin with *Midnight's Children.*

The crucial difference between the two phases, however, lies in the fact that the post-Emergency texts constructed a new lens for viewing the nation and its history. Writing in a different moment, most of Indian English novels of the past three decades portray nationalisms as being inherently fanatical and violent. Historiography is important here, but reflections on the politics of history-writing are raised in opposition to the understanding of history itself as dynamic, as the product of contending human and structural forces. Characterization, voice, plot, and theme are fashioned in ways that represent, for instance, anticolonial nationalism as being always already suspect as a utopian, elitist, and/or atavistic project; postcoloniality as a condition of endless violence and crises; the cosmopolitan-elite subject as victimized by the nation for her/his hybridity and cultural "impurity"; and migrancy and "rootlessness" as the only genuine conditions for knowledge of postcolonial oppressions. Very often, the nation is constructed as the enemy of both transnational and subaltern-centered views, and Indian crises can be grasped only from spaces outside the nation. The (unacknowledged) *telos* of postnational texts is the construction of an implied audience that can transcend the nation; we are encouraged to support cosmopolitan-elite protagonists who come to recognize not only the "pitfalls" of national consciousness but also its reactionary nature. Indeed, in most novels after the Emergency, models of mass, national struggle are generally dismissed as utopian; when masses of people do appear, they are often portrayed as violent mobs. For the most part, representations of ordinary people are of distant, victimized figures whose agency, when it emerges at all, is limited to the minimum: the act of survival.

And yet commonalities persist, too. Early postcolonial novels, as we shall explore in the next two chapters, run the risk of essentializing the nation and its traditions as positive force for good. But it is also true that a unitary, monolithic representation of India often pervades more recent novels, often linked to similarly flat representations of the West (Meenakshi Mukherjee, *Perishable* 174). Indeed, as I discuss in chapter 4, despite their often explicit desire to transcend the nation, post-Emergency novels remain haunted by it; as with "postcolonial" and "postmodern," the category "postnational" continues to be constituted by the entity it aims to supersede. Moreover, many post-Emergency novels belie the reputation of radical political oppositionality mistakenly associated with their radical aesthetic experimentations, as they articulate a rejection of the present through a fairly mainstream political discourse that—at times—is indistinguishable from what I call in chapter 3 an "NRI [Non-Resident Indian] nationalism." Rather than a new articulation of "hybridity," we are led by novels such as Rushdie's *The Moor's Last Sigh* into the arms of a fairly liberal understanding of community under the rubric of "unity in diversity"—an idea that had emerged in Indian political and cultural discourse alongside the earliest expressions of anticolonial nationalism and was, often problematically, enshrined in Nehruvian state institutions.[31] Make no mistake: the slogan is a welcome and necessary one in a practical sense as communalist and other reactionary forces continue to disfigure the subcontinent. But the positing of a unitary nation to defuse conflicts of social and cultural difference does not answer the question of why the "imagined community" of the Indian nation was an insufficient basis for liberation in the first place.[32] In fact, my effort to establish the presence of an alternative, *namak-halaal* tradition in the Indian English novel draws attention to a paradox. In many cases, Indian English novels that "look away" from the nation in the context of neoliberal globalization are, in fact, less perceptive about the workings of the postcolonial nation than early, *namak-halaal* texts that, in the aftermath of decolonization, allied themselves with the national project but "looked back" with full awareness of its ongoing challenges.

When "Rough Beasts" Slouch In

The 1980s were monumental for postcolonial (Indian) English literature. Eurocentric grand-narratives were questioned and "Commonwealth Literature" was challenged. Ghettoization was reviled. Rough beasts slouched in. In a reversal of the dynamics of modern history, a sort of poetic justice perhaps, Rushdie and "Rushdie's children" have dominated global English literature, producing, as many have attested, some of the most important and exciting fiction in the English-speaking world since World War II. When Lord Thomas Babington Macaulay infamously asserted in his "Minute on Education" (1835) that "a single shelf of a good European library was worth the whole native literature of India and Arabia," he certainly didn't have in mind a shelf full of novels by today's postcolonial Anglophone authors, descendents of parents and grandparents who had the direct experience of the Raj and had, perhaps, participated in overthrowing it.

But what happened to those beasts as they took over the master's house, slept in the master's bed, wore the master's clothes? They talked of revolution and transformation, but what changed and what remained the same? Did the rebellious beasts start turning human, like the Orwellian pigs of *Animal Farm,* or—yes, why not?—did they start losing their pigmentation, as it were, like the postindependence Indian businessmen in *Midnight's Children*? Did they begin to resemble those they had replaced, creating new canons and ghettos and hierarchies, renaming "Manor Farm" to "Animal Farm" but then reverting back again? When the greatest of these beasts were feted and honored, what happened to those who, despite making the voyage in, were forced to watch the coronation from the outside? How might a literary genealogy that seriously considered the work of pre-Rushdie, non-postmodern, *namak-halaal* authors change our view of which things fell apart and which things remained quite intact despite the literary revolution of the 1980s? How might we challenge the postmodernized notions of the postcolonial and the cosmopolitan that, ironically, have helped build rigid binary oppositions between national/ cosmopolitan, vernacular/English, and realist/magical-realist texts?

At the very end of *Animal Farm,* the only sliver of hope that remains is expressed by the fact that the implied author of the text describes the debacle of Napoleon's transformation from *outside* the farmhouse. In light of the uncritical reduction of the Indian English novel to its post-Emergency phase, it is this sort of outside space we need to recover in order to reassess the genre and its relationship to shifting aesthetic, historical, and political contexts. In doing so we would only be insisting, as Rushdie does in his critique of Orwell in "Outside the Whale" (1984), that artists and critics remain aware of the intimate and unavoidable links between literature and the world in which it is produced and received.

2

Dawn of Freedom

Namak-Halaal Cosmopolitanisms in *A Time to Be Happy* and *The Coffer Dams*

"One can have an ugly child, but it's one's very own."

—Veena Shivpal, in Nayantara Sahgal, *A Time to Be Happy* (1958)

"For there was a problem unresolved: the cord that threaded through [Indians and the British], making them one, like an ill-sorted bundle of sticks that stood or fell together [. . .] [He looked] forward to a time when they could walk, ride, fly, and build solo, gathering strength and pride and thereby grow mighty."

—Krishnan, in Kamala Markandaya, *The Coffer Dams* (1969)

On August 14, 1947, at the midnight hour marking India's independence from Britain, Jawaharlal Nehru, the incoming prime minister, delivered a memorable speech describing the significance of the moment to the nation and the world at large. Its opening lines, rich in figurative language, reveal the populist and internationalist orientations that had become embedded even within official Indian nationalist discourse by the late colonial and early postcolonial periods:

Long years ago, we made a tryst with destiny, and now the time comes when we shall redeem our pledge [. . .] At the stroke of the midnight hour, when the world sleeps, India will awake to life and freedom. A moment comes [. . .] but rarely in history, when we step out from the old to the new, when an age ends, and when the soul of a nation, long suppressed, finds utterance. It is fitting that at this solemn moment we take the pledge of dedication to the service of India and her people and to the still larger cause of humanity. (Nehru, "Tryst with Destiny" 3)

Nehru's words crackle with revolutionary intensity in describing the long-awaited moment, a world-historic and rare opportunity for human beings to "step out from the old to the new." But he hastens to say that this is also a "solemn moment," a moment of pledges and responsibility, the first step in a longer journey whose goals are even more lofty. As Nehru bluntly states later in the speech: "The service of India means the service of the millions who suffer. It means the ending of poverty and ignorance and disease and the inequality of opportunity" (4). Referencing M. K. Gandhi's aim to "wipe every tear from every eye," Nehru states that "as long as there are tears and suffering, so long our work will not be over" (4). Finally, he emphasizes, such dreams "are for India, but they are also for the world, for all the nations and peoples are too closely knit together today for any one of them to imagine that it can live apart" (4). National independence, then, should not simply benefit the elites of the Constituent Assembly, Nehru's immediate audience, who were poised to take state power. Rather, self-governance demands that these elites partake in an "incessant striving" (4) for popular welfare and global solidarity.

More than sixty years later, in light of the persisting inequalities within postcolonial nations and the manifold critiques of nationalism that have developed in its wake, scholars in the humanities and social sciences will tend to Nehru's words with skepticism. Leaving aside the questions of implementation (did Nehru's policies follow these ideals?) and intention (did Nehru really mean what he said?), a rhetorical and ideological analysis reveals that the Indian nation as represented in the "Tryst with Destiny" speech is a textbook example of Benedict Anderson's theory, oft-cited in Anglo-American Postcolonial Studies, of nations as "imagined communities." Like nationalists everywhere, Nehru seeks to convince ordinary Indians that they will find true freedom and unity, to use Anderson's words, within the "deep horizontal comradeship" of the nation "regardless of the actual inequality and exploitation that prevails" in their day-to-day lives (7). Part of this project entails representing the nation as being both a product of history ("long years" of patient struggle) and an entity that transcends history, as if sovereignty were inevitable (a "tryst with destiny"). In rewriting political independence as a narrative in which "the soul of India," at long last, "finds utterance," Nehru posits a deep, essential unity on a people sharply divided by class, ethnicity, language, caste, gender, region, and religion. And this against the backdrop of the bloodbath and mass displacement engendered by the partition of British India into the nation-states of India and Pakistan—the gory price of political sovereignty in South Asia. Dispelling romantic myths of origins,

Partition revealed the fractured nature of national identities, and the violence that is inflicted on ordinary people when nations are made real through the force of laws and armies.

Beyond the necessary critique of elite nationalism, however, certain aspects of the context and content of Nehru's speech demand that we analyze it more closely. First of all, despite the horrors of Partition, millions of Indians who had just defeated a mighty empire tended to agree with Nehru's claim that independence was a step forward, and that the nation could become a vehicle for popular progress. According to Mildred Talbot, an American woman who stood with 500,000 others all night outside the Assembly Hall to participate in Independence Day ceremonies:

> [T]he multitudes had gathered as far as the eye could see in the two-mile long parkway approach to the Secretariat, on tops of buildings, in windows, on cornices, in trees [. . .] [As the flag was raised] there was almost a subdued hush over the whole crowd; then a soft bass undertone slowly swelled until, perhaps when the flag reached the top, . . . there was a breathtaking roar of cheering, shouting, and excited cries which others said penetrated to the hall inside and made their spines tingle. (qtd. in Tharoor, "1947, First-Hand")

The excitement about the national flag emerged from the recognition that its new status represented a sea change in history. After all, the same flag for which activists had been jailed, beaten, and killed in the immediate past now represented the law of the land. Similar scenes of euphoria were to take place in the next few decades in independence ceremonies across Asia and Africa amidst the wave of decolonization following the Second World War. If we are to accept that the participants in such events were not simply dupes who mindlessly followed their leaders, then we must consider the possibility that nationalism in the context of a mass anticolonial struggle is a heterogeneous entity: appealing to elite desires for power as well as popular desires for emancipation.

Antonio Gramsci's categories of "common sense" and the "national-popular" offer ways to understand this amalgamation of interests. For Gramsci, "common sense" signifies "the terrain of conceptions and categories on which the practical consciousness of the masses of the people is actually formed [. . .] the 'taken-for-granted' terrain, on which more coherent ideologies and philosophies must contend for mastery" (Hall 431). Nehruvian nationalist ideology became dominant because it was able to "take into account, contest and transform" the terrain of common sense more effectively than other ideologies (431). Over the late nineteenth and early twentieth centuries, as several historians have shown, nationalism developed by linking with, rising above, absorbing, or marginalizing a number of related and/or autonomous movements (for class, gender, caste, and sexual equality) and ideologies (from Hindu-revivalism and cultural nationalism to secularism, feminism, and socialism).[1] In the process of gaining hegemony, nationalism was able to forge and reshape a sense of the "national-popular," that is, to make the aspiration for national freedom a crucial part of popular "common sense," tying together (subaltern) desires and struggles for control over material resources to (elite) hopes for political and economic sovereignty.[2] Nehruvian nationalism, in particular, contested ideas to its left that sought to construct a different notion of the "national-popular"—one that was more attentive to caste and class inequalities, the contradictions of capitalist modernization, the marginalization of Muslims and other minorities, and the oppression of women. But it also placed itself against the more reactionary versions of nationalism and society emerging from groups such as the Hindu Mahasabha and the Rashtriya Svayamsevak Sangh (RSS). I do not mean to overstate the radicalism of Nehruvian theory and practice here; I am merely indicating that the progressive content of "Tryst with Destiny" ought to be read as being a bit more than political posturing. Nehru owed his popularity to his prominent role in engaging with this anticolonial "common sense," and he was forced to respond to the mood for continuing change. Nehru's populist rhetoric is, thus, a measure of the pressure that rising expectations placed on nationalist elites by ordinary people who had been involved for decades in various struggles against oppression. "Disavowing decolonization" because of the fact of elite leadership or its failures risks minimizing the historic and organic links between anticolonial nationalism and mass desires for democracy and social justice.[3]

Namak-Halaal Cosmopolitanisms of the Nehruvian Years

In keeping with *Decentering Rushdie*'s focus on cosmopolitanism, we can look at Nehru's speech from another angle: as an example of the cosmopolitan-elite writing and thinking that dominated the late colonial/early postcolonial period. Remarkably, "Tryst with Destiny," one of the core texts of Indian nationalism, was delivered in the English language by an individual who grew up in a family of Anglophiles, who studied in English-medium schools in India, who attended Trinity College, Cambridge, trained as a

barrister at the Inner Temple, and represented, in short, the classic Anglicized Indian cosmopolitan. Leaders such as Nehru immediately complicate
the binary opposition between cosmopolitanism and nationalism that is
often taken for granted in postcolonial and cultural theory. On the one
hand, Nehru shows that mainstream Indian nationalism was quite recep-
tive to cosmopolitan-elite participation and leadership despite the populist
and nativist assertions that often accompanied anticolonial sentiment. On
the other hand, progressive cosmopolitans found in the nationalist movement a space for expressing their own global, secular, and democratic
goals. This conjunction of nationalism and cosmopolitanism was familiar across the colonized world: like Nehru, for instance, M. K. Gandhi
and Muhammad Ali Jinnah in South Asia, Kwame Nkrumah in Ghana,
Sukarno in Indonesia, and Leopold Senghor in Senegal were also drawn
from European-educated, elite classes. The historical processes of colonialism and the anticolonial struggle themselves forced this development,
pushing many progressive-minded, Westernized elites toward the nation.
Discriminatory laws in colonial society regarding employment, education, housing, and social mobility demanded that elites, in their own self-
interest, consider questions of national autonomy and sovereignty. No
single yardstick can be used to measure the pace with which such developments took place in various colonized spaces, and how nationalist
elites sought to link themselves and their organizations to the anticolonial
theory and practice developing among oppressed and marginalized popu-
lations. In British India, at least, it soon became evident that mass involvement was crucial to any advancement toward such political autonomy.
For example, the Indian National Congress, an organization created by
Westernized elites in the late nineteenth century, became relevant only after
Gandhian populism connected it to the concerns of ordinary Indians and
their own, independent legacies of resistance.[4] A *namak-halaal* orientation
emerges, indeed, only out of this temporary alliance of classes around the
anticolonial movement.

The *"namak-halaal* cosmopolitanism" that I identify among postcolonial Indian English authors in *Decentering Rushdie*—a cosmopolitanism
that is "true to its salt"—is thus the expression in literature of a larger
phenomenon among Anglicized Indian elites as a whole, rooted in the
colonial experience and continuing on to the early postcolonial period.
This orientation developed in the context of a larger milieu of Indian writers in all languages that, under the aegis of the Progressive Writers' Association (PWA) and affiliated groups, explicitly linked literature, art, and
culture to the political developments of the time. As Priyamvada Gopal

argues, the period leading up to and immediately following independence was a "cultural and political moment where the best writing in different Indian languages, including English, intersected with and was inflected by the diverse political exigencies of those times and the radical literary currents that responded to those exigencies" ("'Curious Ironies'" 63). Not only "the best" texts but, I would like to suggest, novels of *all* sorts were inflected thus. Nayantara Sahgal's *A Time to Be Happy* (1958) and Kamala Markandaya's *The Coffer Dams* (1969), which I examine in this chapter, belong to a plethora of pre-Emergency Indian English novels that link their cosmopolitan concerns and sensibilities about a range of social issues to the national question. To give a sampling: Bhabani Bhattacharya's *So Many Hungers!* (1947), Markandaya's *Nectar in a Sieve* (1954), Bhattacharya's *He Who Rides a Tiger* (1954), R. K. Narayan's *Waiting for the Mahatma* (1955), Khwaja Ahmad Abbas's *Inquilab* (1958), Narayan's *The Guide* (1958), Atia Hosain's *Sunlight on a Broken Column* (1961), and Bhattacharya's *Shadow From Ladakh* (1966). Many of these texts were originally published in England or America; many of these authors were situated abroad. And yet they consistently "look back" toward the nation in positive ways, often mourning the cultural and/or actual distance between cosmopolitan-elites and ordinary Indians. In each of these very different novels, and scores of others like them, "the nation" appears neither as the cause of continuing social inequalities and conflicts nor their easy resolution but as a potentially emancipatory framework through which crises around class, caste, gender, sexuality, modernity, and cosmopolitan identity might be resolved.

Often, even critics who do reference Indian English novels before *Midnight's Children* tend to minimize or even skip over the early postcolonial texts, moving from the nineteenth century (Bankim Chandra Chatterjee's *Rajmohan's Wife*) to the so-called Big Three of the 1930s (Anand, Raja Rao, R. K. Narayan) to the 1980s and Salman Rushdie. Rather, I suggest, considering early postcolonial texts allows us to form a bridge between the politically charged period of the 1930s and 1940s and the metacritical narratives and nuanced representations of subjectivity and identity that mark post-1980s literature. Like the late colonial texts, early postcolonial novels sought materials and gained inspiration "from the nationalist mobilization and 'upliftment' of women, workers, untouchables, and peasants. At best, these narratives tend to represent the colonial encounter itself as a shadowy subplot to the larger story of socio-economic transformation" (L. Gandhi 171). Far from counterposing the nation to subaltern demands, in other words, writers of all stripes were driven to the paradigm of the nation precisely because it offered, in its cross-class and universalist demands and claims, a vehicle for broader emancipation.

In keeping with my larger goal to demonstrate the *multiple* cosmopolitanisms of the Indian English novel, the central feature of *namak-halaal* texts that I explore in this chapter is the presence of ideological diversity despite a common orientation toward the nation. Sahgal's *A Time to Be Happy* does put forth a perspective that is, like "Tryst with Destiny," both *namak-halaal* and nationalist, seeing the modern nation-state as an inviolable unit that can resolve class and gender inequalities. But Markandaya's text sits with the many postcolonial leaders, intellectuals, and artists who were quite critical of official nationalist discourse and the contradictions of Nehruvian India—even as they embraced the radical possibilities engendered under the rubric of anticolonial nationalism.[5] Questioning the postcolonial present, and leaning toward a Gandhian/romantic critique of capitalist development, such texts reflect on Indian and local contexts and developments positively but seek to develop an alternative version of the "national-popular," refusing to subordinate class, gender, ethnic, and religious differences to mainstream nationalism.

In order to illustrate both the prevalence and diversity of this *namak-halaal* orientation, I offer a brief comparison of three texts from the 1950s with very different ideological underpinnings: Bhabani Bhattacharya's *He Who Rides a Tiger*, Khushwant Singh's *Train to Pakistan,* and Faiz Ahmad Faiz's famous poem "*Subh-e Azadi*" ("Dawn of Freedom," Urdu 1952). *He Who Rides a Tiger* can be categorized as a nationalist text in that its narrative resolutions to the problems of rural poverty and caste oppression, set in the Bengal Famine of 1943, crystallize in the efforts of Biten, a militant rabble-rouser who transforms into a nationalist agitator. Focused on the lower-caste, subaltern characters Kalo and his daughter Lekha, the novel draws out the hypocrisies of the modernity-as-progress narrative of the colonizers and aligns itself with a Gandhian opposition to caste discrimination. But despite the novel's formulaic approach to nationalism in terms of plot and theme, the text "actively engages the contradictions and complexities engendered by its historical moment" (P. Gopal, "'Curious Ironies'" 79). Even though the text seems eager to bundle anticaste radicalism under the banner of nationalism, it differs from Bhattacharya's earlier novel about the Famine, *So Many Hungers!,* in that it cannot offer any direct, nationalist closure (76, 79). Nationalism is certainly privileged as the sign of militancy and collective organizing in this novel: Bhattacharya appeals to nationalism to disrupt Kalo's attempts to subvert hierarchies through individualist acts of mimicry and performance (he pretends he's an upper-caste Brahmin in order to escape rural destitution). However, at the same time, the subaltern-centered nature of the novel's representations, and the acknowledgment that Indian rural elites are also contributing to the Famine, lead to a series of ironies and ambiguities that do not sit well with mainstream nationalist ideology (P. Gopal, "'Curious Ironies'" 78–79).

Indeed, by the time of *Shadow from Ladakh,* published soon after Nehru's death in 1964, Bhattacharya's Gandhian critique of Nehruvian modernity is at its height despite the novel's uneasy attempts to unite the two. What Leela Gandhi says about the ambiguous affiliations of novels of the 1930s and 1940s is only intensified in the early postcolonial period: "While the bulk of Gandhi novels faithfully narrative the conversion of the Westernized 'foreign-educated' protagonists to simple rural ideas, in reality those stories are often unable to eschew the cosmopolitanism of the Nehruvian alternative" (171). The actuality of independence and the onset of Nehruvian modernity, in fact, resulted in either a much more confident embrace of Nehru combined with a fond nostalgia for Gandhi (as in Sahgal's early works) or a much deeper cynicism about the present day in which hope persists but is muted (as in Markandaya's *Nectar in a Sieve* or Narayan's *Waiting for the Mahatma*). My juxtaposition of Sahgal's *A Time to Be Happy* and Markandaya's *The Coffer Dams* explores how narrative strategies and representations of cosmopolitan-elite identity reflect and animate this spectrum of ideological debates on the nation.

Train to Pakistan can be called "non-nationalist" or even "antinationalist" in the sense that it mourns the violence resulting from the imposition of Indian and Pakistani national identities on the border town of Mano Majra.[6] It presents an interesting version of a cosmopolitan text (a "self-hating cosmopolitanism," perhaps?) that is so focused on its romantic portrayals of the rural that its biggest villains are "outsiders": city-dwellers, politicians, and activist do-gooders. With deep sarcasm, Khushwant Singh rewrites Nehru's "tryst with destiny" metaphor, asking whether the Prime Minister was referring to his alleged popularity with the wives of foreign diplomats, or to the many brutal "trysts" represented by the rapes of Sikh, Muslim, and Hindu women during Partition.[7] Despite its rejection of official nationalism, however, *Train to Pakistan* is a *namak-halaal* text par excellence, so focused on exposing the destruction of local space and recovering its authenticity—often in a politically reactionary way, as far as gender is concerned—that no one from outside the village can do any good. The chief among these is Iqbal, the Westernized, pro-nationalist communist who talks big about bringing freedom to "the people" but cannot mingle with them in the least; his snobby lectures about national liberation are so abstract that they do not speak to the villagers' material needs. Unlike the particular transnationalism of post-Emergency texts, in which elite movements between Indian and Western spaces produce new insights into the problems of postcoloniality, *A Train to Pakistan* projects more local acts of border-crossing in its resolution. Its everyman hero Juggat Singh, now marked as "Indian" by virtue of being Sikh, is compelled by his love for Nooran, his pregnant, Muslim girlfriend (now "Pakistani"), to take decisive action in opposition to national and religious divisions. Juggat's selfless act at the railway crossing, preventing Sikh communalists (also "outsiders") from slaughtering the Mano Majra Muslims on the train to Pakistan, leads to his death but enables readers to project a future for Nooran and her child beyond the text. Indeed, by describing Juggat in this final scene as merely as "a man," silhouetted against yet another dawn, the implied author generalizes this action beyond the text, producing a model of transnational and transcultural subjectivity that is, nevertheless, firmly grounded in the border towns between India and Pakistan. The critique of nationalism and nation-states in this text does not translate into a valorization of the outsider but, through a masculinist romanticization of the peasant, produces a fierce commitment to an imagined local space of harmony.

The poem *"Subh-e Azadi"* is penned by Faiz Ahmad Faiz, the celebrated writer and intellectual—both a Marxist and a PWA member—who lived in Pakistan after Partition. For many like Faiz and Singh, 1947 is represented not as a moment of euphoria but one of sorrow and bitterness: the millions of people who were displaced, raped, and killed by Partition made a mockery of official pronouncements of freedom. Written while Faiz was in prison for his leftist political affiliations, "Dawn of Freedom" reflects back on the moment of Partition and distinguishes the Pakistani present from genuine liberation (cf. Genoways 110–12). Read alongside "Tryst with Destiny," "Dawn of Freedom" reveals the same use of the romantic metaphor and light/dark imagery—but these are now turned to a critique of official nationalisms. The speaker of the poem declares: "These tarnished rays, this night-smudged light— / this was not that Dawn for which, ravished with freedom / we had set out in sheer longing" (1.1–3). As in "Tryst with Destiny," freedom—feminized as the desired goal of the implicit male-heterosexual speaker—can come only from a long struggle: "our eyes remained fixed on that beckoning Dawn / forever vivid in her muslins of transparent light" (2.5–6). The nationalist leaders' insistence that "our feet [. . .] are now one with their goal" (3.3), however, is characterized as a "terrible, rampant lie" (3.1). By declaring success, in Faiz, the leaders "polish their manner clean of our suffering" (3.4) and minimize the violence of the events of an independence that came at a terrible price.

And yet "Dawn of Freedom" does not dismiss the goal of freedom itself. Despite the incredible difference in their ideological perspectives, Faiz's speaker, like Nehru, points to unfinished business and the long road ahead. Insisting that his body is "[s]till ablaze for the Beloved," the speaker tells his audience to restart the journey: "Friends, come away from this false light. Come, we must / search for that promised Dawn" (4.2, 4.6–7). While the poem ironically twists Nehru's symbols and contests the idea that freedom has been attained, it remains quite sincere about seeking the "promised Dawn" and confident in the possibility of reaching it. By implication, marking the leaders' new positions as acts of betrayal suggests that the two groups of Dawn-seekers once shared a common path and yearning. It is this common commitment to the legacy of the national liberation struggle, an acceptance of its populist roots, and belief in the possibility of national regeneration that I discover in the novels before the Emergency period. Like Ammu at the very end of Arundhati Roy's *The God of Small Things*, they "look back" confidently even as they look away and ahead to a tomorrow that has yet to come.

An "Ugly Child" but Our Child

Despite their very different positions on postcolonial modernity and the new nation-state, then, *A Time to Be Happy* and *The Coffer Dams* share strategies of representation that produce an ethical and activist sensibility among their cosmopolitan-elite characters (and readers) in the interest of national regeneration. While *A Time to Be Happy* exhorts the contemporary postcolonial elite to emulate, in whatever possible way, the elites who directed their abilities toward the overthrow of the British Raj, *The Coffer Dams* targets elite Indians and the nation-state themselves as being complicit with postcolonial violence. Nevertheless, both texts emphasize the possibilities for solidarity and transformation even as they draw attention to the fact that the project of national liberation remains incomplete.

In fact, despite differences from postnational texts, Sahgal's and Markandaya's novels develop their *namak-halaal* perspectives through investigations of postcolonial subjectivities whose conflicts of identity and affiliation will be quite familiar to readers of the contemporary Indian English novel. *A Time to Be Happy* highlights the internal struggles of

Sanad Shivpal, an up-and-coming manager at a British multinational firm, as he considers quitting his job in order to better serve the nation. Through his direct experiences of Indian poverty and British racism in the late colonial period, in the context of the Quit India uprisings of 1942, the Bengal Famine of 1943, and independence/Partition in 1947, Sanad realizes the extent of colonial oppression and mourns elites' alienation from the Indian masses. The unnamed and completely reliable narrator, a veteran of the Gandhian movement and a friend of Sanad's father, helps Sanad sort out his existential and political dilemmas. *The Coffer Dams* features the crises of two characters whose efforts to inhabit their ascribed "cosmopolitan" and "elite" identities are thwarted by both their evolving notions of self and the material realities of gender, ethnicity, and class. The first, Helen Clinton, is the wife of a British contractor whose firm has been hired by the Indian government to build a series of dams in southeastern India. As Helen becomes friendly with and sympathetic to the local Adivasi (aboriginal) inhabitants whose villages will be flooded by the dams, she struggles against the limits of her white, elite identity as well as the gender restrictions placed upon her by British society. At the same time, Bashiam, an engineer of Adivasi origin and Helen's lover-for-a-day, finds that modern Indian society will not allow him to escape from the Adivasi subject position that he despises, associating it with poverty and humiliation. Cut off from his roots but still regarded as a savage "*jungly-wallah*" by his British and Indian managers and co-workers, Bashiam finds that neither education nor training can rid him of his ethnicity—a fact that becomes increasingly apparent as the conflict between the dam-builders and the Adivasis intensifies. Though *The Coffer Dams* is far less confident than *A Time to Be Happy* in the prospects for national regeneration, both texts seek narrative closure by projecting a postcolonial future in which their new identities might be accepted.

The epigraphs above illustrate these pre-Emergency novels' hopeful commitments to such a future as well as their ideological differences on the question of postcolonial modernity. The context of the first quotation is a conversation toward the end of *A Time to Be Happy* between the narrator and Veena Shivpal, Sanad's younger sister, who is on a visit home to Sharanpur from the capital city of New Delhi where she works as a broadcaster for All-India Radio (AIR). The culinary standards of a local café, formerly "Claudette's," have clearly diminished since the departure of its British owners, and the insipid menu options provoke a more general reflection on the problems inflicting the new India, including the refugee crisis after Partition. But the incompleteness of the national project ("[o]ne can have an ugly baby"), in this *namak-halaal* rendering, does not diminish the fact of national self-determination and sovereignty ("but it's one's very own"). Veena, representing a twenty-something generation that is free from Sanad's angst, clearly expresses the exuberance about the new India that is conveyed by the title of the novel itself. In terms of the narrative sequence, Veena's brief appearance in the novel follows the narrator's extended meditation on elite complicity with colonialism in times past and the need for postindependence businessmen, politicians, and intellectuals who are independent and committed to building the new nation. Veena is a response to this problem: as an AIR broadcaster, she is directly involved in the national project at the infrastructural and ideological levels. Urban, sophisticated, and described as physically attractive, Veena enters the dusty, small-town atmosphere of Sharanpur as a dreamlike, magical figure, embodying the new nation's potential to resolve postcolonial "ugliness."

The second epigraph reveals a similar acknowledgment of postcolonial contradictions, but it emphasizes the difficulties of transcending them. Krishnan, the main nationalist voice of *The Coffer Dams,* shares Veena's desire for Indian progress but is still waiting, a decade later, for the sovereignty and independence that she so proudly champions. Though a veteran of the anticolonial struggle like Sahgal's narrator, Markandaya's Krishnan is positioned in a very different place: he can imagine postcoloniality only as the continuing denial of the promise of national liberation. For Krishnan is employed by Clinton and Mackendrick, Ltd., the British builders working with the Indian government. Subject once more to the orders and insults of British overlords and seething from feelings of historical dependency and inferiority, Krishnan is trapped in a quintessentially postcolonial conundrum. Though he uses his skills as an organizer to unite skilled and unskilled labor and wrests some concessions from the British bosses, the scope of Krishnan's rebellion is limited since he ultimately views the success of the dam as linked to Indian progress. For him, Indians and the British now "stood or fell together."

The difference between Veena and Krishnan, thus far, seems more temporal than ideological: the nationalist euphoria of the 1950s, dying down, has become the nervous despair of the 1960s. However, the contrasting ways in which these nationalist characters are situated reveals the deeper ideological differences between the two novels. While Veena simply confirms and augments the nationalist position championed by the narrator of *A Time to Be Happy,* Krishnan's nationalism is marginalized in *The Coffer Dams.* His dreams, of "a time when [Indians] could walk, ride, fly, and build solo, gathering strength and pride and thereby grow mighty" are portrayed as examples of the violence and hubris contained in nationalist thought. At the ethical and political core of *The Coffer Dams* are not nationalists but the Adivasis who inhabit the hills and valleys where the dam is to be built. The entire novel is a sustained criticism of Indo-British cooperation in accelerating such a brutal modernity, and Krishnan's contemptuous attitude toward the Adivasis underlines Indian-nationalist complicity with their marginalization. The critique of nationalism and modernity in Markandaya exposes a hierarchy of power that is missing in Sahgal.

Nevertheless, what joins these two viewpoints together and separates them qualitatively from many post-Emergency treatments of the national question is their activist concern with questions such as "What went wrong?" and "What can be changed?" Despite the explicit differences on representing modernity, Sahgal's novel is far more critical of the nation than its title might indicate, as it mercilessly exposes the hypocrisies of Anglophile elites and remains fearful about the onset of modern industry. And Markandaya's text opens up many doors for regeneration, constructing characters with different backgrounds (Indian nationals, Europeans, or urbanized Adivasis such as Bashiam) as being capable of empathizing with the plights of the Adivasis in the hills, of challenging what Patrick Hogan calls their "categorial identities" (notions of self derived from relatively fixed, socially defined categories) through developing alternative "practical identities" (aspects of self created through what one does and what one can learn). The category of "*namak-halaal* cosmopolitanism" is designed precisely to account for such deep differences between pre-Emergency texts while grasping their common emphases on elite responsibility and future possibilities.

Sanad's Political Awakening

In the words of one critic, *A Time to Be Happy* features "the awakening of young Sanad, the 'Brown Englishman,' to the social and political realities of newly Independent India" (Naik 239). Mapping this awakening is central to discovering the novel's *namak-halaal* and nationalist commitment, as Sanad represents the first generation of elites who came into adulthood in an independent India. However, while the author's political affiliations appear everywhere—the novel is even dedicated to "Mamu," Sahgal's affectionate name for Nehru, her maternal uncle—a true sense of its *namak-halaal* orientation emerges when we take account of the novel's narrative strategies and articulations of character and voice. The way in which the first-person Gandhian narrator relates and shapes Sanad's story is as important to the text's achievement as the story itself. Alternating between and linking together the voices of the narrator and Sanad—the finished product and the work-in-progress, respectively—the novel constructs a veritable handbook for the English-educated cosmopolitan who wants to contribute to the new India. It is ultimately, however, unable to resolve the contradictions of modernity that are often expressed under the signs "Gandhi" and "Nehru."

With the novel set in the years just after independence, the narrator begins by reporting the question that Sanad posed to him: should he leave his prestigious job in Selkirk and Lowe, Ltd., a British multinational textile firm, in order to better serve the nation? In effect: does the nationalist, cosmopolitan-elite have an ethical and political obligation to quit his/her employment with British companies now that independence has been achieved? In order to answer this question, the narrator reflects on the late colonial period, situating Sanad's query in the context of a much larger history of cosmopolitan-elite experiences. The narrator describes Sanad's experiences in the 1940s, reporting on and citing letters and conversations, and links these to stories of his own transformation from the son of an Indian textile magnate to a Gandhian activist in the 1920s. Amidst his many digressions, asides, and flashbacks, the narrator also recounts the tale of his own mentor, Sohan Bhai, yet another cosmopolitan-elite who had become an activist after a personal encounter with M. K. Gandhi. The reference to Gandhi, in turn, recalls his own narrative of elite metamorphosis that arguably sits at the heart of Indian nationalism. Gandhi's widely read autobiography, *Satya-na Prayogo* (*The Story of My Experiments With Truth,* Gujarati, serialized from 1925–28), details his transition: from an Anglophile lawyer of the late Victorian period who spent hours starching his collar and learning ballroom dancing to a nationalist who donned the garb and lifestyle of the Indian peasantry in order to demonstrate his solidarity with them. This circulation and recirculation of narratives of elite political awakening across many generations of Indians, linking Sanad's story to Gandhi's own, is central to the ways in which the novel "validates [. . .] the Gandhian strategies for emancipation" (Bhatnagar, *Political* 137).[8] Having shored up these many overlapping narratives, the novel returns to the post-1947 moment toward its end, with the narrator giving his blessings to Sanad's decision to remain at Selkirk and Lowe as long he works at deepening his cultural and political associations with India and the Indian people. Sanad still has many questions but, the novel suggests, he is learning how to integrate the Indian and Western aspects of his identity and culture in the interests of self-advancement and national progress.

I am insisting on the primacy of the narrator's role in the novel because he does not, on the surface, appear so crucial to it in comparison with Sanad. On the one hand, the narrator is unnamed and may appear to be a sloppily constructed character whose function is simply to report on and aid Sanad's development toward an appropriate nationalist consciousness. At one point, the narrator even interrupts himself during an autobiographical aside in order to insist that this is "really Sanad's story" (*A Time* 6). On the other hand, the novel appears to have two narrators, as the narrator cites Sanad directly quite often, having him speak to the reader in the first person for about one-third of the book. Accordingly, many of the novel's critics regard the narrator's haphazard methods of storytelling as evidence of Sahgal's bad writing in this, her first novel. Meenakshi Mukherjee writes, for instance, that the novel suffers from a "basic confusion of point of view" as it "shifts uneasily between an impersonal observer, a narrative agent, and an omniscient author" (*Twice-Born* 50). Upon examining these uneasy narrative shifts more closely, however, we recognize that although the novel flits back and forth between the narrator's and Sanad's stories, it always remains under the firm control of the first-person narrator, who steers Sanad's voice in a nationalist and even radical direction. By keeping the narrator nameless and offering Sanad's story in the first person—that is, by employing "free indirect style"—the implied author seeks to make the narrator a relatively invisible agent. But it is under cover of this invisibility that the novel does its ideological work.

Free indirect style allows the implied author to employ Sanad's voice in two ways. At times Sanad joins the narrator in his critique of both colonial oppression/racism and Indian sycophancy/self-centeredness. In these instances, Sanad is the model for what postcolonial elites ought to be like, for they are given a voice and an interiority only if, like Sanad, they begin to question the consequences of a life that takes them away from the nation. At other times Sanad himself exemplifies the conflicts and challenges of Indian elites, pulled away from a consideration of popular suffering by his desires for personal advancement. On the whole, Sanad is attempting to learn from the narrator how to comfortably move between "looking away" and "looking back"; the narrator's steady and unwavering critique of colonialism and his portrayal of independence as the joyous subversion of racist hierarchies is offered as a reference point for the reader's assessment of Sanad's evolving consciousness. The following examples show how the narrator and Sanad work together in drawing out the novel's aims: that Westernized elites ought to construct a new cosmopolitan-elite identity in order to comprehend the people's victimization under colonialism properly, learn the people's culture, and become committed, as "Tryst with Destiny" puts it, to the "service of the millions who suffer."

The narrator's reflections on the Sharanpur Club, represented as a graphic site of the racial and economic hierarchies of colonialism, exemplify how the novel's anticolonial critique is embedded in the narrative itself. The narrator walks into the Club, newly desegregated after independence, with a sense of curiosity—to see what it was that the British had been so anxious to keep secret. The narrator's memories of exclusion from the Club go back to his childhood when he was forbidden to play on its "velvety lawn," a world apart from the dry, brown field that he was used to (*A Time* 202). In fact, the narrator marks this incident as his first introduction to racial discrimination: he had seen white children playing there but found that he could not. His physical reclamation of this forbidden space of childhood, therefore, not only becomes a metaphor for Indian decolonization but provides a depth to political freedom, recasting it as the recovery of cultural and psychological space.[9] The narrator recognizes, for instance, that his "*dhoti*-clad presence" in the Club is an act of blasphemy, and that the ghost of Sir Charles Kittering, a "hero" of the British counterinsurgency during the 1857 Revolt whose portrait hangs in the Club, must be "thoroughly disapproving" of it (214). Besides the assertion of cultural pride, the emphasis on the narrator's *dhoti* and Kittering's likely reaction to it alludes to an event of significant symbolic and ideological importance in the anticolonial struggle: Winston Churchill's famous dismissal of Gandhi as a "half-naked fakir" as the latter prepared to attend the London Round Table Conference of 1931.

The physical retaking of occupied spaces at the end of the novel enables a thorough deconstruction of British-colonial identity. The placement of Kittering's portrait reveals the central role that colonial historiography played in the day-to-day life of the British community, cementing Club-goers' loyalties to counterinsurgency. In turn, the narrator's casual dismissal of Kittering in the context of a victorious anticolonial struggle signifies a rewriting of that history. The narrator further tears down the façade of empire in commenting on the Club's library, with its deep leather chairs, fireplace, and crimson carpets:

> The library had obviously been designed by a man who dreamed of snow-
> flakes drifting past the windows, of vintage port sipped in the depths of

an armchair, of warmth and plush on a wintry day. I wondered why he had not gone home to what he missed so much. For a moment the overpowering nostalgia of all those generations of exiles who had conjured up snowflakes in Sharanpur gripped me, and I felt sorry for them. How the demon sun must have mocked their fancies! (205)

These phrases and images invoke, and then invert, the discourse of colonialism. They reveal that the imperialist imagination that had turned India into an "island of make-believe" and adventure (205) was itself grounded in childish fictions. The phrase "demon sun" ironically positions us, for a moment, in the mindset of the imperialist before giving that Indian sun the agency to mock them. This critique of the British-colonial imaginary, reflected in the opinions of most of the British characters in the novel, is pointedly supported by repeated references to the fact that Indians had bodily taken over colonial spaces. Independence, here, is not an abstract political concept but the fact that, as the narrator gleefully reports, there were now "bare brown bodies beside the white ones splashing in the pool" at the Club (206). The narrator projects such a democratic glee regarding a whole range of social and political inversions. The late colonial days that, for him, had been full of hard work with little time to even think of pleasure "had for others been a time of gaiety," whereas the moments he had entered into now were a "prelude to hard times" for loyalist Indians and the remaining British (236).

For the novel makes clear that it was not only British elites who saw independence as a "prelude to hard times." Sanad's Anglicized uncle, Harish, has finally moved up in the ranks of the Indian Civil Service only to find that the man on the rung above him was a despicable *dhoti-wallah*: the sort of person Harish had tried to avoid all his life (*A Time* 248). Meanwhile, Sanad's father, Govind Narayan, cannot accept what Sanad calls "the age of the Common Man" and the new government's plans to abolish the *zamindari* system of landownership that has been the cornerstone of his family's wealth (243). The narrator and Sanad engage in full-frontal assaults on such loyalist and apolitical Indian elites. The narrator describes how Harish sees himself as playing a crucial part in Britain's "civilizing mission": "It was as if the white man, weary for a little while of his burden, had passed it on to Harish and he felt it an inestimable privilege to stagger under it [. . .] [His] entire outlook and manner had been so molded as to leave not the suspicion of an Indian about him. Had his complexion not been darker than the Englishman's, not one distinguishing feature would have existed to vouch for his separate identity" (16–17).

Perfectly capturing the unique liminality of the sycophant, the narrator identifies the narrow "cocktail party–gymkhana-club–Government House-circuit" that produced such a creature (17). Like his British bosses, Harish would flee to the hill stations to avoid the heat of Indian summers, would never go to an Indian doctor, never wore Indian clothes, spoke with a British accent, and couldn't appreciate Indian languages or poetry.

Sanad's first-person accounts of his experiences in colonial cities such as Calcutta serve to augment the narrator's critique of Anglicized Indians, for he can directly report from places where the narrator, with his *dhoti* and generational/cultural differences, cannot go. Calcutta's "neon-lit nights, its air-conditioned cinemas, its exclusive clubs" (*A Time* 88) are a complete shock to Sanad. With "at least a half dozen night spots to choose from" (compared with Sharanpur's single Club), Calcutta was a place, Sanad tells the narrator, where Europeans mingled with Harish-type men who "thumped one another on the back, called one another 'I say, old chap,' and sported the right school tie" (90).[10] Sanad notes that only one year before the worst famine in the history of Bengal these individuals could avail themselves of tins of asparagus, caviar, and foie gras. The insularity and parochialism of this "cosmopolitan society" (89) suffocates Sanad: every day brought visits to the same clubs with the same people, talking about the same things.

Such criticisms underline the *namak-halaal* attitude that dominates the novel's framework. But since Sanad himself is in a transitional stage, retelling his stories to the narrator in almost a confessional mode, the reader is made privy to the process by which political consciousness develops. Sanad is thus often both the subject and the object of critique. In another incident in Calcutta, accordingly, Sanad has an encounter with severe poverty that plays a crucial role in his political awakening. The setting is a dinner party at the home of Sir Ronu and Lady Lalita Chatterji, the center of Calcutta high society for Indians. Recently knighted for his services to the Empire, Sir Ronu sought contributions to help war widows of the Netherlands and starving children in Belgium—but with no attention, it is implied, to Indians who paid for the costs of World War II with their taxes, with food shortages, and with soldiers' lives. The Chatterjis' palatial house is marked as cosmopolitan and Western-oriented, featuring Italian upholstery, Venetian glass, and portraits of Lalita by French artists. Tired of the Chatterjis' pretentiousness, Sanad drifts away and amuses himself "by watching the reflection of the chandeliers twinkle in the window panes" (*A Time* 100). He looks out one of the large windows that open onto the street and finds himself in the middle of a typically Sahgalian moment of epiphany:

> I saw a little girl outside, begging, I suppose, with an even smaller child
> on her hip, looking up at the lights. If she was asking for alms I couldn't
> hear her because the music was so loud. [. . .] Seeing me looking out, she
> raised [the child's] filthy shirt, the only garment he had on, and showed
> me his jutting ribs. There was the barest covering of flesh on them. [. . .]
> Then one of the Chatterjis' liveried *chaprassis* [guards] hurried out of
> the house and drove the child away [. . .] [When I angrily asked why he
> hadn't given food for the child] the *chaprassi* looked at me in surprise.
> "The food would have done him no good, sahib. He was already dead.
> [. . .] He has been dead for hours. [. . .] The girl was here this morning
> and he was dead then."
>
> I had an insane desire to rush into the salon, stop the music, and
> shout "Silence!" (98)

Sanad's first-person narration allows us direct access to his sudden shock,
not only regarding the depth of poverty and deprivation but also at the
macabre acts that the poor need to perform in order to get even a cursory
recognition from the wealthy.

But the driving force of the passage is not the "barest covering of flesh"
on the child's "jutting ribs" but the ways in which Sanad tries to grapple
with this brush with extreme hunger. Sanad's attempt to communicate
beyond the charmed circle of elite space is repeatedly frustrated. Initially,
we are hopeful that the gap between Indian elites and the poor might
be bridged. Sanad is forced to shift his gaze from elite, private spaces,
"watching the reflection of the chandeliers twinkle" in the windows, to
public ones: to look outside to the street in order to see the girl who is also
"looking up at the lights." Oppositions of class are mapped onto the imagery of light/dark, as the reflections in the windows and the girl's attraction
to the lights imply that it is dark outside but bright within. For an instant,
the very lights that divide elite/poor, inside/outside seem as if they will
unite them, as the scene creates a cinematic eyeline match between Sanad
and the girl ("seeing me looking out"). Immediately, however, a series of
obstacles to Sanad's empathy appears as the elite space goes into lockdown
mode. It becomes impossible to know what the girl wants; he "couldn't
hear her" because of the loud music. Then the *chaprassi*, whose job is to
patrol Lady Chatterji's borders, steps in and removes the girl, closing the
spatial breach she had briefly created.

Since Sahgal constructs the *chaprassi* as more than a faceless guard,
however, the latter allows the reader to linger around the dead boy a bit
more. A liminal figure by virtue of his position—he communicates with

elites but is also situated on the margins—the *chaprassi* actually interacts with the girl, and it is *his* knowledge that enables Sanad's politicization. Initially, thinking himself to be the enlightened one, Sanad had come running to the door of the house and scolded the *chaprassi* for showing the girl the door and saying that he "would have given her something to eat" (*A Time* 98). But it is the *chaprassi* who is constructed as being much more in touch with reality as he reveals the secret of the girl's performance with the corpse. To restore the last set of ellipses in the passage above: "'He has been dead for hours,' he said matter-of-factly. 'The girl was here this morning'" (98). These phrases illuminate, with the suddenness of a rifle shot, the depth of the elites' disengagement with both the girl and the *chaprassi,* as Sanad is literally shocked into silence. For the *chaprassi,* who responds "matter-of-factly," the girl's situation is not an occasion for melodrama or ontological crisis but one of the many, daily tragedies emerging with the onset of famine. Sanad thinks about taking action, desiring to "shout 'Silence!'" in an attempt to bring the "outside" in, but even now his elite conditioning prevents him from embarrassing his hosts. Humbled, he stays with the *chaprassi,* who says, bitingly, that there is "not enough human pity for all the corpses we shall soon see [. . .] Already the people are straggling in from the villages. The smell of death is about them" (98–99).

This passage, narrating the suffering of the people with tremendous sympathy and calling for the elite to learn how to recognize this pain, draws forth a trope that exists in many pre-Emergency texts and hearkens back, indeed, to late colonial Indian English novels such as Mulk Raj Anand's *Untouchable* (1935) and Raja Rao's *Kanthapura* (1938). Taking the narrator's and Sanad's stories together, *A Time to Be Happy* champions the reclamation of Indian spaces and histories against colonial racism, the criticism of Eurocentric Indian elites, and the recognition of the extreme impact of colonialism on the poor. With Sahgal's novels in particular, there is a consistent attempt to expose and disrupt the cloistered experiences of elite characters through moments that reveal the daily tragedies and emergencies of subaltern life; the texts' explicit aim to challenge elitist bias despite focusing on elite characters. Nevertheless, the ways in which the novel resolves Sanad's crises raises questions about the narrator's understanding of the nation in relation to the people. Increasingly, the novel's acceptance of elite nationalism and the subsequent diminishing of class conflicts lead to a privileging of elite voices. Despite its sympathy toward the marginalized and oppressed, the text is unable to envision them as central to the project of liberation.[11]

McIvor's New Cosmopolitanism

In *The Black Man's Burden,* Basil Davidson distinguishes elite national-ism from populist, revolutionary nationalism by dubbing the former as "nation-statism." I use this term to signify a perspective whose ultimate concept of liberation from colonialism entails the achievement of a capital-ist nation-state that can eke out a space for itself within the global market-place. As *A Time to Be Happy* draws to its conclusion, the "nation-statist" elements of the Nehruvian nationalism to which it adheres become more apparent, rendering it more of an elite-centered, rather than subaltern-cen-tered, text. Three basic elements of this shift away from the people stand out, modifying the novel's earlier, intransigent critiques of British racism and elite self-centeredness: 1) the prominence that the implied author eventually grants to the voice of McIvor, Sanad's new boss at Selkirk and Lowe; 2) the text's insistence on compromise and not confrontation with loyalist elites; and 3) the marginalization of subaltern voices. Under the guise of a progressive critique of nativism, the text ultimately turns ordi-nary Indians into the backdrop against which elites perform their histori-cal roles.

Despite the discourse of Indian self-determination that constitutes the novel on the most basic level, it is McIvor—not the narrator—who best articulates the framework through which the novel portrays the his-toric task of elites in postcolonial India. Soon after independence, Sanad, McIvor, and the narrator begin to spend time socially, often talking deep into the night about the problems of postcoloniality. In one instance, Sanad talks about subaltern suffering and openly expresses his exaspera-tion with his isolation and impotence as an Anglicized elite:

> You know, Mr. McIvor, it is a strange feeling to be midway between two
> worlds, not completely belonging to either. I don't belong entirely to
> India. I can't. My education, my upbringing, and my sense of values have
> all combined to make me un-Indian. What do I have in common with
> most of my countrymen? And of course there can be no question of my
> belonging to any other country. I could not feel at home anywhere else.
> (*A Time* 147)

Sanad's lament stems from a sense of commitment to the nation: the elites ought to have "something in common" with their countrymen but do not have "the gift of mixing outside their own class" (147). This confusion is the postcolonial echo of the native intellectual's concerns in the colonial period, what Frantz Fanon calls the "second stage" of politicization: "[A]t the moment when the nationalist parties are mobilizing the people in the name of national independence, the native intellectual sometimes spurns these [Western cultural] acquisitions which he suddenly feels make him a stranger in his own land" (*The Wretched of the Earth* 219). Significantly, Sanad says not that he no longer feels at home in India but, in fact, that he "could not feel at home anywhere else"; his alienation still comes from a space of postcolonial mourning that is oriented toward the nation, not away from it. This sense of "not completely belonging" anywhere is more like the aesthetics of interwar modernism, in which "desolations of the self were still experienced quite frequently as a loss," than like the post-modernist model, in which "belonging *nowhere* is [. . .] construed as the perennial pleasure of belonging everywhere" (A. Ahmad, *In Theory* 157).

The text's expression of the dilemmas that inflict Western-educated, colonized elites, at this point, is not elitist in and of itself. But it becomes so when the narrator and Sanad uncritically accept McIvor's response as a way to resolve these tensions. McIvor provides a veritable manifesto for elites—whether belonging to the early postcolonial period or today's class of "Global Indians"—who seek to garnish their transnational profiteering with a nationalist flavor:

> [Y]ou have the great advantage, with your background, of being able to feel at home among people of your class anywhere in the world. [. . .] Treat [your upbringing] as the link between India and the rest of the world, an indispensable link because so few of your countrymen [. . .] dress as you do, so few [. . .] speak English, and so few have the educa-tion which you say sets you apart from India. [. . .] It is incumbent upon you to maintain this link and strengthen it. The world is in need of a uni-versal culture, a universal language. (*A Time* 147–48)

McIvor rewrites what Sanad had expressed as the cosmopolitan's handi-cap of "not belonging" as a "great advantage," a tool by which Sanad can belong to both India and the world. McIvor's observation that Sanad could "feel at home among people of [his] class anywhere in the world" is actually an invitation, an effort to impress upon Sanad that his Eng-lish education and Western dress given him the unique opportunity to be an Indian representative in a transnational club of elites. Indeed, McIvor gives the forging of such links between the national and the international realms an activist charge by articulating it as a categorical imperative ("It is incumbent upon you . . .").

Sahgal's *A Time to Be Happy* and Fanon's *The Wretched of the Earth* were published only a few years apart, but the McIvor passages illustrate the vast ideological gap between them. McIvor's proposed cosmopolitan identity for Indian elites of the early postcolonial period—one that corresponds to their subject positions as managers and capitalists in the new nation—is the inverted image, point-by-point, of Fanon's "first-stage" native intellectual who, though beginning to think self-critically, remains oriented toward the West:

> The intellectual who is Arab and French, or Nigerian and English, when he comes up against the need to take on two nationalities, chooses, if he wants to remain true to himself, the negation of one of these determinations. But most often, since they cannot or will not make a choice, such intellectuals gather together all the historical determining factors which have conditioned them and take up a fundamentally "universal standpoint." (218)

In criticizing this "universal standpoint" Fanon is not celebrating parochialism: the argument of *The Wretched of the Earth* ultimately rests upon the need for a radical anticolonial nationalism to develop into a genuine internationalism based on popular solidarity across national borders. At this point, however, Fanon portrays the impulse toward "universalism" as the inability or unwillingness ("cannot or will not") to ally oneself with a rebellious nationalism. But what Fanon describes as a political deficiency is, in *A Time to Be Happy,* precisely what McIvor prescribes as a solution: Sanad ought to *refrain* from "the negation" of one of the worlds to which he belongs. If we look at this through Fanon's schema, Sanad is moving backwards from a realization of his alienation ("second stage") to a desire for a "universal standpoint" that, in McIvor's discourse, is to be equated with the perspective of a transnational elite. In Gramscian terms, this is an "imperial-universal" standpoint that is diametrically opposed to the secular and progressive versions of the "national-popular" that are forged by the subaltern-centered, "organic" intellectual.[12]

Indeed, McIvor's suggestion that Sanad is an "indispensable link" between ordinary Indians and the world can be read, ironically, as the postcolonial fulfillment of the British administration's goals during the activist phase of "cultural reform" that had ended with the Revolt of 1857. In his infamous "Minute on Education" (1835), Lord Thomas Babington Macaulay had written:

We must [. . .] do our best to form a class who may be the interpreters between us and the millions we govern; a class of persons Indian in blood and color, but English in taste, in opinions, in moral, in intellect. To the class we may leave it to refine the vernacular dialects of the country [. . .] and to render them by degrees fit vehicles for conveying knowledge to the great mass of the population. (Macaulay)

Although the colonial administration's policies regarding intervention in Indian education and culture fluctuated between direct involvement and (alleged) noninterference—a tension that ultimately resolved itself in the formation of English literary studies (Viswanathan 38)—Macaulay's class of Indians with English tastes became a reality of colonial India. As studies of early- to mid-nineteenth-century debates on Indian education make clear, inculcating Englishness was widely seen as crucial to fortifying the hold of the East India Company on its colonies. In the struggle to overthrow colonialism, accordingly, an important segment of this English-educated class enacted Fanon's "negation," advocating various strands of cultural nationalism. Sanad's confusion initially appears to be the narrative of such a negation—the novel is replete with self-critical statements such as "I might as well be an Englishman except for the color of my skin" (*A Time* 232)—but his final acceptance of his Englishness in the interests of becoming a representative for the Indian bourgeoisie represents the negation of that negation. The class elements of this discourse about culture, which McIvor openly recognizes, ought not to be forgotten: in the context of Sanad's employment as an officer in a multinational textile corporation, his Englishness is not really a link between the people of India and the world but instead is that between a potential Indian market and a British firm seeking to maximize its profits. McIvor's cosmopolitan paradigm is one that completely fits Indian "nation-statist" goals, as well as British imperialist ones.

One consequence of the novel's acceptance of McIver's paradigm as a resolution to Sanad's dilemmas is the surprising resuscitation of characters previously discarded as racist and elitist. As the novel progresses from the late colonial to the early postcolonial periods, Sanad and the narrator engage in friendly debate and dialogue with characters who mourn the passage of the British, including Tom and Dora Grange, Harish, and the Chatterjis. We are reminded of Krishnan's insistence, from the second epigraph, that after independence the British and Indians "stood or fell together." Tom Grange, for instance, is absolutely prejudiced against

Indians' ability to rule themselves effectively—but Sanad continues to meet with him socially in order to argue politics. The reduction of the sphere of nationalist struggle to the level of friendly disagreements with pro-colonial elites undermines the other crucial aspect of the novel's representation of the committed cosmopolitan: a sense of responsibility to ordinary people. For all its value in terms of Sanad's politicization, the Calcutta scene involving the beggar girl, cited above, ends with a whimper. Sanad stays for dinner with Sir Ronu and his wife, Lalita, and participates fully in the dancing and merriment that follows—with no attention to his earlier critique of elite self-absorption. There is little textual indication that the implied audience ought to be critical of Sanad for this obliviousness.

What I am reading as a mark of the text's ambiguous politics is, in fact, explicitly constructed as a willful lack of closure. For instance, despite having decided to stay at Selkirk and Lowe, Sanad still represents a work-in-progress—but it is unclear, now, whether the narrator regards this as a failure or as evidence of a necessary process in the configuration of a new identity. On the one hand, Sanad desires to assert his Westernness: he joins the Club as soon as he can and is elated when Kusum Sahai, his newly married wife from a staunchly Gandhian and traditionalist family, agrees to wear high heels and drink liquor at office parties in order to fit into his world. On the other hand, he refuses to go abroad on company work until he can "go as an individual instead of as the carbon copy of an English man," and tries to learn a little Hindi from Kusum in order to read the recently published book of patriotic poems by her brother Sahdev, martyred in the Quit India uprising (*A Time* 267). Sanad, thus, has acquired all of the various accoutrements of cultural and political nationalism: he learns how to sit cross-legged and how to wear a *dhoti,* and his alliance with Kusum's nationalist and indigent family is clearly marked as a political act. The narrator observes all of this but explicitly refrains from counseling Sanad too much, seeing his development as part of a process that "will work out in time" (231). Echoing McIvor exactly, he rewrites Sanad's frustration about his divided self into strength: "The more elements that combine to make us, the more integrated we shall be as human beings, with a better understanding of those elements" (232). We have, then, both the desire for coherence and an explicit avoidance of closure. The novel continues to emphasize the process over the product, which applies as much to Sanad as to the nation itself ("One can have an ugly child [. . .]"). The lack of closure is portrayed as an expression of the narrator's patience with emerging developments—solutions will emerge "in time." As we have seen, however, what is being presented as the integration of diverse elements is actually the construction of a nation-statist cosmopolitanism.

The ending of the novel attempts to exhibit the productive tensions engendered by the lack of closure and continuation of dialogue, but its representation of Indian modernity reveals a suspicion, in spite of itself, that the modern nation had already discarded subaltern concerns. The handicrafts fair that culminates Village Industries Week, an event the narrator has organized, functions as a microcosm of the ideal nation that the novel has sought to achieve—in which differences and dialogue are encouraged as the mark of progress. On the one hand, the Fair is charged with anticolonial symbolism. The items on display, handicrafts and handspun cloth used to great effect in the anticolonial struggle, glorify the culture of the *kisan* (peasant) as both artisan and producer. The site at which the Fair takes place symbolically reclaims what was an exclusive enclave for British leisure; as the narrator triumphantly tells the portrait of Sir Kittering, "It is time to relent, Sir Charles. [. . .] [T]he natives are swarming all over the Polo Grounds [. . .]" (*A Time* 272). On the other hand, the narrator welcomes and even highlights the asymmetries and ironies involved in the coming together of persons of different nationalities, classes, and ideologies. In one booth, for instance, we see Sanad squatting in his neatly creased trousers and shiny black shoes, failing miserably at using a *charkha* (spinning wheel) yet waving proudly at the shocked British bosses of Selkirk and Lowe who walk by, disturbed by his "primitive" behavior. Again, there is more than a little irony reserved for the "distinguished patron[s] of the cottage industry" (260) who arrive with much fanfare—including Sir Ronu and Lady Chatterji, who have transformed into nationalist philanthropists now that the ruling party has changed. Nothing here is contradictory to the imagined nation of *A Time to Be Happy,* which constructs closure as the cessation of dialogue. Through the spectacle of the Fair, the novel aims to leaves its implied audience with a question that it does not seek to resolve: how will the urban-capitalist modernity emerging in the first decade of Nehru's India relate to the Gandhian economic models that tied the countryside to the nation throughout the anticolonial struggle?

The uncertainty surrounding this question, however, suggests that the novel secretly knows the answer: modern industry has already won. The narrative shifts from a celebration of "unity in diversity" to a troubled meditation on the implicit contradictions between the new Nehruvian India of modern industry and the one imagined by the romantic anticapitalist visions of Gandhi. The many ideological and symbolic contradictions in Village Industries Week rebound upon the narrative, as it were, by presenting questions that its framework, resting on the narrative of development-as-progress, cannot process. At one point, the novel allows us to listen in on a debate between Sir Ronu and Sanad, in which Sir Ronu openly mocks Village Industries Week as an archaic anomaly. The exchange is still friendly, but the novel now depicts as problematic the way in which formally loyalist capitalists both claim association with Gandhism, the peasantry, and handicrafts, and mock them, pouring investments into large-scale textile magnates such as Selkirk and Lowe. The narrator does not know what to do with this fact. His description of the Fair increasingly takes on a defensive tone, and he conjures up a romanticized vision of the purity of peasant work in order to drive away the suspicion that village handicrafts are merely symbolic and will always be marginal to the Indian economy. Making his rounds through the Fair, the narrator insists that he is filled with peace: what mattered was not the quality of the handicrafts but their very existence. This was proof, he contests, that "the machine age had not robbed the people of their prowess or their faith. The *kisan*'s [peasant's] art would survive as long as he himself survived" (273). The "ugliness" of the handicrafts must be tolerated, just as Veena tolerates the refugees fleeing Partition violence and arriving in Delhi. The narrator's comment on the *kisan* is indicative of a *namak-halaal* sensibility unavailable to most post-Emergency novels, but the passage is unaware of the simultaneous processes of romanticization and objectification of the *kisan* that it engenders.

The narrator's vision then pans up and out to give us a topography of the polo grounds, acknowledging the tension in the new nation and assuring us of the continuing presence of the people and their art: "The polo grounds were ringed about by a circle of tall trees, and beyond them rose smoke of the mills and factories. But here within this peaceful circle were the enduring things, the immemorial Indian things, tranquilly displayed. To me each painted toy and article of wood was a symbol of courage and the determination to survive" (*A Time* 272). The implicit critique of the factories and smokestacks surrounding the Fair is a testament to the narrator's desire that the modern nation remain people-centered, that the mills not wipe out the *kisans* and their handspun cloth. The narrator tries to invert the power relations, to decenter modernity—configuring the handicrafts that lay in the "peaceful circle" as the real, "immemorial" core of the new India. But this attempt to construct a safe haven for rural India only mirrors the fictitious world of the library in the Club: a space of escape from the brutal realities of modern life. The narrator insists upon reading the Fair as the fruit of the anticolonial struggle, buttressing his argument by returning to the Club and talking tough to Sir Kittering, but this confrontation seems far less real than the one between Sanad and Sir Ronu at the bar—in which Indian elites, not the British, stand in the way of a people-centered nation. The narrator is effectively caught in a contradiction, for Sanad, his protégé, is, after all, nothing but "the representative of a textile empire" (230). The narrator, though he does not admit it often, knows how different Sanad is from Sahdev, the former still "struggling to reach" the plateau achieved by the latter (230).

The narrator can only leave Sanad behind and escape from the suffocating Club into the "hot, jasmine-scented darkness" of an Indian night (272), embracing the heat and smells of an indigenous space whose construction as exotic, here, distances it from everything that is Western and modern. The anticlimactic ending unintentionally leaves us with an impression of Indian postcoloniality that is far less jubilant than one suggested by the novel's title. It says implicitly what the narrator refuses to say: the mills and steel towns have already won.[13] While the rural handicrafts are held up as a symbol of true self-reliance and reminders of the heroic anticolonial struggle, the reality is that capitalist modernity, led by Indian elites and aided by British firms, was already looming over the new nation, inevitable and forbidding like the smokestacks over the polo grounds, ripping the old Gandhian vision apart.

Interrogating Postcolonial Identities

Like *A Time to Be Happy,* Kamala Markandaya's *The Coffer Dams* is also committed to a version of national freedom that does not leave behind subaltern groups. It too combines a critique of British imperialism with a rejection of a narrow anti-British chauvinism, championing interracial and interethnic dialogue and seeking out transnational alliances. But *The Coffer Dams,* like Markandaya's *A Handful of Rice* (1966), is a subaltern-centered novel that portrays Indian modernity and its complex subjects very differently than *A Time to Be Happy.* The novel pits the aggressive industrial-capitalism of the Indian government and its British partners, the dam-building firm of Clinton and Mackendrick, Ltd., against the Adivasis (indigenous peoples) who inhabit the marginalized zones of the new nation-state and are being driven off their settlement. Markandaya's text leaves no doubt, as it were, that the factories and smokestacks of modern industry have already choked and engulfed the "peaceful circle" of the people.

The Coffer Dams tells a story, in fact, about that postcolonial violence. Every challenge that the British firm must overcome—building on
the difficult terrain of a forested hillside, planning a timetable around the
monsoon, maintaining the pace of the work, and keeping labor peace—
is embedded with the problems of postcoloniality. Constructing the dam
means displacing the Adivasis, a fact that creates ethical conflicts between
the characters and exacerbates, in turn, the racial and ethnic divisions
among managers and workers and between workers themselves. At times
the opposition between capitalist modernity and humanity comes to a
head and characters are faced with stark choices: should they "look away"
toward a modern Indian future, or "look back" to lives that would be displaced? For the completion of the dam project entails looking away while
Adivasis are displaced and killed—and fighting obstacles such as the monsoon and mudslides that are portrayed in the novel as the resistance of
the land and environment themselves to capitalist modernity. While these
larger oppositions (industry/humanity; machines/nature) establish the basic
conflicts of the text, the novel maintains a focus on characters who begin
to question their given roles in the drama, to challenge the prison houses of
the identities that have been assigned to them by history and society.

Like *A Time to Be Happy*, *The Coffer Dams* does its work through an
investigation of its characters' shifting identities, and their perceptions of
these shifts, over the course of the narrative. The moments of tension in
the text emerge when the two protagonists are forced to question social
hierarchies and expectations. Helen Clinton, the chief builder's wife, educates herself about the Adivasis' plight and becomes a fierce advocate for
them even at the risk of breaking up her marriage. Bashiam, an Adivasi
himself and now a crane operator for the British firm, excels at his work
but finds that no amount of technical skill can prevent him from being
denigrated, by the British and Indians alike, for his origins. Helen's and
Bashiam's trajectories cross somewhat as they become friends and, temporarily, lovers, but their challenges are different. Helen recognizes and
struggles against her Orientalist tendencies as she defends the Adivasis
against an encroaching modernity, whereas Bashiam, relatively uncritical
of modernity and a subscriber to a Horatio Algerian myth of bootstraps,
seeks to prove that Adivasi birth is no barrier to becoming a skilled, modern worker. Nevertheless, the actions of each—dialectically linked to those
of nature itself, the transcendent antagonist of modernity as the text represents it—are central to the plot and drive the novel to its divided and
ambiguous conclusion.

The representations of postcolonial identity in *The Coffer Dams* develop amidst the severity of its critique of modernity and its contradictions. When an early monsoon disrupts the best-laid plans of the increasingly despotic Clinton, the builders are forced to make several decisive choices. The first is to increase production to a twenty-four-hour cycle, breaking the natural sequences of time and dragging more and more impoverished Adivasis out of the hills to meet the labor shortage. Adivasis thus receive a wage for the construction of the very dams that are destroying their homes, "a perpetuating circle that gained momentum as the dam drained men from the tribe" (*The Coffer Dams* 167). The breakneck speed of production results, in turn, in a number of workplace fatalities and injuries, with the biggest explosion resulting in the death of forty Adivasi workers. Recovering the bodies of the dead in accordance with Adivasi traditions, however, would require moving a massive boulder and setting back the timetable—so Clinton and his associates decide to forgo the effort. The boulder can be made part of the dam, they reason, and the men's "bodies can be incorporated. Into the structure" (188). The short, choppy sentences articulate the cold, deliberate logic of modernity, in which the dams literally swallow up indigenous bodies.

As tensions rise between the British, the Adivasis, and the Indians, who have decided to put aside their prejudices and unite with the latter in protest of British inhumanity, Bashiam steps in *on the side of the dambuilders*—partly in secret atonement to Clinton for sleeping with Helen and partly in order to recover the bodies, but largely because he wants the challenge of operating the new Avery-Kent crane that no one else can handle. This element of Bashiam's characterization is extremely important, for it shows Markandaya's sensitivity to a contradiction that cannot be easily answered, namely that in a world dominated by modern, capitalist structures, progress on the level of both society and the individual becomes defined in terms of advancement within those structures—no matter how violent and disruptive they may be. For Bashiam, his personal liberation from poverty is always tied to his ability to master Western machinery, and Clinton and Rawlings take advantage of his eagerness, allowing him to operate the crane even though they know that it is defective. His devotion to modernity betrays him: Bashiam eventually moves the boulder out, anchoring the faulty crane with the strength of his body, but his backbone breaks, adding another Adivasi casualty to the total. Still, even though he returns to the Adivasi village for rest and recovery, Bashiam sets out to work on new modernization projects as soon as he is well. The novel clearly depicts postcoloniality as violent and the new nation-state as treacherous, seeking the aid of and enriching the former colonizers in the effort to control nature at all costs. But there are no easy resolutions, and the ambiguity of the ending also confirms this. It becomes clear that the dams still will not be completed on time, and that the "coffer dams" at the foundation will have to be broken apart immediately if the coming monsoon rains are not to drown the Adivasi villages. Clinton, increasingly dehumanized in his desperation to conquer India, its people, and its weather, refuses to breach the coffer dams for any reason whatsoever. The tension is defused, however, when the rains, existentially allied with the Adivasi cause, end unexpectedly. We are left with an ambiguous ending as categories and spaces previously constructed as oppositional are shown, suddenly, to coexist: the village is saved *and* the coffer dams remain standing. We have then the clear outlines of a politics that draws attention to the excesses of postcolonial modernity and the problems of identity it throws up—but also an unwillingness to resolve these questions in any simple way.

Thus, in terms of how it depicts protagonists and antagonists, *The Coffer Dams* offers fairly clear-cut dichotomies between capitalist modernity and popular welfare, between the interests of elites and nonelites, (ex-) colonizers and (post)colonized. Unlike the more sympathetic approach to Selkirk and Lowe in *A Time to Be Happy,* British characters in Markandaya's novel are constructed as sympathetic only to the extent that they shift their positions *against* the British complicity in postcolonial suffering. Helen, for instance, moves further and further away from her husband and the dam project as she develops a greater understanding of Indian realities and boundaries. She earns her place in the novel, as it were, by refusing the role of neocolonial *memsahib*: mingling with the Adivasis, learning their language, and ultimately becoming a spokeswoman for them. She is thus in basic opposition to McIvor in *A Time to Be Happy,* who is allowed to hold forth on the benefits of British firms to the new India. Helen knows the material facts beneath the rhetoric: along with the Americans, West Germans, Russians, and the Dutch, the British are simply seeking "to gain a foothold in an expanding subcontinent of vast commercial potential" (*The Coffer Dams* 12). Subsequently, Helen also stands in opposition to Sanad, as her version of becoming an "indispensible link" between the people and the world is centered around the people and not herself—and this despite the fact that she is not Indian. Indeed, there are no nationalist saviors here, as it is the Indian elites themselves who are welcoming the multinationals into the nation. The deep critique of imperialism in *The Coffer Dams,* thus, emerges out of a representation of the new nation-state as a willing participant in the Western exploitation of its own resources and people.

One might expect that in a social-realist novel, such a stark political opposition to postcolonial modernity would result in a cookie-cutter approach to characterization and voice. No so. Despite its thorough critique of the ongoing British interest in India and the characters who defend it, paradoxically, it develops British characters to a far greater extent than does *A Time to Be Happy*. While Sahgal's text resuscitates and makes sympathetic all of its British characters, engaging in friendly debate with them, their viewpoints are firmly ensconced within those of the first-person, reliable narrator. The reader of *A Time to Be Happy* always approaches British characters from the outside. On the contrary, *The Coffer Dams* is much more didactic. Its third-person, omniscient narrator has no difficulty in marking characters as racist, sexist, or generally unlikable. But the interiority of British characters, such as Clinton, Helen, Mackendrick, Rawlings, the chief engineer, and Millie, Rawlings's wife, is developed to such a degree through the usage of free indirect style that they become three-dimensional, with human frailties and motivations mixed in with their political and cultural outlooks. This narrative strategy disrupts any easy association between racial, ethnic, or national identity and political outlook, and places greater value on where a character stands on the question of modernity than who s/he is. Certainly, the novel's politics tell us clearly where our sympathies should lie, but in terms of character and voice the text is far more interested in movement than stasis. Clinton's trajectory from liberalism to brutality is given more attention than the motivations of the consistently open-minded and kindhearted Mackendrick. The brooding Krishnan has much more of a voice than his Indian co-workers Gopal and Shanmugham, despite the fact that it is the latter who slowly learn to overcome their prejudices against Adivasis. Bashiam challenges stereotypes by actually glorifying the dam project—with classic Nehruvian gusto—and exhibiting a real distaste for Adivasi life. Helen's complete rejection of modernity makes her, in fact, a better spokesperson for the indigenous cause than Bashiam—even though the text is self-conscious about the problems of Orientalism.

The Coffer Dams, therefore, does not privilege any particular aspect of identity, whether nationality, race, gender, ethnicity, sexuality, or class, as automatically endowing a character with a critical knowledge of modernity's consequences—or, for that matter, as barring him/her from such a knowledge. Rather, it investigates the relationship between identity and ideology and the potential for change. While some characters are clearly fixed in order to anchor the novel's politics (Clinton, the Adivasis), the characters who do transform are drawn from the same identity groups

(Helen and Bashiam, respectively) in order to combat essentialist representations. The novel thus exhibits both a firm loyalty toward the Adivasis and recognition of the dynamism of cultural and political identity. It draws a firm line between the powerful and the powerless, even while offering, on the level of narrative, a perspective into the viewpoints of people who are on either side of that line—and thereby opening up the possibility that they might shift across it.

The question thus becomes not simply about locating the presence of "hybridity" but in asking about the *kinds* of hybrids that exist and can come into being, about the limits and possibilities of cross-cultural mixing. While those who champion and benefit from modernity are able to turn their cross-cultural experiences to nefarious ends, Helen and Bashiam are "elite" only in a relative and contingent sense as their gender and their ethnicity, respectively, turn them both into "freaks" (157). Their marginality is emphasized decisively by the two main dramatic moments of the text: when Helen is raped by her husband after an argument about the British role in a free India, and when Bashiam breaks his back. The rape puts Helen outside the pale of "Englishness" and everything it signifies, a punishment for mixing with the natives and refusing to recognize Clinton's firm order to stay away from them: "Not our country, not our people. Nothing to do with us" (145). Likewise, the accident—severely injuring Bashiam and taking away the abilities that allowed him to rise above ethnic and class oppression—thrusts him out of the dam-building modernity that he so admires and back into the Adivasi identity that he had been trying to escape (234). Hybridity and newness, here, are not special modes of cultural mixing or consciousness that can cross all borders. Rather, they are by-products of modern life that can be used either to cement hierarchies or to challenge them. While the representatives of modernity employ their cross-cultural experiences and knowledges in the interests of the status quo, Helen's and Bashiam's "hybridities" are portrayed as threatening and in need of correction because they stand against the violent logic of that modernity.

The Postcolonial Memsahib and the Adivasi Engineer

Let's investigate a bit more closely the kinds of hybridity expressed by Helen and Bashiam as they shift and transform through the text. With Homi K. Bhabha's work in the 1990s, especially *The Location of Culture* (1994), "hybridity" began its long reign as a dominant theoretical term in Postcolonial Studies—one that is, in turn, central to concepts of cosmopolitan experience and knowledge. As a student in the field quickly learns, "hybridity" is posited as the "good" term that stands in opposition to "bad" ones such as "binary opposition" and "essentialism." Bhabha's specific role in the postmodernization of Postcolonial Studies has been to problematize the colonizer/colonized dyad. Borrowing liberally from both Foucauldian and Derridean discourses, Bhabha has argued that there is no clear dividing line between colonizers and colonized, that such terms are homogenizing and essentialist, and that a great variety of alternative, hybrid subjectivities have existed across this false divide. As several historicist critics have noted over the years, while Bhabha's model may have helped to raise important questions about the construction of both colonial discourse and its national antagonist, his method tends to minimize the materiality of colonialism and colonial oppression: the ways in which a series of specific economic, political, and legal processes did, in fact, dichotomize colonial societies into the subjectivities of colonizer and colonized. Hidden beneath debates around Bhabha's hybridity, quite often, are disagreements about the relative materiality of different sets of oppositions. Are all binary oppositions equally constructed and, implicitly, equally false ways of viewing the world? On the flip side, are all hybridities equally liberating, and what exactly does the mixture consist of? How does one judge the truth-values of different hybrid configurations?

Reading *The Coffer Dams* suggests that we question a critical model in which all binary oppositions are marked as being worthy of debunking, that some oppositions exist in order to obfuscate the operation of power while others have actually helped to analyze and critique a world of oppression, suffering, and war. The novel's characters allow us to conceptualize a more materialist and historicist notion of hybridity by revealing that social and political identities can be fluid even when the lines between oppressor and oppressed are fairly thick and deeply rooted. In *The Coffer Dams,* binary oppositions that justify oppression are dismantled as false, but those that reveal its presence are maintained and emphasized. Crossing boundaries in the face of a rigid hierarchy of power is upheld in the interest of preserving notions of truth, justice, and the possibility of knowledge. On the flip side, a championing of hybridity and cross-cultural experience that leads to the perpetuation of oppression is represented by the novel as being either manipulative or ignorant.

In Helen and Bashiam, *The Coffer Dams* offers a careful study of different hybridities and their manifestations. Let's take, for instance, Helen's initial curiosity about the Adivasis and the way in which she negotiates the line between genuine cross-cultural understanding and the opportunistic appropriation of another culture. With time on her hands and an unfamiliar world to explore, Helen comes to know about the "hill-people" and tries to find out more about them, visiting a few settlements and reminding us forcefully of the kinds of Orientalist sentiments that have become associated with journals such as *National Geographic*. Here, Helen is deliberately constructed as naïve, unmindful of history and the political and cultural tensions underlying the relationships between the British, the Indians, and the Adivasis. At one point, for instance, she asks Krishnan about his opinion on the "impermanent, flyway foundations" on which the Adivasis built their homes and their lives (51). Helen does not know what the third-person omniscient narrator promptly tells us, that Krishnan, a Tamil Brahmin from the plains, "despise[s] Helen for thinking that he [. . .] could be familiar with any aspect of the half-savage hill people's lives" (51). And yet, despite his own loathing for the Adivasis, Krishnan "close[s] the Indian ranks [. . .] decisively" and replies in a polemic whose roots Helen cannot comprehend: "'Of course they seem flyaway to you, you are used to better things. Unfortunately our people are not. They've become used to being done out of their rights'" (51).

The third-person narration performs several tasks simultaneously. In terms of Helen, it reveals her concern for the Adivasis but also her complete lack of knowledge about historical and cultural differences among the inhabitants of the Indian subcontinent. History, we are told, "still largely lay between the covers of a book" for Helen, "dissociate[d] from [. . .] human reality"; learning about the "humiliations of being an underdeveloped and pauper nation" might allow her to understand Krishnan's bitter reply (52). And yet, even while asserting the importance of understanding the colonizer/colonizer divide in postcolonial encounters and Krishnan's greater knowledge in this regard, the narrator reveals the arrogance of Krishnan's construct of "civilized Indians" and "savage Adivasis." We are shown that both Helen and Krishnan operate around false constructs about "Indians," even as it is emphasized that the *history* of colonial and ethnic oppression in India is real and important. We are shown both that Helen's curiosity smacks of Orientalist ignorance *and* that her continued search for knowledge about the Adivasis is superior to Krishnan's, because his opportunistic closing of "Indian" ranks ultimately legitimates the violence of mainstream nationalist discourse and nation-statism. "Our people," in Krishnan's usage, is shown to be just empty rhetoric that masks the oppression of Adivasis by the nation.

Thus, Krishnan's specific way of employing the opposition between

"Indians" and "British" is shown to be a false construct even as the division of colonizer and colonized, as engendered by history, is represented as real. We have, as it were, different gradations of binary oppositions: colonial oppression creates the context for the formation of a national identity which is useful in overthrowing that oppression, but buying into that identity in perpetuity, especially after decolonization, suppresses racial and ethnic variety and difference within the nation. Initially, Helen seeks to leap over the historical divide through an idealist act of will and is rebuffed by Krishnan. But because Helen does not then revert back to the *memsahib,* ruling-class subject position that is available to her but actually pushes ahead for greater knowledge and communication, she is able to go beyond Krishnan's national fictions. In Hogan's terminology, Helen reshapes her "practical identity" by gaining "competence" in another culture. It is in this capacity that she is made sympathetic to the implied audience.

Helen soon encounters Bashiam, who becomes, the narrator informs us, her "link man" to the Adivasis' language and cultural practices (52). Again, given the deep entrenchment of Foucauldian paradigms of power/knowledge in literary and cultural studies, it might seem impossible to view the term "link man" as a neutral one. Two possibilities present themselves: either that 1) "link man" is Helen's term and the text is further exposing Helen's naïveté, as it did in the dialogue with Krishnan; or that 2) it is the narrator's term and the text is demonstrating *its own* lack of understanding about the impossibility of knowing without dominating. But we are being given, in fact, a much more nuanced model of representation and knowledge. Helen shows that she is quite aware of the manipulation of knowledge for power and mastery, but this does not prevent her from working hard in the interest of communication. I take up the dialogue between Helen and Bashiam in some detail as it is among the best illustrations of the novel's representation of the different possibilities inherent in (postcolonial) identity formation.

Struggling to study the Adivasis' language, which was "different in rhythm and structure from any that she knew," Helen refuses to take the shortcuts of "sign language and a smattering of a few words" for fear that she would become like Rawlings and Mackendrick, whose "thundering hodge-podge of *jaos* and *jaldis* [. . .] bewildered their South Indian labor" (52). The term "South Indian labor," voiced by Helen, immediately distinguishes her relation to Indian languages from that of the other British characters. Rawlings and Mackendrick know a few words (*jao* means "go" and *jaldi* means "quickly") but these words are Urdu/Hindi words, widely spoken in northern regions of India but probably incomprehensible to the Tamil workforce. Helen shows that she has no interest in this sort of border-crossing, in gaining a "command of language" that simply serves as the "language of command."[14] And yet Helen does not read *all* knowledge of other people and places as appropriation. Genuine communication and knowledge would be possible, Helen insists, if one achieved a higher level of competence in linguistic ability. This idea is not represented by the novel as a manipulative, "Western" model of knowledge, and Bashiam, suitably impressed by Helen, agrees: "one learns if one wishes to learn" (52). Indeed, Helen has high standards for herself, desiring "the minimum fluency without which [. . .] communication degenerated into grinning goodwill and one-syllabled monotony [. . .]" (53). We are being shown, on the one hand, that all acts of representation are not necessarily appropriative; on the other, that real communication across class and cultural borders, even if possible, is quite difficult. Expanding identities and consciousness in ways that actually leads to greater understanding requires developing more than the surface points of (linguistic) affiliation.

The Coffer Dams does not rest at this provocative point, but continues to interrogate Helen's desire to learn about the Adivasis by forcing her to explain to a quizzical Bashiam why "she found interest in a village for whose standards [. . .] he had little left but a near contempt" (53). Now, the text raises the issue of her romanticization of the Adivasi settlement by presenting her with an estranged member of the hillside who couldn't wait to leave it behind. Initially, it irks Helen that Bashiam "doted on [machines] as passionately as Clinton" (53). Ever attuned to the nuances of her own discourse, however, Helen realizes that she's falling into an Orientalist trap: she "expected people like Bashiam—a backward people [sic]—to be content with natural things like hills and woods and a water pump or two [. . .]" (53). Arriving at one of the most profound insights of Leon Trotsky's theory of "combined and uneven development," as it were, Helen sees that the Adivasis, too, were "creatures of the nuclear age however much it had bypassed them" (53).[15]

At this point the narration is still ensconced within Helen's consciousness as she thinks *about* Bashiam. But Bashiam then speaks, providing a forceful argument for the validity of Indian modernity and his desire for "upward mobility." Bashiam insists, challenging Helen, that machines had given him "a better way of life" (54). He understands why Helen pitied the destruction of "the ramshackle, fly-by-night settlement," a symbol of the way in which modernity forced a transience on the community. But nothing could "dispel the horror that *dwelling* in [Adivasi huts] infused in his mind" (54, italics mine). Helen pursues the issue, asking whether it had not been more quiet and peaceful before the blasting began, but Bashiam is not so sure, remembering, with a shiver, "the sodden huts, the cold, the uncertainty, the comfortless ritual of a departure, the incantations of a bewildered clan to an immune god" (55). Bashiam tries to explain to Helen why he loves the machines so much despite the fact that his "roots were attenuated" and he was an outsider everywhere (55). What is important to recognize here is not whether Bashiam "gets it right" in terms of our own political perspectives on "upward mobility" but the fact that the implied author is able to represent, from an imminent perspective, a real debate between characters who are at a remove from the Adivasis whose interests they each claim to represent. Bashiam's articulation of the different pressures that had driven him way from the settlement—a distaste for poverty and hunger, an unwillingness to pray to an "immune god," and a love of modern progress—acts as a check on Helen's desire to know. With Bashiam, she comes to understand that the material experience of being victimized, the experience of actually living in the huts that Helen can only talk about, might drive one toward a rejection of "the indigenous" as a sign for the "nonmodern." Making Bashiam more than a token figure forces Helen to see that Adivasis, too, were a complex group and had different opinions about their circumstances. Bashiam raises questions about Helen's complete dismissal of modern development—and thus makes it hard to read the novel as simply voicing a romantic anticapitalist critique.

But it is not only Helen who is forced to shift her perspective. Bashiam's frequent interactions with her make him discover aspects of his identity that he has suppressed. First, Bashiam realizes that "in his bones, however de-tribalized he might be, birth and upbringing within the tribe had given [him] race knowledge and instincts that could never be acquired by real outsiders" (93). Markandaya's essentialist language is apparent here, and raises questions about the Adivasi identity that she is projecting. It seems, for instance, that his attempt to "look away" is constructed as more of an act of false consciousness than others' gestures toward the modern, and one can argue that a romantic antimodernity is operating here. In terms of what the text is attempting to accomplish, however, its assertion that Bashiam's ethnic identity is an inescapable material fact highlights the difficulties of transforming one's identity, especially in a modern world that has institutionalized ethnic divisions. Bashiam simply cannot break into a modern Indian subjectivity. Even though he is even more adept at handling machines than his co-workers, they prefer to call him not just a *jungly-wallah* ("jungle-man") but, with greater irony, a "civilized *jungly-wallah*"

(52). Further, Bashiam comes to understand the differences between knowledge based on free association and opportunistic knowledge. Before Bashiam's interactions with Helen, his experience with non-Adivasi outsiders had included two sorts of people: those "whose outlooks barred them from allowing their interest to be sparked by anything," and Orientalist scholars "who alarmed him by taking down everything he said for use in the books they were going to write, attaching an importance to every trivial detail" (93–94). Helen came to him, Bashiam reflects, not because of his English, for "her grasp of dialect made her independent of him" (93), but because she identified with his rebelliousness.

The text constructs Bashiam as reflecting explicitly on the commonality between their different paths, on "[t]he divergent channels they had carved for themselves—he the skilled and competent technician away from his jungly-wallah tribe, she the No. 1 memsahib who refused to bear the memsahib's load—so that there was an acreage of common rebellion which both were stimulated by and respected in one another" (93). What ties Helen and Bashiam together, despite the "divergent channels" of their own choosing, is a refusal to remain within their prescribed identities. Each seeks wholeness, but must rebel in order to find it. Bashiam, whose "roots were attenuated," longs for the "fusion" and feeling of "one-ness [*sic*]" that happens at the construction site, bringing together machines and men of different backgrounds (55). The narrator employs the same term, "fusion," to describe Helen's experience after sleeping with Bashiam: she feels "a peace that was to do with her mind as consummation had been for her body, the fusion making her whole in a way that she could not recall having achieved before" (160). Indeed, a similar "acreage of common rebellion" is also the political basis for the illicit, cross-class and cross-caste relationship of Ammu, divorced and disgraced, and Velutha, the Dalit carpenter, in Arundhati Roy's *The God of Small Things* (1997). Politics saves these elite female characters from what might otherwise be a kind of "slumming." As Ammu realizes her desire for Velutha, she hopes that "under his careful cloak of cheerfulness he housed a living, breathing anger against the smug, ordered world that she so raged against" (*The God of Small Things* 167). Similarly, it is just after Bashiam's meditation on their commonalities that he feels "the flame [that] licked over him, over his limbs and mind" (*The Coffer Dams* 95).

A very specific model of identity formation and its complexities, then, lies at the basis of the *namak-halaal* perspective in *The Coffer Dams,* allowing critique of both a reductive nativism and a blind nation-statism. Helen and Bashiam, first, are marked as characters who are cosmopolitan and elite, but only in relative and limited ways given their race, gender, ethnicity, and politics. Despite these limits, they employ the skills provided by their cosmopolitan experience to reach out toward new possibilities and the formation of more complex identities. Their two trajectories seem to be in opposite directions: Helen moves toward the Adivasis and develops a critique of modernity and its excesses, while Bashiam seeks to escape this very violence by transforming himself into a "modern" subject and leaving behind his Adivasi identity. However, their interaction with one another over the vast "acreage of common rebellion" helps to refine their knowledge about modernity's violence. It is at this point, in the narrative sequence, that Helen and Bashiam are punished for their transgressions, as if modernity exacts revenge for exposing its processes. Helen's cultural explorations are tolerated until she actually stands up against Clinton's plans to halt the effort to recover the bodies of the dead Adivasi workers. The narrator depicts Clinton's rape of his wife as a deliberately political act. He literally chants the phrase "not our people" throughout the scene—the words he used earlier to warn her against associating with the Adivasis—as if to make her aware that she is being punished for her transgression of national, racial, and class borders. Similarly, though abused and resented, Bashiam is tolerated for his technical skills only to be cast aside like a broken machine when he confronts the juggernaut of "progress" by trying to move aside the mighty boulder. There is no reconciliation between Helen and Clinton and no quick recovery for Bashiam.

With Helen and Bashiam, then, *The Coffer Dams* offers careful, contextualized representations of identity: transformations are possible, but one cannot imagine oneself, on the individual level, across subject positions overdetermined by society. Elites who are uncritical of their role in oppressing Adivasis or who actively maintain the unequal relations of power are depicted, in contrast, as putting their intercultural knowledge to poor uses. However, they are also contextualized carefully. For instance, Rawlings—he of the *jao*s and *jaldi*s—has lived in many lands and climates but his "cosmopolitan reflections" are limited to thinking about "the women whose shining skins had gone from copper to ebony" as he exerted his "double mastery" over them as a man and as a landlord in Asia and Africa during colonial times (222). Rawlings is given a voice, but his sexism and colonial mentality render him as unsympathetic. In this context, the novel does not hesitate to point out that decolonization, for all its limitations, actually placed a limit on such a man's barbaric trysts. Rawlings bemoans the fact that things were no longer the same now: "the spirit is different [after] the freedom which [. . .] had been delivered on a plate [and] ma[de] people uppity" (222). We are encouraged to read against the grain of Rawlings's words and to champion the fact that independence, having tapped into the "common sense" of ordinary Indians, made them sufficiently "uppity" to refute the advances of the Rawlingses that peopled the world. The implied author, thus, encourages us to investigate the complex identities produced in postcolonial contexts and their fluidity, but within an explicit political framework. The violence of postcolonial modernity ought to be criticized, but decolonization represented a step toward freedom.

The Coffer Ribs

The resolution of the conflicts in *The Coffer Dams* presents us with a few problems on the level of narrative and representation of the nation, not unlike the ending of *A Time to Be Happy*. The pressures of nation-statism, as it were, produce in the text an inability to sustain its critique of modern India. By this time, Clinton has refused all alternatives and spoken the words of doom—they will not break the coffer dams though this will mean the submergence of the Adivasi village. As the headman lies dying, symbolizing the utter victimization of the village as it awaits the flooding, Helen defies the driving rainstorm to march up the thundering hills and show her solidarity with the Adivasis, accompanied by a newly rebellious Mackendrick. Bashiam is nowhere in these final scenes, as he has already said his farewells to Helen a few chapters ago; she will go back to England, and Bashiam, when he gets well, will look for more building projects in postcolonial India. While Helen sits quietly with the headman, having learned from Bashiam how to be tranquil in the face of crisis, Mackendrick paces back and forth impatiently, waiting for a word from the Adivasi leader regarding the future of the village. Shaking the headman awake from his semiconscious stupor, an act that is marked as one of Western impatience, Mackendrick lifts up his frail frame so that he can see the distant mountains and judge, from his experience, the state of the storm. The exertion ends up killing the Adivasi leader, but his final prediction—that the rains will end when the faraway ridges are clear—provides great joy. By the next dawn, Helen, "having kept her vision whole" and in tune with the Adivasis, can also see that the rain has stopped at the distant ridge and that the monsoon will soon be over (255).

Amidst the general euphoria after the end of the heavy rains, Mackendrick "enclose[es] [Helen's] hand in two jubilant palms" (256). The novel concludes:

They picked their way out, into the watery landscape and through the aftermath of the storm to the river to look, and saw that the banks held firm and the water levels were falling, which was of moment to them. While others who looked, their concerns being different, saw only the coffers, whose formidable ribs rose bleached and clean in the washed air above the turbulent river. (256)

This potential scene of tranquility and hope—binding together Helen and Mackendrick with the pronoun "they"—emerges quite unexpectedly in a novel whose main themes had been the rejection of modernity and the utter alienation of Helen from the other British characters. The passage evokes the mythical scenes, common in many religious traditions, of the human survivors of a devastating flood, of new beginnings that proceed slowly, "pick[ing] their way out" of the "watery landscape." Indeed, there is a humanist, Miltonian resonance here, recalling Adam and Eve holding hands and looking out toward a world that they must create anew after being exiled from Eden at the end of *Paradise Lost*. As in Milton, there is a spirit of adventure, excitement, and hope in Helen and Mackendrick's departure from the village, a celebration of humanity in the midst of crisis. But what do we make of this diffusion of the opposition between modernity and the Adivasis? Or this newfound association of Helen with Mackendrick, who remains a partner in Clinton and Mackendrick, Ltd., now associated directly with rape and homicide?

There is much evidence to suggest that after its incessant critique of the brutality of modernity, the text is finally compromising with it, recognizing the limits of the Adivasis' position and keeping faith in the possibilities of a gentler, kinder modernity. Mackendrick's shift toward Helen, in this view, would symbolize the hope that modernity could be reformed, piece by piece, by the interventions of sympathetic elites. Indeed, despite all of the attempts of Helen and Bashiam, the Adivasis lose their agency; they are not represented as actually *doing* anything to force Clinton's hand. When Clinton coldly lays down the rigid laws of bourgeois rule—"We make the calculations, it is they who run the risk" (250)— the Adivasis and their allies are reduced to waiting for the weather to change. Indeed, even after having his teeth kicked in by postcolonial modernity, Bashiam resigns himself to his work after Helen says she will leave the village: "I shall go, too. There are many projects [. . .] It is a big country" (235). The rebelliousness that had shaken up the steady march of development seems resolved too quickly, with Helen returning to a British friend and Bashiam being trapped, once again, in the service of the modern nation. One of the effects of the ending is to make modernity appear so threatening and unchanging that it can serve to undermine the radical critique made by the book and rid the oppressed of any agency. The coffer dams become an organic and permanent feature of the geography, as it were, as they are described as having "formidable ribs [that] rose bleached and clean" from the river.

The disappearance of Bashiam toward the end of the novel, the incessant critique of Krishnan's attempts to organize labor as opportunistic, the reliance on British agents such as Helen and Mackendrick—all of these elements in the plot and characterization undermine the crucial element that differentiated it from *A Time to Be Happy*, namely the construction of the oppressed as active subjects who think, question, and resist. In Sahgal's novel, the problem is persistent: the text condemns poverty but has no characters that are poor; it proclaims the greatness of "the *kisan's* art" but develops no *kisan* voices. In the process, the tendency to compromise with loyalists and imperialists is the only option, as these elites are seen as the only avenue for change. In Markandaya, the presence of Bashiam, the impact of the headman on Helen, and Helen's own critique of Bashiam allow a much more complex picture of Adivasi politics and, crucially, allow the development of agency while guarding against romanticization. But all of this is dropped, as it were, by an ending that neither imagines Adivasi resistance and agency nor remains fully critical of the dam project—the symbol of nationalist and imperialist teamwork in the postcolonial era. It is possible, in fact, to read this gesture as a final return to the nation-state, as depicted at the end of Sahgal's novel, even while insisting that the marginalized and oppressed ought not to be forgotten.

However, the one element that might allow for a different reading of this ending is the possibility that the text's return to modernity and the nation emerges from such a stark realism—eschewing all easy utopias—that nothing is possible besides irony and the hope of ongoing confrontation and resistance. The novel rarely turns to the ironic mode but there is certainly a trace here, as there is in Sahgal's topography of the Village Industries Week, of what Theodor Adorno calls "negative dialectics," a mode in which critically drawing out contradictions until their logical conclusion leads to a radical, if pessimistic and even nihilistic, critique of the status quo. At Helen and Bashiam's final meeting, for instance, Helen asks why Bashiam tried to move the boulder after all. Says Bashiam: "There are some things which one has to do" (234)—a phrase that Helen repeats to Mackendrick in order to try to explain why she goes up to the village, which meant risking death since Clinton had refused to break the dams and release the rapidly rising river. In each case, the speaker is conscious of the fact that the phrase does not explain his or her actions in logical terms, but is content with its pure expression of resistance and willpower. Bashiam and Helen are simply silent after articulating this, as "each understood the other had gone as far as it was possible to go, for the present or perhaps even forever, and were quiet" (234). It is a silence that lies at the end of a dialogue in which a deep communication has been reached, and which gives strength for bearing the brunt of modernity's future attacks—a silence whose power Helen learns only gradually.

Rereading the final paragraph of the novel from this point of view, *The Coffer Dams* offers no triumphant tale—celebrating neither modernity nor effective resistance—but a representation of the impasse between the oppressors and the oppressed in postcolonial conditions. The end of the rains symbolically conjoins two events that were originally opposed to one another; the threat to the Adivasis ends, but the dam project continues forward. Helen and Mackendrick are joyous about the former as they see that "the banks held firm and the water levels were falling" (256). But there is no question that this is only a small victory because the "others who looked," with different eyes and much more power in the world, "saw only the coffers." Through such eyes, that rendered human beings invisible, dams were like live creatures (with ribs) and represented only reality. The ongoing presence of the coffer dams might now be read as containing a threat as dire as Sahgal's looming smokestacks. The main difference is that while modernity in *A Time to Be Happy* completely encircles the space of the indigenous, *The Coffer Dams* reveals that modernity can be looked at from two different perspectives, a subaltern-centered one whose main interest is halting its destructive path, and a nation-statist and/or imperialist one in which development itself signifies progress.

3

Twilight Years

Women, Nation, and Interiority in
The Day in Shadow and *Clear Light of Day*

> "I might have known love would dawn on you in the chilly chamber of the House in the middle of a debate about oil."
>
> —Raj to Simrit, in Nayantara Sahgal, *The Day in Shadow* (1971)

> "[W]hy talk of local politics, party disputes, election malpractices, Nehru, his daughter, his grandson—such matters as will soon pass into oblivion? *These* aren't important when compared with India, eternal India."
> "Yes, it does help to live abroad if you feel that way," mused Bim.
>
> —Bakul and Bim, in Anita Desai, *Clear Light of Day* (1980)

On June 25, 1975, at a different midnight hour in postcolonial India, the populist leader Jayaprakash Narayan was awakened by the proverbial knock on the door. Perhaps JP, as he is often known, was not surprised to be summoned so rudely by the government despite being a septuagenarian veteran of the struggle against the British. After all, JP had been leading mobilizations against Prime Minister Indira Gandhi's policies and methods for several years now. That very evening, at a massive rally at the Ramlila Grounds in New Delhi, he had called for a week-long civil disobedience campaign against Indira Gandhi after her corrupt practices in the 1971 elections came to light. This was the last straw, apparently. The night before declaring a state of emergency, Gandhi ordered the arrest of hundreds of leaders, including JP, members of the opposition, and the rebellious "Young Turks" of her own party. Over the next nineteen months, Jawaharlal Nehru's daughter conducted a barefaced assault on democracy: abolishing freedom of the press and civil liberties, centralizing state

power, confronting protesters with police repression and mass imprison-
ment, bulldozing slums for "beautification" projects, and conducting a
forced sterilization campaign. New economic policies were designed, leading to the privatization of some sectors and the nationalization of others.
Although the Emergency was lifted in January 1977 and Gandhi lost the
February elections in a landslide, its aftereffects continue to haunt India.
The rise of Hindu communalism since the 1980s and the post–Cold War
neoliberal policies that have accelerated class inequality can both be traced
back to the Emergency and Indira Gandhi's return to power in 1980.[1] The
fact that no viable alternative existed to prevent Gandhi's second coming
seems to have wiped out the historic 1977 vote, once described as "democracy's finest hour" (Tarlo 22).

The Emergency was not simply an aberration but was an attempt by
Indian ruling elites to resolve the escalating political, economic, and social
crises that began in the mid-to-late 1960s.[2] Initially, in the early decades
after independence, India may have appeared to be on its way to fulfilling the aims of Nehru's "Tryst with Destiny" speech, shrugging off two
centuries of colonial discrimination and exploitation. The Indian Constitution had enshrined the political equality of all Indians under the law,
regardless of class, caste, religion, or gender. The first two Five-Year-Plans
were fairly successful, and Nehru's central role in forging the Non-Aligned
Movement, a gathering of nations seeking independence from Cold War
allegiances, raised India's profile globally.[3] However, as with decolonized
Asian and African nation-states everywhere, India's state-capitalist economy was coming under increasing pressure by the 1960s to pull down
its protectionist walls.[4] Wars with Pakistan and China, and the nationalism and xenophobia that accompany wars, punctuated the period (1962,
1965, 1971). A long economic downturn developed after the failures of
the third Five-Year Plan (1961–66), resulting in soaring prices and severe
cuts to public investment. To quell the waves of resistance in this period,
most famously the Naxalbari rebellion in 1969 and the Indian Railways
strike of 1974, the state struck back with deadly force. By removing the
"obstacle" of democracy, the Emergency allowed the government to be
more effective in carrying out its tasks of capital accumulation and social
control.[5]

The broad shift from *namak-halaal* to postnational cosmopolitanisms
in the postcolonial Indian English novel, I argue, developed in the context of the ideological crisis around the national question that was generated during this period. Only a few decades removed from the euphoria
of Independence Day, many were quick to contrast those two midnights

in 1947 and 1975. An excerpt from JP's prison diary, cited in Nayantara Sahgal's *Indira Gandhi's Emergence and Style* (1978), captures the mood:

> It is not for this that I, at least, had fought for freedom [. . .] The people have to travel many long miles to reach that freedom for which thousands of the Congress' youth made sacrifices. [. . .] Hunger, soaring prices and corruption stalk everywhere. [. . .] Unemployment goes on increasing. [. . .] Land-ceiling laws are passed but the number of landless people is increasing [. . .]. (121–24)[6]

The deconstruction of nations and nationalisms in novels such as Salman Rushdie's *Midnight's Children* (1980) was also a response to this very specific moment in Indian history. Indeed, one of *Midnight's Children*'s many accomplishments is that it offers a portrayal of the ideological and ontological crises of its own time, reading Nehru through the lens of his daughter. The idealism of Saleem Sinai, its *namak-halaal* protagonist, is steadily beaten out of him by postcolonial realities.

Nevertheless, for a great many Indians of the twilight years, a historical memory of the anticolonial struggle did not yet allow for the cynicism that was to come. The militant strikes, rural uprisings, and mobilizations of the late 1960s and 1970s—in reaction to class inequalities, lack of access to education, tuition hikes, gender oppression, deforestation, and corruption—revealed a popular desire to reclaim the emancipatory visions of the past, often by directly adapting old slogans and tactics.[7] As Sahgal suggests in *Indira Gandhi's Emergence and Style,* the frequency and militancy of these actions sent "a shiver down the official spine" because their very existence disproved the idea that Gandhi—who cast herself as a left-wing populist and the guardian of her father's legacy—was "pro-people" (127). It was through such opposition that Indira Gandhi was defeated, if temporarily, in 1977. Indeed, Sahgal's persistent and public opposition to her first cousin illustrates that many mainstream nationalists were radicalized and thrown into activity—thus joining those who had continued to fight for genuine national liberation after the historic elite-subaltern alliances of the anticolonial struggle had split up. Sahgal's novels and writing from the late 1960s to the present still aim to recover the nation, but with an increasingly skeptical edge—a far cry from the relatively uncritical portrayals of the nation in *A Time to Be Happy* (1958) and her early memoirs.

It is with regard to the ongoing ideological debates about the meaning of 1947 that I am inclined to call these years of the 1970s and early 1980s the "twilight years," on the cusp of the old and the new. The grand visions of revolutionary nationalism were severely discredited, but many still responded to the call to build that "noble mansion of free India where all her children may dwell" ("Tryst with Destiny" 4). The passage from JP above, for instance, obviously mourns the postcolonial present but from the perspective of hope, saying that "the people have to travel many long miles to reach that freedom." The phrase echoes Faiz Ahmad Faiz's metaphor of the ongoing journey to freedom in *"Subh-e Azadi"* ("Dawn of Freedom," Urdu, 1952), written from a different prison: "Come, we must / search for that promised Dawn" (4.6–7). Both of these texts, though quite critical of the present, retain a *namak-halaal* orientation; freedom can and will be achieved. Rushdie's attraction to yet ultimate dismissal of Saleem's nationalist hopefulness in *Midnight's Children* registers this *namak-halaal* desire but belongs to a new moment, anticipating and ushering in the postnational perspectives that became much more dominant through the 1980s and 1990s. In the discourse of *Midnight's Children,* as I discuss in the next chapter, JP and Faiz represent not commitment and steadfastness but the susceptibility of Indians to the "optimism disease."

My juxtaposition and comparison of Sahgal's *The Day in Shadow* (1971) and Anita Desai's *Clear Light of Day* (1980) aims to demonstrate the liminality of the twilight years and its impact on the Indian English novels in terms of the development of new perspectives, themes, and forms—foregrounding, in the process, the place of women's writing and gender analysis in *namak-halaal* texts and in the development of the Indian English novel as a whole. On the surface, Sahgal's and Desai's novels are different from one another in quite obvious ways. *The Day in Shadow,* often read by critics as a "political novel" (when it is considered at all), is concerned with the Hindu Code Bill, the Indian government's new policies on oil and weapons, and the passing of Nehruvian idealism. When Sardar Singh, the aged and dying Petroleum Minister, asks, "[H]ow did such a future emerge from such a past?" (125), he is giving voice to the ideological crises described above. But Desai's text seems to avoid any discussion of the political. Although Partition violence forms the backdrop of the protagonists' memories of their childhood, critics have argued that since the novel is "primarily interested in human relationships, not in history," it cannot be considered a "historical novel" (Crane 10). Rather, terms such as "psychological novel" and "the Virginia Woolf of India" come to the fore in assessments of Desai's novel. In terms of narrative strategies, admittedly, *The Day in Shadow* cannot compare with *Clear Light of Day*'s celebrated and subtle strategies of interiority that illuminate its characters' motivations, desires, and fears.

But when read in the context of the twilight years—including the rise of the women's movement and of women's writing itself as an identifiable genre—the novels exhibit important ideological and aesthetic commonalities. Both texts focus on the visible and the intimate aspects of women's oppression, challenging gendered divisions of the private and the public, the personal and the political, and encouraging the development of new strategies of characterization and voice. Simrit of *The Day in Shadow* and Bim of *Clear Light of Day* continually challenge male chauvinism, gender inequalities, and the role of the traditional family in perpetuating these. Furthermore, such devastating critiques of Indian/Hindu gender norms do not produce a postnational dismissal of the nation and its traditions but an attempt to refashion the nation into a gender-egalitarian space. A distinct *namak-halaal* framework is discernible: male characters who exhibit a crude sexism in their private and public lives are inevitably marked as cosmopolitan-elites who favor Western cultural spaces over Indian ones, defend militarism and authoritarianism over democracy, and/or romanticize the nation from an outsider's vantage point. In this way, the novels represent a moment between things ended and things begun, considering the nation with a skepticism that foreshadows the postnational perspectives that will soon dominate the genre but also displaying *namak-halaal* ethics of solidarity and communication seen in the early postcolonial novels. Although, in my reading, *The Day in Shadow* and *Clear Light of Day* are not ultimately successful in imagining gender-inclusive national spaces, such feminist-nationalist representations force us to rethink theoretical frameworks in which nations and nationalisms are regarded as being inherently opposed to women's liberation.

Feminist Resolutions of the National Question

Postcolonial women writers have often constructed the decolonized nation as a vehicle for future emancipation, even when it is also shown to be a site for oppression. For instance, Buchi Emecheta's *The Joys of Motherhood* (1979), Nadine Gordimer's *Burger's Daughter* (1979), Jessica Hagedorn's *Dogeaters* (1991), and Edwidge Danticat's *The Dew Breaker* (2004) are products of different contexts, ideologies, and aesthetic traditions, but each novel seeks to rewrite the nation despite its sharp criticisms of it. Although none of these texts can be described as "nationalist" in a limited sense and each remains interested in cultural and ideological exchanges across national borders, each also recognizes that national contexts are crucial in shaping the lives of its characters and future possibilities. Nevertheless, the opposition between "woman" and "nation" pervades Postcolonial Studies: a theoretical framework that often rests on an ahistorical notion of nationalism as being always already reactionary.

Consider, for instance, Partha Chatterjee's "The Nationalist Resolution of the Women's Question" (1990), an essay about colonial India whose paradigm about woman and nation is often cited in the contexts of Postcolonial Studies and South Asian Studies. Chatterjee describes how male nationalists' views of women's status were shaped by gendered concepts of *ghar* ("home") and *bahir* ("the world"):

> The world is the external, the domain of the material [and gendered male]; the home represents our inner spiritual self, our true identity [. . .] The home in essence must remain unaffected by the profane activities of the material world—and woman is its representation. And so we get an identification of social roles of gender to correspond with the separation of the social sphere into *ghar* and *bahir*. ("Nationalist" 238–39)

Anxious about their lack of power in the colonized world around them, Chatterjee asserts, male nationalists became interested in "home rule" in a domestic sense as well as a political one, tying women to the home and private sphere by making them representative of the nation's pure, "inner spiritual self" that must not become sullied by the world. Undoubtedly, Chatterjee's description is useful in understanding women's secondary status in many visions of "national liberation." It reminds us how the "imagined communities" of nations operate, claiming to provide resolutions for all inequalities within the nation but actually subordinating those concerns and silencing conflict. Chatterjee's paradigm also describes feminist voices that limit women to subject positions associated with the feminized, private sphere. Liberal feminist movements and writers in colonial India, for instance, often internalized and naturalized the discourse that Chatterjee describes as they staked their claims to the nation (P. Bose 117–18).

Chatterjee's formulation, however, tends to minimize both the resiliency of nationalisms and the variety of ways in which they have shaped themselves in relation to questions of gender—both historically and in literary imaginings. For instance, historians have critiqued Chatterjee for "an exclusive emphasis on the discursive contests between colonialism and nationalism that neglects the political economy of colonial rule" (Sreenivas 9), a methodology that fails to explain how nationalist discourses were produced in very specific colonial contexts. In *Hindu Wife, Hindu Nation*

(2001), for example, Tanika Sarkar particularizes Chatterjee's observations of the home/world discourse as one prevalent among nineteenth-century Bengali elites, and argues that it emerged in the contexts of their manifold struggles against the colonial state, upwardly mobile lower castes and classes, and radicalizing women (T. Sarkar 38). Rather than investigating how a particular nationalism became dominant over time in a given instance, Chatterjee generalizes his reading to "nationalism" itself. But other nationalisms have produced other ideas about women and the family. Mytheli Sreenivas's *Wives, Widows, and Concubines* (2008) describes, for instance, the ways in which the Tamil Self-Respect movement and its radical notions of the family and conjugality actually contested, for a time, the sort of mainstream Indian nationalism that Chatterjee describes (92–93).[8]

The intersection of the categories of "woman" and "nation," then, ought to be understood as a site of struggle and change, configured differently in different ideological and historical contexts. In literary analysis, positing the nation as being always already inimical to women's progress and liberation sets up a false dichotomy in which nation-oriented writing is regarded as necessarily uncritical of women's oppression while texts that challenge gender norms are inevitably anti- or postnational. In Indian women's writing of the 1970s, however, we see different permutations of woman and nation. It recognizes the failures of Indian nationalism, broadly speaking, to include women's liberation within its framework of emancipation, but then seeks to rewrite the nation in the interests of women. The results of this combination are often mixed, sometimes producing ideological and narrative tensions with the texts. Nevertheless, the theoretical and critical refusal to allow a text to be both feminist and nationalist or nation-centered ultimately limits our understanding of the range and complexity of women's writing.

The ideological contexts of the twilight years—increasing skepticism toward the nation but continuing hope in its future—can help explain why Indian women's writing of this period remains so tied to the nation. The 1970s, indeed, were central to the revival of the Indian women's movement, and women's writing flourished in its wake. Women participated in all of the revolts of the time, and often shaped their direction.[9] These efforts received an ideological boost from the publication of *Towards Equality* in 1974, a report by a government-appointed committee charged with studying the status of women in India. On the one hand, it claimed that twenty-five years of independence had brought no improvement for women; on the other, by praising nineteenth-century reformers and nationalisms for their progressive positions on women's equality, it placed its demands for change within the paradigms of anticolonial nationalism.[10] *Towards Equality* was momentous in its impact in terms of creating programs and policies for women, funding more research on women's lives and work, and opening up disciplines such as women's history and women's studies (Forbes 223). The end of the Emergency "was like the bursting of a dam" in terms of social movements (Vanaik 197; R. Kumar, *History* 106), and the women's movement won important victories against social and legal inequalities in a variety of areas including rape, inheritance, prostitution, and marriage practices.[11] Rather than rejecting a nation that had clearly left them behind, women's movements and the other struggles of the 1970s revived and redirected the old discourse of emancipation, continuing to see the nation(-state) as a site for future progress and to act upon the opportunities afforded by the framework of secular democracy.

This was the context in which postcolonial Indian women's literature, in all languages, came into its own.[12] In Telugu literature, for example, serialized periodical publications by women writers in the 1970s were the basis for successful novels (Subbarayudu and Vijayasree 323). Similarly, in Tamil literature, the organization Ilakkiya Chintanai began publishing yearly anthologies of short stories in 1970, making accessible the work of the increasing number of writers of that genre, especially women writers (Sri 295). By 1973, in a seminar titled "Indian Literature Since Independence" held by the Sahitya Akademi in Bombay, Prema Nandakumar could say, "The most significant development for Indo-Anglian fiction in the last twenty-five years has been the emergence of a group of women novelists" (56). Anita Desai, Atia Hosain, Ruth Prawer Jhabvala, Kamala Markandaya, Nayantara Sahgal, and Shakuntala Shrinagesh had each published one or more novels in English by 1973. Institutions that encourage and make Indian women's writing accessible today on a global scale developed out of this period, including the English-language journal *Manushi* (1979) and the publishing house Kali for Women (1984).

Thematically speaking, the personal was political in India, too. Women writers of the 1970s tended to write about women's lives in a self-confident, if not outright radical, tone. Just as the women's movement brought dowry death and rape out into the public sphere, writers such as Sahgal and Desai consistently took up themes such as the burden of (arranged) marriage, the massive responsibilities of the joint family, and the repression of sexual desire. Novels before this period had certainly discussed themes relating to women, but it was only with the work of the 1970s that women's oppression gained legitimacy as a topic that novelists could explore in its own right, and not as a passing problematic on the way to discussing "larger" issues such as modernization or political turmoil. To write about women also meant to question "seriously and systematically, and at times to reject outright, traditional interpretations of women's role and status in society" (Gupta 299). And so, the very figures writers used to depict the oppression of women were transformed, from the simple glorification of women's forbearance under a "halo of noble self-sacrifice" in earlier representations to those in which a "great diversity of characters and situations" was employed to reveal the complexity of the situation (299–300). Indeed, despite notable variations in ideological perspectives, women's writing in the charged context of the 1970s was "engaged in negotiation, debate, and protest invariably in areas that directly concern, or are closely related to, what it means to be a woman" (Tharu and Lalitha 115).

In Indian novels in English, the thematic shift toward women's oppression developed alongside new strategies of narrative and representation, allowing for the examination of the psychological and personal impact of women's oppression and the spectrum of women's responses to it, from acceptance to compromise to rebellion. Two tendencies seem to evolve in the woman-centered Indian English novels of the 1970s, seemingly contradictory but often contained within a single work. On the one hand, the interior turn corresponded to a radical desire to investigate and reclaim the two crucial spaces of repression (in terms of psychology) and oppression (in term of physical cloistering in the home), a product of the gendered division of the world into private/public spheres.[13] Like Shashi Deshpande's portrayal of Sarita in *The Dark Holds No Terrors* (1980), for example, such representations grapple with the relationship between psychological and deeply personal knots (Sarita's suicidal loneliness and distress over her marriage and career as a doctor) and illuminate the conditions that help shape them (Sarita's family's opposition to her intercaste marriage and profession). On the other hand, the interior turn often has a conservative tendency that cannot imagine a space beyond the traditional boundaries of gender and even dissuades readers from doing so. A good example of the latter is Rama Mehta's *Inside the Haveli* (1977), a text whose consistent criticism of a patriarchal Rajasthani family is inexplicably undermined in its resolution when its long-suffering protagonist, Geeta, becomes the new head of the household upon the death of her mother-in-law. Failures on the ideological and aesthetic levels are intertwined; with no indication of an ironic switch in focalization, the novel suddenly closes the implied audience's access to Geeta's thoughts and appears to suggest that the *haveli* had now been reformed. Emerging strategies of interiority, in other words, spanned the ideological spectrum in their conceptualizations of gender oppression and resistance.

These new ways of writing about women laid the groundwork for contemporary investigations of overlapping zones of power, a central trope in women's writing and postcolonial literature in general. Women's writing since 1970, Vinay Dharwadker argues, "focuses mainly on the unequal distribution of power across gender differences within middle-class Hindu, Muslim, and Sikh societies [. . .] [but] also deals with more complicated situations in which gender inequities combine with asymmetries between upper and lower classes, higher and lower castes, urban and rural environments, older and younger generations, and so on [. . .]" (239). In other words, women writers began not only to resist their exclusion from "the nation," but to refute the restrictive division of the world into gendered public and private spheres by viewing their own oppression in light of other social factors. Ketu Katrak's analysis of postcolonial women's writing in the 1980s and 1990s describes the process that came into being in the 1970s: "representations of the deeply personal, even intimate issues facing their protagonists in their novels, poems, short stories are historicized within their particular socio-political milieu" (244). Thus, the same impulse that drew thousands of women into activism in the 1970s, namely, disillusionment with a postcolonial ruling class that colluded with traditional structures of women's oppression (R. Kumar, *History* 97), also drove women writers' search for a literary space in which to write out their lives and those of their sisters (and brothers) in increasingly complex ways.

Katrak's observation, that women's writing historicizes "representations of the deeply personal, even intimate issues" in "their particular socio-political milieu," is central to my reading of Sahgal and Desai. First, it implicitly rejects the false divide of the "political novel" and the "psychological novel" that has saturated the critical readings of their work.[14] In doing so, it allows us to ask important questions about the novels and the gendered division of the private/public spheres. In what way does Desai historicize Bim's personal crisis? Conversely, what representations of the personal and the intimate drive Sahgal's plotline: the situation of a divorced woman amidst the decline of Nehruvian India? In each case, despite their differences, we find that the nation serves as the privileged site upon which public/private spheres are critiqued and renegotiated. When Katrak rightfully defends the *political* and *historical* value of literary explorations of the personal, then, she limits the scope of women's texts when she says that they "explore the personal dimensions of history *rather than* overt concerns with political leadership and nation-states" (234, my italics). The words "rather than" suggest a thematic division between female and male writers that threatens to reinscribe the gendered divisions of the personal/political. Agreeing with Katrak's assertion that "postcolonial women writers enable a reconceptualization of politics" when they focus on the personal, on the intimate, and on the body (234), I would like to add that they *also* do this when they choose to talk about governmental policy. The nation ought not to appear as the Other for critics who are, quite correctly, arguing for the political value of women's writing.

Narrating the Public/Private Spheres

In *The Day in Shadow* and *Clear Light of Day,* the reimagining of a gender-egalitarian nation occurs not only in terms of plot and mimesis but also through the ethical and political sensibilities produced by their narrative strategies. The implied audiences are confronted with third-person narrations that are strategically limited, as they are either closely associated with or directly filtered through a female protagonist who has an incomplete understanding of herself and her situation. The effect is to create, at once, both a distant and an intimate understanding of women's oppression in postcolonial India by revealing the processes through which characters come to political consciousness—a strategy we have already seen with regard to *The Coffer Dams.* Indeed, the limited dramatic action that does occur in the novels takes place within the protagonists' flashbacks and memories (Livett 52; Banerjee 130). By hitching the implied audiences' perspective onto protagonists whose knowledge expands through the narrative, the texts invite the readers to participate in the process—and to receive a political education themselves. Readers are persuaded to imagine, by the end of the novels, a harmonious, decompartmentalized world/nation/family that might regard women as equal to men. And this space of liberation, as it is imagined in the texts, is constructed as a freedom from both rootless cosmopolitanisms *and* orthodox traditions as each is associated with the corrupt and violent nation-state of the post-Nehruvian present.

The following sketch of the narrative strategies in the two novels offers some insight into how these processes of knowledge and self-consciousness work. Set in the late 1960s, after Nehru's death and at the early stages of Indira Gandhi's ascendancy, *The Day in Shadow* draws us into the life of Simrit, a journalist, in the immediate aftermath of her divorce from Som, a jet-setting businessman. The third-person omniscient narrative is focalized through Simrit via the repeated use of free indirect style—a device by which a narrator moves into the consciousness of a character temporarily and sporadically. This develops the implied audience's close identification with the character as well as the ability to critique that character from an "outside" space that exists within the structure of the narrative itself. On the one hand, the implied author gives readers direct access to Simrit's changing mental state as she rehearses the events and emotions leading up to and immediately following her divorce, gradually freeing herself from the guilt and anger caused by its harsh terms. On the other, by using free indirect style rather than character narration—which quite often means reducing to zero the space between the narrator and the protagonist and maximizing the readers' empathy with the latter—the implied author creates a distance between narrator and protagonist and invites our evaluation of Simrit's developing knowledge.[15] The novel concludes with Simrit's marriage to Raj, a close friend and upright, Nehruvian MP, who is crucial to the development of her political consciousness and is never criticized by the novel.

Similarly, *Clear Light of Day* also employs a third-person narrative and free indirect style, but the narrator's voice is so intertwined with the voice of Bim, the protagonist, that the free indirect style approximates the interior monologue produced in classic character narration.[16] The novel is divided into four chapters: the first and last take place over a few weeks in what we may presume to be the early 1970s, framing the two middle chapters in which Bim, her sister Tara, and/or the third-person narrator reflect upon the summer of 1947—when the sisters were young and the nation-states of India and Pakistan were first established. Initially we see that Bim, a caustic, unmarried history professor, has taken responsibility for her ancestral, Old Delhi house, living there long after her siblings had left to pursue their own futures, throughout India and the world. Bim is forced to confront the roots of her bitterness by the visit of Tara, her younger sister, who lives abroad with her husband, Bakul, a jet-setting, Westernized diplomat. The narrative voice here allows us to critique Tara and Bakul through Bim's perspective, but the very cynicism and bitterness of that perspective forces us to regard Bim, too, with critical distance. In particular, Bim is angry that her brother Raja, having inherited their old house after the death of his father-in-law, the previous landlord, wrote her a patronizing letter, "permitting her" to continue to live in their childhood house at the same rental rates. Bim must learn how to make peace with Raja, and the process begins at the end of the first chapter. Bim finally softens up, giving in to Tara's demand that they remember their youth in the Old Delhi house and come to terms with the traumas of the past. In the next two chapters, the narrative reveals to Bim and to its implied audience the origins of her oversensitivity and symbolically links the violence of the family to that of the original violence of Partition at the birth of the nation(s). In the frame narrative in the fourth and final chapter, Bim gradually heals her rifts with her family and its traditions, concluding that she needs to be less critical of them.

The two novels are remarkably similar on the level of plot and characterization, consisting of a central, female protagonist (Simrit, Bim) who must break out of the passivity and isolation imposed upon her by external forces, a supplementary character who helps her do so (Raj, Tara), and a resolution, driven by scattered, cathartic flashbacks, in which a synthesis through "communication" is finally achieved. More broadly, the novels present a spectrum of (elite) women's oppression as characters struggle against a socially demanded subservience to their husbands (Simrit, Tara), the crushing burden of household responsibilities (Bim), sexual repression (Simrit), the cruelty of divorce laws (Simrit), the experience of widowhood and arranged marriage (Desai's Mira Masi, Sahgal's Shaila), and the feelings of martyrdom (Bim) and guilt (Simrit, Tara) that emerge from an internalization of traditional gender roles. In each case, the desire to gain freedom from the confining, domestic sphere forms the dramatic and emotional crux of the novel. The action and causation that drive the narratives are mainly psychological and discursive, with reinterpreted memories, remembered fears, and conversation playing prime roles. However, the novels explore and resolve the private/public division through different narrative arcs. *The Day in Shadow* enacts a centripetal movement in which the narrative consistently forces Simrit to exteriorize her sorrow, to recognize that her private oppression is linked to larger structures in a society that is willingly blind to the realities of women's lives. Conversely, *Clear Light of Day* exhibits a centrifugal narrative, in which Bim must go deep within her family relations and familial past—which is also the nation's past—in order to recognize and recover from the hidden traumas of life as a woman in a traditional family. Throughout, a fierce *namak-halaal* ethics is in play, though it is variously articulated.

To Be "Fully a Person"
Locating Simrit's Voice

From the very opening of *The Day in Shadow* we are introduced to the novel's strategies of free indirect style and how it turns Simrit into both the subject and object of critique. Immediately after her divorce, Simrit attends a fancy party in New Delhi and finds that such social gatherings are replete with "reminders of the husband-centered world she had forsaken" (2). Focalized through Simrit, the narration shows how the simplest conversations can entrap women within an inexorably circular discourse of marriage and work:

> "What does your husband do?" one of [the society women] wanted to know.
>
> Wasn't it odd, when you were standing there yourself, fully a person, not being asked what you did? [. . .] Simrit herself had never accepted a world where men did things and women waited for them. Hadn't she? She could hear Raj demanding, never letting her get away with any neat hem-stitched notions about herself. Whatever her views on emancipation were, she had kept them well-buried.
>
> "I am divorced," she said.
>
> "Oh," said the woman.
>
> "Then you must be working," said her companion.
>
> They had fixed her with a [. . .] look [that] made her feel she had broken out in spots and scales.
>
> "I am a writer." [. . .]
>
> "I have a niece who writes now and then," one of them said. "She writes the cleverest little pieces. It gives her something to do till she marries."
>
> She stopped abruptly. (*The Day* 6–7)

In terms of content, we learn that Simrit is a divorced woman, working as a writer (a journalist), who repeatedly finds herself marginalized within a conversation in which women like her have no ontological status. But it is the narrative strategy, exclusively granting Simrit interiority and agency and blocking out the consciousness of other partygoers, that allows the text to do its work.

Simrit's emphasis that she is "fully a person" reveals her self-consciousness about her invisibility in a society that makes normative the gendered opposition of marriage/career. Her critical perspective draws out the way in which her very existence confounds the accepted logic of this opposition, that 1) women are either married or on their way to be married, 2) married women are merely appendages of their husbands who don't work or "do" anything, and 3) writing, marked as frivolous ("cleverest little pieces"), is not a career but only something a woman might do before she gets married. Simrit's interiority is not supplementary to the passage's critique of gender ideologies but foundational to it. While both Simrit and her questioners speak in short, chopped sentences, Simrit is the only one of these characters who is given a set of thoughts and emotions that not only explain her reactions but illuminate why she finds the conversation so unproductive.

Further, the focus on Simrit's thoughts suggests a map of the process by which she has developed a political consciousness from within the constraints of the very society that she inhabits. The key here is the rhetorical question—"Hadn't she?"—that interrupts what initially looks like a didactic passage (however welcome) in which a feminist, divorced career woman self-righteously criticizes a group of mean, married, social butterflies. Without surrendering an inch of ground to Simrit's interlocutors, the implied author deepens our understanding of women's oppression and resistance by conjuring up the figure of a "demanding" and challenging Raj within Simrit's head. "Raj" is thus introduced to us as a sign that points to the still-transitional state of Simrit's political consciousness. On the one hand, "Hadn't she?" construes Simrit as being dependent on Raj; problematically, we often see Simrit escaping to him throughout the novel for emotional and intellectual support when faced with sexism. On the other hand, "Raj" appears here as *Simrit's* construct and as a mark of her capability for self-critical reflection; it is Simrit who is reminding herself that developing an oppositional consciousness is an uneven process and that she cannot settle for the "neat, hem-stitched notions of herself" as the ever-rebellious woman. Indeed, by employing a metaphor associated with domestic work ("hem-stitched") to describe the process of identity formation, Simrit implicitly links the desired *deconstruction* of that identity with the rejection of "proper" femininity itself. This texturing of Simrit's interior at the very beginning of the novel makes her quite sympathetic to the audience and provides the charge for the overt critique of gendered public/private spheres that follows.

Simrit further commands our sympathies because she appears to be not only the protagonist but the guiding intelligence behind the narrative. Not only is she a character who is marginalized, who is aware of this process, and who is self-critical about her self-perceptions, but she is also a good storyteller. The narration leads us to attribute the clever arrangement of the passage, with its frequent interjections and the ironic placement of voices, to Simrit herself. The dry sense of irony that we see in Simrit's thoughts ("Hadn't she?") is reflected in the dramatic arrangement of the dialogue, in which the insularity of society's logic is reflected in the circularity of the conversation. Even the dull-witted partygoer is allowed to realize, momentarily, that she and her friends had been putting their feet in their mouths by telling a divorced writer that writing was a decent activity for a "girl" before marriage. Such metacritical moments increase the audience's pleasure and bind us closely to Simrit; for instance, the spurt of figurative language in the passage ("as if I had broken out in spots and scales") is immediately followed by the line "I am a writer." In this manner, like a first-person character narrator, Simrit accomplishes all of the narrator's tasks, described in narrative theory as reporting (telling us the bare facts), interpreting (giving us a standpoint from which to view them), and evaluating (suggesting what we ought to make of the story).[17]

And yet, even in this passage, it is apparent that *The Day in Shadow* is not a first-person character narration but one told from a third-person perspective that frequently employs free indirect style. A sliver of space between the narrator and the protagonist opens up with the question "Hadn't she?"—a momentary but jarring question that seems to come from outside of Simrit as the text invites us to critique not only the party-goers but Simrit herself. Although we quickly realize that Simrit is questioning herself, we see that, self-reflexive or not, Simrit is still a work in progress and we are asked to separate ourselves, however minutely, from her consciousness. The gap between Simrit and the narrator through the novel is often razor-thin, but even this slim presence is notable. It makes Simrit both the subject and the object of the narrator's gaze: the medium through which the narrator can observe and convey the reality of women's oppression and the character whose limited but growing self-consciousness offers insight into the development of oppositional consciousness. By making Simrit a dynamic, self-reflexive character and yet refusing to conflate her with the narrator, the implied author is able to chart her tumultuous shift from the discourse of victimization to that of empowerment—the *telos* of the text—without completely entangling the implied audience in every moment of that transition. In terms of literary-critical analysis, *The Day in Shadow* cannot be "simply" read as a classic social-realist text interested in linear models of character development over time: diachronic time (the story of how Simrit comes to consciousness) is combined with the synchronic (the Simrit who reflects on each moment of her life is herself in flux). Politically speaking, this method of narration 1) allows the exteriorizing of internal, private conflicts, challenging the public/private divide that makes women's oppression a dirty little secret; and 2) puts a spotlight on the processes by which consciousness about this oppression develops.

In the earlier portions of the novel, before Raj takes center stage, Simrit's growing consciousness about her own life as an unhappy wife becomes the basis for her understanding of national politics. These insights into the public sphere, in turn, allow her to rearticulate the way she understands her problems with Som. The construction of Simrit's voice—flexible, introspective, and always in the process of learning—allows her to move freely between the sexual politics of the bedroom, emotional stress, political corruption, and war profiteering. Simrit has already learned, for instance, that Som's inability to communicate directly with her lies at the root of their problems (Livett 54–55), and that this is a direct result of a world always compartmentalized into "his" and "hers." By chapter 7, the violence underpinning this world becomes more apparent; Simrit notices that Som would get quite angry "when something did not obediently fit into the compartment provided for it" (*The Day* 77, 79). It is this *private* violence that engenders Simrit's new comprehension about Som's business dealings, a "male" space that Simrit had never considered entering before. As she witnesses Som's celebration with Vetter, his German business partner, after securing their armaments contract with the Indian government, Simrit marks them as the "envied, successful, appalling creatures of her time, caught up in a sickness they did not even recognize" (86–87). The violence, she comes to see, extends across the private/public divide. Som and Vetter dismiss Simrit's articulate objections to living on blood money and patronize her for having political opinions in the first place, but Simrit, refusing to celebrate with them, stakes out her own political space. Simrit rewrites India's arms economy as a macabre one in which "[b]its of child [. . .] could be exchanged for a whole new drawing room, furniture, and upholstery, silk and velvet cushions for gracious and civilized living" (85–87).

This critique of national policy is explicitly articulated through reference to families and homes, allowing for a link between public and private on the level of language that reflects the thematic pairing of the two. Significantly, the association is developed not through metaphors but through politicized metonyms whose task is the unmasking of appearances. In Simrit's words, "bits of child" *are* weapons, and her "gracious and civilized living" hides the processes of exchange that underlie her family's wealth. Broadly, the emotive reference to children as a way of talking about weapons sales itself acts to break the divide between the private world of family and the public world of war and armaments; every casualty of war represents a violently fragmented child and family. Closer to home, Simrit's language reveals that the violence of compartmentalization in the family and domestic sphere is linked to violence perpetuated within the nation itself. It is only fitting that Simrit brings the language by which she described

private oppression into the public sphere, wishing for an entirely different, noncompartmentalized, nonviolent world "whose texture is kindly"
(85, 89). Simrit begins to think of Som's notions of women's economic
dependency and subordination to the husband as his *particular* view of the
world, not a natural state of being, and can represent her own vision of a
peaceful, united world as a competing view. The leaking of political questions about the military and economics into Simrit's personal life on the
level of plot forces her to rethink the viability of having separate spheres at
all.

In fact, the final split between Simrit and Som comes on the very night
of Som's and Vetter's celebration of the military contract, when Simrit
refuses to sleep with Som. Again, Simrit thinks through the discourse of
decompartmentalization as she ponders how even a sex life "with laws of
its own, kept apart from the rest of life, must wake up on a night such as
this with all the doubts and fears of the years knocking against it" (*The
Day* 90). The narrator traces how in the very act of particularizing Som's
world as a construct, Simrit engenders her own: "She was no longer able
to follow the goals Som had set for himself, and the inability seemed to be
spreading through her veins, affecting the very womb of her desires, dry-
ing up the fount within her" (90). Simrit thus portrays Som's world as a
parasitical one that uses the rhetoric of separate-but-equal spheres in order
to dominate Simrit's entire life. In both *The Day in Shadow* and Sahgal's
previous novel, *This Time of Morning* (1965), "the final break [between
husband and wife] comes because of the violation of the unstated rule of
obedience which the husbands think their wives must follow" (Paranjape,
"The Crisis" 294). Earlier, Simrit had characterized sex with Som as an
act of obedience and passivity, "centered [. . .] on anticipation of his next
move and his next" (*The Day* 49). Refusing sex, in this context, is nothing
short of an act of resistance on the level of the narrative, destabilizing the
entire structure of the domestic sphere. Indeed, the passage above characterizes Simrit's refusal as a whole-scale, bodily rejection of Som's world,
one that was "spreading through her veins." She disagrees, at once, with
what he wants in both the public and private spheres: his desires for the
nation, his means of bringing in wealth, and the demands he makes of her
body.

Even as the broad arc of Simrit's politicization clearly moves from
acceptance of rigid gender divisions to a rejection of them, the strategy of
free indirect style in *The Day in Shadow* draws out the uneven process of
this politicization. It takes a series of vicious blows for Simrit to truly comprehend the violent nature of the gendered private/public divide and to

develop a new perspective. Despite her criticisms of him, Simrit still wants Som as he was before, and it is Som who finally asks for a divorce. And even after the divorce, Simrit keeps faith in Som's basic humanity, refusing to believe Raj when he says that the "Consent Terms" are murderous, placing millions of shares in the name of her children, but making her pay the heavy tax on it for nine years while not receiving a rupee (39–40). Consciousness does not change all at once. It takes time for Simrit to learn that decompartmentalization means forging communication, not making compromises at all costs. Simrit finally achieves a synthesis of her tendency to compromise and Raj's advocacy of making "savage breaks with the past" by carefully "carry[ing] it along" as a memory that she firmly rejects (225).

One of Sahgal's comments on her fiction, appearing in her introduction to *Relationship: Extracts From a Correspondence* (1994), gives insight into her portrayals of the difficulties of coming to political consciousness.[18] The protagonists of *This Time of Morning* and *The Day in Shadow*, novels written during Sahgal's own divorce,

> limped their bewildered way to a new definition of virtue, one that meant leaving home. They had no idea there were human equations that did not extort obedience as the price of love and shelter, but they chose to take risks rather than settle for the shaky security only obedience would ensure. Like myself they had a tendency to grieve over broken bonds, and a longing for ordinary, uninterrupted living. Like myself, too, they were undramatic creatures on whom drama had insisted on descending, to beckon or goad them to decision and action. (ix)

This wonderful phrase—"longing for an ordinary, uninterrupted living"— allows us to bring together the novel's narrative strategy and its political bent: to focus on the internal processes of a woman's coming to feminist consciousness. Simrit is not an utter victim of circumstance, though the facts of her victimization do leave marks upon her consciousness. She is not a born radical though she develops a radical consciousness and becomes an agent, taking decisive action. The careful treatment of women's oppression here breaks the dichotomy of representing women as either victims or heroes. The desire for "ordinary, uninterrupted living" and the attempt to represent it reminds us of Njabulo Ndebele's call for a "rediscovery of the ordinary": acts of representation that emphasize the complex dialectics of everyday living, not just narratives of spectacle, when portraying oppression and resistance.

Raj and the Nation

But there are clear limits to the text's concept of fighting women's oppression. The character of Raj in *The Day in Shadow* is one in a series of liberal, male characters in Sahgal's early novels whose task is essentially to save her heroines (Paranjape, "The Crisis" 295). Raj's interventions are central to Simrit's struggle and to reconstructing the "backbone" that her life with Som had crushed (*The Day* 38). While Simrit's break from Som begins with her *own* refusal to have sex with a man whose wealth is made through armaments, it is Raj who is presented as the driving force behind Simrit's mental and physical emancipation, always possessing greater knowledge and foresight. Further, it is through Raj that *The Day in Shadow* most clearly and decisively weaves together its narratives of women's oppression and national crisis. Indeed, Raj's voice is hardly challenged by the third-person narrator; there is virtually no space within it to raise questions about his role either as Simrit's advisor or as a Nehruvian politician. A more careful investigation of Raj is, therefore, necessary to see how the novel begins to shift toward a more mainstream notion of gendered private/public spheres despite its explicit efforts to dismantle such compartments.

When Simrit first meets him, Raj is in the midst of a two-pronged parliamentary war against Sumer Singh, the young radical Petroleum Minister who wants India to sign an oil exploration contract with the Soviet Union, and businessmen such as Som who would destroy India in their desire to accumulate capital. Raj attempts to resuscitate the classic principles of Nehruvian nonalignment, a balance "between Marx and anti-Marx," to draw forth "a new breed of India-lovers" from the plethora of "America-lovers" and "Russia-lovers" (*The Day* 155, 158, 20). What is truly significant about the position taken by Raj, however, is that it represents a *nationalist* (really, nation-statist) critique of the postcolonial nation and, at times, the national liberation movement. While Raj and Ram Krishan, his Gandhian mentor, are firmly committed to the principles of 1947, they admit to being disappointed by the current state of the nation and cast Sumer Singh as the product of failed nationalist visions. Sumer Singh's critique of Gandhi marks him as an antagonist in the text—he wants to "bury Gandhi" and have "real revolution—not eyewash" (*The Day* 186, 192)—but the text acknowledges that Gandhian-Nehruvian voices offer no alternatives. Raj and Ram Krishnan wonder whether the gradual rise of authoritarianism (recall that the novel is published in 1971, four years before the Emergency) was the price India had to pay for a revolution that did not "involve enough people deeply enough or long enough" (230, 233). Indeed, they see the tumultuous present as a reaction to what they regard to be India's own historical and cultural weaknesses, including a legacy of subservience to foreign powers like Britain, the U.S.S.R., and the United States, on the one hand, and the ideological pull of Hinduism toward compromise, passivity, and acceptance, on the other.

This nationalist critique of the nation provides the backdrop for Raj's explicit pairing of the public, national crisis with Simrit's private one. Explaining the oil debate to Simrit, for instance, Raj comments that "independence has no meaning unless it's economic. You're realizing that now yourself" (*The Day* 10). Against Simrit's protest that the Consent Terms were a personal matter, he continues, "Signing on the dotted line is the hallmark of the defeated [. . .] whether they're trusting souls like you or governments without know-how" (10). Simrit, in other words, becomes both a metaphor for India and a case study of "the Indian woman," an example of what happens when emancipatory projects falter. Raj comments that economic victimization had produced both in Simrit and in India an "overwhelming passivity" in the face of brutality and a dependence on other people's solutions (40, 155). The "mute, acquiescent" nation, "letting things happen to it, from a country to the mind and body of a woman" (*The Day* 37), is constructed by the narrator as both a parallel, analogous subject to Simrit and the *cause* of Simrit's victimization. In an India caught between "its brave modernity and its gross old superstitions" (150), many laws defending women's rights had been passed, but an underlying social and structural misogyny still positioned women seeking equality against the state. For instance, as Simrit notes, even the right to divorce had become part and parcel of women's continuing oppression. The Hindu Code Bill (1954) had "jumped two thousand years of tradition to confer that particular twentieth-century blessing [of divorce]"—obtainable faster than the four years it took to get a Fiat and eight years to get a telephone (4–5). Simrit's account drips with irony: "here we were [. . .] the females among us, in the state of revolutionary emancipation, out on our ears on the street" (4–5).[19]

In response, Raj exhorts Simrit (and India) to reject the allegedly Hindu notion of restraint and the "endless, spongelike capacity to absorb," especially "at this particular juncture in our history where we have to act [. . .] [where] passion and deeds would serve us better" than simple compromise (13, 102). Indeed, the dichotomy that Raj draws between Indian society's alleged passivity and Western individualism and activity is often so ruthless that it often invokes the (gendered) discourses of Orientalism. Indian/

Hindu lethargy, Raj avers, rests on fatalism and an inability to generate new ideas, reflecting "a whole culture [of] people—especially women—forever taking things lying down" and a "race" that "has yet to produce a modern thesis of its own" (140, 18). The alternative is signaled through characterization: Raj's father had converted to Christianity because he saw Hinduism's respect for renunciation as a fetishization that "ma[de] a man draw back and do nothing" (171). Although Raj is usually sympathetic to Simrit and contextualizes her unwillingness to act as a *product* of society, he sometimes becomes impatient, patronizingly contrasting her fatalism with his (Christian) resilience. Raj's words invoke a broader discourse that has shaped male nationalists from the nineteenth century to the present—exhorting the feminized and demasculinized nation to rise and make its own destiny.[20]

In this context, when women's victimization becomes both the symbol for and the proof of national degeneration, Raj can rewrite Simrit's fight against Som as a matter of deep importance to the nation. Refusing to bend to the violence of the Consent Terms would be performing "non-violence in action" (*The Day* 181) and would strengthen the nation, Raj reflects, for "if this nation were ever to come to life, the educated and privileged like her must make the most [. . .] of what they had" (36). People like Simrit—whom the text associates with orderliness and permanence, and "unspoilt, untouched, non-human things" such as nature and books (34–37, 4)—would have to live in the country as she lived in her half-settled apartment, "in a bit of a mess, with things not in their places, and not nearly enough of them to go around [. . .] There are no magic formulas. We can't make coaches out of pumpkins except by our sweat" (14–15). Raj speaks beyond Simrit to the implied audience as a whole, especially English-speaking Indian elites who understand the Cinderella reference and have experienced the complications of balancing "West" and "East." Like the narrator in Sahgal's *A Time to Be Happy* (1958), Raj beckons this audience of the educated and the privileged to struggle on behalf of the nation. Cosmopolitanism and "hybridity" are not opposed to nationalism but depicted as essential for national regeneration: for Raj, the hard work of national wholeness also means being comfortable with the process over the product, with fuzziness and grayness over compartmentalization and rigidity.

It is Raj's engagement in the politics of the nation—in terms of both the debate over oil and the handling of the Consent Terms—that makes him attractive to Simrit and ultimately cements their relationship. Raj's "compelling passion so like [Simrit's] own for [India]" becomes their common bond (15). Again, while Simrit's own concern about the nation and its poor emerges repeatedly through the text, it is only after meeting Raj that she realizes that she "has never cried about such things before" (87). It is thus through Raj that Simrit finds a complete unity of her personal and political goals, the ones that she had articulated in the fight with Som over the arms deal. Like Simrit, he also believes in totalities and not fragments, that there exists "a world like that [of freedom] very near us, just around the corner if you look for the signs. You in your lifetime may reach out and touch it, if you have the courage [. . .]" (*The Day* 177). The sense of wholeness enters into their personal lives as well: in direct contrast to her experience with Som, Simrit characterizes lovemaking with Raj as a joining of two souls, a wholeness completely distinct from "segmented ordinary life" (206). The "great, objective inheritance" in the nationalist vision of the two ostensibly disinherited lovers is the nation, in all its natural and cultural richness (35–36). Ram Krishan himself—the dormant, Gandhian figure in this novel similar to the narrator of *A Time to Be Happy* and K. L. in *Rich Like Us*—"begins to emerge from his self-imposed confinement [after his wife's death] to take up the fight for India with new energy" and "begins paradoxically, to inherit the future" through Raj and Simrit, his adopted children (Livett 61).

Simrit's move from dependence to independence, from Som to Raj, is in effect a feminist rewriting of the national question, a framework in which national progress is impossible as long as Indian women are being treated as unequal members of society. But falling in line with the *namak-halaal* cosmopolitanisms of the pre-Emergency period, this rewriting entails not a rejection of the nation but an imagined resurgence toward what the implied author constructs as the original goals of national liberation. In this process, cosmopolitanism and hybridity are not dismissed in and of themselves; indeed, Raj's devastating and "Christian" critique of Indian/Hindu culture is foregrounded as providing a necessary "outside" viewpoint on the nation. However, as I have been emphasizing in this book, such cosmopolitan openness is not incompatible with nationalism but falls comfortably within the Nehruvian ideological framework that is explicit in Sahgal's work.

For instance, when speaking at the foundation-laying ceremony for a women's college in Allahabad in 1928, Nehru was appalled to find out that the college prospectus outlined the most backward ideas about women's role in the private sphere. He angrily retorted that such ideas of women's education meant not only that a woman was fit only for the "profession of marriage" but also that "[e]ven in this profession her lot is to be of secondary importance. She is always to be the devoted help-mate, the follower, and the obedient slave of her husband and others [. . .] The future of India cannot consist of dolls or playthings [referring to Ibsen's *Doll's House*]" (qtd. in Jayawardena 98). We see here the blend of cosmopolitanism, nationalism, and commitment to women's equality that is central to Nehruvian discourse, distinguishing it from Gandhian and other cultural-nationalist ones. First, it reveals not only Nehru's support for women's education but also 1) his willingness to challenge curricula that turn such schools for women into sites for the teaching of traditional gender roles, and 2) his insistence on linking Indian progress to the rejection of ideas that render women into "dolls or playthings." Second, while the passage remains firmly within a nationalist discourse and its concerns are clearly "the future of India," Nehru does not hesitate to enlist the services of a European play in making his point against Indian traditionalism and—given the context of his speech—putting forth such cosmopolitan knowledge as a model for an alternative pedagogy. Women's freedom from gender oppression and national freedom from colonial rule were thus intertwined and resisted the essentialist labels of "Western" and "Indian." As Nehru writes in *The Discovery of India*, this sentiment reflects how the "call of freedom" had a "double meaning" for women fighting the colonial regime; their energy and enthusiasm for the nation "had no doubt their springs in the vague and hardly conscious, but nevertheless intense, desire to rid themselves of domestic slavery" (qtd. in Jayawardena 98–99).[21]

"Staying Home"
Bim's Critique of NRIs

Clear Light of Day seems to belong to a different universe. Its plot, characterization, and theme make paramount the characters' internal lives and the repairing of broken familial bonds, apparently marginalizing the public sphere of national politics. While it is significant that the rupturing of Bim's family occurs in 1947, the year in which British India was split into the nation-states of India and Pakistan, the Partition in *Clear Light of Day* appears to function mainly as a historical backdrop to dramatize the characters' personal crises. For instance, when the text employs Bim's voice in a didactic mode toward the end of the book in order to find solutions to interpersonal problems, it does not address—as does *The Day in Shadow*—whether and how national tensions might be related to those of the individual within the family. Nevertheless, I maintain, the implied author's strategic choices in terms of characterization and plot force key political questions around gender and nation onto the table in explicit and implicit ways. On one level, *Clear Light of Day* details the negative experiences of daughters, wives, widows, and unmarried adult women, and only a severely limited and gendered notion of "the political" would exclude this novel from that category. On another level, although references to the world of governments and policies appear to be incidental and slight, there is enough textual evidence to suggest that the novel represents the nation as the historical and cultural ground upon which the family and its hierarchies are formed. The family and nation are united through characterization, voice, and symbolism, making it possible to read *Clear Light of Day*'s concerns about gender through the prism of the questions around cosmopolitanism and nationalism—especially as they were being articulated in the twilight years.

The key to an ideological and political analysis of the novel is recognizing that Bim, like Simrit above, is not only the object of the text's critique but also the main voice through which the novel articulates its transformative visions. The many critics who read *Clear Light of Day* as mainly a narrative about Bim's transformation from bitterness to calmness—with her sister Tara tutoring her along the way—usually minimize Bim's importance in transforming other characters and, thus, in voicing the central political frameworks of the text.[22] While Bim is clearly represented as an arrogant, angry woman who needs to learn how to cope with her past, she is also a clever observer of human behavior who, on the narrative level, gains an authoritative voice on questions of gender and the nation. Given this positioning, Bim's growing awareness of her own foibles instigates, for her and for the implied audience, an understanding of the deep links between the family and the nation. By understanding the larger contexts of women's isolation, the novel suggests, we might reimagine familial and national spaces that treat women with respect. And Bim is the only character who is sufficiently self-reflexive to develop such an understanding.

The first chapter of *Clear Light of Day* gives a sense of how difficult it is to disentangle the narrator's perspective from that of the characters. Initially, it seems as if Bim and Tara are given equal weight as the narrative shifts from one character to the other, voicing their responses to one another. It might appear that the dialogue establishes a two-way relationship between Bim and Tara that drives the plot forward—or even that Bim's obvious cruelty toward Tara makes her an antagonist. But the narrative voice, I contest, is focalized mainly through Bim. Undoubtedly, Tara is crucial to the narrative: it is her visit that unleashes Bim's self-criticism and critical memory, allowing her release from her ostracized existence. But it is Bim's independence, her outright rejection of women's oppression in the family, and her critique of a disengaged cosmopolitanism that drive the novel's mimetic and political tasks. While Bim certainly shifts her perspective by the end of the chapter, it is really Tara who begins to arrive at a new consciousness: she can recognize her subordination to Bakul, stop feeling guilty for leaving Bim burdened with responsibilities, and move toward self-confidence.[23]

The opening pages shuttle the narrative back and forth between the sisters through free indirect style and interior monologue, conveying how they watch one another intently and react to each other's words and subtle elements of gesture and body language. On the day after her arrival to the Old Delhi house from the United States, Tara runs out to the garden as happy as a child, oblivious to the viciousness of the morning sun "slicing down like a blade of steel" or to the deteriorating plant life all around her (*Clear Light* 1). Cynically observing Tara's nostalgic performance from a few feet behind her, Bim reaches out and pointedly crushes a rose in full bloom, an action that adds emphasis to her comment that the garden was degenerating annually (2). Tara is dismayed but carries on with a cheery, NRI exuberance about the garden that momentarily seduces even the earthly Bim, reminding her of a Lord Byron poem that she had read by Raja's bed "that summer" of 1947 (3).[24] But the Bim of chapter 1 must violently repress all nostalgic memories of family, and she angrily spreads the broken rose petals over the soil, trying "to bury it all again" (3). Panning out and zooming in, even as far as Bim's subconscious, the third-person narrator deftly provides us with a wide range of emotions and memories that are stirred up when the diasporic Indian comes "home."

At the core of the sisters' divergent attitudes is a conflict around location and its meaning in terms of the family and the nation: the question of who has gone and who has stayed, and how each remembers the past.[25] The narrative still moves between characters' viewpoints but Bim increasingly takes on the role of questioning Tara's utopian notions of home— revealing, at once, Bim's greater knowledge as well as her arrogance. At one point, for instance, the nostalgic Tara exclaims with a sigh:

"How everything goes on and on here, and never changes [. . .] I used to think about it all," and she waved her arm in a circular swoop to encompass the dripping tap at the end of the grass walk, the trees that quivered and shook with birds, the loping dog, the roses—"and it is all exactly the same, whenever we come home." (4)

The third-person narrator in this passage, emerging between the quotation marks, describes the garden through the lens of Tara's nostalgia, transforming the garden into an Edenic space. The "dripping tap" and the quivering and shaking of the bird-filled trees suggest a scene teeming with lushness and vibrancy. But the narrative voice is soon harnessed by Bim as she raises criticisms of Tara's exoticization of "home." Giving Tara "a quick sideways look," Bim begins to provoke her: "'Would you like to come back and find it changed?'" (4). When Tara, confused, replies in the negative, Bim laughs: "'But you wouldn't want to return to life as it used to be, would you? [. . .] All that dullness, boredom, waiting. [. . .] Of course not [. . .] [You wouldn't prefer it] to going on—to growing up—leaving—going away—into the world—something wider, freer—brighter'" (4).

Bim has caught Tara in a discursive trap, exposing the elite expatriate's longing for the nation as an inherently paradoxical one: situated abroad but repeatedly glorifying "home" in order to reaffirm national identity and affiliation. Poor Tara's NRI nationalism, which is inherently a cosmopolitanism, is caught between two wrong answers. She cannot answer yes to Bim's query about whether she desired to find things in India changed, as Tara's version of cosmopolitanism requires that "home," the family and the nation, remain frozen in time in order to be properly loved from afar. Bim's query and her "quick, sideways look" draw attention to the patronizing implications of Tara's "circular swoop," that haughty, effortless gesture of the neither-native-nor-tourist figure that feels entitled to encompass Bim's present as its past and to call Bim's space "home" whenever it likes. But by replying that she does *not* want to see things change, Tara would be implying a negation of her identity as well, for Tara left, we later learn, because she did *not* love "home" the way it was. Bim attributes an oppositional framework to Tara that she cannot afford to acknowledge, in which "staying home" signifies dullness and waiting, while "going away" leads to excitement and freedom. In response to Bim's prodding and sarcasm, Tara's subsequent explanation for why she comes home inadvertently reveals the NRI national identity as a slippery performance, requiring regular, ritualized pilgrimages to the nation.

We will recall, however, that the arc of the first chapter moves from Bim and Tara's early antagonisms to their united resolve to revisit the past. One of the key elements in this incremental drawing-together of the sisters is that the narrator, along with Bim, gradually disassociates Tara from Bakul. By the end of the chapter, this NRI nationalism (or vapid cosmopolitanism) is gendered male; Tara's earlier attitude upon coming to

New Delhi is depicted as the product of domestic oppression, for she is the trophy wife who must mimic her husband's cosmopolitan attitudes about the nation. Bim notes that when Tara, refusing to join Bakul in a New Delhi shopping excursion, says she prefers to stay home, Bakul berates her for degenerating in the Indian climate: he "only had to bring [her] home for one day" and she became "as weak-willed and helpless and defeatist as ever," wanting to "sit about with her brother and sister all day, doing nothing" (*Clear Light* 17, 11). Bakul tempts her to enter into a different world, marked as urban, Western, and active: "If only you would come with me, I would show you how to be happy. How to be active and busy—and then you would be happy. If you came" (18). As we have seen, the words "coming," "going," and "staying" here are overcharged with meaning and rigidly dichotomized.[26] Tara wants to stay home and to bite the fallen guava fruit in the luxurious indolence of Old Delhi/India while remaining with her family; Bakul wants her to be "happy," away from home and in the bustle of New Delhi/cosmopolitan social life. As Bakul's and Tara's positions disentangle, under Bim's watchful gaze, Westernization and urbanization are now linked with women's subservience as well.

The triangle between Bim, Tara, and Bakul—and the gendering of cosmopolitanism—develops most sharply during a visit to the Misras, their neighbors. When asked about how he represents India to a U.S. audience, Bakul says, in his most dignified manner: "'I refuse to talk about famine or droughts or caste wars or—or political disputes [. . .] with foreigners, in a foreign land [. . .] I choose to show them and inform them only of the best, the finest'" (*Clear Light* 35). Bakul misses Bim's sarcastic tone when she provocatively asks whether he is referring to the Taj Mahal, and the ensuing debate dramatizes two very different ways of imagining the nation:

"Yes [. . .] The Taj Mahal—the Bhagavad Gita—Indian philosophy—music—art—the great, immortal values of ancient India. But why talk of local politics, party disputes, election malpractices, Nehru, his daughter, his grandson—such matters as will soon pass into oblivion? *These* aren't important when compared with India, eternal India—"

"Yes, it does help to live abroad if you feel that way," mused Bim, [looking] carefully away from Tara, who watched. "If you lived here [. . .] I think you would be obliged to notice such things [as] bribery and corruption, red-tapism, famine, caste warfare, and all that [. . .] In all the comfort and luxury of the embassy, it must be much easier, *very* easy to concentrate on the Taj, on the Emperor Akbar. Over here I'm afraid you would be too busy queuing up for your rations [. . .]. (35–36)

Once again, it is Bim's perspective that is championed by the text; she interrupts repeatedly and sarcastically and forces Bakul to unleash all the aspects of his national imaginary. Bakul, in contrast, is a character with no interiority. Bakul simply responds arrogantly and on cue ("promptly," "firmly") while Bim "muses," reflects on the dialogue's impact on her thawing relationship with Tara, and asserts her dialogic equality with him despite his arrogance at being a (male) diplomat. Bim gives Bakul a rhetorical thrashing. She criticizes Bakul's vision of the nation for being ahistorical ("eternal India") and apolitical and gives this reading a materialist gloss by suggesting that the "comfort and luxury" of a diplomat's life abroad has much to do with his easy dismissal of real-world problems. Rejecting Bakul's contention that his depiction of the nation is a functionalist one to combat Orientalist notions of India abroad, Bim emphasizes the importance of thinking about the crisis of Nehruvian politics, corruption and bureaucracy, famine, and caste inequalities. The nation is of utmost concern to Bim, but it is the day-to-day realities of the nation, not its image in the expatriate mind as a pure, eternal essence.

Significantly, the text is quite interested in drawing out Tara's position here: she watches the debate and is being watched by Bim. The passage reminds us that Bim's relationship to Tara is not oppositional but dialectical; their familial bond and common experience of women's oppression allows for a dynamism and movement that is unavailable to Bakul. The deliberate noncommunication between Bim and Tara—Bim sees that Tara is watching but avoids her eyes—is itself a communication borne from years of a shared life, a knowledge that locking eyes would be like speaking, engendering interpretation and response. In fact, the context suggests that Bim looks away to limit potential misinterpretation of her statement. The specific moment at which Bim accounts for Tara's presence is the line "it does help to live abroad [. . .]"; by looking away, Bim says, as it were, that her challenging of Bakul does not extend to Tara. Bim's knowledge of Tara's presence suggests a performative aspect to her debate, as if she is modeling behavior for Tara by standing up to Bakul as his equal. And when Tara, still sensitive, does react angrily to the rhetorical ending of Bim's speech by reminding her that she was too wealthy to ever have to stand in line for rations, Bim's reaction is not to get angry but to laugh and defuse the situation (36).[27]

As this self-critical laughter toward the end of the chapter suggests, Bim is starting to soften toward Tara, seeking to engage her in dialogue, to move her away from Bakul's patronizing influence, and to open herself up to criticism as well. Her thoughts at this juncture turn away from Bakul to reflect on Tara's "not quite assimilated cosmopolitanism that sat on her oddly, as if a child had dressed up in her mother's high-heeled shoes— taller, certainly, but wobbling" (*Clear Light* 37). Problematically, neither the third-person narrator nor Bim is critical of Bim's own patronizing atti- tude toward Tara, just as *The Day in Shadow* is unmindful of the way that Raj talks down to Simrit in "liberating" her. Nevertheless, by viewing Tara's cosmopolitanism as a performance for her husband, a mark of her oppression as a woman, Bim stops thinking about her in essentialist terms and opens up the possibilities of change and transformation. Communi- cation, not sarcasm, begins to emerge as a value as we move toward the cathartic moments of chapters 2 and 3. Upon returning from the Misras, Bim and Tara are able to begin a conversation in which the power dynam- ics between them subside in favor of the joint project of recovering the past and the link between familiar and national problems. But although they enter into the past together, it is Bim's realization of Tara's subject position and her growing awareness about her own that opens up this space for remembering the family and the nation.

Families and Nations

The analeptic, middle chapters of the novel establish the links between familial conflicts and national ones; the family is both a product of national crises and a metaphor for the fragmented nation. And central to the disintegration of and violence within the family, as Bim comes to real- ize, is the oppression of generations of women. Bim's reflection on her own alienation from her family in the middle chapters emerges, in fact, from the deepening of a feminist or antisexist political consciousness that contextu- alizes individual experiences within larger histories. Following the novels' various chains of signification, we can read the family and the nation as analogous objects for renewal and transformation. First, the "deep stone well [in the back garden] that held green scum and black deeds" (*Clear Light* 117) symbolically links together the main female characters' stories and opens the door to a broader understanding of women's oppression. Further, as Huma Ibrahim has shown, the well is also a symbol through which the story of the deteriorating nation is woven into the fabric and even the psyche of the female characters' daily lives. At the same time, various male characters' visions for solving familial/national crises are marked as idealist and utopian, as emphasized in the narration of Raja's and Bakul's youthful responses to Partition violence. Only selflessness and sympathy stand out as potential avenues for healing and wholeness, as represented by Bim's work as a volunteer to aid Partition refugees. While no explicitly political statements appear here, the tracing of Bim's growing understanding about her own life becomes the basis of the novel's politics and ideology.

The well is at once a symbol and a site of women's oppression and of the repression of that oppression within the traditional family, an act that produces various shades of guilt, paranoia, and neuroses among the female characters of the novel. Indeed, this interpretation is strongly suggested to the reader by Bim herself, who emphasizes how the well was a site of calamity for the female characters in the Old Delhi house. The association begins with the death of the "bride-like cow" of the family, the producer of much milk and sustenance, that had wandered off and tumbled into the well and drowned, poisoning and blackening the water (*Clear Light* 99, 107, 117). The description of the cow as "bride-like" emphasizes its value, in Hindu iconography, as a symbol of femininity, fertility, and motherhood. The cow's unfortunate death and the family's inability to remove the rotting carcass make the well a source of fear for female characters; only Raja and the (male) gardener ever go even near the well, though the young Bim pretends to in an attempt to seem brave (99, 117). When Tara and Bim find themselves there once as children, they return screaming "at the horror behind the hedge, the well that waited for them at the bottom of the garden, bottomless and black and stinking" (118).

The narration explicitly recasts the well as the unconscious, the site of repression and its potential return as horror. The impact of the well is deepest on Mira-masi, Bim's aged and widowed aunt, whom the family makes responsible for the cow's death by accusing her of negligence. Mira-masi dreams nightly of the cow's drowning and imagines her own destruction/suicide (99). Haunted by the well, the mature Bim herself fears that she is headed there toward the end of the novel (157), an idea that is resuscitated when Tara's daughters, her nieces, call her "Bim-masi" (170). The language of drowning and death by water is invoked at other times throughout the novel as a way to describe coercion and suffocation, often prompting characters to refer to the well. For instance, Tara once describes Bim's hold on her as "that rough, strong, sure grasp" that was dragging her down; the "waters of her childhood [were] closing over her head again—black and scummy as the well in the back" (149). The well is the site of violence against the feminine as well as the repression of that violence, one that rebounds back on the female characters as a warning and a fear. As Bim reflects: "the horror of that death by drowning lived in the area behind the caravanda hedge like a mad relation, a family scandal or a hereditary illness waiting to re-emerge" (107–8). Indeed, each item of this triple simile alludes to the family, conjugal and joint, as the source of conflict and deterioration and binds it to the well. The family itself is turned into a prime site of repression and horror.

Ibrahim skillfully argues, further, that the well ought to be read as the site of the post-Partition national degeneration that is haunting the Old Delhi house and its women. As she puts it, *Clear Light of Day* is about "how a Hindu family negotiates the reality of everyday life before the Partition and how loyalties and emotions are disturbed and reconfigured after the Partition" (306). The cow had been brought into the home with much fanfare and was thought to be a provider of sustenance for the children (*Clear Light* 107); it can thus be read as an "icon for the carefully anticipated and finally decolonized nation" (Ibrahim 306). Watched carelessly, the cow drowns and symbolizes "the continuity of violence between families/nations and religions that began with Partition" (306). Ibrahim reads the cow's unrecovered carcass as a symbol of the unrecovered wholeness of the new nation, "festering in the historical consciousness of the severed family/nation," now viewed with a "participatory dread" that cannot be exorcised (307). The morbid attraction that Mira-masi and Bim have for the well, Ibrahim argues, is analogous to that of the crowds who were drawn, inexplicably, toward Partition violence; and, in that case, violence against the other was also violence to the family and to the self (307). *Clear Light of Day* reads the rupture of the nation not only as being analogous to the rupture of the family, but also as the very physical and imagined ground upon which familial oppression occurs. The violence of Partition is now located as the source of the violence against women in the family. This is how Ibrahim explains the intensity of the narrative voice when describing how Bim and Tara would shudder while watching the fires of the Partition rioting burn from the rooftop of the Old Delhi house: the event stands in for the nonfictional narratives of actual women who were victimized and terrorized by the communal violence, and the sisters' recognition of that horror (Ibrahim 308).

Reading the well in this manner allows us to link the text's desire for a reconstructed family to the desire for national wholeness that appears in bits and pieces throughout the novel—and against the "horror" of Partition violence that lies at the very foundation of the nation. One such scene is described from the vantage point of a bus traveling through Partition-era Delhi, as Bim remembers viewing the massed jungle of rag-and-tin huts that had grown beneath [the city walls], housing the millions of refugees who were struggling in across the new border [. . .] They swarmed and crawled with a kind of crippled, subterranean life that made Bim feel that the city would never recover from this horror, that it would be changed irremediably, that it was already changed, no longer the city that she was born in. She set her jaw and stared into its shadowy thickness. (86)

The violence of the nation is being mourned in both meanings of the word "of," both in terms of the violence caused by the nation ("the new border") and upon it ("changed irremediably"). Caught in the contradictions of this "of," however, are the refugees. Between Bim's shock and her nostalgia for the pre-Partition nation, the meaning of "this horror" becomes ambiguous, pointing to both the conditions that created refugees and the refugees themselves. Seeing the refugees as the "outsiders" makes even Bim—a volunteer in refugee camps—describe them as a swarming, crawling horde of insects or animals, inhabiting a space inferior to the real subject of this passage: the city/home/nation. The elitism of bourgeois-nationalism emerges here clearly. Nevertheless, Bim means to be compassionate. Her determination to bear the sight of the refugees, setting her jaw against the inevitable changes, feeds her youthful resolution that she would never leave her home even if that limited her opportunities for marriage (*Clear Light* 140). For Bim, therefore, the family and home are always overwritten by the nation, and vice versa—and it is through the desire for recovering that imagined nation of the past that the *contemporary* nation is implicitly critiqued for its violence.

Only Bim can hold together the family/nation, and the gendering of her position is clearly revealed through the opposition of her materialist, locally grounded view of the nation against idealized forms expounded by male family members such as Bakul and Raja. The two characters, in a sense, could not be more different, though both are associated with antiparochial notions of identity. Bakul, the urban cosmopolitan, celebrates the new nation (Partition and all), and its Hindu heritage. Raja falls in love, as a boy, with the figure of Hyder Ali, the family's landlord, on his horse; Urdu poetry and (elite) Muslim culture a bit later; and, inevitably, Hyder Ali's daughter, Benazir. Terrified by the Partition riots and what it would mean for Hyder Ali and his family, Raja expresses his solidarity with him through supporting the creation of Pakistan (*Clear Light* 57). He finally goes to live with Hyder Ali, marries Benazir, and starts a family. Despite their differences, both Bakul and Raja are depicted as being useless at the time of Partition and the disappearance of Hyder Ali's family, their idealized visions of the nation dissolving in the fact of actual conflict. Bakul, a young civil servant in the late colonial era, doubts the reports of Partition violence and declares his full faith in Nehru, Viceroy Mountbatten, Mohammed Ali Jinnah (Pakistan's first prime minister), and the "police protection" of the state (71). Raja, called "Lord Byron" by his classmates, announces to the world that he will protect Hyder Ali and Benazir (59). The younger Bim is critical of this bombast but not yet bitter. Positioned in opposition to these two men as the novel's only realist, Bim exposes the material structures that allow such male romanticizations of the nation: the domestic work of Tara and Bim, respectively (cf. 100–101). The investigation of the past, of the roots of the family's current fragmentation, leads to an explanation of Bim's bitterness as a product of the pressures on the family/nation, linked through symbol and character.

The narrative resolution of *Clear Light of Day*, however, presents some textual obstacles for the implied audience, drawn in by the novel's woman-centered representations of oppression in the family/nation.[28] For, quite inexplicably, Bim's critical lens is suddenly turned away from examining the social and familial structures that women inhabit and is directed, instead, at her individual psychology. Initially, as Bim seeks to "apply" the lessons learned from the flashback chapters, the old critical attitude persists; she is, at once, caustic as a person but also perceptive as an observer of social life. Bim recognizes the need to confront obstacles and to attempt communication, but is still quite aware of how she was wronged. Having learned the introspective, meditative quality of Bim's voice, and the novel as a whole, the audience does not expect any dramatic breakthrough. But Bim suddenly arrives at an epiphany that transforms the text—and disrupts Desai's characterization. When Bim lashes out at her autistic brother Baba one day, an image of the "smashed egg and the bird with a broken neck" that she had just seen outside flashes in her mind, a sight that had made her wonder what bird had "made its nest so crudely, so insecurely" (165, 163). And she sees herself in that bird:

> Her eyes opened up at this sight against her will, and she looked around the room almost in fear. [. . .] [S]he saw how she loved [Baba], loved Raja and Tara and all of them who had lived in this house with her. There could be no love more deep and full and wide than this one, she knew. No other love had started so far back in time and had had so much time

in which to grow and spread. They were all really parts of her, inseparable [. . .] so that the anger or disappointment she felt in them was only
the anger and disappointment she felt at herself. (165)

The (joint) family is apparently *not* a site of conflict, oppression, and
repression, a false ideal that masks the material realities of women's labor.
Rather, the family is always already whole, "inseparable," linked to the
Old Delhi house and bound together by a "deep and full and wide" love
and rooted in common location and history. The statement that "the anger
or disappointment she felt in them was only the anger and disappointment
she felt at herself" transforms the text from one that criticizes women's
internalization of gender norms to one that justifies it. Indeed, Bim's recognition of her culpability is marked as the pinnacle of her new understanding of the family. She notes that if there were "gashes and wounds in her
side that bled, then it was only because her love was imperfect and did
not encompass [her family] thoroughly enough [. . .]" (165). Earlier, the
text focused on bringing to light those "gashes and wounds," suggesting
that their cause lay in the violence of familial oppression, which was itself
intertwined with the violent convulsions of the postcolonial nation as a
symbol for it. Bim's recognition of these systems of violence was presented
as a mark of her growth. But these concluding passages offer the implied
audience a new framework for gauging Bim and her progress. The "gashes
and wounds" were only the product of her lack of understanding familial
wholeness, a mark of her imperfect love.

In the aftermath of Bim's new realization, a second event occurs, ending the novel, that seems extraneous but actually serves an important function: to expand Bim's resolution on the level of the family to that of the
nation and national culture. Bim and Baba go out to a concert at the Misras where their neighbor Mulk, previously described as a lazy and sexist boor who lives off the labor of his sisters, is going to sing after many
years of fruitless practice. The setting of the outdoor, evening concert is
described, without irony, as a "picture as perfectly composed as a Mughal
miniature of a garden scene by night, peopled with lovers, princes, and
musicians at play" (*Clear Light* 180). The scene evokes the poetry readings at Hyder Ali's house, previously marked as idealist and romantic,
that Raja had attended. A bit of the old Bim remains, thankfully: she is
attracted not to Mulk's "sweet and clear" voice but to his aged teacher's,
"sharp, even a little cracked, inclined to break [. . .] with the bitterness
of his experiences, the sadness, the passion, the frustration. [. . .]" (182).
However, Bim will now seek compromise at all costs. Listening to the

guru, Bim sees "how one ancient school of music contained both Mulk, still an immature disciple, and his aged, exhausted guru, with all the dis-illusionments and defeats of his long experience" (182). The association between this scene, Hyder Ali's poetry readings, and "Mughal miniatures" evokes a sense of national culture as diverse, syncretic, and transcendent, and Bim immediately links these properties to the family: "her own house and its particular history linked and contained her as well as her whole family, with all their separate histories and experiences" (182). So when Bim hears the guru singing "verses [. . .] that remind her of her brother's (and her own) childhood romantic aspirations, she no longer rejects the memory" but "brush[es] aside the grey hair at her face and [. . .] lean[s] excitedly towards Baba. 'Iqbal's,' she said. 'Raja's favorite'" (182). Work-ing as a balm to soothe Bim's frustrations with her family, her neighbors, and her nation, the concert leaves the critical, independent Bim, inexplica-bly, contented and whole.

The Return to Tradition

Both *The Day in Shadow* and *Clear Light of Day* are profoundly and uniquely political in terms of theme and perspective, and their develop-ment of female characters' interior lives actually enables their challenge to the gendered public/private spheres. Each novel, in different ways, holds the traditional family and the postcolonial nation-state responsible for vio-lence toward women. However, each also returns to fairly unreconstructed models of familial and national communities in order to reimagine them as potentially emancipatory spaces. In *The Day in Shadow*, right-thinking politicians and husbands such as Raj are imagined as reforming the nation and gender relations. In *Clear Light of Day*, women who resolve to be less stubborn and more forgiving, as Bim finally does, allow the family and nation to heal. The texts' failure to critique the traditional nation and fam-ily—ideological failures—produces unresolved contradictions and tensions on the aesthetic level. Ideological analysis becomes important not only for the discussion of politics and content, I suggest, but also for an analysis of the novels' aesthetics.

Let's first articulate what the novels themselves aim to do: they fore-ground a sympathetic approach to traditions even while being deeply com-mitted to a nation and society that would treat its women justly, and that would stand for syncretic and nonparochial notions of culture and society. While *The Day in Shadow* critiques Hindu traditionalism, for instance, it also cites quotations for Hindu scriptures such as the Upanishads in order to make its point about the need for syncretism. On the flip side, while *Clear Light of Day* critiques Bakul's cosmopolitan idealism and champions "staying home," Bim's position, as the final resuscitation of Raja, Iqbal, and Lord Byron emphasizes, certainly does not emerge from a narrow perspective about cultural purity. Taken together, the novels rewrite the critique and reform of tradition as a process that is derived from Indian/Hindu tradition itself—and not as a deviation from it. For all her criticisms of tradition, as Sahgal explains in "My New Novel: *The Day in Shadow*" (*The Hindustan Times,* 18 December 1971), she sees in Hinduism a "powerful potential to provide men and women with a buoyant base for action" (*Point of View* 18).[29]

It bears emphasizing that in taking up such a perspective toward Indian tradition, Sahgal and Desai place themselves within a long line of modern Indian nationalists, from Swami Vivekananda to M. K. Gandhi to Jawaharlal Nehru, who discussed the need for India to amalgamate "Western" values (activity, rationality) with "Eastern" ones (patience, spirituality). Such a discourse allowed, at once, an Enlightenment-style critique of traditional hierarchies and a valorization of precolonial practices. Take the following excerpt from Nehru's *The Discovery of India:*

> National progress can [. . .] lie neither in a repetition of the past, nor its denial. New patterns must inevitably be adopted but they must be integrated with the old. Sometimes the new, though very different, appears in terms of pre-existing patterns, and thus creates a feeling of continuous development from the past [. . .]. There was [in the Indian past] a reverence for the past and for traditional forms, but there was also a freedom and flexibility of the mind [. . .]. In no other way could that society have survived for thousands of years. Only a living and growing mind could overcome the rigidity of traditional forms, only those forms could give it continuity and stability. (*Discovery* 517)

The passage goes on to emphasize scientific learning over "religiosity" and the need to fight the effects of backward traditional forms: caste, class, and gender oppression (518–20). In effect, "national progress" is linked to an approach that 1) values synthesis and syncretism, in which the "new" is valued but "must be integrated with the old"; 2) recognizes that the "pre-existing patterns" are *already* implied in the "new"; and 3) asserts that ancient Indian society "survived for thousands of years" precisely because the "freedom and flexibility of mind" that Nehru is prescribing was practiced. "Freedom and flexibility," newness and syncretism, are thus central aspects of "thousands of years" of Indian society, which was not stagnant but "living and growing."

The passage critiques tradition, but, paradoxically, regards the critique and reworking of tradition as one of the central features of Indian tradition. On the one hand, Nehru challenges Orientalist oppositions between Western/dynamic and Eastern/stagnant. On the other, he raises questions about *how* tradition ought to be criticized. Who gets to decide what needs to be preserved, and what ought to be changed? Nehru resolves the question conservatively: making an ahistorical appeal to a unitary tradition as being sufficient in and of itself. Such modern-nationalist paradigms, despite their appeal to social reform and transformation, end up legitimating and reifying "Indian tradition." As such, the passage serves to limit critique—and stands in tension with the quotation from Nehru discussed earlier on the topic of women's education. The approach to Indian religious and cultural traditions in both *The Day in Shadow* and *Clear Light of Day* embodies a similar set of tensions. The ultimate championing of such ahistorical notions of tradition means that protagonists resolve crises by returning to mainstream traditions, whether political or cultural, with nothing more than a change in outlook. The key is the moral, upright individual, a good citizen who unselfishly acts for the betterment of all and interprets/reforms tradition in "appropriate" ways. The idealism and ultimate conservatism of these political ideologies produce certain textual ruptures that weaken the novels' own literary projects. Most importantly, the return to tradition in these novels requires the taming and marginalization of the female protagonists whose paths to political consciousness were initially marked by a greater understanding of the *structures* of gender oppression in the family and the nation.

In *The Day in Shadow* the explicit adherence to Nehruvian approaches to political and cultural tradition both enables a critique of authoritarianism and women's oppression and ultimately limits the novel's development of character and voice. Take, for instance, Ram Krishan's formula for personal and political action that synthesizes Raj's ("Christian") tendency to act decisively and Simrit's ("Hindu") unwillingness to make complete breaks with the past (*The Day* 235). Such a synthesis, in the novel's imaginary, allows the nation to recover its Gandhian and Nehruvian political traditions and break from the post-Nehruvian dependency on the either/or future of "Marx and anti-Marx," the Soviet Union and the West, Sumer Singh and Som—and therefore to build a nation that is more equitable. The union of Raj and Simrit symbolizes this idea of creating new political paradigms through the combination of existing ones, and suggests the kind of individuals who might make such changes. But the novel's ultimate focus on moral individuals undermines its own political analyses and forces the novel's characters into molds that do not necessarily fit them. Simrit articulates this morality as a way to get around the confusing world of Indian politics, arguing that the "real dividing line in Indian politics would soon be between the ruthless and the compassionate. All the other labels and variations would not count" (*The Day* 222). In a time when significant leftist and secular forces uncritically supported Indira Gandhi's authoritarianism, such a paradigm allowed *The Day in Shadow*'s prescient observation that so-called socialism was working hand-in-glove with domesticated international capital. But the imprecision and subjective nature of the categories "compassionate" and "ruthless" also ends up labeling as "compassionate" forces that are quite ruthless in terms of their oppression of women and ordinary Indians, and vice versa.

For instance, the reader is asked to sympathize with the plight of Sumer Singh's aging and wealthy father, who fears that the new, "robber government" (of which his son is a member) will tax too heavily whatever inheritance he leaves for Sumer. Sumer's father asserts that his problem is not that the government is "socialist": "It has been [socialist] for twenty-five years. It is somewhat different today" (132). A moral yardstick is being used for the purposes of political theory: there is apparently a socialism of the present that is associated with hypocrites such as Sumer who find ways to keep their own inheritance even as they rob others, and a socialism of the Nehruvian past that defended property rights—one that a rich old man could get used to. But the moral yardstick is not applied consistently, for while we are asked to sympathize with Sumer's father's desire to transmit his personal wealth to his son, Som's passing along a huge financial inheritance to Brij, his eldest son, and thus cutting out the divorced Simrit, is marked as immoral. The moral-political critique of the inheritance, that "no one should have *that* kind of money with no effort when so many still lived tortured lives" (*The Day* 56, 147), stands in conflict with the representation of Sumer's father, in which the quantity of his wealth has no bearing on whether he gets to keep it in the family.

Perhaps the best evidence of the unreliability of the moral litmus test is the fact that even Som is partially resuscitated as an ally for Indian progress, as he turns out to represent the kind of "radical, self-sacrificing individualism" that the novel's political ideology demands (*The Day* 235). Such individualism becomes so valued in the text that Raj and Som, in fact, are finally made to appear quite similar: "self-made men" with all familial property and inheritance lost during Partition (104, 24), men who "could be formidable instruments of progress" (226). Indeed, unlike the "Russia-lover" Sumer Singh, sparks of Indianness emanate from behind Som's cosmopolitan façade. It manifests itself in unexpected moments, especially through his Panjabi heritage, but his regional and national identities are depicted as being smothered amidst the frills of cosmopolitanism: German phrases "on the tip of his tongue," French ties, Italian shoes, and a son going abroad to school (91, 216). As the novel proceeds, Som is increasingly described in a tone that almost pities him for the absence of the nation in his life. For instance, the inquisitive Brij watches Som eat Indian bazaar food just before a trip to Europe:

> Now he was eating heavily [. . .] almost like a man in prayer, chewing every mouthful with deliberation, savoring every morsel, as if the whole world were shut out. It was so strange, Pa sitting away in his own room, away from the others [European friends], about to leave for Europe, so terrifically dressed . . . but eating bazaar food like that, the only food he ate like that, as if it filled some enormous chasm in him with much more than food. (216)

Brij's suspicion that the "chasm" represents the absence of his mother in his father's life is only partially right; in the novel's system of signification, missing Simrit is also missing India. A new compartment in Som's fragmented life is opened up, a private, Indian space that is "away from the [European] others" in which bazaar food is consumed prayerfully, as an act of national longing. Indeed, if we follow the clues of Simrit's own thoughts about Som, his "chasm" may be linked to the loss of his inheritance at Partition, a Panjabi life that represented his "real hunger," far from the "monogrammed china and linen" of his cosmopolitan present (*The Day* 26). While this passage is incredibly valuable for its perceptions about the national longings of even allegedly antinational cosmopolitans, its eagerness to put aside criticisms of capitalism and sexism in the interests of a rehabilitating nationalism is suggestive of an ideological framework that creates instability on the level of plot, character, and voice, and is not consistent with its emancipatory claims.

If the return to tradition in *The Day in Shadow* is somewhat expected, being the result of a gradual progression, in *Clear Light of Day* it is an inversion that is quite shocking. On the level of character development and resolution, readers of all political persuasions might draw comfort from Bim's ability to confront her repressions and anxieties, to go into her new term as history professor at Indraprastha College and rearrange her decaying, "stifling, dust-choked room," throwing away her old papers, trying to "jettison everything, lighten the bark, and go free" (*Clear Light* 168–69). But as Bim "goes free" she also loses her voice. The knots and complications in Bim's thoughts disappear even as the gap between Bim and the third-person narrator virtually vanishes: throughout the fourth chapter, Bim's role is to articulate surprisingly simple platitudes, however touching, about the love that families must have for one another. As with Simrit in the later chapters of *The Day in Shadow,* an apparent consequence of liberation is the utter loss of a textured interiority, the achievement of which remains the strongest and most unique feature of the novel. The sophisticated implied audience that was imagined by the text in its earlier chapters—one that learned to accept Bim's cynicism and her critique of traditionalism—is now forced to accept Bim's absorption into a static tradition. But what are we to make of the fact that at least some of the basis of Bim's initial alienation was her relatives' own narrowness and conservatism with regard to women's roles in the family? What do we make of the fact that the implied author—who initially revealed Bim's shrewdness and her arrogance simultaneously by emphasizing the gap between her voice and the narrator's—now dissolves the gap and offers a univocal story of Bim's transformation?

We are left with a surprising reinscription onto Bim of the figure of the self-sacrificing woman, a figure that Gupta relegates to the period before the 1960s (299)—and this at the conclusion of a novel that explicitly criticizes the violence that such "ideals" cause in women's lives. Bim, Miramasi, Tara, and the Misra sisters are shaped and crushed by the burdens of being the good widow, the good wife, the good mother, the good daughter, and the good sister. But Bim's "epiphany" valorizes the woman's subservience to the family and the idea that she ought to blame herself for being dissatisfied by its individual members. The quotation from Iqbal that ends the book emphasizes and glorifies subservience on an ontological level: "In Your world I am subjected and constrained, but over my world You have dominion" (*Clear Light* 183). Addressed to God and/or a lover, the line glorifies self-sacrifice and voluntary submission; the speaker is "subjected and constrained" in the listener's world, and the latter has complete "dominion" in the speaker's world.

This valorization of willing subservience attenuates another possibility for resolving Bim's frustrations that had been raised earlier: the rejection of traditional notions of women's self-sacrifice but *not* the idea of freely performed acts of service and solidarity. As Bim reviews her life and begins to heal, she remembers what the frustrated Dr. Biswas, a jilted suitor, had said to her: "'Now I understand why you do not wish to marry. You have dedicated your life to others—to your sick brother and your aged aunt and your little brother who will be dependent on you all his life. You have sacrificed your own life for them'" (*Clear Light* 97). What Bim dislikes in this characterization of her is not the idea of helping others, but the prescriptive element in them: the words were "so leadenly spoken as if engraved on steel for posterity" (97). Her service to her family implicitly becomes, in this refutation of Dr. Biswas, a voluntary act. But by representing Bim as "flawed" for being angry at Raja's condescension and NRI arrogance, the novel undermines its own critique of women's oppression. Indeed, the reduction of Bim toward the end of the book into an embittered old spinster who has missed out on her dreams is more in line with Tara's own fixation on the idea of Bim's being unmarried (151–52) than with Bim's fierce independence. Before her conversations with Tara, Bim seems to be quite happy with her own "family" of history students who have come to her home for their lessons, exhibiting a persona of informality of which Bakul, with his fixed notions of how women should behave in public, does not approve (20). She appears to be far from desirous of being in either Tara's or Raja's situation. Are we to reread the entire novel, understanding Bim's spirit of independence as a mark of her flawed nature?

In light of these novels' final return to political and cultural traditions, it may be tempting to read them as two more examples of the how the nation and its traditions are inimical to women's emancipation, revealing the taming influence of national thinking on feminist and antisexist critique. The texts' desires for wholeness through regenerated models of the nation, whether in the arms of a male Nehruvian nationalist such as Raj or in reconstructed models of the family/nation, place their female protagonists firmly back into gendered private spheres. However, I read their final turns toward tradition as contradicting and displacing earlier insights. The initial critiques of women's oppression are themselves linked to critiques of the postcolonial nation, specifically militarism, foreign policy, divorce laws, corruption and rations, Partition violence, and the refugee crisis. Furthermore, these critiques of the present emerge not from postnational positions but from *namak-halaal* and nationalist ones: the postcolonial nation had betrayed the ideals of the past, whether these were embedded in Gandhi and Nehru (Sahgal) or Akbar and cultural traditions (Desai). The fact that these novels do not produce alternative, gender-egalitarian models of nations and families ought not to minimize their efforts to seek such spaces. At the very least, we need to record the presence of feminist-nationalisms in postcolonial women's writing and explain, with references to historical and ideological contexts, why it is that old models of the nation and of gendered private/public spheres assert themselves even when such texts clearly desire something new.

The authors themselves, disinterested in whether they are regarded as radical critics of nationalism or not, provide more direct responses to such questions. In interviews and articles, both Sahgal and Desai have defended their portrayals of women's characters by suggesting that compromise, and not radical antagonism, is the basis for women's emancipation. As educated, urban, professional women, they represent themselves as being personally outraged by social and political oppression but, at the same time, as individuals who choose compromise (often marked as "nonviolent") over radicalism (often marked as "violent"). The authors also point out that there is continuity between their own perspectives and their fiction, as their (urban, middle-class) characters constantly choose reconciliation and dialogue over self-annihilation. However, as I have tried to suggest, historical and ideological developments in the early decades of Indian postcoloniality push these authors to express ideas that are far more radical than they may seem, even to the writers themselves. Or perhaps Sahgal does recognize this, as she writes in a 1991 letter: "I am a conservative (i.e., careful about stepping out into the new) who has been constantly driven to be a revolutionary by the force of circumstances and the nature of events around me" (Paranjape, "Crisis of Contemporary India" 298). This striking self-definition is consistent with my discussion of how *The Day in Shadow* and *Clear Light of Day* do emerge into the new, investigating gender and sexuality through giving greater depth to female characters. Amidst the ideological turmoil and confusion of the 1970s, however, a time when Communists (among others) supported authoritarianism and Hindu fundamentalists (among others) opposed it, that newness was delimited by historical and ideological contradictions that literature could not necessarily overcome.[30]

4

After Midnight

Class and Nation in *Midnight's Children* and *Rich Like Us*

> "I was already well-schooled in looking away, the jungle-craft of gentility."
> —Narrator, in Amitav Ghosh, *The Shadow Lines* (1988)

Salman Rushdie's *Midnight's Children* (1980) and Nayantara Sahgal's *Rich Like Us* (1985), published soon after Indira Gandhi's Emergency (1975–77), offer memorable and critical representations of that watershed event. Both novels portray the suppression of parliamentary democracy and civil rights under the Emergency as an acute crisis in Indian history. Both also depict the oppressive conditions for political dissidents and the poor in Indira Gandhi's regime, invoking its repression and corruption, its bulldozing of slums, and its forced sterilizations. By making the Emergency central to the plot and structure of their stories about postcolonial India and its people, the novels instigate queries that push beyond fiction, operating on the levels of historiography and political consciousness.[1] Did Indira's India of the 1970s represent a qualitative break from Nehru's India, or just a new wrinkle amidst a fundamental continuity? Could India go back to the Nehruvian and Gandhian visions of a subaltern-centered nation that would seek "to wipe every tear from every eye" (Nehru, "Tryst With Destiny" 4)? Or did that idea, too, represent just another fiction? *Midnight's Children* and *Rich Like Us* present characters and voices that demand answers to such questions—and construct implied audiences that must consider them seriously in the realms of both fiction and reality.

But the texts' orientations toward and resolutions to these questions differ dramatically as their critiques of the Emergency emerge from very different perspectives on the nation and its history. Saleem Sinai,

Midnight's Children's nationalist, first-person narrator, comes to see the Emergency as the culmination of a long crisis that began with the "optimism disease" of anticolonial nationalism itself. For this postnational novel, the *namak-halaal* narratives that appear in the plot—representing the characters' various efforts to be "true to their salt," to be committed to the nation and its people—are portrayed as dead ends. Saleem's search for an egalitarian nation, across the divisions of class, religion, and culture, is depicted as utopian, and his prediction that he and India will soon implode serves to warn the implied audience about the dangers of nation-oriented thinking. In *Rich Like Us,* on the other hand, it is precisely *namak-halaal* characters such as Sonali who are important: extremely critical of the actually existing nation-state, but firmly ensconced in a nationalist framework. The year 1975 is portrayed as a diversion from 1947 and the Gandhian-Nehruvian visions of a free India, not as their logical conclusion. By tracing Sonali's politicization, calling for a Gandhian struggle against the Emergency, and drawing attention to the daily emergencies of suffering subalterns, the novel asks its implied and real audiences to bring the derailed nation back on track.

In the first chapter, I argued that the postnational cosmopolitanism of *Midnight's Children* marked the beginning of a shift in the Indian English novel after the Emergency, one that has shaped current critical understanding of postcolonial cosmopolitanism itself as being inherently postnational. In this light, the *namak-halaal* and specifically nationalist cosmopolitanism of a text such as *Rich Like Us* represents an anomaly: a post-Emergency novel that continues to see the nation as a legitimate space for postcolonial renewal. My comparison of the two novels here serves to draw out the differences between *namak-halaal* and postnational cosmopolitanisms more precisely. However, as in previous chapters, I am also interested in drawing out the nuances that lie beneath the surface distinctions. Each of these texts emerges from a similar frustration and disappointment about the nation and a concern with subalternity, and this chapter explores their similarities despite their different orientations and discourses. On one level, I discuss how the nation also continues to haunt *Midnight's Children,* becoming constitutive of its postnationalism. The ways in which Saleem is debunked place him under erasure as S̶a̶l̶e̶e̶m̶: a palimpsest whose desire for the nation, though overtly suppressed, emerges so strongly that *Midnight's Children* can be read as trafficking in the *modernist* discourses of what Timothy Brennan has called a "national longing."[2] Further, I show how the postnational and *namak-halaal* orientations, despite their differences, often converge in terms of their politics of class. Despite their common interest in the impact of the Emergency on subalterns and marginal subjects, each text operates on the terrain of elite-centered representation and historiography that invokes subaltern suffering through characterization and voice, only to deflect and marginalize it once more. This examination of the intersection of class and nation in *namak-halaal* and postnational texts forces us to consider that 1) post-Emergency and postnational novels such as *Midnight's Children* that critique elite manipulation of histories and peoples are not necessarily progressive and oppositional, and 2) *namak-halaal* cosmopolitanisms such as *Rich Like Us* might seek to highlight the deficiencies of the nation in the interests of the oppressed but often remain elite-centered as well.

A clarification of my usage of the category of "subalternity" is in order in light of its prevalence in the very postnational, postmodernist theoretical practices that I have diverged from in this book. Given the widespread familiarity of the term in Postcolonial Studies, I use "subaltern" as a general, descriptive category that refers to the oppressed, marginalized, and exploited even while acknowledging the multiple and overlapping categories of oppression. I am not, however, employing the category in the strict sense that Gayatri Spivak does in "Can the Subaltern Speak?" and "Subaltern Studies: Deconstructing Historiography," that is, as a discursive space of silence that lies outside the realm of representation. If anything, my usage is close to that of Ranajit Guha and the Subaltern Studies school of Indian historiography before its postmodernist turn in the late 1980s, when it deliberately contested elitist historiography by excavating narratives of subaltern resistance, survival, and rebellion. In these texts, representing the voices of the oppressed is possible but requires careful investigations of the complex processes of power across overlapping and uneven social and economic arenas. While even the early *Subaltern Studies* scholars were making a self-conscious break from Marxist theories of class, as I have argued elsewhere, I remain attracted to their interest in the possibilities of writing "histories from below."[3]

I am further interested in the link that the early Subalternists suggest between a subaltern-centered methodology and the study of anticolonial nationalism, as they provide a direct contrast to prevalent theories that cast socioeconomic inequalities and the "ignoring of the subaltern" (Spivak) as the "categorical feature of all nationalist decolonization" (Chrisman 195). While the effort to draw out spaces of subaltern struggle and mobilization leads to critiques of both imperialist and bourgeois-nationalist strategies of representation, anticolonial nationalism is not dismissed in its entirety. Indeed, Guha and others are at pains to emphasize the active and independent participation of subaltern groups in anticolonial and nationalist agitation. The problem, according to Guha, is a *political* one: that the Indian working class and peasantry failed to gain ideological and practical hegemony ("On Some Aspects" 7–8).[4] Failure was not a foregone conclusion, in other words, because nationalist agitation both allowed for and depended on mass involvement in the struggle; indeed, Guha writes elsewhere, to reduce nationalism to its elite component is to minimize the role of nonelites in the struggle.[5] This understanding of the decolonized nation as a product of subaltern activity informs my assessment of Rushdie and Sahgal here. Postnational positions on the Left extend their class critique of bourgeois nationalism to all forms of nationalism. But the historiographical rejection of nationalism as being inherently elitist "turns out to have as its unwitting consequence the duplication of the established trajectory of liberal historiography, which also casts nationalism as an elite, homogenizing imposition upon more or less disunited [. . .] communities" (Lazarus, *Nationalism* 117). Like bourgeois-nationalist historiography, such an orientation depends on models of popular consciousness that construe the masses of people involved in national(ist) struggle as either nonagents in their own history or as autonomous subjects, involved in spheres of struggle that are, by definition, construed as being discrete from elite spheres.[6] Erasing the history of subaltern participation in anticolonial struggle, the emancipatory potential of decolonization, and the many reforms engendered by the process, postnational perspectives tend to reinscribe the elitism that they correctly ascribe to bourgeois nationalism.

My characterization of *Midnight's Children* and *Rich Like Us* as elite-centered, then, is based on specific readings of the ideological positions and narrative strategies of the two texts—not a general rejection of the possibility of subaltern-centered representation itself. Given the many failures of decolonized nations, often through the actions of the very figures and parties that led the anticolonial struggles, and given the ways in which nationalist representations continue to appropriate subaltern voices in media and cultural representations, I value Spivak's warnings about elite representations masquerading as populist ones. However, following Guha's approach to historiography, I submit that one can trace and differentiate between various instances of elite representations of subalterns, marking representation as a site of struggle and conflict. The usefulness of this approach, in terms of literary criticism, is clarified in my discussion of Arundhati Roy's *The God of Small Things* in the next chapter as both a *namak-halaal* and subaltern-centered text. Roy, I argue, develops a narrative structure that contends with the problem of elite mediation even while outlining a method for recovering important truths about subaltern oppression through history. This is not because representation becomes miraculously unmediated in such instances, but because it is possible for novelists to create narratives in which subaltern characters are explicitly or implicitly shown to be rounded and not flat—that is, to be thoughtful, to be driven by desires and interests, to be conflicted and human, and not to be mere spectacles for either Resistance or Oppression. "Subalternity," in this book, describes a state of oppression that can be grappled with and challenged in history and culture, not a name for that-which-we-cannot-know. The political overlap between the novels in this chapter, therefore, is that they marginalize subaltern voices even as they remain quite aware of what Amitav Ghosh calls, in the epigraph from *The Shadow Lines* (1988) above, the "jungle-craft of gentility," the art of "looking away" from scenes of poverty and devastation that is constitutive of bourgeois narratives of self and society (134).

Comparing Cosmopolitanisms

Comparing two retrospectives—Sahgal's introduction to the 1965 edition to her memoir, *Prison and Chocolate Cake* (1954), and the opening lines of Rushdie's 1984 essay on Günter Grass—provides a way of tracing the differences and commonalities of *namak-halaal* and postnational cosmopolitanisms around questions of class and nation. Sahgal's text opens with a section entitled "Home and the World," a direct allusion to Rabindra-nath Tagore's famous novel, *Ghare Baire* (*The Home and the World*, Bengali, 1915). Explaining why Mumbai (Bombay) felt foreign to her while foreign cities abroad did not, Sahgal suggests that her upbringing as the niece of Jawaharlal Nehru problematized the home/world dichotomy:

[E]verything outside the contexts and concerns of the environment of my childhood [. . .] had, for me, a foreign, exotic dimension. By this curious reckoning Madrid and Barcelona, cities halfway across the world, had an intimate ring to them, and the Spanish revolutionary cry, "No paseran!" could have been a cry from my own heart, so anxiously had talk of the Spanish Civil War and other international events figured in the talk at home. Home, in this sense, was wide open to the world and there was no clear dividing line between the two. A typical example was a letter from my father [Nehru's brother in law] written from Almora saying that he did his daily quota of spinning at the hour of the Moscow broadcast in English "so that I can hear of the collective farming of the Soviets while I ply the *charkha* [spinning wheel] of Gandhi Baba." Likewise, the Chinese, European, English, and American visitors who came to Anand Bhawan [Nehru's home] did not seem in the least foreign or different from ourselves in any way that mattered, joined as they were to us by a common view and vision of the world. (*Prison* i–ii)

The spaces denoting "home" and "world," thus, are redrawn such that Madrid is less "exotic" than Mumbai. "Home" expands as the passage proceeds, incorporating geographically disparate locations (Allahabad, Barcelona, the USSR, China, Europe, the United States) along with their respective signifiers (Gandhism, Republicanism, Communism, Maoism, capitalism). It is not national or cultural boundaries that define what is familiar to Sahgal's elite, nationalist family but an eclectic mix of international and political ones.

Sahgal grounds her version of *namak-halaal* cosmopolitanism in the political attitudes of late colonial, nationalist elites—and points to a cosmopolitanism that is qualitatively different from the postnational one. First, although members of this elite class, educated in England, the United States, or English-medium schools in India, were obviously comfortable with Anglo-American culture even in the 1930s, they saw themselves as being intimately linked with revolutionary movements in Europe and national liberation struggles in the colonies. This blend of nationalism and internationalism is actively foregrounded in the narrative through the marshalling of the slogan of the Spanish republicans, Sahgal's father's letter, and the explicit reference to *Ghare Baire* and its own negotiations of such questions.[7] In contrast, as Timothy Brennan argues in *At Home in the World*, today's cosmopolitans happily perform the role of an intermediary between the West and the "Third World," displaying "impatience, even at times hostility, to the legacy of decolonization," parodying or dismissing the writers and theorists of decolonization, and seeing themselves as inimical to all national and state formations (38–42). If postcolonial cosmopolitans since the 1980s are self-exiled in a middle ground that signifies being "highly critical of imperialism" but also having "lost faith in independence" (40), the anti-imperialism of the corresponding class in 1930s India was shot through with a supreme faith in decolonization and, in many cases, tinged red with an affiliation to socialism.

Another distinguishing mark of *namak-halaal* cosmopolitanism as seen in this passage lies in its effort to construct smooth, concordant relations between the implied audience and the implied author, narrator, and/or protagonist in the effort to convey an ethics of commitment. Sahgal's prose is completely sincere in its treatment of the struggles of the past, produced through a congruence between the flesh-and-blood author (Sahgal in 1965), the implied author/narrator (the autobiographical voice), and the character who experiences and learns from the narrated events (the young Sahgal of the 1930s and 1940s). It is thus at odds with the aesthetic of detachment that dominates postnational writing. Certainly, the "subtlety, irony, and understatement" that Brennan finds in contemporary writing is also important to Sahgal (*At Home* 40), and of course it would be inopportune to divorce "irony" from "commitment."[8] The entire passage, for instance, highlights a playful and eclectic juxtaposition of signs—the intimacy that an Indian feels with a Spanish slogan, the pairing of Gandhian and Soviet practices—in order to explore the initial paradox about the "foreignness" of Bombay and the "intimate ring" of Barcelona. However, the figurative and self-reflexive language here is directed toward narrative closure and a definite *telos:* the construction of a global consciousness amidst a staunchly nation-centered one.

Consider, in contrast, the opening lines of Rushdie's essay on Grass:

> In the summer of 1967, when the West was—perhaps for the last time—in the clutches of the optimism disease—when the microscopic, invisible bacillus of optimism made its young people believe that they would overcome someday, when unemployment was an irrelevance and the future still existed, and when I was twenty years old, I bought from a bookshop in Cambridge a paperback copy of Ralph Manheim's English translation of *The Tin Drum*. In those days everybody had better things to do than read. There was the music and there were the movies and there was also, don't forget, the world to change. Like many of my contemporaries I spent my student days under the spell of Bunuel, Godard, Ray, Wajda, Welles, Bergman, Kurosawa, Jancso, Antonioni, Dylan, Lennon, Jagger, Laing, Marcuse, and, inevitably, the two-headed fellow known to Grass readers as Marxengels [. . .]. A book is a kind of passport. And my passports, the works that gave me the permits I needed, were *The Film Sense* by Serge Eisenstein, the "Crow" poems of Ted Hughes, Borges' *Fictions*, Sterne's *Tristram Shandy*, Ionesco's play *Rhinoceros*—and, that summer of 1967, *The Tin Drum*. ("Gunter Grass" 276)

Rushdie's playful-cynical tone when speaking of the political climate of his childhood, and his positioning of a global map of culture in *opposition* to one of struggle, forms the basis of a very different worldview than Sahgal's. I am admittedly reading against the grain here: the passage's tongue-in-cheek quality, established by the opening sentence, seeks to disarm a reading that is as unfunny as mine. For instance, the cynical characterization of the desire for change as an "optimism disease" is mitigated by the repetition and development of the metaphor (e.g., the "microscopic, invisible bacillus" of optimism that attacked the young). The reader is invited to trust the narrative as it enters into a familiar discourse: the fondness with which adults reflect on the follies of their youth.

But I am suggesting that this tone is actually constitutive of the passage's politics. As in many contemporary representations, "the 1960s" function here as a symbol, marking an age of innocence and adolescence from which Rushdie—and the entire West, apparently—have moved on, however unwillingly. Rewriting the contagious radicalism of the time as an "optimism disease," however, adds a new, more serious dimension to the notion that the desire to change the world was (is?) ephemeral and childish. (Apparently, even champions of "hybridity" and cross-cultural contagion such as Rushdie don't like certain parasites.) Inverting a line from the famous Civil Rights movement hymn in order to make his point ("that they would overcome someday"), Rushdie risks minimizing the hurdles that oppressed groups *did* overcome in the 1960s, such as racist Jim Crow laws in the United States. But more troubling than the mocking tone of the passage (e.g., "there was also, don't forget, the world to change") is Rushdie's utter obliviousness to the fact that the Anglo-American multiculturalist platform from which he is able to speak is itself a product, directly and indirectly, of the cultural changes wrought by the struggles of the 1960s.

Aijaz Ahmad, in drawing attention to this passage, suggests that having dismissed the political movements of the 1960s, Rushdie places world literature and culture in the position of "an antidote to such follies" (*In Theory* 153–54). Indeed, both Sahgal and Rushdie identify comfort zones of "home" in a global way, traversing the world in the process of mapping the spaces that are dear to them. But whereas Sahgal points to global flashpoints of struggle, Rushdie's stimulants are books, films, and intellectuals *in opposition* to struggle. There is no inherent opposition between political activism and the world of ideas and culture, of course, and many of the texts Rushdie cites are political in their own right. Rather, the attitude appears to be, as Amitav Ghosh puts it, that "writers don't join crowds" ("Ghosts" 56, 61). The literary and cinematic cartography that Rushdie constructs, naming influences from across North America, South America, Asia, and Europe, thus develops as an *alternative* to movements. And it is only at this juncture that the tone of the passage changes, gaining the sincerity and excitement that we saw earlier in Sahgal's memory of political events. As in the Sahgal excerpt, Rushdie continues to deploy clever, figurative language even here ("I spent my student days under the spell of [. . .]") but it is clear that we are not to mock this fascination with books and film but to partake in the magical new world that they involve. The philosophical idealism here, and the class moorings that underpin it, are readily apparent: Rushdie's metaphor of books as "passports" and "permits" to travel the world invokes the classic Kantian figure of the transnational, cosmopolitan, bourgeois intellectual, but now as the agent of newness and transgression.[9]

Sahgal's reflections on her youth, in contrast to Rushdie's, are more attentive to questions of subaltern agency as she invokes populist and internationalist discourses concerning anticolonial nationalism, democracy, and economic self-reliance. Nevertheless, I would argue that the subaltern is ultimately invisible and silent here, too. If Sahgal's reminiscences display how cosmopolitan elites involved with mainstream nationalism in the 1930s were conversant with Left politics, they also reveal how nationalist intellectuals, by the 1960s, tended to uncritically bundle together populist demands and the workings of (postcolonial) nation-states. Thus, for instance, the Spanish republicans are placed alongside the Soviet Union with no sense of the latter's role in the republicans' defeat. The differences between Gandhian and Soviet practice become less important than the aesthetic affect of placing them side by side. By the time we get to the last sentence of the passage Sahgal does not even feel compelled to define what constitutes the "common view and vision of the world" between the Chinese, European, and American guests; her familiarity with their foreignness is sufficient in establishing a sense of joint purpose.

From Sahgal's other autobiographical texts, however, we get a sense of who the visitors to Anand Bhavan were and what their "common view and vision" might be. Nehru often hosted elite circles of foreign visitors before and after independence, as we gather from Sahgal's writings and other sources—including ambassadors, UN officials, and international dignitaries. In the aftermath of World War II, the end of British, French, and other colonial empires, and the onset of the Cold War, a progressive, "common vision" for postcolonial elites often translated, for better or for worse, into membership and participation in the United Nations and its affiliated organs, in the Non-Aligned Movement, and in other bodies that brought together people (usually elites) from different nations and backgrounds. The sign for "internationalism" shifts from the Spanish Civil War to the dignitaries in Anand Bhavan, tracing anticolonial nationalism's slide from an oppositional movement linked to internationalist and anti-imperialist currents to bourgeois-nationalism.[10] It is precisely this narrowing of nationalist ideology, reflected in *Prison and Chocolate Cake*, that laid the groundwork for the cynicism that we see in the Rushdie passage. Undoubtedly, the representations of the Sahgal piece draw their force from the living memories of struggles from the past—Sahgal's own father, described fondly there, was an anticolonial activist who died in a British prison in 1944. But the consequences of the Guha passage cited earlier, in which he described how "the Indian working class and peasantry failed to gain ideological and practical hegemony" in the Indian anticolonial struggle, are that the freedom of 1947 was sorely incomplete. Leaving aside their individual political proclivities, the memories of writers such as Rushdie, a generation later, are often drawn from the contexts of historic betrayals and failures: Partition, the end of 1960s radicalism amidst the global economic downturn of the 1970s, and a political and economic scenario dominated by, for instance, Indira Gandhi in India, Zia ul-Haq in Pakistan, Margaret Thatcher in Britain, and Ronald Reagan in the United States.

An incident from Sahgal's early memoirs along these lines reminds me of the tragicomedic scenes in the opening credits of Ousmane Sembene's *Xala* (1975), in which West African elites, immediately after decolonization, enlist the services of the ex-colonizers who, in turn, entrap them in neocolonial relations. Sahgal, her uncle Nehru, and her cousin Indira, we learn, were invited to dine at the Mountbattens', Viceroy and Lady, shortly after independence. Unmindful of the ironies of the moment, Sahgal simply reports how "Mamu [Nehru] and Indi[ra] were calling [the Mountbattens] by their first names, and the four of them were joking like old friends" (*Prison and Chocolate Cake* 216). The Prime Minister of the newly decolonized India, his family, and his "old friends" then rise to toast the King at the end of the meal—with nary a comment from our young nationalist narrator. Instead, what really disturbs Nehru's niece—reflecting back on the moment as an adult—is that she "had not distinguished [her]self in the social graces" since she had forgotten to take her shoes off during the toast (218)! Recall Rushdie's comments about the Raj-nostalgia films produced in Britain during the Thatcherite 1980s, which represent decolonization as if "the British and Indians actually understood each other jolly well, and that the end of the Empire was a sort of gentleman's agreement between old pals at the club" ("Outside the Whale" 101).

The contemporary attraction to Rushdie's fiction and nonfiction, as we see in this critique of imperialist and nationalist historiography, lies in its ability to deconstruct myths of the nation and to discern the contending interests within it—for we are still living through the consequences of the incompleteness of the national liberation projects, and new paradigms are only starting to emerge amidst the current global recession. But both Sahgal's and Rushdie's frameworks operate in a liberal ideological framework that places the individual above all collectivities. In Sahgal's version of this liberalism, ordinary Indians are simply the "huge, brown blur," the backdrop against which Nehru and other leaders act upon the stage of history (*From Fear Set Free* 30). In Rushdie's, the nation is either doomed by history in perpetuity or is little more than a chaotic, magical, and imaginary entity, available for manipulation at the behest of the middle-class protagonist/writer. Despite producing memorable portraits of the predicament of the Emergency and its aftermath, therefore, neither *Midnight's Children* nor *Rich Like Us* is able to represent the people from a perspective that opens up space for them to be agents in these stories. For these are, after all, not meant to be their stories at all.

Saleem's Story and Postnational Narrative

In the following reading of *Midnight's Children,* I draw out its larger elite-centered perspective through an analysis of its narrative structure: a configuration of characterization and voice that evokes subaltern figures only to ultimately shunt them aside. I begin with a discussion of the complicated, first-person narrator that the novel constructs: the nationalist, unreliable, yet sympathetic Saleem Sinai, whose autobiographical retrospective both develops and deconstructs a narrative of the Indian nation. On the surface, the allegorical association between Saleem and India is simple and direct. Saleem and the nation are born exactly at the same moment, on the stroke of midnight on August 15, 1947, and the main events of Saleem's life are paired with the key historical moments of postcolonial India until the late 1970s. We quickly find, however, that the narration actively seeks to disrupt any assumption that the novel is offering an archetypal nationalist allegory in which the development of the individual is linked to the progress of the nation. For in this particular bildungsroman, we are explicitly warned that the narrative present from which the mature Saleem relates his story is a precarious space, portending the demise of Saleem and the failure of the national project. Since Saleem himself is telling the story, we know that at least he and the nation will survive—but how should we read this tenuous survival? Does the ultimate stability of Saleem's voice denote the novel's turn toward the nation as resilient and praiseworthy?

Or is the implosion of Saleem, which he predicts with great pathos in the final pages, a reversal of his continuing, misplaced faith in the nation? Tracking how Saleem's character narration works, I suggest, is necessary to analyzing the text's orientation toward the nation and, as related to this, its attention to but ultimate marginalization of subaltern characters such as Padma and Shiva.

The narrative structure of *Midnight's Children* forces readers to recognize and develop critical reading skills on at least two levels. The first order of critique emerges through the simultaneous offering and debunking of a nationalist narrative. As in all first-person bildungsromans, readers must learn the basic story as it is being relayed through two filters: the mature narrator in the frame narrative and the youthful self that is portrayed as experiencing the core story firsthand. But being a metafictional text, *Midnight's Children* deliberately foregrounds the operation of both of these filters, rendering problematic the very division between "frame narrative" and "core story" by giving equal time to the mature Saleem, as it were, by allowing multiple interruptions and digressions. In this way, the undermining of the nationalist allegory suggested by the core story begins from the very first paragraph: its hesitations and ellipses mar even the narration of basic facts such as Saleem's date of birth (*Midnight's Children* 2). Indeed, the allegorical links between Saleem and India are so exaggerated that the effect is comical. But a serious edge to the tale enters very soon: Saleem describes himself as being "handcuffed to history, [his] destinies indissolubly chained to those of [his] country" (3). And so when we learn that Saleem's birth has been blessed by Prime Minister Nehru and when we read the framed note from the PM that hangs in Saleem's room, we cannot help detecting a warning about state surveillance: "'We shall be watching over your life with the greatest attention; it will be, in a sense, the mirror of our own'" (143). Saleem is thus depicted as being appropriated into the matrix of Nehruvian nationalism, against his will, from the very start. As such, he carries the weight of representing the ideal of a democratic and secular India—an ideal, as we can already sense, that is bound to fail.

Forced to read Saleem's beginnings through his end, the implied audience is trained to read all instances of hope and promise as signs of future defeat; the "dialectic of suffering and redemption" that operates in *The God of Small Things*, as discussed in the next chapter, does not exist here. For instance, the magical elements of Saleem's characterization capture the immense potential of the nation as it comes into being. Saleem discovers, around age ten, that his gigantic, sensitive nose will allow him to telepathically connect with all of the other 1,000 children in a "Midnight's Children's Conference" (MCC). He hopes that the combined and organized use of these powers might help (re)build the nation, as the children belong to various regions, classes, religions, and castes. But the real world stamps out all magic. The potential for unity falls apart through the tumultuous 1960s and 1970s, as the MCC fractures along the fault lines of its diverse subject positions and political factions. In Saleem's nonmagical life, his relatives—part of an elite, Muslim family that remained in India after Partition—are internally divided by affairs, betrayals, oppressions, and political debates and externally pressured by wars, communalism, and nationalism. Tossed between the governments and nations of India and Pakistan, each of which is depicted as hypocritical and vile, most of the family is wiped out by a bomb in the 1965 war—illustrating the extreme limitations of secular (Muslim) subjectivity in postcolonial South Asia. Saleem then enters a new phase in which he bears witness to the Pakistani versions of the trauma of postcoloniality, depicted most poignantly in the "Sundarbans" chapter when, as a special-operations Pakistani solider in rebellious East Pakistan in 1971, Saleem is transformed into a rebel-sniffing dog and becomes a tool of the government.

One last possibility for national reconstruction emerges with the figure of Parvati—an old MCC comrade and potential lover who rescues him. Along with Saleem, we hope that the Communist-influenced Delhi slum of magicians and circus performers might lead to a new, subaltern-oriented future through its alternative politics and artistic creativity. But this final utopian loophole, too, is tightly closed. Indira Gandhi, appearing as both a fictional character ("the Widow") and as herself, methodically co-opts and/or eliminates all of the members of the MCC under the rubric of the Emergency. Saleem undergoes not a vasectomy but a complete "sperectomy," a "draining of hope" (coined from the Latin *speros*). The sperectomy deftly ties together the political and personal traumas that have characterized Saleem's life in postcolonial India, with impotence and disrupted/unnatural genealogies serving as motifs and metaphors for sociopolitical and cultural crises. Indeed, *Midnight's Children* treats us to a history of the processes that have produced its own postnational orientation. Rather than simply asserting its claims, the novel takes its implied audience through the experience of having one's expectations dashed. Through Saleem we move back and forth between cynicism and hope, until we finally learn that the nation cannot deliver on its promises.

The very mechanisms by which the young Saleem's life and views are critiqued lead us to the second order of analysis: a skepticism toward the mature Saleem himself. *Midnight's Children*'s narrative method encourages this, mirroring the process of a postmodernist epistemological critique. The novel first demonstrates that all truths are claims to truth and that all entities that appear whole are actually constructs—and then undermines the plausibility of *its* truth-claim through an ironic, self-reflexive aesthetic in which the narrative voice itself is deconstructed. The mature Saleem, thus, in retelling the story of the younger Saleem's frustrated attempts to build a secular, democratic, egalitarian India, duly deconstructs national mythologies. At the same time, on the level of character, voice, and narrative sequence, the novel overtly seeks to portray the mature Saleem himself as a flawed and unreliable narrator, disrupting the notion that he holds the key to a greater truth, that the novel is moving toward a *telos* (which is, in fact, its *telos*). Besides being frail and impotent, Saleem is literally cracking apart as he tells/writes the story of his life. Saleem's running self-critique while he narrates, the repeated movement back and forth between frame narrative and the core story, Saleem's mistakes about dates and facts— all of these serve to explicitly minimize the authority of Saleem and his critical counternarrative. Indeed, Saleem's long "courtship of fragmented experience" is heralded from the very beginnings of the novel, with his grandfather Aziz's "laborious courtship of Naseem, conducted through a perforated sheet that allows only partial glimpses of her body" (Keith Wilson 62). No adequate historiography is possible when history-writing itself is depicted as a cosmic joke that "create[s] past events simply by saying they occurred" (*Midnight's Children* 529). The implied audience, consequently, is made to repeatedly reflect upon its own gullibility for believing in both the youthful and the mature Saleem. All of this, crucially, happens on the surface of the novel and as part of its explicit project.

The cleverness and artistic mastery with which Saleem deconstructs himself, however, leads to a fundamental paradox: one which threatens to reassert the centrality of Saleem and the nation itself. Saleem, we find, is utterly compelling, even as he critiques himself. In *Living to Tell About It*, Jim Phelan suggests that first-person character narration builds a bond of trust (an ethical bond) between the implied author, the narrator, and the implied audience—both because it fully divulges the interiority of the character (developing empathy) and because it ensures that the character will survive whatever trials and tribulations s/he describes. In the sort of postmodern character narration we have here, though, there is a tension between our attraction to Saleem as a survivor and skilled storyteller (whose self-deprecation disarms our mistrust) and the way that the novel trains us as readers: to question all truth-claims including those of the narrator and the text itself. The prominence of Saleem's character narration, in other words, threatens to eliminate the second order of critique. After all, like a smart, postcolonial version of Forrest Gump, Saleem survives the 1956 Marathi-Gujarati language riots in Bombay, the 1965 India-Pakistan war, the violent birth of Bangladesh in 1971, and torture during the Emergency. Perhaps, we are led to think, the fact that Saleem can recognize his condition and "live to tell about it" is itself, at last, a victory over the tumultuous history of the postcolonial nation-state.

This implicit reinstating of Saleem's voice on the narrative and epistemological level threatens to reinstate the nation as well. Saleem deconstructs himself in the process of narrating his story, but as a *character* he is never quite cured of the "optimism disease," never quite as detached from the Indian scene as is the implied author, the one who constructs Saleem as the ultimate victim of the postcolonial nation. Indeed, we might say that much of the novel's appeal is drawn from its deep engagement with the nation—even when that position is overtly rejected. At the end of the novel, too, when Saleem predicts his (and India's) implosion, there is a pathos amidst the cynicism. In relating to us the story of his repeated disillusionment with the nation, then, Saleem (inadvertently) conveys how difficult and painful it is to stop believing in the idea of a national unity that transcends communal, class, and ideological divisions. The repressed nation returns and haunts this postmodern bildungsroman as a desire that simply won't die. Indeed, like its cousins "postcolonialism" and "postmodernism," the term "postnationalism" must define itself primarily in relation to that from which it seeks to escape. In this way, at the cusp of the historic shift away from the nation in the postcolonial Indian English novel, *Midnight's Children* abides by it in the form of a character narrator whose desire for national wholeness persists despite being victimized by postcolonial violence. Dohra Ahmad's reading of *The Satanic Verses* pins down the alleged indeterminacy of Rushdie's narrative constructs exactly: "The elusive, contradictory, and finally assertive manner in which Rushdie wields his unwelcome authority comes through in the way he treats oppositions. He deliberately establishes dualities like minority/majority, purity/corruption, and fundamentalism/hybridity, and then undermines those dualities, as part of a strategy of laying out and claiming for himself all possible interpretations" (16). Saleem becomes unassailable because he presents himself as containing, Whitman-like, all contradictions and critiques.

It is because of this continuing trace of the *namak-halaal* orientation in the novel and its palpable longing for a lost India, I suggest, that several critics have simply read *Midnight's Children* as a nationalist text, minimizing the novel's deconstruction of the nation and national history.[11] Such readings have much to support them. They fit nicely, for instance, with Rushdie's own articulations of a fairly mainstream nationalism in essays and interviews; like many a diasporic Indian, Rushdie, too, "looks back" to the nation frequently, often with a surprisingly misty fondness. Indeed, this recognition of nationalism in Rushdie supports my broader arguments, in this chapter and in the book as a whole, about the organic links between early and contemporary postcolonial novels and the preponderance of fairly mainstream politics within both. In the latter case, such novels reflect the left/progressive intellectual who is disillusioned with the nation but who has continued to look back to it and to speak for it. Undoubtedly, therefore, India is very much present in *Midnight's Children* as the trace of a desire. But what is at issue is not simply the novel's interest in India but the perspective through which it views the nation. India, in contemporary texts, is often an ahistorical abstraction and exotic space in which cultures, languages, classes, religions, political ideas, and individuals endlessly clash and intermix in creative, garish, beautiful, and/or violent ways. Its value lies mainly in its spectacular failures—which, significantly, are best seen from outside the nation. While the nation, and the modernist longing for a lost time of wholeness, are evoked in *Midnight's Children*, the novel cannot be called nationalist in its orientation because its main effort is to debunk this desire.

I conclude this section with two arguments against the reading of *Midnight's Children* as nationalist: the first on the level of narrative and the second in terms of the novel's strong associations with contemporary ideas about the postnational. To consider *Midnight's Children* as a nationalist text means, first of all, to orient oneself around Saleem's compelling role as character narrator and not to the text as a whole. But the gap that exists between the character narrator and the implied author must be taken into account—despite the fact that the novel seeks to elide this distinction. Thus, we are encouraged to regard Saleem as the intelligence that constructs the text and even as the real author: Saleem appears as the writer/teller of the story on multiple levels; Saleem's prediction of his annihilation also ends the novel itself, leaving no space outside of his voice; Saleem narrates from the very same time frame within which the novel is published, that is, immediately after the Emergency; Saleem and Salman are both born in 1947, as emphasized in Rushdie's discussions of the book; and so on. But in fact, Saleem is a character in the novel and, as such, occupies a limited and particularized position. Much happens in the text that he does not and cannot construct, including the characterization of Padma in the frame narrative, the working of the pickle factory in which he is writing, the jail from which he has been released, the reality of Shiva, and so on.

The ending of the novel does much to hide Saleem's status as a character; functioning as an epilogue, it projects Saleem as a spokesperson for the text and even for History. Saleem predicts his death in a booming voice that, like a filmic voiceover, graphically describes a coming postcolonial dystopia in which he and the generations to follow are mercilessly crushed. However, as a character, Saleem is still "saying" all this from his desk in the pickle factory. It seems to me that we have two choices: either we can read this final dystopia as Saleem's ultimate turn, after the sperectomy, toward a postnational cynicism, a look away from a nation where (individual) freedom and progress are impossible, or we can highlight the modernist longing for a lost wholeness that continues to haunt Saleem, even after the Emergency. In either case, the (predicted) end of the character narrator and the nation emerge as a clear indicator of the implied author's turn away from the nation as a viable space for rehabilitation and progress. The centrality of Saleem's voice in the epilogue contains a sense of national longing, but this does not determine the novel's overall orientation to the nation. The brilliance of the novel, indeed, lies in being able to draw upon both national and postnational desires through its construction of Saleem as character narrator.

A second point that leads me against the reading of this novel as nationalist has to do with the clear links between Rushdie's narrative discourse and the ideological contexts in which he is writing. The representation of the nation in *Midnight's Children,* indeed, fits with the claims that have been made since the 1970s, from various political angles, concerning the imminent crisis of the nation-state. Financial institutions such as the World Bank and the International Monetary Fund (IMF)—as well as the advanced capitalist countries that underwrite them—have invoked a postnational narrative of "failed states" in the Third World in order to justify neoliberal policies for the expansion of capital. For U.S. politicians and the military, as we have seen over the first decade of the twenty-first century, being postnational means being able to bring "democracy" anywhere at any time, setting aside "fictions" like national sovereignty. Left/ progressive theorists such as Arjun Appadurai, Michael Hardt, Antonio Negri, and Gayatri Spivak—categorically opposed to the forces described above—have deployed a postnational discourse quite differently, arguing that amidst a new postindustrial and postmodern capitalism, new methods of communication across nation-states have led to a vast democratization, possibilities of agency and even "speech" for subalterns and "the multitudes," and demands for justice that can circumvent the narrow constraints of nation-states. In each case, it is in the name of subaltern welfare and human progress that a postnational view of the world is proposed. Undoubtedly, the postnational orientation of contemporary Indian English writers and cultural theorists is motivated by an admirable ethical-political desire to criticize oppressions that occur within nation-states, cloaked by the rhetoric of national sovereignty and cultural difference. I am opposed to the notion that discursive commonalities between these starkly different postnational visions imply some sort of complicity between them on the material level; indeed, we need to make use of all of the new avenues available to contest global and local hierarchies. But following Partha Chatterjee's critique of Appadurai's postnationalism in "Beyond the Nation?" we ought to ask whether this desire to "look away" from the nation-state reflects not a given writer's critique of national elites and existing structures but a dissatisfaction with the forms of *political society* that are being churned out in the postcolonial world—forms that, since colonial times, have involved nonelites in movements for democracy against the modern state (both progressive and reactionary) in ways that the institutions of *civil society,* dominated by Westernized elites, have not.

While I am not convinced by Chatterjee's implied theoretical premise that universalist notions of individual and group rights (marked as "Western") *necessarily* dismiss the particularities of community formations in colonized and postcolonial spaces, I share his concern that when left/progressive voices demand that we look beyond the nation-state, they are often speaking from a "transnational public sphere [. . .] whose moral claims derive from the assumed existence of a domain of universal civil society" ("Beyond" 67).[12] Paying scant attention to the complex efforts for democracy and change within national borders, often developing outside the purview of the global media and the various human rights groups and NGOs, such a position can find itself unable to challenge imperialist incursions that, like the colonial rhetoric of "the civilizing mission" in years past, further global hierarchies in the name of a world without borders.[13] On the flip side, as events following the 2003 invasion of Iraq have highlighted, we still live in a world system of nation-states in which imperialist violence, progressive national visions, and revolutionary struggles continue to shape the lives of millions (Gopal and Lazarus 8).

It is not, then, that the nation does not appear in postnational novels or that its appeal to ordinary people (and subsequent betrayal) is not recognized; in fact, postnational texts seek out and meditate on this appeal precisely in order to problematize and investigate the continuing pull of various nationalisms. If we read Rushdie's *The Moor's Last Sigh* (1995) as a sequel to *Midnight's Children,* given the brief but powerful cameo appearance in the former text of Aadam Sinai, Saleem's son, it is obvious that Rushdie remains quite invested in tracking the nation's trajectory, especially to find spaces for secularism, humanism, and art. The book's clear, anticommunalist message and nostalgia for a lost secular India even allows it to rehabilitate the Nehruvian past with its explicit commitments to national unity and syncretism. However, this doomed nation is little more than a fiction waiting to be reimagined by the artist, teeming with diversity and conflict but able to offer no solutions internally. As Tabish Khair writes of *The Moor's Last Sigh,* its concerns with communalism in India are welcome, but its portrayal of the battle as being always already lost presents a flawed view of the ongoing struggle against communalism through the 1990s, minimizing the agency of Indians while reinscribing the historical inevitability of defeat. Escaping to Spain and leaving India, once again, is the sad but necessary fate of the secular, cosmopolitan-elite subject. In Rushdie's essay "Imaginary Homelands" (1982), as discussed in the introduction, the expatriate writer's turn to "fictional Indias" was depicted as the result of a "physical alienation" that made it impossible to grasp the real thing. In the postnational orientations of Rushdie's novels, these "imaginary homelands" seem to be as real as, or perhaps even more real than, the "actual" places being referred to, both allegorically and directly. In such places, subalterns can be victims and objects of pity, but never agents of change in their own right.

Padma
Subaltern Voice and Implied Audience

In the character of Padma, *Midnight's Children* links "the ordinary Indian" to linear models of causation and storytelling ("what-happened-next")—both of which are then positioned for erasure. Padma represents the novel's recognition of its difficult task: to construct an aesthetically complicated novel about India for an English-speaking global audience that, in the main, desires directness and political clarity from Third World texts. By expertly accounting for these desires, the Padma scenes enable the text to construct an implied audience that is self-reflexive about them. It is through the mature Saleem's conversations with Padma at the very beginning of the novel, which interrupt its flow and establish the contingent nature of Saleem's narration, that the implied author trains his audience in the novel's narrative processes. But it is also through Padma that we can begin linking the novel's narrative processes with its elite-centered politics of class. The novel's ultimate transcendence of Padma—and therefore of realism and linearity on the level of narrative—is central to the novel's marginalization of subaltern characters.

Temporally, Padma is situated in the narrative present. While cooking for Saleem, tending to his fracturing body, and completing household chores, Padma listens to and comments on Saleem's story as he narrates, influencing its form and content. In the early part of the novel, Saleem is repeatedly forced to cut away from his story to respond to Padma's "loud" interruptions: her frustrations with his delays, digressions, and obfuscations, and with his ambiguity with respect to causation, genealogy, and even the basic elements of event and story. Padma's questions force Saleem to address the reporting function of the narrator: answering the basic questions of "Who?" "What?" and "Why?" Much to the delight of my students as they wrestle with the novel, Padma presents a counternarrative and counteraesthetic to Saleem's. She challenges him, orders him to get on with the plot, asks him to summarize, and forces him to shift course and break his stride. Padma's common sense rewrites Saleem's story as nonsense, forcing him to reckon with the esoteric and incomprehensible nature of his meandering reflections on life and society. Padma, then, seems to possess a great deal of power in relation to Saleem on the level of narrative, character, and voice. Physically stronger than Saleem and sexually hungry, she seems to intimidate the small, impotent, and disintegrating narrator whose cucumber-shaped nose (hint, hint) has lost its magic. Since Padma appears to be the agent for the text's second order of critique (i.e., its critique of the mature Saleem), she might appear to have more power than he. One might even read Padma, in this light, as the speaking subaltern who subverts the power dynamics of gender and class that ordinarily might exist between a male writer/employer and his female reader/nurse/cook.

One might, but one would be wrong. For, as we can deduce from the patronizing way in which Saleem allows himself to be corrected by Padma, her actual function in Saleem's story is to reveal the superiority of his narrative methodology over her own. Padma's palpable materiality and strength symbolize, as it were, the enormity of the novel's attempt to develop a postmodernist historiography against the prevalent desire for linearity and simplicity. And Saleem ultimately succeeds. Becoming less and less combative as the story goes on, Padma finds herself getting engrossed

in the story despite her ongoing dissatisfaction with its style and its conflict resolutions—and thus serves as a model for the type of reader that the
novel imagines for itself. Ultimately, Saleem's dialogues with Padma allow
the implied author to have both his metacritical narration and his linearity. Her insistence that Saleem clarify the lines of causality and provide a
clearer plot *does* serve to drive the novel forward, even extracting useful
summaries from a reluctant Saleem. But these interventions represent not
an independent challenge to the novel's project but a device for drawing
the audience's attention to mainstream reading practices so that they might
be overcome.

Saleem introduces Padma at the beginning of the second chapter of
the novel thus: "Padma—our plump Padma—is sulking magnificently.
(She can't read and [. . .] dislikes other people knowing anything that
she doesn't. Padma: strong, jolly, a consolation for my last days. But definitely a bitch-in-the-manger.)" (*Midnight's Children* 20). The passage is
not hard to unpack. Padma's "sulking" at Saleem's refusal to eat while
he is writing is described as a childish response, rooted in illiteracy. While
Padma is "strong" and "jolly," Saleem also describes her as an angry, vindictive "bitch." Naturally, Padma is prone to melodrama, as her responses
include snorts, stormy exits, and specific gestures meant to convey the
image of "the angry South Asian woman": "her right hand slicing the air
up-downup in exasperation" and her "[w]rist smack[ing] against fore-
head" (20).

Even when he appears to be sympathetic to Padma, considering the
daily working conditions that make her irritable, Saleem falls into familiar
elitist and gendered discourse:

> She stirs a bubbling vat all day for a living; something hot and vinegary
> has steamed her up tonight. Thick of waist, somewhat hairy of forearm,
> she flounces, gesticulates, exits. Poor Padma. Things are always get-
> ting her goat. Perhaps even her name: understandably enough, since her
> mother told her, when she was very small, that she had been named after
> the lotus goddess, whose most common appellation amongst village folks
> is "The One Who Possesses Dung." (20)

Besides some degree of pity for Padma's daily drudgery, she is denigrated
here by occupation, appearance, and origins; at best, she is viewed from
a distance, as a curious creature exuding an exotic physicality and earthiness. Further, Padma is gendered by her labor, in ways that are sometimes
complicated but always sexist. On the one hand, Padma is defeminized

by her work, as stirring the bubbling vat is linked to her being "thick of waist" and "hairy of forearm." On the other, following a long legacy that discursively links workers to "femininity," Padma is associated with melodrama, sentimentality, and irrationality. Finally, the issue of Padma's name highlights the ways in which Saleem and the implied author mock Padma even as they claim the role of speaking on her behalf. The translation from "lotus goddess" to "The One Who Possesses Dung" is given the veneer of authenticity through reference to the "village folks" and the awkward phrasing that makes it sound like a translation from another language. Through this association with "dung," the text legitimates the links it repeatedly makes between Padma, physicality, and earthiness.

This opening scene creates thus a definite distance between Padma and the implied audience. She is to be pitied, perhaps, but is certainly not one with whom the English-speaking reader, whether South Asian or not, ought to identify. But Padma's place in the novel soon becomes more complicated than this, and the next step in her character development triggers her role on the level of narration. As Padma brings dinner and demands that Saleem at least let her listen to his book, Saleem considers: "perhaps our Padma will be useful, because it's impossible to stop her being a critic" (29). The entry of Padma into the role of reader/critic then opens up new relations between the implied audience, Padma, and Saleem. While the implied audience has been trained to associate itself with Saleem and not Padma, on narrative but also class grounds, Padma's new role as narratee (the in-text audience of the narration) places the implied audience in a common structural location with her. The audience's affiliations are now split and uncertain, especially when Padma begins to contest Saleem's authority as a storyteller. For after Padma reacts angrily to Saleem's portrayal of her (described above), she breaks out of the mold of "poor Padma" and asks us to see her with new eyes. With a blistering and unexpected critique of Saleem's treatment of her name as well his elite gaze, Padma at once undermines his authority and asks the audience to consider his class biases. What angers Padma is not that Saleem makes fun of her name behind her back, but that the "city boy" thinks that her name could be a source of frustration to her (29). "'In my village there is no shame for being the Dung Goddess,'" Padma exclaims, "'Write at once that you are wrong, completely'" (29). Saleem's (and the gullible, implied audience's) incorrect representation of Padma's feelings about her name is marked as the imposition of elites' *liberal* standards onto a world that they pretend to understand but do not.

Saleem's subsequent response, however, problematically closes up the gaps in his knowledge that Padma had forced open, quickly resolving the ambiguity by appropriating Padma's alternative explanations and reifying rural stereotypes. Class and narrative hierarchies are reestablished with Saleem's mocking "apology":

> In accordance with my lotus's wishes, I insert, forthwith, a brief paean to Dung.
>
> Dung, that fertilizes and causes the crops to grow! Dung, which is patted into thin chapatti-like cakes when still fresh and moist, and is sold to village builders, who use it to secure and strengthen the walls of kachcha buildings made of mud! Dung, whose arrival from the nether end of cattle goes a long way toward explaining their divine and sacred status! Oh yes, I was wrong, I admit I was prejudiced, no doubt because its unfortunate odors do have a way of offending my sensitive nose—how wonderful, how ineffably lovely it must be to be named for the Purveyor of Dung! (29)

The ironic nature of the passage is explicit: the word "paean" that introduces it, the archaic and formal language indicating the fulfillment of a duty ("forthwith") or scriptural obfuscation ("arrival from the nether region"), the capitalization and deification of "Dung," the repeated use of exclamation points, the emphasis on the messy qualities of dung ("fresh and moist"), and so on.

But beyond this irony, what really marks the passage's marginalization of Padma is its suggestion that Saleem 1) recognizes the properties for which Indian rural communities recycle (cow) dung, and 2) is actually self-critical of urban-elite stereotyping of rural practice. Saleem reestablishes his credibility here by asserting that it is the *audience's* ignorance about dung that is being questioned, not his own. Saleem returns to his role as pseudo-ethnographer/pseudo-anthropologist in this passage, quickly listing the uses of dung—as fertilizer, as building material—in order to educate his English-speaking, elite audience. His use of a nontranslated word such as "*kachcha*" to describe the rural dwellings (Hindi for "unripe" or "raw") establishes him as a linguistic and cultural insider. At the same time, the ironic mode also assures the English-speaking audience that one can know about rural life and still comment on the "unfortunate odors" of cow dung. Indeed, Padma's reaction does not appear in opposition to Saleem's comments, since it underlines the villagers' veneration for the "Dung Goddess" and reifies the association of her character with earthiness/bodily functions. What was lacking, perhaps, was a proper respect for rural difference, and Saleem's lip service to this difference is constructed as being sufficient.

Padma, then, merely gives greater credibility to Saleem's original binary opposition of elite/urban complexity and subaltern/rural simplicity. Saleem's voice, in effect, subsumes Padma's so that *he* can function as the true "native informant" to the English-speaking reader; he establishes epistemic authority over her through his inflated rhetoric.[14] But when we investigate Saleem's representation of dung with a critical eye, it becomes apparent that he and the implied author have simply exploited, if not completely swallowed, the Orientalist expectations that readers have about Indian rural life. The very association of the name "Padma" with "dung," for example, encapsulates an artistic sleight-of-hand that readers unfamiliar with South Asian languages and practices might accept since Saleem's narration seems to be the conveyor belt of truth about Indian names and practices. When we first meet Padma, Saleem suggests that she is named for the "lotus goddess" (Lakshmi, the Hindu goddess of wealth) but that villagers commonly call Lakshmi "The One Who Possess Dung." And so Padma is called "dung goddess" throughout the novel. There is some real-life justification for the metonymical association between "Lakshmi," dung," and "wealth": Hindu villagers who are dependent on the cow and committed to what Vandana Shiva calls organic and eco-friendly methods of agriculture may hold ceremonies that literally worship cow dung as wealth (e.g., *gobar-dhan puja*), and, therefore, as Lakshmi, the goddess of wealth ("In Praise of Cow Dung"). But translating this into "dung goddess" deliberately taps into Orientalist and/or urban expectations of the backwardness of rural Indians, and the rearticulation of the name as "The One Who Possesses Dung" ironically poses, in its very awkwardness, as a potentially authentic translation of a South Asian name. In this form, Saleem and the implied author strongly suggest an etymological link between the names Padma and Lakshmi where, in fact, none exists.[15]

Soon after this episode, the implied audience is explicitly made to understand that Padma is a foil for Saleem's critique of linear narration. The movement of the passage at the opening of the chapter "Hit the Spittoon" is extremely complex, as Saleem needs to reveal the superiority of his narrative method even while avoiding the black-and-white dichotomy that such a declaration would entail. Padma interrupts one of Saleem's self-referential rants on the process of pickling: a messy method of preservation that, in transforming the stored object into a new one, acts as a metaphor for Saleem's storytelling. Padma demands that he hurry up and get to the plot, "bullying [Saleem] back into the world of linear narrative, the universe of what-happened-next" (37). Seeing her interest, Saleem announces his victory: "she is [. . .] hooked. No doubt about it: my story has her by the throat" (37). Immediately, however, Saleem becomes self-conscious about his new power; he tries to "[fight] down the proper pride of the successful storyteller [and] attempt[s] to educate her" in the art of pickling (37). Instructing Padma that "[t]hings—even people—have a way of leaking into each other [. . .] like flavors when you cook," Saleem must admit also that "certainly Padma is leaking into me. As history pours out of my fissured body, my lotus is quietly dripping in [. . .] (37–38). The text continues to ironically mock and play with Saleem's sense of self-importance; Saleem is not shy about calling himself the "successful story-teller" and cannot hide his excitement that Padma is "hooked," but his very assertions about the value of dialogue and heterogeneity require him to develop an openness toward what he calls Padma's "down-to-earthery" (38). As proof of Padma's importance, this interlude ends with an accelera-tion of the plot and, apparently, a fulfillment of her wishes, "[b]owing to the ineluctable Padma-pressures of what-happened-nextism" (38). Never-theless, even though the narrative takes a more linear turn at this juncture, the implied audience has been forced to confront the desire for linearity as a mode of thinking, as an "ism," and not simply as the natural way to tell stories. The implied author can now have the narrator get back to his reporting function and reestablish the plotline while placing the responsi-bility for this return to linearity on the bossiness and bullying of Padma herself.

By linking the desire for linearity and progress—and for a coherent allegory of the nation—to an unsophisticated, working-class Other, the novel ultimately draws a thick line between the class identities of Sal-eem and the English-educated implied audience, on the one hand, and of Padma, on the other. Whether she is being praised or mocked, Padma is explicitly constructed as an illiterate, simple-minded, subaltern character whose "power" lies in her down-home anti-intellectualism. No matter how much the audience is led by Saleem to appreciate Padma's "down-to-earthery," it is certainly not expected to identify with her. Rather, we are asked to link ourselves with Saleem, whose fragility, antirealism, and circuitousness contrast with Padma's solidity. Paradoxically, it is *because* Saleem "stutters, bumbles, and digresses" that he is positioned as one who can strike "a carefully poised balance between concealment and disclo-sure" (Batty 74). Saleem encourages Padma to be skeptical of narrative power and reliability: "Padma: if you're a little uncertain of my reliability, well, a little uncertainty is no bad thing. Cocksure men do terrible deeds.

Women, too" (*Midnight's Children* 254). But he ultimately revels in his narrative mastery: "call it education, or class-origins [. . .]. By my show of erudition and by the purity of my accents, I shamed them into feeling unworthy of judging me" (254). This dynamic trains the implied audience into being skeptical of the narrator, and to laugh at his hubris—but also, in the very process, to give the narrator, and not his subaltern interlocutors, its trust and allegiance.

Shiva and Subaltern Agency

The dynamic of the narrative process in *Midnight's Children* as seen through the Saleem-Padma exchanges, therefore, is 1) to challenge Saleem's perspective and to problematize the reliability of his narration, but then 2) to also contest the reliability of those alternative voices, especially ones from below, for the purpose of deconstructing any and all truth-claims. While the first move destabilizes the mythologies of the family and the nation that the young Saleem falls into, the second paradoxically reasserts the voice of the mature narrator, since change from below is cast as a utopianism that is utterly unviable. The novel's treatment of Shiva—a magical child, Saleem's "equal and opposite," and the most powerful and independent subaltern character in the main story of *Midnight's Children*—illustrates most clearly the impact of the text's elitist perspective on the question of subaltern agency, because Shiva, unlike Padma, is part of the core story itself.

As the second-eldest member of the MCC, Shiva is endowed with a tremendous strength that emanates from his powerful knees. He transforms in the course of the narrative from an ordinary Bombay slum kid into a powerful gangster, eventually becoming a military officer during the Emergency. Brought up as a poor child in the same neighborhood as Saleem and a constant witness to his elite lifestyle, Shiva harbors a deep resentment for Saleem, an emotion that finds its fulfillment when the elimination of the MCC becomes his main task under the Widow. Indeed, Shiva's very presence mocks and subverts Saleem's straight-laced ideas about nations and progress because, as the implied audience and Padma come to know, Shiva and Saleem had been exchanged at birth by their nurse, Mary Pereira. Although Shiva remains ignorant of Mary's act, the knowledge that Saleem's wealth and privilege was to have been Shiva's injects an extra level of narrative tension in the audience's and Padma's experiences of the Saleem–Shiva confrontations. Saleem's constant guilt about the situation adds yet another dimension to his crisis of authenticity. The pairing of Saleem and Shiva thematizes the problematic notions of genealogy and narratives of origin that overlap with the crisis of nationalist historiography and truth itself.

And yet Shiva is no subaltern hero. Certainly, his unapologetic, class-based critique of Saleem's optimism about democracy and freedom reveals them as the luxurious fictions of elite classes—and shows Saleem to be aware of the "jungle-craft of gentility." But Shiva can provide no alternative to Saleem, as the novel is resolutely against Shiva's class-war attitude and ultimately links his politics with the ruthlessness of the Emergency. Shiva is both the antithesis of Saleem's nationalism and a reminder that nationalism of all kinds eventually leads to authoritarianism and nihilism. The way in which the novel pairs these two together, using Shiva to critique Saleem but then also harshly undermining Shiva, is best seen in the chapter titled "Alpha and Omega," describing the birth of the MCC. On both narrative and political levels, Shiva's subaltern critique of Saleem proceeds through dynamics similar to those we saw with Padma's: he offers a corrective to Saleem's naïveté but then is characterized as part of the problem.

Shiva's challenge to Saleem's abstract idealism is fully displayed in their first meeting—a session of the MCC which, fittingly, can only occur in Saleem's head. Saleem, like a nationalist organizer, must seek out each magical child and help her/him to acknowledge that s/he is not simply an isolated weirdo but is part of a larger collective entity. As these children span the geographical breath of India and represent a variety of political and philosophical platforms, they literally and symbolically undergo the process of constructing the "imagined community" of the nation. But questions about power inevitably emerge and Saleem wonders, in an ethical mode, whether he is "immune to the lure of leadership" (*Midnight's Children* 260). Shiva, in contrast, thirsts for power: he quickly calculates that he and Saleem are naturally the most powerful and proposes that they should be "the joint bosses" of this gang (263). Saleem steadfastly argues against Shiva's anti-idealism, in outlining what the national tasks for the children of midnight should be: "something more like a, you know, sort of loose federation of equals, all points of view given free expression [. . .] we must be here for a *purpose*, don't you think? I mean, there has to be a *reason*, you must agree? So . . . we should try and work out what it is, and then, you know, sort of dedicate our lives to . . ." (263). But Shiva, with a slur similar to Padma's "city kid" but much more critical, counters with: "Rich kid [. . .] You don't know one damn thing! [. . .] What thing in

the whole sister-sleeping world got *reason,* yaar? For what reason you're
rich and I'm poor? [. . .] Man, I'll tell you—you got to get what you can,
do what you can with it, and then you got to die. That's reason, rich boy"
(263).

The young Saleem describes this exchange and his struggles to square
what India was supposed to be with what India is: "And now I, in my
midnight bed, began to shake [. . .]. 'But history,' I say, 'and the Prime
Minister wrote me a letter . . . and don't you even believe in . . . who
knows what we might . . .' He, my alter ego, Shiva butted in: 'Lissen little
boy—you're so full of crazy stuff, I can see I'm going to have to take this
thing over'" (263–64). Looking for reason, hope, and meaning, Saleem
comes off as optimistic but is naïve and unsure of himself. Shiva, driven
by poverty and the knowledge of inequality, rejects the idea of a rational
world and the egalitarian possibilities of the nation, sees a chance at power
and control, and is single-minded in getting it. Speaking in ellipses, Saleem
cannot even articulate a cohesive argument as he holds on to the talismans
of "history," the Prime Minister's letter, nationalist belief, and an activist
will ("who knows what we might . . ."). But Shiva interrupts frequently,
in a powerful and dominant voice, and gets the last word. Shiva appears
to have Saleem under his thumb, just as Padma initially appears to boss
around Saleem the narrator. In fact, however, the dynamic of this exchange
encapsulates the text's ideological dilemma, of which the implied author is
not necessarily aware: the text is critical of nationalism and idealism, but
also fearful of the angry poor.

As with Padma, the implied audience hardly comes to this interrupt-
ing, dictatorial, angry slum kid as an alternative voice to Saleem's. Indeed,
Shiva's "rich boy" insult is tremendously more threatening to Saleem than
Padma's "city boy" because it directly exposes the class basis of Saleem's
philosophy. And yet, while Shiva as a character is positioned to offer a
devastating critique of Saleem, it is Saleem who comes off as calm-headed
despite his confusion. As Saleem's antithesis and "alter-ego," Shiva is diametrically opposed to Saleem not because he is antinationalist but because
he is anti-idealist, nihilistic, and anarchistic. Shiva—the name of the god
of destruction in Hindu mythology—constantly disrupts and critiques Saleem's nationalist plans throughout the novel, as a subaltern figure connected to the real world of poverty and the fight for survival. To some
extent Shiva's criticisms of Saleem and the legacy of 1947, emerging from
his marginalization, are portrayed as being quite legitimate, even when
they come at Saleem's expense. But Shiva can only engender a critique; he
does not form any alternative basis for understanding the nation. In this

way Saleem's voice reestablishes itself as the voice of reason even as it is undermined by the text.

In fact, rather than a complete and utter destabilization of all voices—the project that the novel sets up by making Saleem an unreliable narrator—*Midnight's Children*'s character narration actually forces a recentering of Saleem's voice upon the marginalization of subaltern ones. Saleem hints at this paradoxical dynamic when, in light of a worsening situation, he wonders whether "the purpose of the Midnight's Children might be annihilation; that we would have no meaning until we were destroyed" (273–74). On the surface, the implied author seems to be as nihilistic as Shiva in his treatment of Saleem. As the fissures and cracks slowly take over the body of the narrating Saleem, it appears that the text is sacrificing him to avoid a cohesive, *alternative* narration of the nation—embracing, instead, the "liminality of cultural modernity" that emerges through the slipperiness of national narratives (Bhabha 140). After being imprisoned by Shiva, with his expanded powers of policing under the Emergency, and after undergoing the "sperectomy," "the draining-out of hope," Saleem feels the old tug of optimism but realizes there is no escape:

> Yes, here is optimism, like a disease: one day [Indira Gandhi will] have to let us out and then, and then, wait and see, maybe we should form, I don't know, a new political party, yes the Midnight's Party. . . .Children, something is being born here, in this dark time of our captivity; let Widows do their worst; unity is invincibility! *Children: we've won!* . . . Too painful. Optimism, growing like a rose in a dung-heap: it hurts me to recall it. (*Midnight's Children* 520)

Saleem realizes the falsity of rewriting defeat as victory and embraces the failure of his vision, the failure of India, and the failure of storytelling: "gone forever [. . .] the originally-one-thousand-and-one marvelous promises of a numinous midnight. . . . Who were we? Broken promises; made to be broken" (523). We are back to the metaphor of the "optimism disease," a conceptualization of dissent and struggle referred to throughout the novel and, as we have seen, in Rushdie's essays as well. The novel thus conducts a trenchant criticism of the betrayals of the contemporary postcolonial nation, but through the lens of a more foundational pessimism about activism, struggles from below, and even the possibility of whole subjectivities. In this light, it is not surprising that subaltern figures have no agency. What's more surprising, perhaps, is that Saleem does (in a limited sense). Revealing the indeterminacy of all voices actually depends on valorizing the clever voice of the elite narrator and thus, paradoxically, revealing this postnational text's attraction to a fairly mainstream vision of the nation.

Saleem Will Die (Long Live Saleem)

While it may appear that subaltern voices are not being singled out for deconstruction—that Saleem, too, is being brushed aside—his fracturing and anticipated annihilation at the end of the novel is actually the precursor to wholeness in terms of the ability to narrate. Saleem's elite voice retains its credibility even when the joke is on him—or, more precisely, *because* the joke is on him. However, as I have suggested above, Saleem's role as character narrator as expressed in the epilogue raises questions as to whether he stands as a nation-oriented figure in mourning to be cast aside or as an enlightened postnational figure himself. In either case, the novel recenters him at the expense of both subalterns and historicist portrayals of the nation.

The final, dystopic paragraph of Rushdie's novel illustrates how the paradox of Saleem's recentering through his prediction of annihilation is also a recentering of the elite individual:

> Yes, they will trample me under foot, the numbers marching one two three, four hundred million five hundred six, reducing me to specks of voiceless dust, just as, in all good time, they will trample my son who is not my son, and his son who will not be his [. . .] until a thousand and one midnights have bestowed their terrible gifts and a thousand and one children have died, because it is the privilege and curse of midnight's children to be both masters and victims of their times, to forsake privacy and to be sucked into the annihilating whirlpool of the multitudes, and to be unable to live or die in peace. (552)

The people, described in a Malthusian mode as an "annihilating whirlpool of the multitudes," are part of the problem, and they—not the state, as with the Emergency—will trample Saleem and his children in perpetuity, tearing them apart, rendering them voiceless, and robbing them of privacy and identity. Indeed, these multitudes are literally the Indian people: 600 million or so was the population of India at the time of the Emergency. The cadence of this long, one-sentence passage, punctuated with only commas, emphasizes the inexorable and definite nature of the future. The passage recalls Amitav Ghosh's comment about mood in the early years of the post-Emergency period, of which Indira Gandhi's assassination was both a reflection and a stimulant: "[I]t was a sense of something slipping loose, of a mooring coming untied somewhere within" ("Ghosts" 48). Saleem will be destroyed in this prophecy of doom, but whether or not he articulates this in despair, his ability to foresee it is the sign that he has arrived at the *truth* about the nation as an absolute and unredeemable failure—which is the implicit and unacknowledged *telos* of the postnational argument.

The epilogue thus produces not a fragmented narrator/subject but a supersubject: a seer and a soon-to-be martyr whose powerful voice, cast from beyond the formal ending of the novel, can describe his own (coming) annihilation in the first person. However, unlike Anglophone novels such as Ayi Kweh Armah's *The Beautyful Ones Are Not Yet Born* (1968), Ngugi wa Thiong'o's *A Grain of Wheat* (1967), Buchi Emecheta's *The Joys of Motherhood* (1979), and Roy's *The God of Small Things* (1997), this paradox develops not as a dialectic that opens the possibilities for transformation and egalitarianism but, rather, as an opposition between the realm of suffering (history, the nation) and the realm of freedom (storytelling, writing, reading). Whereas the subaltern-centered novels mentioned above seek to open up the spaces of subaltern victimization in colonial and postcolonial history in order to reveal spaces of possibility and alternative histories—even when there is no "happy ending"—a postnational text such as *Midnight's Children* produces an individualist model in which history and society conspire to crush the hopes of one solitary figure.

Indeed, the "multitudes" of the epilogue resolve, in an elitist direction, a more ambiguous representation of the people offered earlier in the novel. Before Saleem's birth, his mother, Amina, wanders into the slum area behind the General Post Office, a recurring locus of popular agency, creativity, and resistance in *Midnight's Children* that, as can be expected, ultimately fails to deliver any alternative to postcolonial crises. The representation of the people, focalized through Amina, emphasizes their diverse subjectivities and ideologies: they are victims, rendered invisible by class society; they are agents of progressive change and resistance, like Picture Singh and Parvati; and they are a potential base for reactionary ideas. All of these elements are invoked as, in the communalized climate of the mid-1940s, the Muslim Amina is attacked by a Hindu mob—and then protected by Das, a poor Hindu, who puts his life on the line by protecting her. Like the many leftist/liberal writers who have decried communal violence in South Asia, Rushdie carefully constructs this scene in order to record the presence of anticommunalism among the people. As readers of anticommunalist texts from the 1940s on will know, the sympathetic Das *must* be a Hindu in order for this novel by a Muslim writer to establish its own anticommunalist credentials.[16] The mob, too, is depicted as being human and malleable, gradually heeding Das's call to leave the pregnant woman alone. The elite Amina struggles with stereotypes about the slum, finding herself unable to look away, to adopt the "jungle-craft of gentility":

> It's like being surrounded by some terrible monster, a creature with heads and heads and heads; but she corrects herself, no, of course not a monster, these poor poor people—what then? A power of some sort, a force which does not know its strength, which has perhaps decayed into impotence through never having been used. [. . .] No, these are not decayed people, despite everything. (*Midnight's Children* 92)

Amina first invokes dehumanizing, generalized descriptions of the poor ("some terrible monster" and "decayed force"), and then appears to move toward a subaltern-centered position ("a force which does not know its own strength"). Amina's view might be seen as patronizing ("these poor poor people"), and the way in which she convinces herself that the poor are all right ("not a monster," "not decayed") recalls the ambiguities of Marlow in Joseph Conrad's *Heart of Darkness* (1902), when he decides that Africans are "not inhuman" after all (32). Nevertheless, there's a self-consciousness here that can be read as depicting the complex, mixed consciousness of elites in the face of suffering—echoing concerns that are scattered across many Indian English novels.

But the "multitudes" of the epilogue contain no such ambiguities, as they reinforce Amina's initial image of the subaltern as hydra, tearing the elite intellectual away from private, peaceful pursuits and making him "unable to live or die in peace." By the end of the novel, we are in the realm of prophecy and myth, where history exists not as the product of human agency and social circumstances but as a natural and timeless force. The Emergency crisis is just the latest installment of the endless strife that is engrained in Indian life. For Sahgal, the Emergency was, as we shall see, a perversion of Nehru's legacy of democracy and equality. Though *Rich Like Us* also remains an elite-centered text, it at least portrays the ways in which elites can engage in transforming the nation. For Rushdie, the perversion of the copy was inherent in the original, and he creatively and fully exploits the biographical aspect of the Nehru–Indira link to suggest the *organic* nature of postcolonial perversions and confusions. But the critique of the nation offered by the epilogue is completely alienated from the peoples who constitute that nation. This ahistorical view of power and time cannot but imagine the people as anything but passive victims or a symbol of destructive rage.

Despite Saleem's continuing national affiliations and the regret that tinges his voice, he is utterly alienated from and victimized by the nation and its people. In postnational cosmopolitanism, indeed, this alienation is experienced as a mark of freedom; after the sperectomy, Saleem is "no longer connected to history" (*Midnight's Children* 526) and is therefore free from the surveillance and coercion that are endemic to being a postcolonial subject. The ending emerges, thus, from a postnational perspective that positions itself against both national historiography and its would-be alternative: a "dissenting citizenship" that seeks a better, more egalitarian nation from within that nation itself (Maira 222). One might say that the homeless and genealogically displaced Saleem speaks with the voice of what Rushdie has elsewhere called "the migrant," "the only species of human being free of the shackles of nationalism" (qtd. in Krishnaswami 126).

When Rushdie talks about India in his essays and interviews, however, an explicit elite-centered nationalism emerges quite clearly, which I read as the real-life consequence of an ahistorical view of the nation's development. For instance, in the introduction to the anthology *Mirrorwork* (1997), Rushdie describes his pride in India's growing importance in the literary world: "The map of the world, in the standard Mercator projection, is not kind to India, making it look substantially smaller than, say, Greenland. On the map of world literature, too, India has been undersized for too long. This anthology celebrates the writers who are ensuring that, fifty years after India's independence, that age of obscurity is coming to an end" (xx). Rushdie's metaphor of the Mercator projection compares the size of India on the map with its size in the (Anglophone) literary world. We can imagine these two in relation to another map of the world in which India is no longer "undersized": one marking the rise of China, India, Brazil, and South Africa as Third World nation-states that have successfully implemented neoliberalist economics and subimperialist policies in the aftermath of the Cold War. Not only does Rushdie uncritically celebrate the problematic rise of India in this essay but, as we have seen in the first chapter, he also limits his notion of Indian literature to only English-language texts (viii). The India he imagines in deliberate terms seems to be peopled primarily of elites, with others providing local color. Other contemporary writers and intellectuals, such as Shashi

Tharoor, have taken their uncritical praise of India a step further, championing the economic liberalization and growth that allow a freer transfer and exchange of goods, visas, and novels to and from India as the culmination of the visions of 1947.[17] While cosmopolitan-elite location in and of itself does not determine novelistic representations and political ideology, interrogating the class politics of contemporary postcolonial writing can help explain the persistence of bourgeois-nationalist views among those whose fiction clearly critiques national mythologies.

Bourgeois Nationalism and the Marginalized Subject

The representation of the Emergency in *Rich Like Us* offers a sharp contrast to that of *Midnight's Children*. As we have seen from the previous chapter, the Emergency represented, for Sahgal and a layer of the politically committed intelligentsia of the 1970s and 1980s, the final betrayal of Nehruvian and Gandhian principles that were at the heart of the Indian national liberation movement. *Rich Like Us* openly indicts the nepotism, abrogation of civil liberties, pro-business policies, and brutality toward subalterns that emerged during the Emergency. More particularly, with its critical focus on the lives of businessmen and government officials, the novel skillfully depicts the internal logic by which pro-Emergency elites rationalized authoritarianism. Its central focus is on Sonali, a government civil servant who is dismissed for refusing to rubber-stamp the production of a fizzy drink called Happyola. The novel thus positions itself against the decline both of democracy and of the economic self-reliance that was a crucial principle of the early postcolonial decades. Sonali exposes capitalists such as Dev, who view the Emergency as "very good for business" (*Rich Like Us* 8), as well as the class of bureaucrats who look away while Dev, in collaboration with the Prime Minister's son, forges checks and makes off with public money for the production of a phantom "people's car."[18] Similarly, the importance given to the viewpoints of Rose, the working-class English woman who is Sonali's friend and Dev's stepmother, repeatedly brings to light the repression and violence that ordinary people face. Rose's befriending of the armless beggar, representing a solidarity across economic, racial, and cultural boundaries, teaches Sonali (and the cosmopolitan-elite audience) about the need to think, beyond one's own subject position, about the multiple emergencies engendered within postcolonial India.

Much more developed than in Sahgal's pre-Emergency novels, the characterization and narrative structure of *Rich Like Us* ask the implied audience to understand the Emergency against a much broader historical and ideological canvas. Sonali's metacritical reflections on history produce a grand narrative of Indian crisis and resistance from the nineteenth century to the 1970s. The question posed by Sahgal's *The Day in Shadow*—"[H]ow had such a future arisen out of such a past?" (125)—emerges here with much greater sharpness. Moving between first-person and third-person omniscient narrators in various chapters and focalizing the tale through Sonali and Rose, respectively, the novel examines Sonali from within and without, capturing the confusions and possibilities of the *namak-halaal,* activist intellectual at the time of the Emergency. Though the periodic use of the omniscient narrator complicates the first-person accounts by Sonali, the novel is unable to establish enough critical distance from her such that it might project the implied audience to a space beyond her elite dilemmas. As a result, the novel reads the Emergency and its antecedents extremely closely and critically but is silent about the processes by which it finally ends. *Rich Like Us* risks undermining its own call to action, reflecting, perhaps, the ideological ambiguities of a period in which Indira was both defeated and re-elected—a time that demonstrated the failure of the various political forces that opposed the Emergency to provide any alternative to it.[19]

Subaltern voices emerge in *Rich Like Us* but are finally subsumed within Sonali's elite-centered and/or individualist models of leadership and change. Certainly, the subaltern subject is crucial to the text as a material proof of the atrocities of the Emergency, and the novel powerfully testifies that, for the poor, "emergencies" are traceable indefinitely into the past and the future. The novel lambastes elites who take servants to get forced vasectomies in the name of national service. The subaltern speaks repeatedly in *Rich Like Us,* usually in Rose's brash, Cockney accent. Sonali herself references the power of mass, grassroots movements as a way to bring forth a nation that cuts across caste, religion, language, and class differences. And Sonali's first and only dialogue with the Beggar, at the very end of the novel, has the potential to transform the text. Even here, however, oppressed and marginalized figures are usually represented as passive victims of oppression who, at most, engage in heroic but isolated and ineffectual acts of resistance. Except on the level of communication with the audience, the only tangible result of Sonali's research into Indian resistance—against colonialism, reactionary traditions, and the Emergency—is that she secures prosthetic arms for the Beggar. Sonali is painfully aware of the smallness of the act, but, in the text's view, she has at least fought against the urge to "look away" from the nation's real problems. However, the structures of power are far too rigid: in terms of plot, the vibrant and anti-authoritarian Rose is killed by Dev for her efforts to bring his forgeries to light, and Sonali escapes from politics altogether by losing herself in the study of precolonial Indian art.

Until we come to the Beggar at the novel's conclusion, therefore, the subjectivity of Indian working-class and poor figures is available only from the outside. I understand and appreciate that the novel's project, accomplished in terms of both the narrative structure and the organization of characters, is precisely to speak through elite voices in an ironic mode in order to jar its elite audiences (implied and real) into self-reflection. The very title of the book, *Rich Like Us,* works by asking the implied audience to read against the grain of an uncritical elite perspective. But—and this is not a necessary consequence of such a project—the subalterns with whom Sonali and we are supposed to empathize are mostly flat characters, cardboard cutouts without psychological lives in a novel that consistently develops the interiority of elite characters *for the very purpose of revealing their elitism.* Within such a paradigm of representation and characterization, *Rich Like Us* is unable to portray the several instances of subaltern resistance that it offers as being anything but scattered, individualistic, and ineffectual. Undoubtedly, a narrative of resistance is formed that connects the Indian present to the Indian past, but its main focus is to instigate the elite protagonist's (and reader's) introspection about her responsibility to resist becoming complicit with authoritarianism. The focus on elite consciousness is not inevitably elitist, but becomes so when, in refusing to give depth to subaltern characters, the novel depicts their actions only through the rubric of stubbornness and spontaneity.

Meditating upon human nature, Sonali remembers an encounter she had witnessed, early in the period of martial law, between the police and a young man being dragged off to the forced-sterilization van: "In my fever I saw the boy in Connaught Place again and again, stumbling half-blind towards his glasses while the policeman wrenched him in the opposite direction. The boy at least had shouted, fought to free himself, while I, I had walked on" (*Rich Like Us* 30). In comparing the boy's shouts with her obliviousness and silence, Sonali condemns the well-educated and well-meaning elite nationalists who believe that their mission is to steer India in the path of democracy but who are actually "all taking part in a thinly disguised masquerade, preparing the stage for family rule" (25). These feelings of guilt are repeated when Sonali remembers how the Beggar also resisted vigorously when Nishi tried to force him into a sterilization van.

Later in the novel, Sonali gains inspiration from an old family manuscript that describes her great-grandfather's heroic but futile and belated
resistance against his family, which makes a *sati* of his widowed mother.
The chapter ends with Sonali's lyrical meditation on the heroism of all
the individual acts of resistance she has encountered, combining them
together:

> On a narrow parapet enclosing a funeral pyre I saw a boy of nineteen
> [her great-grandfather] balancing dangerously, [. . .] as he fought sav-
> agely to kill his mother's murderers. Not all of us are passive before cru-
> elty and depravity. He had not been. Nor the boy in Connaught Place
> who had struggled desperately all the way to the police van. Nor even
> Rose's beggar, undaunted by his armlessness, slipping and slithering from
> his tormentor's grasp while those with arms and legs walked mutely into
> captivity. And I fell asleep to dream of heroisms whose company I was
> scarcely fit to keep. (136)

Sonali's guilt recalls to us the reaction of Sanad, the protagonist of Sahgal's
A Time to Be Happy (1958), to the beggar girl standing outside the lighted
windows of the Chatterjis' mansion. That *Rich Like Us* has advanced
beyond *A Time to Be Happy* in terms of representing subalterns is clear:
despite the focus on elites, the later novel engages much more directly with
subaltern oppression. Nevertheless, the continuous re-emergence of such
scenes of elite guilt speaks both to Sahgal's interest in questions of class
and oppression and to her elite-centered models of change. Sahgal's protagonists are able to see oppression but find it difficult to do more than to
remark on their own futility.

Jasbir Jain sees the disparate, individual acts that are scattered through
Rich Like Us as an expression of the idea that "revolutions can be of
different kinds and levels, but they are happening all the time" ("The
Emperor's New Clothes" 33–34). The point is well taken: the narrative
of resistance produced here allows Sahgal to 1) expand the problem of
power beyond the Emergency period; 2) take up questions of gender, class,
national, and state oppression/repression at once; and 3) mark Indians of
all classes and backgrounds as potential agents of change. By representing
the postcolonial nation as open to historical analysis and transformation,
the text is certainly *namak-halaal,* and its nationalism—in this post-Emergency period—is definitely a nuanced and critical one. But rather than
raising isolated acts to the level of "revolutions," we need to ask what
it means that such acts are depicted against a background of generalized

submissiveness. In the passage above, for instance, the boy who struggles is one out of a group of eight, the Beggar resists but the rest of the servants "[walk] mutely into captivity" (*Rich Like Us* 136), and Sonali's great-grandfather asserts his anger against an entire extended family that is complicit in the performance of *sati* that murdered his mother. Repeatedly, it appears that the novel aims to foreground the need for *individual* heroism as a counterpoint to collective apathy. Such models of individual heroism are connected to the moralism of Gandhian politics, a key component of how Sahgal conceptualizes resistance in India albeit within her Nehruvian and promodern framework.

Significantly, Gandhian strategies of resistance give the highest value to the moral and ethical integrity of the individual leader, but depicting mass action is necessary for revealing the leader's effectiveness. *Rich Like Us* follows suit in its portrayal of the famous mass meeting on the Ramlila grounds just hours before the Emergency, displaying both the potential and the limits of subaltern representation in Sahgal's *namak-halaal* perspective. The rally is Gandhian in two ways: it is replete with the iconography of Gandhian slogans, images, and tactics, and its aim is to conceptualize the fight against the Emergency and "modern authoritarianism" as a repetition of the anticolonial struggle (*Rich Like Us* 23). Sonali notes that the huge banner behind the leader of the meeting, JP (an allusion to the leader J. P. Narayan), says, "Vacate the throne for the people are coming"—a slogan from the national liberation struggle now being used against "another aspirant to imperial power" (156). The puns offered by Indira's name and identity provide other critical slogans—"India is Indira and Indira is India" and "From Mahatma to Madam"—and signify authoritarian rule as a deviation from the goals of the independence movement. While Sonali despairs that the anticolonial and postcolonial contexts might be too different—"[t]here was nothing anyone could do now, no barricades, no open defiance that could not be wiped out in minutes by the armor of a modern state" (156)—she confirms that Gandhian tactics were the only option: "When the Constitution becomes null and void by the act of a dictator, and the armor of a modern state confronts you, *satyagraha* is the only way to keep your self-respect" (157). Gandhism thus provides a framework for both public and personal resistance to the Emergency in *Rich Like Us*— and the *only* framework for it. It allows for a resistance that gives a high place to individualistic acts by elites, such as resigning from government jobs, and mass actions that remain in the bounds of a Gandhian struggle.

Different historical studies have revealed the top-down and elitist nature of Gandhian strategies in the anticolonial movement even while giving due place to its historical and mass impact.[20] The fact that the writings of Gandhi and Jawaharlal Nehru concerning democratic rights and freedom of the press under British rule were banned during the Emergency speaks volumes about the radicalism of those writings (Ali, *Indian Dynasty* 185). The Gandhian JP was seen as a threat to the government, for instance, because his call for "total revolution" in the 1970s—for complete decentralization and local self-government—had mass backing. The government resorted to the repressive Emergency precisely because the movements, Gandhian and otherwise, did not back down in the face of tremendous police pressure. Though the Gandhian framework failed to open spaces for independent subaltern action, its symbols and language enabled a resistance that reminds us how powerful the anticolonial movement really was. It is from this worthy perspective that the novel attempts to grapple with subalternity.

The Many Voices of Subalternity

In terms of its narrative structure, and its development of character and voice, the subaltern figure to which *Rich Like Us* is most committed is Rose, and understanding her character will allow us to approach the Beggar, whom Rose befriends. Rose's importance is established through her centrality to the narrative progression. While she is never granted the status of first-person character narrator, as Sonali is in several chapters, the sections of the novel that feature third-person narrators orient themselves around Rose's viewpoint more than anyone else's—including Sonali's when she appears in them as a character. The alternation between the perspectives of Sonali and Rose reveals how the novel values the exchange between different subaltern voices, allowing them to shape one another; the vast gap between the space given to *Rich Like Us*'s Rose and *Midnight's Children*'s Padma illuminates how much more committed the former text is to representing voices from below. Rose's version of "down-to-earthery" is not mocked but offers a critique of the Emergency, and complements and tempers Sonali's larger and more abstract musings about history, the state of the nation, and democracy. Rose's interventions reveal a sharp class analysis; they function as a vibrant counterdiscourse that challenges Dev and rips through the façade of the Emergency as a benevolent, necessary dictatorship.

Jain goes so far as to suggest that the perspectives of Sonali and Rose form a split narrative, that the two are fully and equally complementary

("The Emperor's New Clothes" 34). Indeed, the text often seems to make Rose's view *more* important than Sonali's, for it is Rose whom Sonali approaches for support and clarity. But no matter how crucial Rose is to the novel, her voice cannot be simply equated to Sonali's, whose cosmopolitan-elite perspective is the touchstone by which the entire novel measures itself. While Rose's gut-level understanding of events is valorized by the novel, whether on the level of plot (advising Sonali) or narrative (the text's frequent solicitation of Rose's voice through free indirect style), her ideas are explicitly shown to be unsophisticated and in need of constant reinterpretation by Sonali. The hierarchy is fleshed out further, and in surprising directions, when we recognize that Rose is more important in terms of voice than other Indians who are marked as being oppressed and marginalized. She acts as the conduit between Indian elites and Indian subalterns; she conveys to Sonali and other elites the plight of those such as Kishori Lal and the Beggar. Sonali, the main narrative voice for communication with the implied audience, is thus structured as being once removed from Rose and twice removed from Kishori Lal and the Beggar, the only subaltern voices in the text that are ethnically South Asian. The place of Rose within this hierarchy of representations reveals Sahgal's awareness of the complexity of mediation in eliciting marginalized voices. The question is whether this attempt to avoid the ventriloquism of subaltern voices ends up suppressing those voices.

How should we read the fact that the spokesperson for ordinary people in post-Emergency India is a working-class immigrant from England? Indeed, it is an ethnic representation of the indigenous Indian subaltern that is most conspicuously absent from *Rich Like Us,* in stark contrast to the abundance of ethnicized representations of elites (for instance, in the careful categorizing of differences between those of Panjabi, Marathi, Kashmiri, and Bengali heritage) as well as the constant emphasis on the particularities of Rose's working-class language, dress, and mannerisms. Undoubtedly, Rose is a fascinating character because her presence among elite Westernized Indians problematizes the neat binary oppositions that might pair nationality with language and/or social status (English/Indian, English-speaking/non-English-speaking, rich/poor). On the level of plot, Rose allows this Indian English novel to represent a working-class character who 1) speaks English (avoiding the question of translation and yet another level of mediation), 2) mingles with Indian elites (because of her family connection to Dev), and 3) communicates with marginalized Indians (since she has also experienced class oppression). By constructing Rose as an *Indian* character—one who lives in India and comes to oppose

British rule—Sahgal emphasizes international solidarity even as she remains concerned with the national space. At the same time, the displacement of ethnically South Asian characters by Rose allows the novel to critique the Indian elite without having to imagine an indigenous alternative. Rose fills in a gap in the iconography of the lower class, but one effect of this is a structural inability to represent the indigenous subaltern as an active agent in history.[21]

Certainly, Rose allows *Rich Like Us* to go much further in "correcting" Indian elite behavior than any previous Sahgal novel. Simply put, Rose performs on a local level the acts of resistance that, Sonali recognizes, Indian elites need to perform on the national level. As an outsider, Rose is disruptive of the status quo. It is Rose who saves the Beggar from forced sterilization, when she "[bears] down on Nishi and physically restrain[s] her, breaking the fanatical chain of command" (*Rich Like Us* 81). It is Rose who prevents the self-immolation of Mona, her distraught and alienated co-wife, upon the death of their husband, Ram—accomplishing, as it were, the task that Sonali's great-grandfather could not when trying to save his mother from *sati*. In every aside and gesture, Rose brings to the novel a consistent class analysis through memories of her family in Britain and her critiques on the level of everyday life, such as cynically observing that her Indian family insisted on giving a venerable servant with "a grey beard and side whiskers" the name of "boy" (57). However, by virtue of being structurally isolated from others of her class and experience, Rose is locked within the paradigm of liberal individualism. She is simply the good person who always fights the good fight, and her analyses, whenever they are not local and practical, get lost in a utopian imaginary. Thus, Rose's rescue of the Beggar from sterilization is represented not as one example of many such acts, but as a single, symbolic act of resistance against the repression of the Emergency.

In the end, Rose is the stereotype of how oppressed classes engage in politics: instinctively political but never self-consciously so. For instance, she constantly depoliticizes situations in the name of "being real." At one point Sonali phones her in disgust after a party with Delhi elites in which "the capital's professional elite gave a demonstration of what the Third World's upper crust talks about when its country's democratic institutions have just been engulfed by a tidal wave" (*Rich Like Us* 85). But the dialogue is emptied of political content after Rose provides her "young and raw" class analysis (85–86). The episode concludes with a romanticization of anti-intellectualism, though it appears as a critique of educated elites and intellectuals: "[Rose] wasn't a great reader [. . .] She didn't need to be. I had seen the great readers at dinner today" (86). The political message is an anti-elitist one, that reading books does not create critical perspectives, but the way in which this (true) statement is made actually risks fetishizing Rose's lack of political knowledge. The very attributes that allow Rose to intervene on the behalf of the people, her class identity and aspects of her vibrant personality, function as limitations on her ability to make change. After rescuing the Beggar all she can do is gaze at him from the bedroom window and "picture him healed and whole, walking upright, running and leaping, and each nightfall becoming exultantly whole once again by the light of the stars" (81). Even Rose imagines resistance and agency in fabulous terms. Rose's naturalized socialism—her natural reactions being always aligned with a left-populist stance—remains unsystematic and unrepeatable precisely because its motivations are portrayed as being spontaneous and nonideological.[22]

It is only near the end of the novel that Rose formulates systematic connections between her various instinctual critiques and the happenings during the Emergency. At a dinner party, her final one, Rose inadvertently links together her functions as a communicator of the stories of the oppressed and a critic of the Emergency with her long, private alienation as an English wife in a polygamous family situation. The series of events that leads to her murder is initiated when Rose ridicules Leila's concern over exposing her servants to love scenes in foreign movies: "They're used to rape, aren't they, so a bit of love making on the screen can't be very 'ard for them to get used to" (*Rich Like Us* 216). She proceeds to narrate to a stunned, elite audience how the police had raped the Beggar's wife and the other women of his village. In the process, we learn to value Rose for building up a relationship with the Beggar, in her broken Hindi, in order to learn the story. But the inebriated Rose unwittingly reveals that she knows about the secret "people's car" project that Dev is involved in. Frightened by Dev's agitated reaction to her queries, Rose wonders whether, at age sixty-three, she can fight the unjust activities of her own stepson. However, the novel has other plans for Rose as she sits in quasi-mystical realization, "as relaxed as a yogi in her cross legged posture, her thoughts beautifully clear" (219). The text martyrs Rose at the very moment that she is "in the act of getting up," rising from her crouched, meditative position (220). Although Rose's role throughout the text has been to combat Hindu obscurantism and the idealization of self-suffering Hindu womanhood through mythological figures such as Sita, she is finally molded into the figure of Sita, realizing, too late, that she had been "accepting" of oppression all her life (220).[23] While Rose's murder serves as a dire critique of the Emergency and its supporters, who would even resort to matricide to make their profits, it also marks the closing-off of the only possibility the novel offered for resistance: the action of a well-intentioned individual.

Like Rose, though in less dramatic ways, Kishori Lal (called "K.L." in the novel) also represents a subaltern voice that is quickly enveloped by the text. K.L. is consistent in his criticisms of the Emergency and, complementing Rose, effectively brings reporting of Indian resistance into the novel, even though he operates from an ideological mishmash: a Gandhian yet an atheist, a supporter of the Hindu organization Jan Sangh, a failed researcher who now sells bathroom cleaning supplies. K.L. is the storyteller of the more general resistance to the Emergency: relating news, for instance, about the anti-Madam student movement in Bihar and of the police *lathi* charges that smashed it (*Rich Like Us* 168). Through K.L.'s meeting with a Naxalite student in jail, the third-person narrator also evokes the history of Indira's suppression of the young student and peasant Maoists in the early seventies (Ali, *Indian Dynasty* 179). Neither the student, with his surrealist play on the Emergency, nor K.L., with his psychological readings of Hitler and Indira, provides any real alternatives, but K.L.'s steadfastness represents some positive model of change. His meeting with Rose, in which she converses with him and attempts to translate the language of subaltern politics to Nishi, is quite promising in terms of producing a reading of history "from below." Unfortunately and inexplicably, K.L.'s story ends with his symbolically powerful but ambiguous decision to stay in jail until the Naxalite student is freed (*Rich Like Us* 216).

It is only after Rose's death toward the end of the book that *Rich Like Us* finally brings the implied audience face-to-face with the Beggar. Until that time, he simply appears, at a distance, as the representation of victimization. He speaks to Rose, but the content of those dialogues is rarely reported (e.g., 68). It is only after the subaltern spokesperson is killed that he speaks for himself, that he appears as a character with a voice for the first time. The Beggar tells his story to the distraught Sonali, who had come to find him in memory of Rose and emphasizes not only victimization but resistance: his arms had been chopped off by his landlords and village leaders in order to suppress a two-year resistance by sharecroppers to keep their share of the harvest. He displays, as Rose had done, a clear class analysis of the situation in postcolonial India—and opens the door to non-Gandhian tales of struggle and a critique of postcolonial India *before* Indira Gandhi. Searching for answers, Sonali asks whether the sharecroppers had taken any legal recourse or asked the help of any political parties. "It is the landlord's *raj* [rule] in my village, record or no record," replies that Beggar. Viciously, he adds, "They [the politicians] are all landlords at heart" (227). The comments spur Sonali to recognize the vast distinction between her idea of freedom and that implied by the Beggars' discourse, thinking, "They, them, the ruling class on one side, the ruled on the other. Power had changed hands, but what else had changed where he lived? If ever there had been an emergency, it was this" (227). Sonali realizes that her "saga of peaceful change" in India, engendered by the end of the Emergency, was not only ending but was false, like a "macabre joke" in light of such daily horrors (228). "The Emergency" is cut down to size, as it were, in light of the recognition of so many emergencies.

The Beggar's perspective actually challenges that of Sonali and has the potential to transform her nationalist notions on a fundamental level. Like the voices of Zirigu and Seta in Ama Ata Aidoo's "For Whom Things Did Not Change" (1970), articulating a critique of decolonization that points to the continuing realities of class oppression, the Beggar's invocation of multiple and ongoing emergencies directs us beyond 1975 to the betrayal of 1947 itself—the Indian politicians were complicit in the "landlord *raj*" even though the British Raj was gone. That *Rich Like Us* achieves this level of interaction with class realities pushes it far beyond the politics of texts such as *Midnight's Children,* which refuse to give any credibility to subaltern voices or to relate to the nation as a historical, malleable entity. For both the politically aware reader and for one who ignores, as Sonali had, all but the largest emergencies, Sonali's conversation with the Beggar gives a glimpse of the larger context of postcolonial suffering upon which the Emergency rests.

Although the Beggar's voice is loud and clear here, the way in which the dialogue is represented as a whole continues to operate within a representational paradigm that minimizes his agency. While Sonali's questions do elicit important responses from the Beggar, his words are constantly interrupted and undermined, filtered through Sonali's reflections on them. The Beggar becomes mostly a participant in and catalyst for Sonali's dialogue with herself. Indeed, the exchange itself does not occur in the narrative present but is ensconced within Sonali's retelling of it, further minimizing the Beggar's voice. Sonali seems, once again, more interested in the difference between herself and the Beggar than in integrating his severe criticism of 1947 into her own understanding of it. This is the context in which Sonali embarks on the individualist solution of buying the Beggar artificial hands—after which he drops out of the story and Sonali's life. The Beggar's main role in the novel is to hover over the text and outside Dev's house as a reminder of the text's critique of the Emergency and the haughtiness of the rich. In their eyes, the Beggar means nothing: he appears to various elite and apolitical characters as a blur, a shadow, an insect. In contrast, the moment of contact with sympathetic figures such as Rose and Sonali reveals that the Beggar has a distinct story, a voice, and a history of agency. And yet, the text cannot give us the Beggar except as a beggar. We can only imagine, leaping away from the scope of the narrative, what this nameless man looked like in the moment of revolt, alongside other share-croppers, against the landowners—whether these moments be dramatic and public (when they seized their rightful share of the harvest) or subtle and internal (when they challenged one another to resist rather than accept their day-to-day experience of oppression).

The omission is not simply a matter of oversight or choice but, I con-tend, is constitutive of the novel's paradigm of class and nation. Elite resis-tance appears in vivid detail and subaltern resistance is relatively obscured, even when these elites are concerned with class inequality. Sonali admits, much before meeting the Beggar, that "[w]e [civil servants] knew this was no emergency," that India's real emergencies have been "Partition, war, famine, refugees on a scale so monumental it had made all disasters till then and many after to look like minor migrations" (*Rich Like Us* 25). Placing the Emergency in the context of the larger narrative of postcolo-nial crises raises fundamental questions about the nation-building project, especially along the divisions of class: "Something was wrong if the fat of the land had settled high up instead of melting and trickling down, if poverty had grown and multiplied" (150). However, the inability to think beyond the limits of bourgeois democracy causes confusion. Sonali fluctu-ates between some optimistic thinking ("some really revolutionary changes might be ahead" [152]) and pessimism ("What if there was a collective will to cowardice . . . ?" [30]). By the time the Emergency ends, and Son-ali admits that "I hadn't realized that the emergency could ever be over" (233), the book also ends, with no attention paid to the numerous other emergencies it has invoked. Sonali's final entry into the privatized world of the academic study certainly has a critical value: much of the text is concerned with the way in which authoritarianism erases and twists his-tory, and *Rich Like Us* rightfully gives importance to the recovery of radi-cal stories as an act of resistance—very much like Guha and the Subaltern Studies project, which also begins in the early 1980s. Nevertheless, the ending of the novel lends itself to a reading of Sonali's academic work as a kind of escapism, as it drops by the wayside the novel's earlier insights about the emergencies that would continue to exist—at the expense of those at the bottom of hierarchies of power.

Nationalism, Postnationalism, Internationalism

Reading *Midnight's Children* and *Rich Like Us* together has allowed a more specific differentiation between *namak-halaal* and postnational cosmopolitanisms, but also an understanding of where they meet. *Namak-halaal* cosmopolitan narratives construct ethical and political universes in which the implied authors employ characterization and voice to exhort the implied audience to support, and potentially engage in, projects of national regeneration—whether or not they are nationalist. But postnational texts explicitly subvert *namak-halaal* narratives, often emphasizing the impossibility of national regeneration through the disintegration of narrative cohesion. While *namak-halaal* texts encourage closure on the level of truth and knowledge, usually by minimizing the gap between the implied audience and the consciousness of the narrator and/or protagonist, postnational texts emphasize the inability to achieve such closure, forcing the implied audience to remain nervous about its relationship to the narrator and/or protagonist. Postnational cosmopolitanisms explicitly reject "national progress" as a *telos* and, often, teleology itself—though this determined rejection itself becomes the goal they seek. Both sets of texts can be metafictional and complex, but *namak-halaal* ones are more concerned, ultimately, with pointing toward future possibilities and the recovery of national/local spaces. We can trace the desire for the nation in postnational cosmopolitanisms too, as expressed through nostalgia, disappointment about the failures of decolonization, and a desire for wholeness. But the tendency in these texts is to foreground tropes of migrancy and exile, valuing the experience of the cosmopolitan-elite who locates herself/himself outside of the nation while speaking on behalf of it. When texts such as Amitav Ghosh's *The Shadow Lines,* for instance, look back to the nation, they tend to grasp it mainly as an abstraction, a set of stories that violent nationalists (often crude, sexist, and communalist to boot) impose on other people's stories. While this novel does critique a certain jet-setting cosmopolitanism, whether British or Indian, it continues to thrive on binary oppositions based on location: national location is paired with narrowness and chauvinism, while moving between nations is associated with liberated and radical thinking. Needless to say, shifts and changes do occur within the work of authors I have called "postnational" as most of whom are still alive and writing. Ghosh's *The Glass Palace* (2000), for example, still shares certain misgivings about the national project—but in impressively staging the shifting political consciousness of its central characters through colonial and postcolonial South and Southeast Asia, the novel offers a much more complicated sense of how national identities and affiliations work(ed) in relation to class, race, and ethnicity. Texts like *The Glass Palace* signal the dynamism of each author in the genre, his or her creativity chafing against prevailing "structures of feeling" in order to produce something new. *Decentering Rushdie* seeks to alert readers to such nuanced developments, not to fix the interpretations of specific authors or modes of writing.

By suggesting that *Midnight's Children* and *Rich Like Us* both invoke subaltern voices only to drown them out, I hope to have shown that neither *namak-halaal* nor postnational cosmopolitanisms ought to be regarded as being politically progressive or leftist in and of themselves. Postcolonial Indian English literature, in general, has always aimed to position itself as a radical literature: challenging Eurocentrism and imperialist attitudes, critiquing indigenous ruling elites, championing subaltern agency, or poking holes in elite rhetoric that *claims* to speak for the people. Produced in the context of a historic victory against colonial authoritarianism, this fiction seeks to be subaltern-centered: sometimes embracing the nation, sometimes rejecting it. However, as my analysis reveals, Indian English novels and the cosmopolitan-elite contexts in which they are produced and consumed have tended toward elite-centered worldviews. While both *Midnight's Children* and *Rich Like Us* open spaces for subaltern characters to voice criticisms of national crises, neither develops these characters as fully as elite chatacters, eventually turning to fairly mainstream modes of stereotyping and romanticization.

The critique of bourgeois nationalism as elitist is familiar in Postcolonial Studies, but the failures of postnationalism as an alternative have been less apparent. As Guha argues, for example, nationalist historiography fails to explain the mass involvement of the Indian people in nationalist activities, portraying explosive events either "negatively, as a law and order problem" or "positively, if at all, as a response to the charisma of certain elite leaders" ("On Some Aspects" 39). The postnationalists, in response to this elitism, not only expose particular nationalist myths of harmonious communities but also claim that the very process of producing coherent narratives and subjects around the nation is responsible for marginalization and oppression, ostracizing those who are not imagined as normative subjects. While this position often leads to a deep criticism of imperialism, Orientalism, and mainstream-nationalist discourse, writing off the nation as "yet another master-narrative" also means dismissing real struggles of subalterns who have used the nation as a space for cohesion and identity. To cite Kumkum Sangari's work in a related context, writing from postnational positions

> gloomily disempowers the "nation" as an enabling idea and relocates the impulses for change as everywhere and nowhere [. . .]. Such skepticism does not take into account either the fact that the postmodern preoccupation with the crisis of meaning is not everyone's crisis (even in the West) or that there are different modes of de-essentialization which are socially and politically grounded and mediated by separate perspectives, goals, and strategies for change in other countries. (183–84)

Valorizing "everywhere" as a space for resistance has often gone alongside recognizing the achievement of resistance "nowhere." Sangari ironically recasts the postmodernist rejection of the nation as a universalist *telos* that suppresses difference and specificity, failing to recognize that "the postmodern preoccupation with the crisis of meaning is not everyone's crisis."

In this manner, not only do postnational critiques of national history tend to elide the distinction between "progressive and retrograde forms of nationalism with reference to particular histories," but they ignore the "even more vexed question of how progressive and retrograde elements may be (and often are) combined with particular nationalist trajectories" (A. Ahmad, *In Theory* 38). Nationalism and national liberation are complex entities that cannot be labeled, a priori, either "progressive" (anti-imperialist) or "retrograde" (pro-imperialist) without reference to their historical specificity and a whole range of sociopolitical contexts. What do we make of Kosovar Albanians' legitimate demands for autonomy in the mid-1990s after the Kosovo Liberation Army becomes a pawn of the CIA? How do we read the anti-apartheid struggle in South Africa in light of the current neoliberal and subimperialist policies of the African National Congress?

No reductionist attitude toward these historic and contemporary demands for national sovereignty can address the needs of the ordinary people in these spaces. Arundhati Roy's comments on the Iraqi resistance to U.S. occupation in a 2004 speech in San Francisco reveal the complexity of the problem:

> Like most resistance movements, [the resistance in Iraq] combines a motley range of assorted factions. Former Baathists, liberals, Islamists, fed-up collaborationists, communists, etc. Of course, it is riddled with oppor-

tunism, local rivalry, demagoguery, and criminality. But if we are only going to support pristine movements, then no resistance will be worthy of our purity. This is not to say that we shouldn't ever criticize resistance movements. Many of them suffer from a lack of democracy, from the iconization of their "leaders," a lack of transparency, a lack of vision and direction. But most of all they suffer from vilification, repression, and lack of resources. Before we prescribe how a pristine Iraqi resistance must conduct their secular, feminist, democratic, nonviolent battle, we should shore up our end of the resistance by forcing the U.S. and its allies to withdraw from Iraq. ("Tide? Or Ivory Snow?")

Roy defends the Iraqi resistance not by simplifying the world into black-and-white categories but by emphasizing its complexity and heterogeneity against (left-secular) desires for "pristine," uncomplicated struggles. Her complex understanding of the situation is self-reflexive about location ("we should shore up our end"), notes the difficulty of fact-finding (media "vilification"), and reflects on how material contexts shape movements ("repression," "lack of resources"). Roy does not sugarcoat the resistance but, in presenting it as the product of historical forces, rewrites the demand for purity as an ahistorical and apolitical move.

As in her essay on the Kashmiri uprising against the Indian state in 2008, thus, Roy recognizes the liberatory and subaltern-centered aspects of the Iraq resistance even as she remains critical of reactionary elements.[24] Roy is no nationalist, but her critical support for movements around democracy and self-determination—even when they speak in the name of the nation—recalls the positions of anticolonial activists and theorists across the twentieth century who sharply criticized bourgeois-nationalism even while arguing that "[i]t is at the heart of national consciousness that international consciousness lives and grows" (Fanon 248). Recognizing what Roy calls the "motley range" of resistance in national movements has a long history in leftist internationalism. In a 1916 article on anti-imperialism and national liberation, for instance, V. I. Lenin argues that anti-imperialism is always marked by a mixture of all kinds of movements and groups, including "revolts by small nations in the colonies and in Europe [. . .] revolutionary outbursts by a section of the petty bourgeoisie *with all its prejudices* [. . .] movement[s] of the politically non-conscious proletarian and semi-proletarian masses against oppression by the landowners, the church, and the monarchy [. . .]" (190, original italics). For instance, the debates between Lenin and M. N. Roy in the Second Congress of the Comintern in 1920, on how Indian Communists ought to relate to the anticolonial movement under the leadership of M. K. Gandhi, offer valuable historical and theoretical reflections on what an international defense of anticolonial nationalism has meant in the past.[25] The underlying conviction here has been well expressed by Aijaz Ahmad:

> [T]he socialist project is essentially universalist in character, and socialism, even as a transitional mode, cannot exist except on a transnational basis; yet the *struggle* for even the prospect of that transition presumes a national basis, in so far as the already existing structures of the nation-state are a fundamental reality of the terrain on which actual class conflicts take place. (*In Theory*, 317–18)[26]

The continuing story of subaltern struggle in the postcolonial world requires that we embrace the "motley range" of resistance *within* the nation-state in order to better understand the contexts from which postcolonial literatures have emerged and toward which they inevitably look back.

5

"Naaley. Tomorrow"

Suffering and Redemption in *The God of Small Things*

> But it appeared that the driver of the truck [that killed the boy] had neither brakes on his car nor a driving license. He belonged to the new, rich civil servant class whose salaries had become fantastically high after independence. [. . .] And thus progress, development, and a pre-occupation with status and living-standards first announced themselves to the village. It looked like being an ugly story with many decapitated bodies on the main road.
>
> —Bessie Head, "The Wind and a Boy" (1977)

> She turned to say it once again: "*Naaley*."
> Tomorrow.
>
> —Arundhati Roy, *The God of Small Things* (1997)

Given Arundhati Roy's stature within today's international movements against corporate globalization and naked imperialism, it is shocking to remember that her Booker Prize–winning novel, *The God of Small Things* (1997), was initially met with a wave of criticism and even hostility from prominent sections of the Indian Left, particularly those associated with the Communist Party of India (Marxist). Indian Communists emphatically and publicly denounced the novel for explicitly mocking E. M. S. Namboodiripad, the late CPI(M) leader, for depicting Communists as being unmindful of caste oppression, and for peddling "bourgeois decadence" through its representations of "sexual anarchy" ("EMS Attacks").[1] Leading the charge against Roy, E. M. S. himself declared that the novel's critique of Communism was central to why it was "welcomed by the captains of the industry of bourgeois literature in the world" (Jose). Similarly, then-Kerala Chief Minister E. K. Nayanar attributed the novel's winning of the Booker Prize to its Western-oriented, "anti-Communist venom"

This chapter expands on my article "Beyond 'Anticommunism.'"

("Nayanar Pours Scorn"). Indeed, Aijaz Ahmad's article in the August 1997 issue of the CPI(M)-friendly *Frontline* magazine, by far the most nuanced of such critiques, had already taken Roy to task for reproducing the "hostility toward the Communist movement [that] is now fairly common among radical sections of the intelligentsia, in India and abroad" ("Reading" 103).[2] Specifically, Ahmad criticized what he regarded as the conservative implications of the novel's representation of sexuality "as the final realm of both Pleasure and of Truth" (104) and "a sufficient mode for overcoming real social oppressions" (107).

However, the post-Booker recognition of Roy's political writing—beginning with "The Greater Common Good"—and her incessant defense of villagers and activists opposing the Narmada Valley Development Project, disrupted any assimilation of Roy into the category of the disengaged postcolonial writer.[3] To their credit, the CPI(M) and the editors and columnists of *Frontline* quickly recognized the radicalism of Roy's political essays despite their earlier criticisms of her novel; "The Greater Common Good," in fact, first appeared in *Frontline*.[4] The rest of the story is, I imagine, quite familiar to those following global leftist political discourse since the late 1990s. Fiercely critical of Western nations for corporate globalization and imperialist wars—but also of postcolonial states for their complicity in the neoliberal project—Roy has developed a unique perspective and emerged as one of the most prominent public intellectuals of the international Left in the first decade of the twenty-first century. What is perhaps most appealing about Roy's political essays, besides their lyrical and confident style, is a theoretical and political framework flexible enough to allow her to comment insightfully on any range of issues, including women's rights, environmentalism, globalization, war and resistance to occupation, caste and racial oppression, and democratic rights.

This chapter asserts that Roy's novel and her political work, far from moving in divergent directions, are bound together by a political paradigm that is unmistakably progressive and leftist. While the genre of the essay allows this leftist voice to emerge more explicitly and directly than that of the novel, *The God of Small Things* allows for a criticism of the status quo that is as devastating as that of the essays—despite either the CPI(M)'s censure or the valorization and appropriation of the novel by the mainstream publishing and academic markets in the West.[5] *The God of Small Things*, simply put, is an anti-authoritarian, antipatriarchal novel, construing a narrative of subaltern struggle and survival in postcolonial India. Like Roy's essays, interviews, and speeches, the novel approaches the world from a perspective that illuminates the role that ordinary people and "small" lives play in history and society, fighting against the attempts of official, "big" histories to suppress their voices. The CPI(M)-affiliated criticism—mired in a nondialectical critical methodology—cannot see this, as it assigns, a priori, a negative political value to Roy's location (as an English-language writer), the novel's reception (its popularity in the West), its explicit statements (criticism of the CPI(M)), and/or its themes (e.g., the liberatory potential of sexuality and desire). The subsequent celebration of Roy's essays, indeed, implicitly employs the same method though with a different result: since the *Frontline* editors broadly *agree* with the explicit statements in the essays, they champion the texts and, once again, fail to analyze the political paradigms underlying them.

In order to properly assess postcolonial texts such as *The God of Small Things,* Marxist and/or political critics need to refute the tautological exercises that make sure writers have the "right" passport and home address, the "right" political affiliations, and the "right" level of skepticism about postmodern aesthetics. We need to develop, rather, a nuanced understanding of the relationship between location, ideology, and aesthetics in which the three categories are not conflated and the meaning of a given text is not automatically determined by one of them. In terms of Roy, for instance, this means recognizing some complexities, including that 1) the leftist essays and speeches are produced from the same elite location as the novel itself, 2) the appropriation of postcolonial novels in English into the global marketplace does not necessarily mean that each of these novels exhibits the values of that marketplace, and 3) not all writers who employ postmodern aesthetics (multivocal texts, nonlinear narratives, magical realism) necessarily replicate the antihistoricist values of postmodern epistemology. If we allow the narrative to breathe and speak its mind, as it were, it becomes clear that far from being a sign of a cosmopolitan-elite anticommunism, the criticism of the CPI(M) in the universe constructed by *The God of Small Things* is actually a marker of its leftist politics. The Marxist literary critic ought to recognize this and hold back from allowing her or his own position on the CPI(M) to overdetermine the analysis. I am not therefore discouraging questions about political ideology, such as "What do we make of Roy's criticism of Indian Communism?" but arguing that they should not be allowed to overwhelm an analysis of the novel as a literary work.[6]

It is worth recognizing that the CPI(M)'s readings represent only one voice in a much larger chorus of critics and commentators who have also tended to read *The God of Small Things* as the fulfillment of the (postmodernist) ideological and aesthetic project launched by Salman Rushdie's

Midnight's Children (1980). In 1997, against the backdrop of the fiftieth anniversary of Indian independence, the Western and Indian mainstream media placed Roy's Booker alongside Rushdie's, reading them as signs of India's rising place in the post–Cold War world.[7] Many scholars since then, though skeptical of the global marketing of Indian English writing, have paired Rushdie and Roy together as participants in a common, *radical* project: disrupting Orientalist and nationalist metanarratives; revealing the "hybridity" of postcolonial subjects and contexts; highlighting intra-national divisions of gender, sexuality, and class; and questioning classic nationalist and leftist discourses. The CPI(M) readings belong to a third group of readers who have associated *The God of Small Things* with today's postmodern writing. In their view, such texts exhibit a cosmopolitan detachment from the nation as their "mastery over the current idiom of metropolitan meta-language of narrative ensures favorable reception in the global centers of publication and criticism" (M. Mukherjee, *Perishable* 179). Despite significant differences, then, these readers have arrived at a consensus: *The God of Small Things* ought to be read alongside novels such as *Midnight's Children* because of demonstrable similarities in genre, form, cosmopolitan-elite location, and Western reception.

However, I suggest, *The God of Small Things* represents an exception to the contemporary Indian English novel and its postnational cosmopolitanism, hearkening back, instead, to the *namak-halaal* sensibilities and frameworks of the early postcolonial period. Though the novel is magical-realist text, its narrative strategies are directed against postmodernist epistemologies that emphasize the impossibility of constructing cohesive counternarratives of truth. *The God of Small Things*'s engagement with and sharp critique of postcolonial Indian modernity flow from a perspective and narrative practice that both mourns the historical, cultural, and geographical loss of indigenous spaces and imagines their recovery. As we have seen in other *namak-halaal* texts—such as Nayantara Sahgal's nationalist and feminist critiques of Indian postcoloniality, Kamala Markandaya's account of how transnational capitalism transforms subaltern lives and bodies in *The Coffer Dams,* and Anita Desai's women-centered representations of family and culture in *Clear Light of Day*—their characterization, voicing, and plot demand that critiques of and solutions to postcolonial crises be formulated from within familial, social, and political contexts that are specifically marked as local and national. While *The God of Small Things* is similar to postnational novels, including *Midnight's Children* and Vikram Chandra's *Red Earth and Pouring Rain,* in its representation of Indian spaces as sites of suffering, despair, and loss, it does not revert to tropes of migrancy and exile or modes of irony and cynicism in order to articulate realms of freedom. Rather, it joins earlier, *namak-halaal* texts in charting paths for the reclamation of national and local spaces, situating itself within the nation itself.

Furthermore, the subaltern-centered and leftist critique of postcoloniality in *The God of Small Things* also differentiates it from most Indian English novels, whether *namak-halaal* or otherwise. Most of these texts develop criticisms of postcolonial society and the ruling elites that maintain it, paying attention to gender, class, sexual, religious, caste, and national oppression, but they are often informed by fairly mainstream nationalist, traditionalist, and/or liberal ideologies. Roy's novel, in contrast, not only portrays inequalities within the nation but also dismantles the entire edifice of elite-centered approaches to history-writing and storytelling. *The God of Small Things*'s narrative strategies allow for a "literature from below," a recovery of small stories that opens spaces for both subaltern-centered critique and the agency of the oppressed themselves. The *namak* ("salt") to which *The God of Small Things* is committed, therefore, is not the nation as such (e.g., *The Day in Shadow*) or the family (e.g., *Clear Light of Day*) but the marginalized and oppressed voices of history.

As in Bessie Head's "The Wind and a Boy," cited in the epigraph above, *The God of Small Things* insistently critiques a postcolonial capitalist modernity in which "progress" and "development" benefit elites while running roughshod over women, working people, and other oppressed groups. Indeed, Roy's novel shares with a host of African texts of the 1960s and 1970s an interest in drawing attention to the subaltern victims of postcolonial modernity and retelling the story of the postcolonial from their vantage point. The narrator of "The Wind and a Boy" does not simply mourn the boy crushed by the truck but explicitly uses the tale to rewrite the reader's understanding of modernity, capitalism, and power in postcolonial Botswana from a subaltern perspective: "It looked like being an ugly story with many decapitated bodies on the main road."[8] The resolutions of nationalist, *namak-halaal* texts (e.g., the return to Gandhian values, the restoration of the family) and the escapes of post-national ones (e.g., the celebration of migrancy and the wit of the implied author) are unavailable to texts whose analyses begin with the everyday, public decapitation of subaltern bodies. And yet, in subaltern-centered Anglophone texts such as *The God of Small Things*, Aidoo's "For Whom Things Did Not Change" (1972), Armah's *The Beautyful Ones Are Not Yet Born* (1968), and Ngugi's *The Devil on the Cross* (1977), the depiction of postcolonial brutality operates alongside a commitment to portraying subaltern agency and resistance. By drawing out the processes by which elite violence develops, and thereby rendering them historical, earthly, and subject to change, they enable what literary critic Njabulo Ndebele calls "the rediscovery of the ordinary." More than most other postcolonial Indian English novels, *The God of Small Things* charts out history's suppression of alternative stories while reconstructing narratives of resistance that are grounded in subaltern-centered notions of truth and knowledge.[9] Furthermore, as I illustrate in this chapter, a *namak-halaal* and subaltern-centered narrative is not incompatible with the development of postmodern metafictional forms such as magical realism.

My reading of *The God of Small Things* thus takes up three related tasks: 1) to argue that a subaltern-centered and leftist political paradigm drives the novel's political ideology and narrative strategies; 2) to contest, in the process, methods of literary criticism that conflate location, ideology, and aesthetics in pairing the novel with other post-Emergency texts; and 3) to read the novel's critique of Indian postcoloniality as an new example of a *namak-halaal* cosmopolitanism. I take up these questions through an investigation of the binary opposition of big things and small things, the metaphorical pairing put forward by the novel itself as a hermeneutic. The big/small dyad structures the text's political content and perspective on Communism; its strategies of plot, character, and voice; and its representations of nature and sexuality. Associated with caste, class, and gender oppression, with nature, and with transgressive sexuality, the small rebels against the big—the traditional laws of caste and sexuality, the forces of capitalist modernity, and ruling parties such as the CPI(M) that, according to the novel, make cynical use of subaltern suffering. At the same time, the big/small paradigm eschews any easy valorization of resistance. *The God of Small Things* offers narratives of failed rebellions and betrayals, forcing its characters and implied audience to think critically about the condition of subalternity and elite complicity in structures of power.

On the whole, I suggest, Roy's big/small paradigm in this novel offers a powerful lens for examining subaltern agency within a "dialectic of suffering and redemption" (Ndebele 54), guarding against either utopianism or pessimism. While this paradigm is not a Marxist one, I am intrigued by the ways in which the novel puts postmodern aesthetics in the service of a radical, historicist epistemology. As Kalpana Wilson suggests in her early critique of the CPI(M) readings, it would be a missed opportunity for Marxist critics to "relinquish—or banish—the concerns which dominate Roy's book, all of which are essentially issues of power, to the domain of the NGOs."[10]

How the Big/Small Paradigm Works

The flexibility of the categories of "big things" and "small things" allows the novel to investigate different sets of power relations simultaneously, championing the voiceless and the marginalized against the forces of caste, class, gender, sexual, ethnic, and racial oppression. Furthermore, like the paradigm of "elite/subaltern" as defined by Ranajit Guha in the early volumes of *Subaltern Studies,* Roy's big/small paradigm insists that characters that are small in some contexts might be big in others. *The God of Small Things* thus describes an intricate web of power in which oppressions overlap and reinforce one another. As the implied audience gradually comes to see, in addition, the various big/small pairings in the novel are not random but organized hierarchically, placing caste and class oppression at the center of postcolonial violence even while carefully investigating other sites of violence. At the novel's very core, thus, is the story of Velutha, a Dalit carpenter and card-carrying Communist who is killed by police in his hometown of Ayemenem, in the southwestern state of Kerala, in December 1969.[11] A brief discussion of the plot and narrative structure will help to illustrate both the complex, multiple oppressions that the novel describes and the construction of Velutha as the smallest of the small.

Velutha's crime is that he dared to pursue a love affair with Ammu, whose upper-caste, Syrian-Christian family owns the pickle factory where he works and which also employs his father, Vellya Paapen. Velutha's open defiance of caste, class, gender, and sexual restrictions cannot go unpunished in the world constructed by the novel, and Ammu's mother, Mammachi, and her grand-aunt, Baby Kochamma, come together with the state in order to enforce hierarchies that are both age-old and completely modern. After Velutha is falsely condemned for kidnapping Rahel and Estha, Ammu's seven-year-old twins with whom he has built a loving relationship, and for killing Sophie Mol, Ammu's nine-year-old niece visiting from England who has died in a boating accident, his brilliant smile is smashed and inverted by six free-swinging cops in thick, hob-nailed boots.

Velutha dies of his injuries in prison overnight, and the event completely shatters the lives of Ammu and her children. Indeed, the children have already been under tremendous emotional and psychological strain: Ammu, socially ostracized for her independent ways, often takes out her frustrations on her children, especially Rahel; Estha, unbeknownst to his family, has been molested by an Orangedrink Lemondrink Man at Abhilash Talkies; Estha and Rahel's boating adventure to the History House has ended with Sophie Mol's death. But, as we gradually learn, all of this suffering pales in relation to what happens after Ammu and Velutha break the Love Laws. Once Ayemenem's elites are finished with Velutha, they come after Ammu and the twins. Within two weeks, Estha is sent away to live with his father, Babu, the alcoholic husband whom Ammu had divorced when he tried to force her to sleep with his boss, the British owner of a multinational tea plantation in the northeastern state of Assam. Estha is completely traumatized and gradually stops speaking: he is separated from his mother, whom he never sees again, and torn away from Rahel until 1993, the narrative present. Rahel also grows up without her mother. After Ammu's affair with Velutha, her long record of rebellion and transgression—choosing her own husband from outside her religious, linguistic, and regional community, and then divorcing him—can no longer be tolerated. Sent away from Ayemenem a broken woman, Ammu dies prematurely and alone at the age of thirty-one. Rahel is described as lost and empty: expelled from her Christian school for "depravity," she serves a long stint as an architecture student in Delhi, enters into and then leaves a loveless marriage in the United States, and is working at a gas station when news of Estha's return to Ayemenem chases her home.

When the twins, personifications of Emptiness and Quietness, make their separate ways back to Ayemenem in June 1993—at age thirty-one—they are unable to even communicate with one another. Over the course of the novel, which shifts back and forth between June 1993 and various moments in December 1969, the third-person omniscient narrator pieces together the events of the past and its aftermath, frequently through the perspective of the self-reflexive, adult Rahel. The 1969 events emerge in a jumbled, nonlinear sequence, reflecting both the traumatized, scattered memory of the adult Rahel and the chaotic/creative reflections of the seven-year-old girl. But the 1993 events, though interspersed with the flashbacks to 1969, are related sequentially, emphasizing the centrality of Rahel's elite voice and allowing us to gauge the impact of her memories on her actions. She and Estha finally end their estrangement and isolation by the end of the novel but in an unforeseen way, engaging in incestuous sex in their deceased mother's old bed in a desperate attempt to find a lost unity in this symbolic womb, hoping to soothe the "hideous grief" that they feel (*The God of Small Things* 311).

Paradoxically, the fact that Velutha's voice is not central to the narration of the story does not take away from the novel's subaltern-centered politics. Certainly, the framing of the story through Rahel's perspective in 1993 grants a certain priority to elite characters and Velutha appears to be only in the margins of the story. The initial foregrounding of Rahel's trauma and the suffering of Ammu and Estha first establishes *them,* not Velutha, as representatives of small things. It is only in chapter 8 that the audience is made aware that Velutha actually bears the greatest brunt of postcolonial violence, which forces us to rearrange our understanding of how the characters relate to one another and what sorts of agency they possess. Thus, the narrative constructs an implied audience that is unable to approach Velutha's story except from a distance, slowly working through the trauma of Ammu's family and discerning the various, overlapping sites of violence and brutality. Rather than producing an elite-centered narrative, however, this progression allows for a complex rendering of power relations in postcolonial society and a lesson in how subalternity is produced through the selective processes of storytelling.

As we learn the truth, that all of these stories of oppression are linked together by the way in which they relate to Velutha's, we also learn that the dark cloud that hangs over Rahel's head represents her guilt about her family's complicity in Velutha's death. Velutha is betrayed not only by those who have an interest in keeping him down—his bosses, the police—but also by intimates and allies such as Comrade Pillai (the local Communist leader), his father (who thought Velutha was getting too "uppity" for a Dalit), and Estha (who was told he had to choose between saving Velutha and saving his mother). Velutha is "abandoned by God and History, by Marx, by Man, by Woman, and [. . .] by the Children" (*The God of Small Things* 294). By representing the murder as the result of a collusion between classic "big things" (history, the state, tradition) and erstwhile "small things" that become "big things" in particular circumstances (Ammu, the twins, Comrade Pillai), the novel moves from a potentially static binary opposition to a dialectical one, constructing a complex hierarchy of perpetrators and victims that places Velutha at the center. By strategically delaying the implied audience's knowledge of Velutha's story and the betrayals of elites—we know what happens to them before we know what they do to Velutha—the novel draws its English-speaking and implicitly elite implied audience into a critical reflection about its own place in (postcolonial) relations of power. The novel does not merely recognize but thoroughly indicts the "jungle-craft of gentility" that forces elites to look away from subaltern suffering (A. Ghosh, *The Shadow Lines* 134).

In showing how the early sections of the novel work to strategically marginalize Velutha, I would like to draw attention to the fact that the foregrounding of caste and class oppression does not mean the minimizing of gender oppression—even when the female characters turn out to be culpable elites—but the linking together of the categories of gender, caste, and class. For instance, the first two chapters, though lengthy and detailed in describing the social, religious, gender, and sexual contexts of the characters' lives, make only passing mention of Velutha. Within the first twenty pages, the implied audience is made aware that some secret story of brutality ("the Terror") hangs over Ammu, Rahel, and Estha, but they themselves appear to be the greatest victims of this Terror in light of Ammu's difficult past and the tragic drowning of Sophie Mol.[12] Brief, scattered statements do foreshow Velutha's story, but the focus remains on other characters. In chapter 1, for instance, Ammu says "I've killed him" after being questioned, harassed, and threatened by the police on the day after Velutha's death (*The God of Small Things* 10). But Ammu's visit to the station is portrayed mostly in terms of the harassment and powerlessness that she experiences there: in order to silence her, the policeman taps her breasts with his nightstick ("Tap, tap.") and calls her a "*veshya*," a word that makes Ammu cry but that she does not translate to her children (9–10). We later learn, of course, that this scene is the linchpin of Ammu's betrayal of Velutha—if she had admitted to consensual sex and accepted the social stigma of being called a "loose woman," he may have been exonerated. But at this moment, the text is focused on Ammu herself, and the episode is related as part of a larger narrative of the conjugal family's suffering in light of gender/sexual bias. In chapter 2, similarly, Velutha is invoked in the description of Ammu's "unsafe edge" as a multiply oppressed woman: "The infinite tenderness of motherhood and the reckless rage of a suicide bomber [. . .] grew inside her, and eventually led her to love by night the man her children loved by day" (43–44). But the text withholds knowledge of who exactly "the man" is and focuses on how Ammu is affected by her repeatedly frustrated attempts to break free from familial and social restrictions. After learning about Velutha's death, we can put these scenes into their "proper" chronological contexts, as it were, and recognize the ghostly presence of Velutha in the early chapters.[13] Nevertheless, orienting the story through the elite female characters has an important function. By suggesting that the sexual affair emerges as a rebellion against gender oppression, the novel is able to deepen our understanding of Velutha's story, linking together gender, caste, and class rather than positioning them as oppositional to one another. By making the implied audience sympathetic to Ammu's oppression as a woman, the text prepares us to empathize with Velutha and to reread his victimization with new eyes.

In this manner, the novel offers a map of diverse and linked social oppressions in postcolonial India and imagines characters that rebel against them. But all of these rebels meet tragic ends. The antagonists of the novel who aid the march of tradition and history brook no disobedience; for every moment of pleasure they exact years of misery. In fact, by arranging the narrative in terms of a look back across decades of Indian postcoloniality, from the post–Cold War and neoliberal 1990s to the late-1960s contexts of emergent authoritarianism and resistance, *The God of Small Things* writes its story of power and powerlessness on a much larger, national canvas. The story of loss and sadness in the lives of the characters extends for decades, paralleling the long crises in the real and fictional India. The adult Rahel and the third-person narrator explicitly link the marginalization of the small with the devastation of capitalist modernity on Partitioned, postcolonial South Asia. As we learn early in the novel, "[i]n the country that [Rahel] came from, poised forever between the terror of war and the horror of peace, Worse Things kept happening" (*The God of Small Things* 20), creating a maddening downward spiral in which each tale of terror is outstripped by the next one.[14]

The novel thus moves between two poles: it represents small things as being infinitely resilient, resisting all obstacles, but also depicts big things as overwhelming all acts of subaltern agency and resistance. Within this dynamic, the implied audience is encouraged to embrace the moments of pleasure and hope that are scattered throughout the text: its characters that refuse to succumb to restrictions on their agency, its dazzling and innovative use of language, its ability to describe both the destructiveness of World Bank loans and the seven-year-old children's Love-in-Tokyo hairbands and Elvis-style hairdos. And yet the decisiveness with which rebellions fail raises question. Is this, after all, mainly a tale of suffering, of the indomitable structures of power?

The appearance of the big/small paradigm in "The Greater Common Good" gives some insight into how the paradigm works, maintaining a space for hope and agency without minimizing the long, wretched historical context that resistance must confront. Commenting on age-old debates between Nehruvian and Gandhian models of development, Roy calls for developing new ways of thinking:

It's possible that as a nation we've exhausted our quota of heroes for this century, but while we wait for the shiny new ones to come along, we have to limit the damage. We have to support our small heroes. (Of these we have many. Many.) We have to fight specific wars in specific ways. Who knows, perhaps that's what the twenty-first century has in store for us. The dismantling of the Big. Big bombs, big dams, big ideologies, big

contradictions, big countries, big wars, big heroes, big mistakes. Perhaps
it will be the Century of the Small. Perhaps right now, this very minute,
there's a small god up in heaven readying herself for us. Could it be?
Could it *possibly* be? It sounds finger-licking good to me. (Roy, *Cost* 12)

A clear opposition is delineated here, with the big standing for the industrial, military, and political devastation of the twentieth century, the result
of the failed, monolithic utopias of heroes with grandiose dreams, while
the small, no less heroic, stands for multiplicity and specificity—for real
solutions to real problems. The power of the big is not minimized, even
as the ability of the small to stand up beyond its powerlessness is asserted.
The small is also associated with femininity and playful excess. "Finger-
licking good" can be read as both a euphemism for "fucking good" and
an ironic invocation of Kentucky Fried Chicken's motto, representing the
big of monopoly capital. A small she-god is invoked in lieu of the predict-
able masculine, serious God. The "dismantling of the Big," then, appears
as both an exhortation for the present ("[w]e have to limit the damage")
and a future possibility (what the new century may have "in store" for us).

The vagueness of categories such as "big things," however, presents
a problem. The line "Big bombs, big dams, big ideologies, big contradictions, big countries, big wars, big heroes, big mistakes" is clever rhetorically but raises more questions. Are all of these "bigs" the same? Are small
countries more just and humane than big ones? Are ideologies of resistance
also guilty of being "big ideologies"? Isn't this the postmodernist/anarchist
notion that all totalities are totalitarian—and a valorization of highly individualist and fragmented notions of resistance? In a more recent interview
with the Indian magazine *Tehelka,* Roy articulates a much clearer statement about power and the state. When asked whether Maoist rebels, who
had killed 55 policemen in a Bijapur attack that month, simply represented
"the flip side of the State," Roy responds:

How can the rebels be the flip side of the State? Would anybody say that
those who fought against apartheid—however brutal their methods—
were the flip side of the State? What about those who fought the French
in Algeria? Or those who fought the Nazis? Or those who fought colonial
regimes? Or those who are fighting the US occupation of Iraq? Are they
the flip side of the State? This facile new report-driven "human rights"
discourse, this meaningless condemnation game that we are all forced to
play, makes politicians of us all and leaches the real politics out of everything. However pristine we would like to be, however hard we polish

our halos, the tragedy is that we have run out of pristine choices. ("It's Outright War")

Roy then goes on to explain how the violence and brutality of the government in Chattisgarh, the state where Bijapur is located, produced such limited options.

The basis of the argument is that "however brutal their methods," the power that the small display in their resistance cannot simply be equated to that of the big; the "real politics" that create situations of oppression and suffering ought to be the basis of our understanding and assessments. Roy first makes her case through appeals to historical struggles, some of which (anti-apartheid, anti-Nazi) are likely to appeal to a more mainstream audience, and others to a specifically left and/or revolutionary-nationalist one (Algeria, Iraq). The selection of examples is interesting as it forces one to think critically about whether one agrees with the historical parallels—thereby rendering the very categorization of bigness and smallness as a matter of one's politics and not self-evident truth. Marking all of these historical struggles as instances of the powerless fighting back, Roy suggests that to equate the violence of the big with the violence of the small would be utopian: to think that our high-minded thoughts ("our halos") would be sufficient to make available "pristine choices" between the best types of resistance. As in the passage from "The Greater Common Good," the solution is not to wait for "shiny new" godlike heroes to come along but to act now and "limit the damage." There is no romanticization of the small here but a hard-nosed, practical allegiance with forces on the ground in all of their messiness.

When the *Tehelka* interviewer pushes further, asking how Roy might imagine these insurgents if they gained state power, she once again underlines the fact that since the Maoists and "various Marxist-Leninists groups are leading the fight against the immense injustice" in India—against the state, landlords, and armed militias—they deserve support. Yet, Roy explicitly criticizes the heroes of some of these groups, such as Mao, Stalin, and Pol Pot, and acknowledges that "[i]t may well be that when they come to power, they will, as you say, be brutal, unjust and autocratic, or even worse than the present government." Since Roy is interested in questions of power and not party affiliations, she feels free to reply: "If they are [brutal, unjust, autocratic], we'll have to fight them too. And most likely someone like myself will be the first person they'll string up from the nearest tree—but right now, it is important to acknowledge that they are bearing the brunt of being at the forefront of resistance." The fact of resisting landlordism and state oppression gives the resistance group credibility, at least for the moment. And yet this is not exactly "solidarity before criticism," in the sense that Roy makes her disagreements quite plain.

Roy's *Tehelka* interview thus augments and updates the paradigm of power as depicted in the earlier passage in two important ways. First, it limits the open-ended nature of the categories of "big things" and "small things," distinguishing between different positions of power and powerlessness, defending a mass movement of the oppressed that seeks transformation, and refusing to write it off as being always already the "flip side of the state." At the same time, this support for resistance remains critical, aware of the possibility that rebellions for change can turn oppressive, that the small can become the big. In this interview, historical contexts and the democratic content of movements become more important than form (big, small). *The God of Small Things,* similarly, does not simply lay out a list of bigs and smalls but presents varieties of power and powerlessness. But this recognition of complexity does not take it away from its central task: to tell the truth about subaltern oppression.

The Dialectic of Suffering and Redemption

Roy's novel and her essays do not simply describe the opposition of big things and small things in a static way but offer a clear dynamic: while small stories can and should be recovered, they are not sufficiently strong to withstand and magically overcome the extreme violence of the big. At best, the subaltern testimony that is produced by *The God of Small Things* achieves, as I have mentioned above, what Ndebele calls the "rediscovery of the ordinary." Ndebele puts forth a representational strategy that— like Gayatri Spivak's criticism of the search for "authentic" subaltern voices—avoids the "literature of the spectacle" but calls for representing the "dialectic of suffering and redemption" that makes up the everyday life of oppressed groups (54). Ndebele, however, wrestles with a question that is different from the one posed by Spivak: he is more concerned with gauging the paradigm of agency and structure through which a given writer seeks to represent the subaltern, not whether such a representation is possible. Keeping the extratextual subaltern referent and the struggle in which s/he participates clearly in view, Ndebele calls for making the "ordinary daily lives of people" the direct focus of representation because the ordinary "constitutes the active social consciousness of people" and is the basis on which a new consciousness can grow (55). In Velutha's love for his carpentry amidst his exploitation by his boss, for instance, we see a perfect correspondence with the character of the miner in South African writer Joel Matlou's "Man Against Himself," in whom, according to Ndebele, "[t]he necessary vilification of exploitation [is] separated from the human triumph associated with work [. . .] which constitutes a positive value for the future" (54).

In Roy's paradigm of big things and small things, therefore, no act of rebellious agency can exist that is not circumscribed by forces of oppression, but no oppression exists that cannot be challenged, that will simply stamp out all traces of the small. Recovering the small, then, is thus an active process of reconstructing subaltern narratives against the grain of the state and its accomplice, history, in whatever way possible. As such, Roy's fictional and nonfictional narratives take up the task of retrieving alternative stories. Against the histories and actions of states and ruling elites, Roy seeks to recover the stories of those who, like Velutha, are forced to wipe away even the traces of their own presence. When Ammu and Velutha see one another as sexual beings for the first time, the intense personal moment is described as a historiographical act, allowing mere individuals to rewrite the past and dream alternative futures: "Centuries telescoped into one evanescent moment. History was wrong-footed, caught off guard" (*The God of Small Things* 167). But agency is always delimited in this novel, and the transgressive gaze lasts only a moment: "History's fiends returned to claim them. To re-wrap them in its old, scarred pelt and drag them back to where they really lived. Where the Love Laws lay down who should be loved. And how. And how much" (168). The loopholes of history through which this cross-caste love has escaped are firmly closed by the end: the beating of Velutha takes place in the History House with the twins as a live audience. They witness "a clinical demonstration in controlled conditions [. . .] of human nature's pursuit of ascendancy. Structure. Order. Complete monopoly. It was human history, masquerading as God's Purpose, revealing herself to an under-age audience. [. . .] History in live performance" (*The God of Small Things* 292–93). The staccato produced by short, one-word sentences provides a soundtrack to the passage's content, in which the police, too, are no longer individuals but performers in a scene whose causes are effects long predetermined. History gets the last word. Period.

Is this, then, a Foucauldian or Althusserian model of the impossibility of agency and resistance in a world fully dominated by the powerful? Not quite. An important aspect of Roy's paradigm is that despite its construction of history as a suffocating tale that only serves the interests of the

powerful, it does not sit easily with postmodernist rejections of historicity. The novel's epigraph, quoting John Berger, reads, "[n]ever again will
a single story be told as though it's the only one"; certainly, this seems
to simply repeat the Lyotardian mantra of being suspicious of all metanarratives. But, like Rushdie's *Haroun and the Sea of Stories* (1990)—the
Rushdie novel I consider to be least interested in rejecting narrativity and
truth-claims—Roy's text is not simply about the power of storytelling in
the abstract but about the need to tell the stories of the small. The novel
has a definite truth that it seeks to divulge, a *telos* toward which it leads,
and its refusal to discount narrativity itself opens the possibility for a subaltern-centered history. What postmodernism sometimes doesn't realize
is that there are many ways to skin a metanarrative; Roy writes more in
the tradition of Howard Zinn than of Jean Baudrilliard. While Roy certainly exhibits what might be called a postmodernist style (highlighting
disjointed narrative streams, fragmented subjects, hybrid literary forms),
this needs to be distinguished from her fundamentally anti-postmodernist
models of knowledge as expressed in the novel's centering of "all those dis-
possessed of an identity or a speaking voice" (A. Singh 133).

In order to articulate this voice, Roy embeds the recovery of small
voices against big institutions within the novel's processes of telling and
the audience's experience of reading. The blueprint for what the text
aims to do is cleverly offered within chapter 2, amidst a passing comment
about caste oppression in Kerala that is symbolically rich in describing the
novel's tasks. Using the metaphor of footprints, *The God of Small Things*
describes how the big institutions of caste, church, and state joined hands
to render Dalits invisible and untouchable. The third-person narrator
explains that Dalits "were expected to crawl backwards with a broom,
sweeping away their footprints so that Brahmins or Syrian Christians
would not defile themselves by accidentally stepping into a Paravan's foot-
print" (*The God of Small Things* 71). After independence in 1947, however, Paravans who had become Christians under the British in a failed
effort to escape the caste system found that they "were not entitled to any
government benefits like job reservations or bank loans at low interest
rates because officially [. . .] they were Christians, and therefore caste-
less. It was like having to sweep away your footprints without a broom.
Or worse, not being *allowed* to leave footprints at all" (71).[15] This might
look, again, like a narrative about the supremacy of the big. But the placement of this historical note, appearing as we are first introduced to the
rebellious, intelligent Velutha, reveals that its purpose is not just to mourn
the past but to set the stage for the struggles of the present and the future.

The narrative does not end, therefore, at the point of history's annihilation of Dalit identity, symbolically carried out by the Dalit's own hand (and replicated, in Velutha's story, by his own father's betrayal). Much like Ralph Ellison's Invisible Man, who declares, "[I] did not become alive until I discovered my invisibility" (7), the novel attempts to subvert the silencing of the subaltern by inscribing the small with the power of omniscience and omnipresence. *The God of Small Things* can now be read as a text that sets as its political and aesthetic task the retracing of the Dalit's footsteps by exposing *how* they were wiped away.[16] The role of the narrator and historian, therefore, becomes like that of an archaeologist: to put together "[l]ittle events, ordinary things, smashed and reconstituted. Imbued with new meaning. Suddenly, they become the bleached bones of a story" (*The God of Small Things* 32). And the complex narrative pattern demands that the reader participate in a similar project when putting together the story of Velutha as refracted through Rahel and other narrators.

The gradual emergence of Velutha as the central figure of the novel fully draws the implied audience into the narrative project of recovering small stories. "Things can change in a day," the narrative warns us at the end of chapter 7, foreshadowing the history-defying gaze of Velutha and Ammu in chapter 8. But what changes is not only on the level of plot but on the level of our understanding of what kind of story this is, one in which Velutha is no longer marginal but *shown* to be marginalized, no longer a minor character but the central one. *The God of Small Things* achieves, through a postmodern aesthetic, the same political and historiographical goals as Chinua Achebe's *Things Fall Apart* (1958) does through its stunning final paragraph, in which the implied author ironically takes up the voice of a colonial officer and considers how the entire story of Okonkwo, the subject of the novel, might fit into one paragraph in a book he would write. Through this paragraph, and indeed the final chapter as a whole, *Things Fall Apart* invokes the marginalization of African stories by European historiography only to turn the tables on it, reducing this officer's story to an ironic footnote. On the narrative level, the unexpected focalization of the narrative through the eyes of the colonial officer at the end of a novel that had strategically given Europeans no interiority whatsoever mimics and calls attention to the historical and historiographical disjuncture caused by colonialism. Both *Things Fall Apart* and *The God of Small Things* highlight the truth of marginalization through the processes of storytelling, but the difference is that in the latter novel, the implied audience remains in the dark for much longer, forcing a lengthier process of rethinking.

After chapter 8, the novel places Velutha himself at the center of the narrative project of recovering the small, as he is rewritten as a storyteller and a nurturer of small tales whose task of recovery mirrors and completes the novel's own. From the descendant of backwards-walking, footprint-sweeping Dalits, he later becomes symbolically associated with the one-armed man of Ammu's dreamworld who "left no footprints on the shore" (*The God of Small Things* 208), who is the God of Small Things and the Keeper of Dreams. Leaving "no footprints in the sand, no ripples in water, no image in mirrors" (250), Velutha learns how to draw power from his smallness. In reflecting on how well Velutha would play with her and the other children, Rahel says that Velutha "[i]nstinctively colluded in the conspiracy of [. . .] fiction, taking care not to decimate it with adult carelessness [. . .]. It is after all so easy to shatter a story. [. . .] To let it be, to travel with it, as Velutha did, is much the harder thing to do" (181). In this manner, Velutha is represented as the antithesis of the state and of history, the artist and storyteller who produces and provides shelter for alternative stories and histories.

The narrative process, in this manner, renders the novel as both *namak-halaal* and subaltern-centered. The distance that the text initially creates between the audience and Velutha heightens an awareness of the difference between its own identity and that of the Dalit character. Like Sanad's frustrating experience with the beggar girl in *A Time to be Happy,* as discussed in the second chapter, it highlights the difficulties of communication across rigid social barriers. This structure develops the novel's *namak-halaal* perspective: as Rahel, the central cosmopolitan-elite figure, takes responsibility for reconstructing the small, suppressed tale of Velutha's murder, the narrative demands that the (cosmopolitan-elite) reader, too, engage with the problems of power and subalternity. But by giving importance to the adult Rahel's perspective and tying the implied audience to her sensibilities, *The God of Small Things* allows for a new possibility: elite characters who reflect upon and become aware of their complicity might develop empathy and even solidarity with subaltern figures, becoming vehicles for the recovery of subaltern stories. For what is ultimately distinctive about Rahel, Ammu, and Estha is that they are capable of recognizing their role in creating the Terror; they mourn for Velutha from the depths of their bodies and minds.

Ammu, for example, is so attuned to how the big/small dynamic operates that she realizes the loss that she will experience from loving Velutha even before it happens. On the very day that Sophie Mol arrives, the day when Ammu and Velutha recognize their mutual attraction to each other's beauty, Ammu takes an afternoon nap in which she dreams of a one-armed man unsuccessfully trying to make love to her, the figure later revealed to be the socially handicapped Velutha. Awakened by her twins, who mistakenly think that she is having a nightmare, Ammu lets them play with the stretch marks scarring her body from their birth, reminding us both of the organic unity of their bodies and the pain that their birth caused to her. Ammu then sees her body in the mirror, admiring herself through the eyes of one who is desired—but then she breaks down, weeping for herself and her children. Vacillating, Ammu forbids Rahel from playing with Velutha and warns her not to get too close to him. But they are all linked to Velutha, bodily and mentally. In the same bedroom twenty-three years later, the organic unity of the four bodies is once again reenacted when the twins sleep together. Rahel, simultaneously performing the roles of herself and her mother, attracts to herself Estha through the recitation of his childhood nickname through lips that, to Estha, seem remarkably like their mother's. It is after this episode, deep into the novel in chapter 20, that the narrator reveals how Ammu had tucked Rahel in bed that night of Sophie Mol's arrival, making up for their fight that day over Velutha and revealing that she "[a]ched for him with the whole of her biology" (312). The spectral reunification of Rahel, Estha, Ammu, and Velutha—the virtual "family" that could never unite in real life—is grafted into the bodies and minds of Rahel and Estha as they continue the rebellious acts that have brought them both misery and joy.

In this manner, Rahel's recognition of her potential complicity in killing Velutha becomes as important as her telling the story of the murder; she plays a central role in the novel's task of writing a subaltern-centered counternarrative to the story of postcolonial modernity. Allied with Velutha despite their betrayal of him, she, Estha, and their mother are shaped by the tragedy and challenge his silencing. As the most developed characters, these figures, along with Velutha, represent the sort of complex interaction of suffering and redemption called for by Ndebele.

"Naaley. Tomorrow."

An understanding of the dialectic of suffering and redemption as it operates in Roy allows for a more comprehensive reading of sexuality in the novel—a theme that is central to the CPI(M) and *Frontline* critiques of *The God of Small Things* as a bourgeois novel.[17] In his review essay, Aijaz Ahmad takes only one aspect of this dialectic at a time, failing to see how they form a whole. First, as we have seen, he criticizes the "conventional" treatment of sexuality in the novel which, like much European-bourgeois fiction, sees "sexuality as the final realm of both Pleasure and of Truth" ("Reading" 104). Undoubtedly, the novel places a high premium on breaking the taboos of cross-caste sexuality and incest, and it is nothing new to use the space of the erotic in order to represent a way to overcome societal grievances (105). Ahmad argues, next, that the satisfaction with the novel among readers of contemporary fiction arises from the fact that its double ending—involving the closure of both the frame narrative (Rahel and Estha's incest) and the core story (Velutha and Ammu's lovemaking)—provides both the "tragic" and "triumphalist" modes of the classic story of the individual facing "intractable social conflicts" (105). The endings invoke, on the one hand, a narrative in which the state and history are seen as monolithic and invincible (the "tragic" mode) and, on the other, one in which human choice—through sexuality—is represented as being able to transcend the injustices of history (the "triumphalist" mode). For Ahmad, representing sexuality as the ultimate act of resistance against the state—whether in the triumphalist or tragic modes—is a failure not only on the level of political ideology, but also of realism.

The implication that Roy tries to maintain a hold on both tragic and triumphalist narratives, however, ignores the basic dynamic of big things and small things that structures Roy's novel. In fact, Roy's double resolution of the plot with two irreconcilable and self-divided narrative strands is an attempt to portray the contradictory tragedy-within-triumph that constitutes ordinary life. The novel succeeds in its project precisely *because* it portrays the inability of sexuality to smooth over the oppression of the subaltern. Ahmad correctly reads the novel as simultaneously valorizing sexuality and lamenting its futility against the state and the Love Laws—but depicting the tension between the two narratives in this way is precisely the space within which the novel does its ideological work. Ahmad's charge of "having it both ways," in this reading, loses its force since it becomes more of a description of the novel's project rather than a critical analysis of it.

Brinda Bose's postmodernist critique of Ahmad's reading fails, paradoxically enough, along the same lines. Bose also sees the novel as privileging sexuality and the erotic but misses the fact that these are not necessarily signifiers of emancipatory spaces. Whereas Ahmad decries the way that "resistance can only be individual and fragile" in the novel, and that "the personal is the only arena of the political" ("Reading" 108), Bose presents a diametrically opposite view, with appropriate markers of her apparently hostile position to Marxism in general and Ahmad in particular:

Roy takes on the histories that perpetuate [oppressive Love] Laws, and to read her novel *politically* [referring to the title of Ahmad's piece] one may need to accept that there are certain kinds of politics that have more to do with interpersonal relations than with grand revolutions, that the most personal dilemmas can also become public causes, that erotics can also be a politics. (B. Bose 68; original italics)

Bose's opposition of "interpersonal relations" to "grand revolutions" is an attempt to mirror the big/small opposition of Roy, with Ahmad's Marxist belief in social revolution standing in as the "big" that displaces "erotics," the "small." Comparing *The God of Small Things* to Milan Kundera's *The Unbearable Lightness of Being,* Bose argues that the politics of the novel lies precisely in "the subversion of this shame and defeat through the valorization of erotic desire" (B. Bose 70). But by prioritizing individual desire and action in this way and seeing individual and private action as the essence of women's resistance (68), Bose shortens the scope of her own feminist project—and misses the novel's larger, structural critique of women's oppression and its relationship to class divisions and modernity itself. Although Bose's reading is explicitly opposed to Ahmad's, both share the sense that the novel's tragedy is ultimately subsumed by its protagonists' erotic agency. Bose attempts to read Roy as performing a postmodernist subversion of social restrictions through sexuality; Ahmad critiques this very use of sexuality, which he sees as a classic trope in twentieth-century literature in English.

While these critics recognize important aspects of the novel's representation of sexuality, they each overestimate its place in determining the novel's politics. First, sexuality is not marked as "the real zone of rebellion and Truth" in the novel (A. Ahmad, "Reading" 108), because it is clearly not the only or even the most important site at which the text attempts to overcome the gap between the oppressed individual and society. Velutha's relationship with Ammu is explosive because it is the culmination of a long list of the proud Dalit's transgressions of class, caste, and sexual boundaries. Velutha's class mobility through carpentry, his membership in the union and the Community Party, his physical, Touching relationship with the children of his boss's family, and his direct, confident attitude have already placed him in a precarious position by the time he and Ammu make love. As we have seen, Ammu's attraction for Velutha, too, emerges out of her own experience of rebellion. Mammachi, Baby Kochamma, Comrade Pillai, unskilled, upper-caste workers, and even Vellya Paapen are so eager to make the affair an occasion for a history lesson precisely because Velutha and Ammu both have a long record of flouting the rules. On the flip side, sexuality is not always portrayed as healthy or positive. Sexuality can be abusive (Estha's being forced to masturbate the Lemondrink Orangedrink Man), empty (Rahel's relations with her ex-husband), and predatory (the attempt by Ammu's ex-husband's English boss to sexually abuse her). These negative portrayals of sexuality in the novel are as fundamental to its larger meaning as the allegedly positive/transgressive moments of incest and cross-caste sexuality. Estha's silence and shame about his encounter in the hallway of Abhilash Talkies, for instance, foreshadows both his shame for betraying Velutha and the long silence that follows. Sexuality in the novel, then, is sometimes aligned with the small and sometimes with the big and needs to be analyzed in its given context. From this point of view, Velutha's rendezvous with Ammu is important because it is furthers the novel's ideological task, to portray hope-within-oppression and, through this portrayal, to locate the novel as the gatherer of alternative, small stories.

In this light, it is not that erotics "is" the politics of the novel or that it represents a postmodernist sign for the viability of "alternative revolutions" (B. Bose 65), but that it is the site at which the oppression of postcolonial modernity is most clearly expressed, the material ground upon which the characters of the novel feel the brunt of powerful institutions. By drawing out the real economic and social relations between the different characters in the novel and, in effect, the "truth" of social oppression, Roy "comes down squarely—if perhaps unconsciously—in favor of a materialist" reading of the questions of gender and caste, as opposed to a postmodernist rejection of structured hierarchies, subjectivities, and material relations (Kalpana Wilson). Roy's novel, therefore, needs to be seen in light of what the big/small paradigm accomplishes, and what it does not. As a rejection of the idea that representation, being impossible, is a site of violence and that all historiography is futile, the big/small paradigm allows for the building of a counternarrative centered on Velutha. Its power lies in the process by which it reads against the grain of history, exposing the processes of erasure that it employs, and reconstructing an alternative. However, while the big and the small are dialectically related on the level of character and narrative—the two categories shape and limit one another—that dynamic stops at a particular point: it does not imagine a resistance that will lead to a fundamental transformation. By the novel's own political logic, therefore, transgressive sexuality is not depicted as providing a final answer—and no other mode of resistance can take its place. Every act of subaltern agency is circumscribed within a system of domination such that Roy is able to avoid the pitfalls of uncritical valorization and/or victimization of the subaltern.

It is within the simultaneous telling and retelling of the story through the crossing narratives of 1969 and 1993 that sexuality emerges as—at once—a powerful and futile act of resistance by the powerless, a balm for soothing the social wounds inflicted on the central characters as well as the immediate cause of Velutha's death. On the one hand, the withholding of the details of the affair and the Terror it unleashes transmits a sense of unease and foreboding; on the other, it allows the coexistence of an entirely opposite dynamic, by which the impact of the Terror is lessened. The more dramatic aspects of the story—Velutha's murder, Ammu's death—pass quickly; the final chapters present the (troubling) resolution of Rahel's Emptiness and Estha's Quietness and the story of Ammu and Velutha's lovemaking. This juxtaposition, concluding with the chronologically earlier scene, allows Roy to rediscover the ordinary, the everyday resilience of popular life that cannot be completely crushed by the big—even as the "happy" ending heightens the sense of what was lost. The move is quite similar to the ending of Toni Morrison's *Sula* (1973), when the moment of Nell's realization of Sula's value is also the moment of her deepest mourning, of "circles and circles of sorrow" (174). Rather than seeing happiness-through-erotics as the transgressive (and thus, celebratory) moment in the novel, one can read the glimmer of hope as being drenched in the "aura of defeat" (Truax). Alice Truax's rendition of the double movement in the novel is as lyrical as it is accurate: "By now we know what horrors await these characters, but we have also learned, like Estha, to take what we can get. And so we hold onto this [final] vision of happiness, this precious scrap of plunder, even as the novel's waters close over our heads." The novel's association of Velutha with the one-armed man, the God of Small Things of Ammu's dream, reveals the contours of Roy's complex representational strategy. He is the true lover and seer—only he can see the shadows and the light—but he "can only do one thing at a time" (*The God of Small Things* 205). His handicap and his forbidden love preordain his defeat—"*If he touched her he couldn't talk to her, if he loved her he couldn't leave, if he spoke he couldn't listen, if he fought he couldn't win*" (207, original emphasis). At the same time, the "if" statements allow for choices and possibilities (B. Bose 70) that are just as important to the novel's politics as the finality of defeat.

The God of Small Things forces the reader to find hope for the small in the midst of an invincible big that has historically never ceased to win and yet to take that hope not as a romanticization of subaltern resistance but merely as a possibility. The same idea is encapsulated in the title of Armah's *The Beautyful Ones Are Not Yet Born;* like the novel itself, the title clearly emphasizes the absence of "the beautyful ones" amidst the rot and corruption of postcolonial Ghana, but allows some space for future hope with the fragile "yet." Neil Lazarus's characterization of the novel as portraying Antonio Gramsci's famous maxim—"pessimism of the intellect, optimism of the will"—is apt (*Resistance* 46), since it encapsulates the two main aspects of the novel's ideological universe. "The man," the unnamed protagonist of the novel, is rewarded for steadfastly holding to hope amidst the rot, but never forgets that a new future is only a possibility (Armah 159–60). To say that Velutha is like Karna, the mythological, lower-caste hero from the epic *Mahabharata,* "[i]n [whose] abject defeat lies his supreme triumph" (*The God of Small Things* 220), is not to read the novel as being "triumphalist," but to see it as maintaining the necessary "optimism of the will" through which subalterns can imagine a different, more egalitarian world.

The final chapter, describing Velutha's tryst with Ammu and with destiny, reveals sexuality to be the novel's ultimate site for representing redemption-amidst-suffering. As Velutha floats on his back in the Meenachal, wondering whether Ammu will come to meet him, the narrator poses a counterfactual question to Velutha that is marked as being unanswerable: "Had he known that he was about to enter a tunnel whose only egress was his own annihilation, would he have turned away?" (*The God of Small Things* 315). Produced at the intersection of the diachronic and synchronic narratives—the 1993 thread has just ended but the 1969 tale, in effect, has only begun—this self-question forces the reader to create a space for agency even when its consequences are already known. Velutha senses where things may go ("*I could lose everything. My job. My family. My livelihood. Everything*" [316]) and the narrator spells it out: "The cost of living climbed to unaffordable heights," including two lives, "two children's childhood," and "a history lesson for future offenders" (318). Velutha and Ammu teeter on the precipice between recognition of the gap between the big and the small, made visible by their actions. Immediately after their liaison, Velutha senses both doom and elation: "[T]he terror seeped back into him. At what he had done. At what he knew he would do again. And again" (319). Ammu feels the euphoria of a "small, sunny meadow" and "blue butterflies" on her road, but "[b]eyond it, an abyss" (319). Fearful of history and knowing that they have no future, the two lovers try to "[stick] to the Small Things [ant-bites, caterpillars, a 'particularly devout praying mantis,' and a spider (who outlives Velutha)]" (320).

The force of Ammu's (and the novel's) final line—"*Naaley.* Tomorrow" (321)—comes from its confident gesture toward a future time of pleasure and hope even when, as the narrator and audience know and the characters suspect, such a future is nonexistent. The subsequent tension, evoking suffering and redemption simultaneously, turns the novel away from both a mere valorization of the erotic (love conquers all) and a fatalistic erasure of subaltern agency (love is futile under oppression). Like the word "yet" in Armah's title, "tomorrow" signifies a self-consciously utopian gesture toward the future, one that is already circumscribed by the oppression of the present, but that gives hope (here, represented by sexual pleasure) to the protagonists. Since the novel always represents human agency as circumscribed by a hostile history, it can engage in a celebration of human resiliency without exaggerating its importance.

Velutha's ability to realize the limits of his subjectivity is thus the paradoxical height of that celebration. When Velutha is led to his destruction, we are told, it is like history "walking the dog" (*The God of Small Things* 272). But it is Velutha, not only the narrator, who sees this, as the narrative flits back and forth between a third-person omniscient perspective and a free indirect style that moves the audience within Velutha's consciousness. Marching toward sexual fulfillment is constructed as being the same as marching toward death, and Velutha is depicted as knowing this: he "felt that his sense had been honed and heightened. As though everything around him had been flattened into a neat illustration" (270). Amidst the whirlwind of thoughts in Velutha's head, his engineer's mind turns his problem into a machine drawing with an instructional manual telling him exactly what to do (269–70). Like Bashiam, the Adivasi engineer who decides to risk his life to save Europeans, Indians, and indigenous peoples from the floods in Markandaya's *The Coffer Dams,* like "the man" who decides to risk "going home" in Armah rather than becoming a recluse like his Teacher, the certainty of annihilation by the big makes Velutha extremely confident in choosing his way. Indeed, as Lazarus writes about Armah's novel, "that way, and that way alone, lies freedom" (*Resistance* 79).

The Postcolonial Pastoral

The rendezvous between Velutha and Ammu takes place at the bank of the Meenachal, underlining the association of the natural environment to "small things" throughout the novel. Velutha and the river are linked together powerfully, and the latter adds a spatial dimension to Velutha's acts of resistance on the level of character and plot. The river offers a rich resource for Velutha where he can replenish his strength and challenge the powers that be; indeed, only he can navigate its feisty currents, find the hidden paths and trails in the woods around it, and bring in the lumber that drives his livelihood. More broadly, Velutha is physically marked with symbols of nature; he carries on his back a light-brown, leaf-shaped birthmark, a Lucky Leaf that made the monsoons come on time (*The God of Small Things* 70). It is such associations, however, that have fueled readings of Velutha as a romanticized and dehistoricized figure, turning him into a "noble savage" (D. Anand 102). One of the most cited passages in such readings comes from the last chapter. As Ammu waits on the bank of the river and sees Velutha approach her for their initial, unplanned rendezvous, she sees that "the world they stood in was his. That he belonged to it. The water. The mud. The trees. The fish. The stars. He moved so easily through it" (*The God of Small Things* 316). One can see why this representation of Velutha, locked into Ammu's admiring gaze, is offered as proof of the novel's othering of Velutha. Depicting the Dalit as a transcendental figure of nature appears to give him praise but actually marginalizes and appropriates him. The subaltern is cast as more elemental and earthy, while the elite character—the subject of the passage—watches and learns.

Viewed through the rubric of the big/small paradigm, however, Velutha's symbolic association with the natural environment is transformed from a romanticized one to a sharp, anti-imperialist reclamation of local and national spaces. The critique of capitalist modernity in Roy's novel often develops through representations of a deteriorating nature; the possibility of transforming that modernity, likewise, is projected through (lost scenes of) lush, natural beauty that are, crucially, linked to (the loss of) Velutha himself. In their discussions of the representations of land and nature by colonized/postcolonial artists, Rob Nixon and Edward Said point to the radicalism inherent in the imaginative efforts to reclaim lost spaces—eschewing easy dismissals of such representations as apolitical or escapist. Indeed, it is through such representations that *The God of Small Things* achieves its *namak-halaal* perspective, locating its resistance to postcolonial modernity within local and national spaces.

In an insightful essay on Roy's novel, Jennifer Herman brings together Nixon's category of the "postcolonial pastoral" with Said's rereading of Irish Romanticism in "Yeats and Decolonization," arguing that Roy's novel "offers an anti-colonial postcolonial pastoral that overtly critiques Western processes of globalization and development, as well as Indian social class and caste systems" (4).[18] Nixon suggests that unlike the English pastoral, whose dehistoricizing effort is to produce "the nation as garden idyll into which neither labor nor violence intrudes," the "post-colonial pastoral" actually "refracts an idealized nature through memories of environmental and cultural degradation in the colonies" (238–99). Postcolonial representations thus (re)infuse nature with politics and history. While not all postcolonial texts might be as explicitly political in their representations of nature, Roy's is an example of the postcolonial pastoral because it captures what Said describes as "the primacy of the geographic element" in the anti-imperialist imagination (Herman 3; Said, "Yeats" 225). In Said's words, employing the first-person plural as a marker of his identity as a colonized Palestinian, "[O]ur space at home in the peripheries has been usurped and put to use by outsiders for their purpose. It is therefore necessary to seek out, to map, to invent, or to discover a *third* nature, not pristine and pre-historical [. . .] but deriving from the deprivations of the present" ("Yeats" 226). For Said, reclaiming "home" through nature in the context of colonialism is not necessarily romanticist in an antihistoricist way nor xenophobic and nationalist, provided that it reimagines home and self as a grappling with and an overcoming of colonial "deprivations" generated by its spatial dominance. In the postcolonial context and subaltern-centered perspective of *The God of Small Things*, Said's discussion of colonial writing can be further expanded. Postcolonial "deprivations" are caused by both the imperialist West and the elites who run the nation-state; the "outsiders" are non-Indians but also upper class, upper-caste, and/or male Indians; the "home" that is constructed around Velutha allows in sympathetic elites (Ammu, the children) but is also marked as separate from them.

As Herman and others have noted, the novel's contrasting representations of the Meenachal River in the 1960s and the 1990s explicitly mark the third-person narrator's critique of capitalist modernity—and open up a "third nature" that is beyond romanticism (the triumphalist mode) and despair (the tragic mode). The novel opens with a description of what the June monsoon usually means in Ayemenem, with the river extending into the streets as "[b]oats ply in the bazaars. And small fish appear in the puddles that fill the PWD potholes on the highways" (*The God of Small Things* 3). "Boundaries blur" everywhere, as "pepper vines snake up electric poles" (3). The passage celebrates the encroachment of nature into the signs of modern, compartmentalized life: the river in the streets, the boats in the bazaar, fish in the potholes, vines on electric poles. At the end of chapter 4, as the young twins lie together in bed in the 1960s, they dream of "their river" in lyrical and romantic language—with swaying coconut trees, with warm water with a texture like "rippled silk," containing a "yellow, broken moon" (116–17).

But the text opens chapter 5 with view of the river in the 1990s, in which the Meenachal greets Rahel with

> a ghastly skull's smile, with holes where teeth had been, and a limp hand raised from a hospital bed [. . .]
>
> Downriver, a saltwater barrage had been built, in exchange for votes from the influential paddy-farmer lobby [. . .]. So now they had two harvests a year instead of one. More rice, for the price of a river.
>
> Despite the fact that it was June, and raining, the river was no more than a swollen drain now. A thin ribbon of thick water [. . .]
>
> Once it had the power to evoke fear. To change lives. But now its teeth were drawn, its spirit spent. [. . .] Bright plastic bags flew across its viscous, weedy surface like subtropical flying flowers. (118–19)

The transformation of the mighty river to a "swollen drain" is clearly tied to the economic and political priorities of capitalist modernity. No longer a vessel of life, the river has been reduced to a site of death and devastation by the greed of agribusiness. "Bright plastic bags," the corpses of commodity culture, adorn the river instead of flowers; toxins from factories upstream, combined with human waste from the shantytowns springing up on the banks, make the water unsafe—even though it must be used, out of necessity, for bathing, cleaning, washing.

Estha's observation of the river is more succinct than Rahel's: the river now "smelled of shit [from the inhabitants of the slums that lined its banks] and pesticides bought with World Bank loans," smells that the new proprietors of the old History House, now a five-star hotel, could not avoid no matter how many walls they built (*The God of Small Things* 14, 119). Indeed, the description of Estha's walk down the now-unfamiliar riverbank in 1993 offers a rich commentary about postcolonial modernity, linking globalization with the transnational movement of peoples. Estha passes "Gulf-money houses built by nurses, masons, wire-benders and bank clerks who worked hard and unhappily in faraway places," a school for Dalits built by his great-grandfather, and a ration shop with "[c]heap soft-porn magazines about fictitious South Indian sex-fiends [. . .] tempting honest ration-buyers with glimpses of ripe, naked women lying in pools of fake blood" (14–15). The riverbank is the preeminent site for the text's articulations of what postcolonial India and Ayemenem have become. While the novel is undoubtedly a critique of the incestuously closed nature of provincial towns and cries out for the crossing of certain boundaries, most of its representations of transnational exchanges mark them as being destructive. The huge volume of traffic between Kerala and Gulf countries produces unhappiness, isolation, and houses whose implicit grandeur is undermined by the deterioration of the nation itself. Commodity culture, with its public hawking of sexual violence, twists the minds of "honest ration-buyers" and makes a mockery of a society that, in secret, beats down those who actually express their sexuality. Dalit schools are built by families that kill Dalits if, like Velutha, they become a bit too confident from all their schooling.

The description of the Meenachal in the novel—as the site of lost hopes and visions—closely parallels that of the Narmada as represented in "The Greater Common Good." The essay, in fact, is dedicated to the Narmada River "and all the life she sustains" (Roy, Cost 5). The displacement of villagers is part of a larger environmental context: threats of deforestation (50,000 hectares of forest between the Sardar Sarovar and Narmada Sagar dams), increased siltation, disruption of ecosystems, loss of wildlife, and flooding of fertile lands. Just upstream from the yet-to-be-completed Sardar Sarovar Dam, huge deposits of silt have cut off all access to the water, forcing women to walk miles to fill their water pots, stranding cows and goats, and creating irregular currents that make the boats of Adivasis useless (49). Even further upstream, the problem is not silt deposits but uneven and unexpected flows of water from reservoirs that wash away crops that have been traditionally planted on the silt banks of the river (49–50). "Suddenly [the villagers] can't trust their river anymore," writes Roy. "It's like a loved one who has developed symptoms of psychosis. Anyone who has loved a river can tell you that the loss of a river is a terrible, aching thing" (50). Certainly, Estha and Rahel's reflections on the river in the 1990s express that deep sense of loss. The effect of personifying the river in this way, I contend, is not to romanticize it and move it away from history but to produce a historicist understanding of change.

The two texts, belonging to different genres, produce implied audiences with slightly different experiences of the river, however. By juxtaposing the 1960s river at the end of chapter 4 with the 1990s river that greets Rahel in chapter 5, the novel does not merely tell us what "[a]nyone who has loved a river" might feel (Roy, Cost 50) but attempts to make us love the river through our reading. Citing Nixon's term "environmental double consciousness," and taking his concept back to W. E. B. Du Bois' original idea of "double consciousness," Herman describes how the readers of The God of Small Things are briefly allowed to enjoy the lushness of the free-flowing Meenachal (already charged with Rahel's nostalgia for her childhood) *before* being forced to view it though the 1990s lens of environmental degradation (Herman 5). One can say, then, that the novel first offers a romanticized image of the 1960s river in order to maximize the impact of its transformation when describing it in the 1990s. After chapter 5, in this view, any appropriate and holistic reading of the many scenes involving the river would have to take this "environmental double consciousness" into account: all representations of the river as being pure and pristine are always already shot through with our knowledge of the tragedy that awaits it.

With the perspective offered by Herman's reading and the theories of Nixon and Said, coupled with our understanding of sexuality as it operates within the big/small paradigm, we can read Ammu's representation of Velutha in the last chapter differently. First, Ammu is viewing Velutha at the very moment in the text where the tension between the big and the small is at its most intense: the moment of sexual agency is also the moment of the Terror (the consequences of resistance). When Velutha emerges from the river, having asked himself his counterfactual question, it is to a scene that is not simply a romp by the riverside but a moment of deep tragedy, a symbol of how big things crushed the radical possibilities of late-1960s India. Second, the fact that Velutha is seen as being part of nature through *Ammu's* eyes is not necessarily elitist. Citing our earlier discussion of Said, we might say that Ammu sees herself, in a flash, as an "outsider" who has been briefly allowed in—and that if this is Velutha's "home" then she has seen him only as an alienated being until this moment. If Velutha is made "other" by this description, then this is in accordance with the distance that the text consistently creates between Velutha and the elite voices through which its narration is focalized: a critical distancing that operates *against* a too-easy, romanticized identification with the subaltern subject.

Communism, Class Politics, and Baby Kochamma's Neckfat

Armed with an understanding of the novel's left-wing and subaltern-centered orientation and its dialectic of suffering and redemption, we can now return to the specific representations of Communism that drive the CPI(M) and Ahmad's critiques, and the larger question of political criticism. Ahmad claims that Roy's rejection of Communism makes her "representative of the social fraction whose particular kind of radicalism she represents" ("Reading" 108). But while Ahmad disparages this "kind of radicalism," I am arguing that in the context of the new configurations of the post–Cold War Left, carefully distinguishing between various non-Marxist radicalisms for the purpose of clarity and dialogue remains quite important for (Marxist) critics of postcolonial writing. In terms of *The God of Small Things,* this means analyzing the novel's representations of Communism in light of its own ideological paradigm, not against the grid of our own political views. In terms of the broader question of Roy's "kind of radicalism," it means engaging more honestly with the fact that an Indian and global Left exists with serious criticisms of Indian Communism and its visions. These two different kinds of analyses—of the novel's representations of communism and of the CPI(M) itself—need to be pursued and brought together, but not conflated. Regardless of how we ultimately understand the novel with regard to its real-world political affiliations, a close reading forces us to concede that its criticism of Communism stands as a marker of its progressive and leftist politics: the rejection of a big idea that masquerades as the redeemer of the small but actually helps to crush it. Indeed, as becomes evident, the critique is forceful but nuanced: it emerges from a perspective that understands the important role Communists have played but feels deeply betrayed by it. This is *not* the same as the anti-Communism prevalent among post–Cold War elites.

On the surface, the basic sense that *The God of Small Things* is anti-Communist in the usual way seems to be true. Roy treats E. M. S. Namboodiripad irreverently in the text ("with spite," Ahmad says ["Reading" 104]), and the novel pokes fun at the ruling party whenever it can. For instance, one passage points out that the greater part of the damage to the garden of Baby Kochamma—Ammu's vindictive aunt—had been done by the weed that people called the Communist Patcha "because it flourished in Kerala like Communism" (*The God of Small Things* 27). Toward the end of the novel, Comrade Pillai's moral and political bankruptcy suggests that Communists are corrupt and use whatever political rhetoric they need to get ahead. Described as a "professional omeleteer" (15)—one who knows the old adage about omelets and eggs—Comrade Pillai opportunistically shifts his position on caste as needed and secures his social status in the community at whatever cost. Comrade Pillai and the leaders of workers' unions in a Communist-led state are portrayed, cynically, as "mechanics who serviced different parts of the same machine" (248).

But the text itself offers up complexities around the issue of Communism that the third-person narrator—effusive and didactic on so many other issues—does not necessarily explain or gloss in any way. For instance, when describing the Communist-led march that swarms around the family car on the way to see *The Sound of Music,* the narrator dismisses some common theories used to explain the deep roots of Communism in Kerala. Some say, the narrator reports, that the relative preponderance of Christians in southwestern India allowed for an easy replacement of "God with Marx, Satan with the bourgeoisie, Heaven with a classless society, and the Church with the Party"—but, the omniscient voice notes, most Syrian Christians were landlords and factory owners who opposed and did not encourage the Communists (*The God of Small Things* 64). Others say that Kerala's high literacy rate may have attracted people to Communism—but the high literacy level, the novel explains, "was largely *because* of the Communist movement" (64, original emphasis). Indeed, the third-person narrator's recognition of the good that the CPI(M) has done in Kerala is an opinion that the real author herself shares. For instance, after moving to Delhi and seeing how elites treat servants and workers, Roy says: "Kerala is a much more egalitarian society. Marxism gave the poor man dignity, if nothing else. It did a lot of good" (Jaggi). That Roy sharply critiques Communism *despite* her approval of the reforms it brought calls for a more serious reading of her position, as well as that of the novel, with regard to the CPI(M).

It is when the narrator divulges the "real secret" of Communism's growth in Kerala that we comprehend the depth of the novel's stinging critique:

> [C]ommunism crept into Kerala insidiously. As a reformist movement that never overtly questioned the traditional values of a caste-ridden, extremely traditional community. The Marxists worked from *within* the communal divides, never challenging them, never appearing not to. They offered a cocktail revolution. A heady mix of Eastern Marxism and orthodox Hinduism, spiked with a shot of democracy. (*The God of Small Things* 64)

The passage contains the text's main criticisms of the Communists: that they were tied to upper castes and did not fight against either caste or communal divides, and that they ultimately never challenged the system itself. The narrator almost sneers when describing how, after E. M. S. Namboodiripad, "the flamboyant Brahmin high priest of Marxism in Kerala," became Chief Minister of Kerala in 1957, the Communists "found themselves in the extraordinary—critics said absurd—position of having to govern a people and foment revolution simultaneously" (*The God of Small Things* 64–65). Clearly, despite the objectivist veneer of the description, the narrator and implied author are among the "critics" being cited, for this representation of the origins of Communism and its compliance with caste hierarchies, established early in the novel, sets the stage for Comrade Pillai's betrayal of Velutha. When Velutha comes to Pillai for help after his intercaste affair is exposed, the latter gravely informs Velutha that the Party would not support him against his employer since it "was not constituted to support workers' indiscipline in their private life" (271).

These are the passages that spark the ire of the CPI(M), and we can safely call the narrator's severe criticism of the Communists as being that of the implied author too, as no contrary opinion that might validate the Communists is really given voice in the novel. By this point, though, it has become clear that the novel's criticism emerges from a leftist perspective that argues that Indian Communism counterposes class to caste and disregards the long oppression of Dalits. Regardless of what one thinks about this position, in the universe and logic of the novel Comrade Pillai has become a functionary of the big, one of "history's henchmen" (*The God of Small Things* 292). To dismiss this position as reactionary or to patronize it as "petty bourgeois radicalism" without recognizing the perspective from which it emanates is, in fact, to risk proving the point: narratives of caste and gender oppression matter less than defending the party.

From outside the sphere of literary-critical analysis one can ask a different question: why is it that a progressive and leftist novel that is *not* dismissive of struggle and resistance and history from below is, nevertheless, hostile to Communism? The fact is that the novel's position on Indian Communism is shared by many on the Indian Left, including Indian Marxists. The history of Communism in India, according to these perspectives, is the history of a largely reformist movement that has become part of the status quo in the states in which it has power. Radical splits from the original CPI, such as the CPI(M) in 1964 and the CPI(ML) in 1967, were either brought into the fold of reformist (mostly electoral) politics, annihilated by repression, or reduced to isolated terrorist groups. As Ross Mallick argues, the success of Indian Communists in a capitalist democracy dominated by middle and upper classes meant their interests were often opposed to the radical actions of poorer sections of society. The landed peasantry—inherently conservative and reformist—became the basis for Communist votes, for it could deliver lower-class votes through its traditional structures of power and have its interests met by a party that no longer needed radical, mass actions to remain in power (Mallick 14). The narrator's contention in *The God of Small Things* that the Party survived in Kerala by ignoring backward social ideas in practice while rhetorically fighting them, "never challenging them, never appearing not to" (*The God of Small Things* 64), reflects Mallick's analysis almost word-for-word: "the CPM abandoned the lower classes in practical terms even while claiming they represent them in rhetoric" (Mallick 14). Indeed, the contradiction between the CPI(M)'s interests as a ruling party and those of lower-class militants often came to a head; in the most extreme case in West Bengal (where the CPI(M) has ruled longest), Mallick contends, "hundreds of untouchables and tribal peoples have been killed by Communist policemen trying to control the radical movements" (16).

Achin Vanaik writes, further, that when the Left parties have participated in the "new social movements" around caste and gender egalitarianism, they

> have too often behaved as if the economic is the only reality or invariably the most important one [. . .]. Thus the legitimacy of autonomous organization by Dalits or women is often denied and the approach of leftists toward such movements essentially manipulative and paternalistic, focusing on giving them the "correct class line" which, of course, they are best able to provide as a result of their "superior" analysis of Indian reality. No wonder participants in such movements look upon traditional left organizations with suspicion. (200)

Those who defend the CPI(M) need to come to terms with how real political disagreements around fighting social oppression have laid the ground for the "anti-Communism" of left-wing intellectuals. The charges that Roy, through the narrator, lays at the door of the CPI(M) cannot be simply dismissed by asserting, for instance, that "it is quite implausible that a Communist trade union leader would actively conspire in a murderous assault on a well-respected member of his own union so as to uphold caste purity" (A. Ahmad, "Reading" 105). Kalpana Wilson argues, in fact, that "[t]he failure of some on the left to grasp the significance of [Roy's progressive politics] springs partly from narrow sectarianism, but also partly from an inability to grasp the importance of patriarchy, the main focus of Roy's attack, to the reproduction of capitalism."

These are undoubtedly ideological questions and open to debate and discussion, but rather than engaging the debate, the CPI(M)-affiliated critique dismisses it out of hand. A more careful reading of the representations of Communism in the novel than the CPI(M)'s reveals an ambiguity in the novel on the question, one that emerges from the incompleteness of the paradigm of big things and small things. Despite being vilified by the third-person narrator, Communism also emerges as the marker of freedom in the novel: for example, Velutha participates in the Party's rallies, Estha uses Velutha's "Marxist" flag to mark his independence (answering affirmatively to Rahel's question, "Are we going to have to become a Communist?" [*The God of Small Things* 191]), and Communism is key to the trenchant critique of Baby Kochamma's class position. The march in chapter 2—the centerpiece of novel's discussion of Communism—exemplifies both the ambiguities and progressive possibilities of Roy's representation of it.

From the outset, the representation of the march is mixed, alternating between an ironic tone consistent with the reading of the novel as "anti-Communist" and one that bears a real sympathy for the Communist-affiliated marchers. The family car—with Chacko driving, Ammu in the front seat, and Baby Kochamma sitting between Rahel and Estha in the back—is held up on its trip to Abhilash Talkies by a march led by the Travancore-Cochin Marxist Labour Union. Although the march is dismissed as cheap theatre—"part of [the] process" of "harnessing anger for parliamentary purposes" with the Communist "orchestra . . . petitioning its conductor [the Communist government]"—the paddy workers' demands for lunch breaks and raises and for a stop to caste-discrimination in the workplace are represented as genuine (*The God of Small Things* 66–67). As vehicles on the road become transformed into "islands in a sea of people" and the march engulfs them, the atmosphere in the family car gathers like a tense fist. The contradictory portrayal of Communism continues. First, we have a continuation of Ammu's mockery of her brother Chacko's pretensions at being a Marxist despite his exploitation of workers (multiplied for women workers through sexual harassment) as a factory boss. When Chacko advises everyone to roll up the windows, Ammu asks, "Why not join them, comrade?" (62); when her Cambridge-educated brother gets angry at a protester who punches the hood, Ammu says, "How could he possibly know that in this old car there beats a truly Marxist heart?" (68). And yet, the narrator does not dismiss the march, but recognizes "an edge to [the] anger that was Naxalite, and new" (67).[19] The march is described in glowing terms, as a site for utopian solidarity and change: it brings together male and female paddy workers, "party workers, students, and the laborers themselves. Touchables and Untouchables" (67). The residual irony in this last statement, if any, is more about foreshadowing the demise of this unity rather than any "anti-Communism."

At this moment, two events happen, apparently unrelated but which the narrative (via Baby Kochamma) ties together neatly. First, Rahel sees

Velutha in the march, hoisting a red flag and with "angry veins in his neck" (*The God of Small Things* 68). Excited, she rolls down the window, sticks her body out, and calls to him; Velutha, surprised, quickly disappears into the mass of people. As her mother fiercely hauls her into the car, Rahel, also surprised, wonders why everyone doubts her claim to have seen Velutha (68); it is only after catching Estha's thought signals that she pretends not to have seen him (77). The car and the march act as the symbols and guardians of class boundaries in the scene, forbidding cross-class alliances between friends when the lines are drawn so sharply. Ammu whisks Rahel into the car; Velutha steps away and tries to avoid recognition.

In describing the second incident involving the march, however, the novel achieves its most brilliant depiction of ruling-class interests and fear. As marchers swarm the car and red flags fill the air—and the possibility emerges that the workers might breach the elite space of the vehicle—Baby Kochamma becomes uncontrollably nervous. "Terror, sweat, and talcum powder [blend] into a mauve paste between Baby Kochamma's rings of neckfat" as she fantasizes about the possibility of meeting the violent Naxalites who were featured in recent newspaper reports (*The God of Small Things* 76). Soon enough, the marchers open Rahel's unlocked door and crowd in to take a look at the family. Drawn to Baby Kochamma's frightened look, they name her Modadali Mariakutty ("Landlord Maria") and make her wave a red flag (later to become Estha's) saying *Inquilab Zindabad*, "Long Live the Revolution!" (76–77). Humiliated, Baby Kochamma focuses all her fury on Velutha; in her imagination, it was *he* who had handed her the flag, who had named her Modadali Mariakutty and who had laughed at her (78). This animosity ultimately seals Velutha's fate.

But Ammu's political feelings about the march are different, and they emerge only later as we witness the beginning of her attraction to Velutha. Seeing Velutha play with Rahel in the woods on the side of the house—just as history is getting caught off guard, as I described earlier—Ammu "hoped that it *had* been him that Rahel saw on the march. She hoped it had been him that raised his flag and knotted arm in anger. She hoped that under his careful cloak of cheerfulness he housed a living, breathing anger against the smug, ordered world that she so raged against" (*The God of Small Things* 167). The march and the characters' different reactions to it correspond to the very different representations of Communism in the text, including those that are not explicitly portrayed as part of the text's debate with Communism. On the one hand, the march is run by the CPI(M), the rulers of the state and the representatives of the big, and the text does not hesitate to suggest, ironically, that the entire event is orchestrated. On the other hand, the narrator aligns Velutha, Ammu, and the children together with the march, and employs the march and the marchers themselves as tools to disrupt the ancient class hatreds of Baby Kochamma—the representative of the vilified ruling elite. Furthermore, the passage in which Ammu hopes that Velutha was in the march (perhaps explaining her abruptness to Rahel in the car) also aligns Ammu and Velutha *politically*, not simply physically, contesting Ahmad's claim that Ammu and Velutha "become pure embodiments of desire" and have no political relationship ("Reading" 105). As Bose suggests, the moment in which Ammu hopes that Velutha was in the march highlights her recognition of a "shared rage" that, indeed, makes it possible for her to "desire the Untouchable Velutha" (B. Bose 64). Indeed, Ammu and Velutha are intimately linked by their ability to rebel at different times, though they do not articulate their rebellions in a recognizably political discourse. The same phrase that Ammu uses to reject the policeman's attempts to squash her voice early in the novel ("Ammu said she'd see about that" [9]) is repeated—or echoed, in terms of a diachronic narrative of events—when Mammachi tells a betrayed Velutha that the consequences for him will be severe ("We'll see about that" [269]). Both fail in their rebellions, but it is their willingness to stand up against power that clearly unites them.

With the linking of Velutha and Ammu around the march, the economic, social, and personal are linked together in a productive way, operating in contrast to Communism but also in a scenario created by Communist agitators. Kalpana Wilson argues that Roy's originality "lies in the way she manages to show us the interconnections between the deep contradictions within this family and those between the social class they belong to and the working people, as she gradually lays bare the tensions beneath the idyllic and nostalgic vision of a 1960s family outing to that clean, white cinematic fantasy, 'The Sound of Music.'" Significantly, the narrative itself does not explicitly highlight these links as an uncovering of class relations, which would require recognition of the centrality of class to the novel and, in turn, would problematize its representation of Marxism (which, for Roy, equals Communism) and raise questions about its free-floating paradigm of big things and small things. Roy's conceptual framework does not allow the paradox she presents to be examined. Still, there can be no greater example than the march to show how strongly Velutha and the marginal voices of the novel are symbolically connected with Communism, problematizing, then, a simple reading of the novel as "anti-Communist."

Namak-Halaal **from Below**

The political contributions of *The God of Small Things* are important to understanding the place of the postcolonial Indian English author today. By drawing out the real economic and social relations between the different characters in the novel and, in effect, the "truth" of social oppression, Roy "comes down squarely [. . .] in favor of a materialist" reading of the questions of gender and caste, as opposed to a postmodernist rejection of structured hierarchies, subjectivities, and material relations (Kalpana Wilson).[20] From this perspective, it becomes clear that the text's political paradigm is more complicated and progressive than its CPI(M)-affiliated critics have supposed. One aspect of the novel's "anti-Communism," for instance, is an excitement about rank-and-file workers, a firm support of their struggle against bureaucracy, and the critique of a narrow class politics that is inattentive to gender, sexual, and caste oppression. In particular, the representation of the Dalit character as central to the story is unique in the genre of the postcolonial Indian English novel. While the novel might appear to represent the "particular kind of radicalism" of the contemporary cosmopolitan elite (A. Ahmad, "Reading" 108), it is important to recognize that the content of that radicalism is rapidly changing in light of a resurgence of activism around the environment, globalization, and war. Roy's early essays translated the political paradigm of big things and small things across genres, from the space of literature to that of nonfiction and political engagement. But her recent work on Iraq and Kashmir, for instance, has pushed far beyond those limits, giving voice to a new, "shared rage" against the violent conditions and deteriorating living standards of people all over the globe.[21] The "fruits of development," as ironically described with regard to the Narmada Dam in "The Greater Common Good," have continued to spread, engendering displacement, rising prices, hunger, brutal wars, and death for millions—along with tougher laws allowing greater surveillance by "history's henchmen" (Roy, *Cost* 41). At the same time, a new radicalization oriented around mass actions in some places and small struggles in others is laboring to come into being. A central aspect of this new moment, not yet fully emerged, is this new confidence in subaltern agency and in the representation of that agency. Roy has been able to articulate the new radicalism of this moment in her political essays. I contend that this perspective is, in fact, rooted in *The God of Small Things* itself.

Indeed, the unsatisfactory treatment of Roy's different writings by CPI(M)-affiliated figures and publications can be understood in a broader context: their uncertainty in relating to the growing prominence of Left intellectuals and leaders in the post–Cold War period who are actively engaged in radical politics and skeptical of postmodernist/new-left paradigms even as they remain unaffiliated with parties such as the CPI(M). Undoubtedly, characterizing the global Left that is forming since the mid-1990s has been a challenging task. It has included forces and ideas that are anti-state (Zapatistas), pro-state (Chavez), and oriented toward radical movements toward reforms in the here and now (Bolivia). Some leftist theorists have emphasized the continuing of imperialist aggression in the context of a hierarchy of nation-states (Gilbert Achcar), while others—unconvincingly, in my view—have declared the end of centralized empires in a "post-capitalist" economy no longer dominated by dominant nation-states (Michael Hardt and Antonio Negri). It is beyond the scope of this chapter to conduct a full-fledged assessment of Roy's position in relation to these various approaches to questions of anti-statism, reform and revolution, postcapitalism, and so on. But it is clear the CPI(M) and Roy enter into these debates about the shape of the post–Cold War Left from distinctly opposed positions. Indeed, the 2007 violence in Nandigram, West Bengal—where villagers and antiglobalization activists met with deadly force while opposing the ruling CPI(M) and its collusion with neoliberal development—have become a flashpoint for a global debate and reassessment about the state of the Indian Left itself and the CPI(M)'s place within it.[22] Roy's active condemnation of CPI(M) actions in Nandigram re-enacts, as it were, the ways in which the implied author of *The God of Small Things* also speaks out against what she sees as the Indian Communists' disregard of ordinary people's lives.[23]

Recovering the radical political paradigm of *The God of Small Things* ought to be distinguished from whether the Marxist or political critic *agrees* with that paradigm. Demanding that literary texts provide a clear political agenda for emancipation, as Frederick Aldama has convincingly argued, both overestimates what literature can do in the realm of society and underestimates what it actually accomplishes in the realm of the imagination.[24] One can discover the political frameworks that a text has to offer and then raise questions about them separately—keeping the two stages of analysis relatively independent from one another. From a historical-materialist point of view, for instance, the big/small paradigm does not adequately answer the question of revolution and transcendence of capitalism. Like Thompsonian "histories from below," Roy's work affirms the possibility of representation (one can be "a voice for the voiceless") and, thus, alternative historiographies (that history can be rewritten from the perspective of the oppressed). But despite this clear break from post-modernist epistemology and historiography, Roy's paradigm runs the risk of delinking the oppression of the subaltern from the structures that create that oppression. While Roy's writings offer a devastating and powerful critique of modernity and help to rally the forces of the Left whenever they appear, they offer no alternative to that modernity, locked as they are into a model that sees all big institutions as being so powerful that nothing remains beyond fighting the good fight to the best of one's ability: mobilizing marches, calling for boycotts, being a public intellectual. I say "beyond" as if what Roy is doing is commonplace; in fact, she stands at the forefront of Left intellectuals who have become public voices for resistance. Still, the view that "power" is a diffuse, omnipresent phenomenon that cannot be explained, and that big answers that attempt to grasp the totality are totalitarian, is ultimately at a remove from Marxist paradigms that place a critique of capitalism at the center of their analysis of oppression. Even though Roy's "narrative from below" model is quite different from the postmodernist rejection of historicity itself, it shares the limitation of only being able to describe differential locations of power struggles without imagining their transcendence. And yet, as discussed above, Roy's discussion of the Indian Maoists in the *Tehelka* interview does point to a nuanced way of understanding resistance movements, representing a position that is far closer to Marxist analyses than most.

The God of Small Things, then, represents an alternative to the dominant tendencies in the post-Emergency novel—and, politically speaking, produces a historicist and subaltern-centered perspective that is unique in the postcolonial Indian English novel as a whole. While we have discussed major characters and themes, it is worth noting that the depth of Roy's political perspectives is often hidden away in minor characters such as Muralidharan, the naked lunatic whom Estha sees as he sits atop a milestone on the Kochin Road, his penis pointing down toward the sign. At first Muralidharan appears to be like "Rose's beggar" in Nayantara Sahgal's *Rich Like Us* in the sense that he too is armless and helpless, little more than a victim. But we learn that like the Beggar—who turns out to have been part of a sharecroppers' rebellion—Muralidharan too has a story: his arms were blown off in Singapore in 1942 as a member of the Indian National Army, the force assembled by Subhas Chandra Bose to fight the British colonizers through an alliance with Japan and Germany. Muralidharan is not only a victim of modernity, thus, but a reminder of resistance and struggle—of an anticolonial but non-Gandhian variety. Despite his madness, and the fact that he "had no home, no doors to lock," he keeps "his old keys tied carefully around his waist," symbolically holding onto hope when it was long gone (61). He is a symbol of those who are displaced, worldwide, but refuse to give up their right of return.

The difference between the strategies of characterization in Roy's Muralidharan and Sahgal's Beggar indicates why the *namak-halaal* of Roy's text is so different despite the fact that it, too, focuses on problems of elite guilt and complicity. In Sahgal, the Beggar is a character whose main function is to tell his story to Sonali, the elite protagonist, for the purposes of her own development. As I discussed in the last chapter, Sonali then grants the Beggar prosthetic arms as the text works him into a narrative of elite redemption through service of the poor. In Roy, however, Muralidharan is much more problematic as a character for elite consumption. That Estha notices him at all is reflective of his character, always attentive to the margins, and the opening that the novel offers for elite solidarity and empathy with the small. But, Estha does not know Muralidharan's story and can only notice 1) that the landscape looks misshapen through the plastic bag Muralidharan wears on his head, and 2) the differences in color and shape of Muralidharan's hair between his head, his chest, and his pubic area. Small himself but shamed by his desire to know more about this difference, he can't think of whom to ask about Muralidharan's hair and looks away instead. Whereas the translation from subaltern suffering to elite understanding in *Rich Like Us* is simply a matter of elite self-reflection and action, in *The God of Small Things* elite knowledge is blocked by class and sexual repression (rich little boys ought not to look at naked lunatics) and ignorance (the grown-ups would not know Muralidharan's story anyway). In both texts we learn about the story behind the subaltern's victimization, but in Roy's he is actually given a name and an identity, and the implied audience is made to reflect upon the processes by which elite blindness actually occurs. Indeed, the references to Muralidharan's past require some independent research on the part of the reader, and, as he never appears again, his story is at risk of being once again marginalized and forgotten. When it is remembered, however, we can comprehend the vast historical canvas on which Roy depicts power and powerlessness, making Velutha's story simply one of the many small stories that need to be recovered.

The explicit critique of Communism, combined with the postmodern aesthetics of *The God of Small Things*, offers an important lesson to Marxist and/or political critics, as it can distract readers from the leftist political ideology of the novel. The links between the novel and Roy's political works raise the stakes even higher. Without recognizing that progressive and even class-oriented political and artistic projects often *reject* Marxism in the aftermath of Stalinism, Marxist theorists and activists risk cutting themselves off from the new movements sweeping the entire world. But when they—we—look beyond the apparent or real "anti-Marxism" of such Left voices and engage them in dialogue and struggle, we can see that they share many common perspectives in battling that new imperialism, as Roy and Ahmad undoubtedly do. As class inequalities grow around the world amidst a new economic crisis, and the ideologies of neoliberalism, privatization, and deregulation expose their flaws, the ground beneath the feet of Indian English writers is shifting. In this context, the *namak-halaal* and subaltern-centered approaches evident in *The God of Small Things* are sure to proliferate, notwithstanding the Western political contexts that dominate the production and consumption of English-language texts.

conclusion

Looking Ahead

In dark times an intellectual is very often looked to by members of his or her nationality to represent, speak out for, and testify to the sufferings of that nationality [. . .] For the intellectual the task, I believe, is explicitly to universalize the crisis, to give greater human scope to what a particular race or nation suffered, to associate that experience with the suffering of others.

—Edward Said, *Representations of the Intellectual* (1994)

I'd say the biggest indictment of all is that we are still a country, a culture, a society which continues to nurture and practice the notion of untouchability. While our economists number-crunch and boast about the growth rate, a million people—human scavengers—earn their living carrying several kilos of other people's shit on their heads every day. And if they didn't carry shit on their heads they would starve to death. Some f***ing superpower this.

—Arundhati Roy, "It's Outright War" (2007)

I had the honor, in December 2004, of speaking at a conference in Tunisia commemorating the work of Edward Said, the celebrated Palestinian-American scholar who had passed away in the previous year. As is well known, Said was a prolific and insightful writer, and *Orientalism* (1978) laid the groundwork for the development of Anglo-American Postcolonial Studies as a field. But it was clear, at the Tunisia conference, that Said was much more than a famous academic. The scholars, writers, and activists attending from around the world were interested in contextualizing Said's work on literature and theory in terms of his writings on politics and history and global events such as the occupations of Palestine and Iraq. Yasser Arafat and Abu Ghraib were as much in the air, in other words, as *Orientalism* and *Out of Place*. Every scholar seemed to be an activist, too: the chair of my session had worked closely with the leadership of the African National Congress in the anti-apartheid struggle, and one of my co-panelists had been imprisoned by General August Pinochet in Chile. The pleasant and unassuming academic couple I met one day turned out to be leaders of mass, secular organizations that participated in overthrowing the Shah of Iran in 1979. As if this were not enough, the conference sessions were packed with hundreds of students, eager to hear about Said and to engage in discussions about his work—and all this in English, presumably their third language. Upon learning the purpose of my visit, the taxi driver who picked me up from the airport conveyed to me, as I put my high school French lessons to use, the widespread respect and admiration that the Arab world had for Said.

Academics die every day, but Said stands out because he embodied the intellectual that he describes in the quotation above. Attentive to the Palestinian nation and its people, with whom he shared racial, ethnic, and historic roots, Said was able "to represent, speak out for, and testify to the sufferings of [his] nationality." Closely linked to global audiences, at the same time, through his academic training and position at Columbia University, he took the opportunity "to universalize the crisis, to give greater human scope" to Palestinian suffering. Said expressed, in other words, the very basic principles of *namak-halaal* cosmopolitanism that I have described throughout *Decentering Rushdie,* a cosmopolitanism that remains "true to its salt" even as it opposes parochialism and yokes itself to other nations and peoples. The tremendous sense of internationalism and solidarity in this position emerges from the notion that the intellectual ought to "associate that experience [of a nation's suffering] with the suffering of others." I particularly appreciate the materialist and historicist basis on which Said constructs these global others: they are capable of empathy because they, too, know what it is to suffer.

The notion that the intellectual can and should translate between worlds in this way is quite far from Gayatri Spivak's trenchant critique of attempts to represent subaltern suffering in statements such as the following: "The ventriloquism of the speaking subaltern is the left intellectual's stock-in-trade" (*Critique* 255). The sincere effort of the intellectual to speak truth to power in Said becomes, in Spivak's formulation, an exercise in bad faith, a trick learned in the process of career-building and self-legitimation. But is insincerity and opportunism really constitutive of all intellectual efforts to bear witness to suffering and oppression? Said's framework opens a space for the *possibility* of representation despite its many pitfalls—thereby positioning itself against contemporary theories about the inherently limited nature of nation-oriented discourse (e.g., Homi Bhabha), the Eurocentrism of historiography and universalisms (e.g., Dipesh Chakrabarty), and Foucauldian paradigms of knowledge/

power that limit our ability to understand others (e.g., Said's own *Orientalism*).[1]

Tracking the Postnational Turn

All postcolonial Indian novels in English, one can argue, are thrust into the position of speaking on behalf of the nation and its people given the contexts in which they are produced, distributed, and consumed. Many of the cosmopolitan and elite writers of the genre, whether based in India or not, deliberately take on the "task"—as Said calls it—of representing the nation and its history; those who do not are often read as "native informants" anyway. But after the publication of Salman Rushdie's *Midnight's Children* in 1980, Indian English novels tended to problematize the decolonized nation itself in their representations of postcolonial suffering, focusing on the problems of narrating history rather than on history itself. While India and Indianness continued to be central to Indian English novels of the 1980s and 1990s such as Amitav Ghosh's *The Shadow Lines* (1988), Shashi Tharoor's *The Great Indian Novel* (1988), Vikram Chandra's *Red Earth and Pouring Rain* (1995), Rushdie's *The Moor's Last Sigh* (1995), and Rohinton Mistry's *A Fine Balance* (1995), such texts tended to identify continuing problems of hierarchy and oppression in India with the nation-state and nationalism as such. In *Decentering Rushdie,* I have suggested that this "postnational" turn was a common response of left/progressive Indian English writers to the crisis of the nation-state that culminated in the Emergency of 1975–77 and developments in its aftermath, including the fragmentation of the Indian polity and rise of communalism, the transition from Nehruvian state capitalism to neoliberal economics, and, on the flip side, the Indian middle classes' increasing access to the West in terms of commodities, culture, and physical relocation. These Indian events were part of larger, global transitions after th downturn of the early 1970s, engendering the failures of nation-states.

As I suggested in the first chapter, however, the specificity of the postnational turn in the Indian English novel has been lost in light of the theoretical paradigms that dominate Anglo-American Postcolonial Studies. Itself a product of the early 1980s, the field quickly aligned itself with postmodernism and developed ways of thinking about representation, the nation, power/resistance, and history in which postnational orientations were seen as being inherently progressive in relation to national thinking.

Even worse, from the perspective of literary criticism, it canonized the postmodern, postnational texts of the 1980s and 1990s and made them— especially *Midnight's Children* and *The Satanic Verses*—the mark of "the" postcolonial. "Postcoloniality" was now a mode of knowledge, and cosmopolitan intellectuals' task was not to represent national and popular suffering but to point to the problems of national thinking and the impossibility and violence of representation. Migrancy, exile, hybridity, transnationalism—these are the tropes that Postcolonial Studies, ironically, has universalized in its unitary conceptualizations of the nation, the cosmopolitan intellectual, and postcoloniality itself. As a corrective, *Decentering Rushdie* historicizes and particularizes the postnational turn in both literature and theory by revealing the presence of *namak-halaal* cosmopolitanisms that dominated the Indian English novel before the 1980s. Novels of the Nehruvian era, like literary and artistic movements during the anticolonial struggle, set out to embrace the very "task of the intellectual" that Said describes—representing national and local spaces as sites for postcolonial regeneration even when they sharply criticized the existing nation and reflected on the difficulties that emerge when English-educated elites attempt to speak for all Indians. The dominant tropes for *namak-halaal* writings have been the struggle to achieve "the ordinariness of living" (Sahgal), fusion (Markandaya, Sahgal), wholeness (Desai), and "shared rage" (Roy). Concordant relations between the implied author, narrator, and implied reader are key to establishing a *namak-halaal* cosmopolitanism and the ethical commitments to the nation. Rather than positioning themselves as nonteleological, these *namak-halaal* texts freely admit their goal and direction: to confront injustice and inequality, to image a more egalitarian nation and world, and to direct their elite readers toward critical self-reflection in this regard.

By "decentering Rushdie," I aim to expand our theoretical categories of postcoloniality and cosmopolitanism in order that we may more fully grasp the heterogeneity of the genre and postcolonial cultural production in general. This means, however, challenging the urge to simplify and valorize *namak-halaal* texts over postnational ones. My readings of novels by Anita Desai, Kamala Markandaya, Arundhati Roy, Rushdie, and Nayantara Sahgal complicate the broad shift from *namak-halaal* to postnational cosmopolitanisms by debunking rigid, deterministic associations of three kinds: history with literature, orientation with political ideology, and either of these with literary form. I contrast the representations of modernity and subjectivity in two *namak-halaal* texts (chapter 2), pursue the development of interiority and characterization in two feminist, *namak-*

halaal texts (chapter 3), pair together post-Emergency novels with very different perspectives on the nation in terms of their class politics (chapter 4), and read a contemporary, magical realist text as *namak-halaal* (chapter 5). In this way, the ideological and narrative analyses of *Decentering Rushdie* portray a map of postcolonial cosmopolitan writing that reveals the shift from *namak-halaal* to postnational visions over time even as it traces the intricate web of elements—ideological, thematic, and aesthetic—that connects them organically. The selection of multiple novels by Sahgal, whose writings span the entire postcolonial period, is meant to offer a small version of the book's larger project; we can see how her texts change even as they remain steadily *namak-halaal* (and nationalist) in their orientation. Indeed, what stands out about Sahgal is not her representative quality but her uniqueness in terms of the explicit attention she pays to the dialectical relationship between individuals and their sociopolitical situations. *Decentering Rushdie* argues for her necessary presence in discussions about the Indian English novel.

The fact that the texts I have selected and read as *namak-halaal* are all written by women is more than a coincidence, even though I did not set out to write a book about "postcolonial women's writing" per se. I do not mean to imply that there is a necessary link between national orientation and women's writing: one could easily find *namak-halaal* texts by male writers (e.g., Khushwant Singh's *Train to Pakistan* [1956], Bhabani Bhattacharya's *Shadow from Ladakh* [1966]). Nevertheless, the selected novels and authors, paired together, stand out for me in terms of what they reveal about the diversity of the postcolonial Indian English over time—including the richness of their narratives, the close attention they pay to questions of elite/subaltern voice and characterization, their concerns with postcolonial inequalities, and the diversity of their approaches to the nation. More specifically, as I have found, turning toward novels from the 1950s and 1960s itself means highlighting novels by women, and it is significant that so many of these, often raising critical questions about unequal gender relations and the continuing hold of traditional attitudes, are unwilling to write off the nation. While postcolonial theory has long insisted on the opposition between a reactionary, sexist nationalism and women's freedom—no doubt because mainstream nationalism has been notorious in orienting around a normative male subject—these novels by women and featuring female protagonists have sought to create gender-egalitarian spaces within the nation, continuing to see it as the terrain for future emancipation. *Decentering Rushdie,* from this point of view, chronicles the development of a powerful set of female protagonists across different novels by women, whose implied and real authors have them take up the tasks of the intellectual as described by Said.

Decentering Rushdie's attempt to complicate the categories of nationalism and national orientation as inherently reactionary and of cosmopolitanism as inherently radical and progressive is, potentially, its most important contribution. The pre-Emergency, *namak-halaal* texts I read in the first two chapters, for instance, do not hold onto the nation for reactionary purposes but—seeking to fulfill Gandhian and Nehruvian ideals of "wiping every tear from every eye" (Nehru, "Tryst" 4)—exhort their cosmopolitan-elite characters and implied audiences to construct subaltern-friendly models of India. On the flip side, postnational positions, explicitly radical in outlook, can become either Western-oriented or, succumbing to the global marketing of India today, slip into modes that, paradoxically, fetishize and romanticize the nation. We come to recognize that *namak-halaal* and postnational orientations ought not to be regarded, a priori, as either inherently radical or conservative. As I suggested at the end of the previous chapter, critics need to maintain a flexibility in our conceptions of political affiliation in order to properly read the meaning behind a given novel's or author's concerns. The following illustration of a complicated interaction between Roy and Rushdie demonstrates the need for a methodological openness to the texts and authors themselves before making political judgments.

"Some f***ing superpower this."

In their joint interview with Charlie Rose on August 14, 1997, the eve of India's fiftieth anniversary, Rushdie and Roy provide a snapshot of two positions that are available to contemporary Indian intellectuals and artists as they negotiate their relationships to the nation and the world.[2] Rushdie is clearly positioned as the dominant voice in the interview—*The God of Small Things* has not yet won the Booker and Roy's major political essays are a few years away. Rushdie is chummy with Rose throughout, often treating Roy in patronizing ways when not cutting her off in mid-sentence. But he becomes increasingly annoyed as Roy continues to raise questions about his pronouncements regarding India, the Indian middle class, and Indian writing. This leads to complicated developments. Rushdie's celebrated postnational cynicism easily slips into a mainstream nationalist discourse that is complicit with Rose's romanticization of India—even though Rushdie is firmly situated outside India. On the other hand, Roy constantly rejects the suggestion that the growing wealth of Indian elites represents Indian progress and critiques the nation—but she makes this criticism by rhetorically affirming her location within and commitment to the national space.

Upon being asked about the future of India in light of internal separatist strife and continuing tensions with Pakistan, Rushdie contends:

> I don't think there was ever a moment when I thought [India] would split [. . .] It just does exist. It just is there, does exist, and it ain't gonna break up [. . .] Maybe the opposite is going to happen [. . .] Anti-Partition, un-Partition, by which I don't really mean political unity. The oldest object I possess, given to me when I was born, is a block of silver on which is engraved the map of undivided India, the real India [. . .] If I was looking optimistically, 50 years from now, maybe we would see Partition as a blip. (Interview with Charlie Rose)

The ideals that Rushdie expresses represent, at once, a desire for the end of nationalist rivalries and a tautological faith in the unity of the Indian nation: it will never split because it "just is there." National borders mean little for this postnational intellectual, but his position is derived from a deeply Indian notion of subjectivity, one that is secured in almost a religious manner through the sacred, silver block, a talisman marked with the nation and handed down through the family. The perspective seems to evoke a powerful *namak-halaal* narrative, one that is specifically tied to a secular Muslim family's faith in the Indian nation in the late colonial period (Rushdie was born, like Saleem Sinai, in 1947).

Roy's response to this comment, however, draws out how disaffiliated Rushdie's view is from the sociopolitical realities of India in 1997:

> Actually [. . .] I would love to feel the way you feel, because it's the right way to feel, and many of us do wish that this barrier didn't exist between India and Pakistan. But what I think is that . . . maybe it's just a perspective from living there and seeing what happens . . . the fact is that what is happening is peculiar. One the one hand you have this internet culture [. . .] and on the other hand you have tribalism [. . .] (Interview with Charlie Rose; ellipses represent pauses in Roy's speech)

Trying not to appear uncharitable toward Rushdie's desire for a larger unity, Roy nevertheless marks his feeling as one that comes from not "living there and seeing what happens." We are reminded strongly of

Bim's repudiation of Bakul's NRI visions of India in *Clear Light of Day*.[3] Migrancy/exile is rewritten here as a space of unknowing, in which memories of the nation—however powerful—are reified to such an extent that they posit the nation as an inherently unified entity. Rather than simply gesturing to the nation as an idea, Roy engages it by discussing the contradictions within it, the class divisions and the contrast between global thinking and "tribalism." And when the reporter Barbara Crossette jumps into the conversation from its margins in order to gloss "tribalism" as a despicable *subaltern* attitude, Roy asserts that she is in fact talking about middle-class elites and politicians who hold right-wing ideas about religious, class, and caste difference.

This dynamic continues throughout the interview, with Rushdie, Rose, and Crossette continually highlighting India's uniqueness as a hybrid nation with "larger-than-life characters" (Crossette) and a perfect "cornucopia" for any novelist (Rushdie), and Roy emphasizing that India is not all that special—that "there are things about India that are just like everywhere else." Frustrated with Roy, Rushdie makes a stark differentiation between her project and his own:

> What I'm saying is this: India allowed me to become the writer that I have become, that I could not have become otherwise. I mean, I know that this is a book [pointing to Roy's novel] about small things, and intimacies, and details, and so on and, you know, good for it. But I'm saying that there is this other project which excited me which has to do with taking on the whole damn thing, you know, and that's what I've wanted to do and tried to do [. . .]

No longer allowed to play the native informant as he usually does, Rushdie is forced to particularize his views about India as those emanating from a specific ideological position as well as—as a result of India's shameful ban of *The Satanic Verses*—his physical distance from the nation. The surface distinction made here between Rushdie and Roy—nation/fragment, big things/small things—might seem to posit *Roy* as representing the real postmodernist and postnational position and Rushdie as exemplifying *namakhalaal* and nationalist cosmopolitanism. But it is in fact Roy's attention to the conditions of Indian life, to the stories of loss hidden behind the image of the nation as cornucopia, that marks her as being situated within the space of India on many levels. It is Roy's materialist critique of postcoloniality, resisting both the transnational dismissal of the nation and the expatriate's abstract longing for it, that produces her subaltern-centered version of *namak-halaal* cosmopolitanism. In this Roy is very much taking up the tasks of the intellectual as outlined by Said.

Roy, indeed, consistently operates from within such nation-oriented paradigms. Certainly, the criticism of Indian postcoloniality in the second epigraph above positions ongoing caste oppression in direct opposition to nationalist mythologies: a million people have to choose between "carry[ing] shit on their heads" and "starv[ing] to death" even while the national and global media trumpet India's economic growth rate and its advancement as a "superpower" ("It's Outright War"). But Roy's consistent use of the first-person plural—"we are still a country," "our economists"—and her engagement throughout the interview with specific Indian questions, aim to transform the nation by reimagining and reclaiming it from within. As Roy asserts on a more personal note in another interview with *Tehelka*, national orientation and nationalism ought not to be conflated: "I don't have a nationalistic bone in my body. It's just not my instinct. Yet it's inconceivable for me to not be [in India], because it's everything that I love [. . .] I'm just a full desi—full-time desi in that way. I just feel, where else can you be?" ("Success").

"Who dared lose heart when there was work to be done?"

Namak-halaal cosmopolitan writers always resituate themselves thus, in the middle of the very sites of suffering that they critique—and hope to change. While this orientation and ethics emerges from a variety of ideological positions, novels and other texts penned in this mode seek to draw the implied audience into asking questions that, demanding a response, aim to move us into critical thought and action. Both *namak-halaal* and postnational novels in English depict gender inequality, caste oppression, elite brutality, poverty, corruption, and the end of the grand promises that had been made to Indians at the "dawn of freedom" in 1947. But it is only the *namak-halaal* texts that seek a path leading away from that devastation—one that emerges from within the national space itself. The concept of *namak-halaal* writing ought not to be restricted to postcolonial India. The powerful spoken-word poem "First Writing Since" (2001) by the Palestinian-American Suheir Hammad, capturing her feeling as a Muslim and a New Yorker immediately after the terrorist attacks of September 11, 2001, powerfully portrays the "dialectic of suffering and redemption" (Ndebele 54) discussed in chapter 5. Toward the end of her piece, for instance, Hammad writes/says: "anyone reading this is breathing, maybe hurting / but breathing for sure" (3). The lines invoke, simultaneously, the pain that the speaker and implied audience are feeling, as well as the ability to withstand that pain. But by grounding the possibility of hope and agency in the implied and real audiences' acts of breathing, the poem seeks to make us realize our own role in changing the world—the real world lying outside the text. The speaker of the poem can do nothing without the reader/listener; their fates are intertwined.

The passage that concludes *Prison and Chocolate Cake* (1952), Sahgal's early memoir, seeks to create the same relationship with its implied audience as Hammad's poem in order to find respite in a similar moment of crisis and tragedy. Sahgal reports on her feelings after witnessing the cremation of M. K. Gandhi, killed by a Hindu fanatic on January 31, 1948. Though too young to have participated in any of the anticolonial agitations—"that had been the work of a different generation"—Sahgal feels the loss on both a visceral and a historiographical level: "It was as if the continuity of a long process begun before my birth had suddenly snapped like a dry twig, leaving me entirely without a sense of direction" (233). We can discern the mainstream nationalist discourse that lies beneath Sahgal's words and the elite-centered models of leadership that her sorrow about Gandhi conveys—but also the desire to respond to subaltern suffering. In short, we can comprehend the power of the *namak-halaal* narrative, an aspect of postcolonial cosmopolitan-elite writing that deserves to be factored into discussions about postcoloniality.

The lines that end Sahgal's book are a testament to the hope that generations of postcolonial cosmopolitanisms have sought in the struggle to reclaim promises that were broken:

> With an effort I roused myself from my imaginings [. . .] Were my values so fragile [. . .] that I could so easily lose courage when he was no longer there? [. . .] He had come to disturb [people] profoundly, to jolt them out of indifference, to awaken them to one another's suffering, and in so doing to make them reach for the stars. Those stars still beckoned luminously [. . .] Who among us dared lose heart when there was this work to be done? The curtain had rung down over a great drama, but another one was about to begin. Gandhi was dead but India would live on in his children. (*Prison* 233–44)

The gap between "Gandhi's children" and "Midnight's children" describes the difference between Sahgal's *namak-halaal* position and Rushdie's post-national orientation. Clearly, all *namak-halaal* novelists would not espouse such a hagiographical representation of Gandhi—and Sahgal, too, moves away from such a stark nationalism in much of her more mature work.

Yet, the idea that there is "work to be done" is exactly the tone with which Said describes the "task" of the intellectual. What will the Indian English writer do today, when—to borrow a phrase from Langston Hughes—India is "in vogue" in the West?[4] Far be it from me to assign a "task," but I have hoped to offer a methodology that can keep us aware of the various experiments that are already underway. First, the first decade of the new century seems to have re-established, in various ways, that a global hierarchy of nation-states continues to underpin the world system, and that struggles for democracy and self-determination in the postcolonial world continue to express themselves on the terrain of the nation. The diagnosis/prognosis of many on the Left that we have now entered a postnational, decentered phase of world capitalism has been refuted, in my view, by the return of a form of territorial imperialism in the U.S. occupations of Afghanistan (2001) and Iraq (2003); by the current global recession, grounded in the failure of the U.S. housing market; and by the various, nation-oriented rebellions against this state of affairs, whether by state actors (Hugo Chavez in Venezuela) or movements of various sorts (Iraqis, Palestinians, Sri Lankan Tamils, Kashmiris, Guatemalans). We may want to examine how postcolonial fictional and theoretical texts, too, are reimagining the nation in these changing contexts.

It may be possible to identify, broadly speaking, a new interest in realism and materialist representations of history in South Asian fiction—even as the lessons of metafiction and the investigations of transnational relations are not lost. Amitav Ghosh's *The Glass Palace* (2000) and his new series beginning with *Sea of Poppies* (2008); Tariq Ali's now-completed quartet of novels on Islamic/Western interactions; Kamila Shamsie's *Kartography* (2002); and Amit Chaudhuri's *Freedom Song* (1998)—such texts pay attention to the problems of historiography and memory without reducing the nation to either an inexplicable site of chaos or a backdrop for elite dilemmas. The stories in Jhumpa Lahiri's *The Interpreter of Maladies* (2000), similarly, are dedicated to exploring the loss involved in transnational migration, rather than its alleged transcendence of national concerns. The realism and even naturalism of Arvind Adiga's *The White Tiger* (2008), privileging a subaltern character even while treating Indians in general with a Naipaulian disgust, raises important questions about ideology and narrative. And through all this we have the steady and reliable Sahgal, exploring the heterogeneity of the Gandhian movement in *Lesser Breeds* (2003) through the eyes of a young Muslim English professor—

skeptical of nonviolent tactics and, with his background of poverty, alienated by the Anglicized ways of the (nationalist) cosmopolitans around him.

Pierre Bourdieu has written that artists and "cultural producers" have the unique power of presenting to their audiences, in a concrete form, their "more or less confused, vague, unformulated [. . .] experiences of the natural and social world" (qtd. in Lazarus, *Nationalism* 142). However, much as Paolo Freire has said about teachers, Bourdieu maintains a distinction between the subject position and ideology/practice of individual artists by emphasizing that "they may put this power in the service of the dominant" or "in the logic of their struggle within the field of social power, they may put their power at the service of the dominated" (142). In this uncertain moment, when racism against South Asians in the West increases even while *mehndi* "tattoos" and *bindis* proliferate as never before, when new global markets allow an Indian middle class to prosper stupendously but also force thousands of farmers to commit suicide, Indian English writers have a wide range of perspectives to choose from— as they always have. We need to develop models of postcoloniality and cosmopolitanism that will be attentive to new formations and the return of old ones. *Decentering Rushdie* has aimed to put forward a critical methodology that acknowledges literature's ability to reimagine its past, present, and future—even while tracing the historical and ideological contexts that shape and limit those imaginings.

notes

Introduction

1. Tagore, *Ghare Baire* (1915, Bengali), was published in England as *The Home and the World* in 1919—the same year in which Tagore renounced his knighthood to protest the massacre at Jallianwala Bagh.

2. Brennan, *At Home in the World*.

3. See Mishra, pp. 24–25.

4. Gopinath, S. Roy, and Varma demonstrate the usefulness of reading early postcolonial Bollywood cinema in discussions of postcoloniality.

5. See Brennan, *Salman Rushdie*, chapter 4.

6. See *The Bible*, Genesis 19:12–29.

7. Compare with Krishnaswamy, "Mythologies," pp. 136–37.

8. Akhmatova's "Lot's Wife" (1922, Russian) constructs a remarkably similar map of memory and space in asserting the value of looking back.

9. Throughout this book, I use "subjectivity" and "subject position" to signify how capitalist society constructs individuals in an *objective* sense, that is, through the state, through institutions, and through structural hierarchies of class, race, ethnicity, gender, sexuality, national status, and so on. The Foucauldian and Althusserian concepts of "subjects" as those who are "subjected" to society are being invoked here, but without the extremely limited space for agency that is implied by those theories. "Identity" is a symptom of subjectivity as it is expressed on the level of the individual—but it is not concomitant with pure volition or agency. Rather, following Patrick Hogan's useful formulation in *Empire and Poetic Voice* and elsewhere, identity itself represents a dynamic and dialectical movement between "categorial identity" (how we think of ourselves through the categories society mandates) and "practical identity" (what we do and learn to do in day-to-day life). Hogan's recognition of both social constructions of identity and its dynamic aspects can be integrated with classical Marxist theories about the relationship between capitalist structures, the workings of ideology and consciousness, and the possibilities of change and transformation. See chapter 6 of Anjali Prabhu's *Hybridity* for a nuanced discussion of identity in relation to concepts of totality.

10. *Midnight's Children* was published in Britain in 1980 and in the United States in 1981.

11. I thank my anonymous reviewers for this formulation.

12. This terminology is taken from narrative theory. The "implied author" is the intelligence that we derive from the text, the one who organizes the relationship between the narrator and characters, the plot, the setting, the themes, the resolutions, and so forth. As a function of the text, the implied author is distinct from the real, or "flesh-and-blood," author. The "implied audience," alternatively called the "ideal audience" or "authorial audience," refers to the reader(s) that the text imagines for itself, a structural position that is more limited than the flesh-and-blood reader (who could be anyone). "Concordant" relations between the elements of the narrative do not imply a lack of irony or drama or humor; they merely describe a text whose overall effort is to put the elements together and to move toward cohesion. "Discordant" relations actively force the reader to pull things together—and often highlight the impossibility of doing so.

13. This phrase alludes to P. Chatterjee's influential essay, "The Nationalist Resolution to the Women's Question."

14. Two recent texts offer a useful comparison. See B. Ghosh, *When Borne Across,* for astute readings of post-Emergency texts that disentangle their global celebrity status from their literary and political achievements. *When Borne Across* rests on a very different concept of cosmopolitanism from mine—employing the category "cosmopolitics," minimizing the contribution of pre-Emergency writers, and assuming that cosmopolitan identity itself produces progressive or radical postnational politics. Another approach can be seen in T. Khair, *Babu Fictions,* a Marxist account that finds Indian English novels, early and contemporary, as so many expressions of the alienation of Westernized, elite, urban, high-caste Indians.

15. See Rushdie's *Step Across This Line* and his 2005 interview with Bill O'Reilly of Fox News.

Chapter 1

1. See http://www.themanbookerprize.com/news/stories/1099. Rushdie's global celebrity can be attributed to the controversy around *The Satanic Verses,* but as the popularity of *Midnight's Children* shows, it is incorrect to suggest that Rushdie was unknown until the *fatwa* (e.g., Dabashi 172).

2. This is not to suggest that Said, Anderson, or Guha can be neatly aligned with the various postmodernisms of theorists such as Derrida, Foucault, Baudrilliard, and Lyotard. Said's humanism and defense of national liberation, Anderson's Marxist paradigm in investigating the modality of the nation, and Guha's materialist approach to questions of subaltern subjectivity and consciousness do not allow for the complete rejection of Enlightenment legacies. That said, the tensions in these texts between materialist and poststructuralist methods of understanding consciousness have often been deemphasized. Little is made of the difference between Anderson's "imagined nations" and Rushdie's "imaginary homelands."

3. See Meenakshi Mukherjee, "Interrogating Post-Colonialism."

4. I explain this term further below.

5. Aldama and Markels offer provocative discussions of the limits and the possibilities of literature and art.

6. Compare Rushdie's portrayals of Islam in *Step Across This Line* with Ali's in *The Clash of Fundamentalisms* for two very different positions on 9/11 and its aftermath, both from secular intellectuals with South Asian and Muslim backgrounds.

7. See A. Ahmad, *In Theory,* chapter 7, and *Lineages of the Present,* chapter 5, for unique discussions on Indian literature. G. Kumar and K. Kumar argue for the inclusion of what they call "native voices" in locating a "new tradition" of postcolonial writing and theory.

8. See P. Gopal, *Literary,* and Krishnaswamy, "Globalization."

9. Meenakshi Mukherjee warns fellow Indian intellectuals about the "trendy label" that "catapults us into the center-stage of an international academic arena" when, as scholars of "Commonwealth Literature" they had been "furtive creatures, lurking in the margins of English Departments" ("Interrogating" 7).

10. For a discussion of state capitalism in the Soviet Union, see Arnove et al. The links between the Soviet Union, China, and Communist parties in the global South are complex, but "while [Russian and Chinese] tactics may have been different, their strategy was ultimately geared toward the same end—consolidating strong national states, with top-down, bureaucratic regimes in control. In other words, they tried to remake Asia in their own image" (N. Rao, Introduction 28).

11. See Jani and Sreenivas for a brief overview of the elite/subaltern dynamic during the anticolonial struggle in British India.

12. The phrase even had a nickname: TINA.

13. Debates around Stalinist "socialist realism" haunt studies of the PWA. See Gopal's discussion about the Communist Party of India's relationship to the PWA, as well as the explicit attempts of Anand, as a founding member, to assert the PWA's support for political heterogeneity. Contrast with others' description of the PWA as a front group for the Communist Party (e.g., Hogan, *Colonialism* 265).

14. Many contemporary theorists think otherwise. See Bhabha, Spivak, Chakrabarty, Appadurai, P. Chatterjee, and Ismail, for instance, for their different critiques of nationalism. My views align more with those of Lazarus, A. Ahmad, Chrisman, Sivanandan, Said, and Brennan.

15. See Tarlo and B. Chandra, *In the Name of Democracy,* for studies that situate the Emergency more centrally. Whereas Tarlo offers a critique of the Emergency through the eyes of subalterns victimized by it, Chandra attempts to analyze how it arose in relationship to the "Total Revolution" movement around Jayaprakash Narayan.

16. See Tarlo, Introduction.

17. Hogan uses "competence," a term from Noam Chomsky's theories of language, to describe the process by which an individual outside of a given community can become intimately linked to it, restructuring her/his "practical identity" (*Empire* 245).

18. See Cheah and Robbins, and B. Ghosh.

19. We see the same ambiguities and hesitations in Said's theoretical treatments of the category of "exile" in "Reflections on Exile."

20. See, for instance, Hogan's discussion of Atia Hosain (*Colonialism* 265–72).

21. Compare with Rushdie's comment: "English literature has its Indian branch [. . .] This literature is also Indian literature. There is no incompatibility here" ("'Commonwealth'" 65)

22. Paranjape allows that the Emergency was a "major exception" to this general lack of commitment because it "threatened [. . .] bourgeois freedoms" for the first time ("Inside and Outside" 216).

23. Chapter 1 of Cheah, *Inhuman Conditions,* reveals his unique blend of historicism with a Derridean critique of humanism.

24. See Steingass, p. 1427. *Namak-halaal* is "Faithful, loyal, true," while *namak-haraam* is "Untrue to salt eaten together, i.e. ungrateful, faithless, perfidious, disloyal; disobedient; evil, wicked."

25. Lelyveld and Devji provide broader contexts for S. A. Khan's thoughts on the rebellion and modernity. Thanks to Shahzad Bashir, Stephen Dale, Priya Gopal, and David Lelyveld for their communications and references on this topic.

26. See also Pliny, *Natural History,* 31.41. Thanks to Dan Seward for this reference.

27. Thanks to V. Sreenivas for the Kannada proverbs in this section.

28. Thanks to Vandana Jani for this proverb.

29. See *Life of Swami Vivekananda,* pp. 616–17. Thanks to Ravishankar Naik for this reference.

30. Even the film *Namak-Halaal* can now be reread. Beneath its dogged commitment to reactionary paradigms of class, gender, and sexuality, the film registers a deep political and moral conflict. Arjun is caught between being faithful to Raja, as he has been instructed to do, and being loyal to his "rural" and "Indian" values by confronting his boss's Westernized, womanizing ways. Amitabh Bachchan also performed in an older film, *Namak-Haraam* (1973), in which "loyalty" once again drives the dramatic tension. The son of a factory boss (Bachchan) must decide whether to crush a workers' strike—and break his friendship with his childhood friend, the union leader (Rajesh Khanna).

31. See S. Roy, especially the Introduction.

32. Recent work being done on secularism points to a more promising end, neither embracing nor rejecting the Nehruvian legacy out of hand. See Needham and Sunder Rajan.

Chapter 2

1. See Brass, Brown, B. Chandra, P. Chatterjee, Guha, S. Sarkar, and T. Sarkar.

2. The "national-popular" is a much-debated concept. As Hall explains, the national-popular is a site of contestation that can be directed toward progressive or reactionary ends (439). See Pearmain's explanation and application of the term.

3. "Disavowing Decolonization" is the title of the second chapter in Neil Lazarus's *Nationalism and Cultural Practice in the Postcolonial World,* featuring a comprehensive study of this orientation in postcolonial theory.

4. The "constitutionalist" bent and communal orientation of the Ceylon National Congress provides a counterexample as an anticolonial nationalism that remained fairly detached from popular pressures. See Russell and A. Wilson.

5. Harris argues in *The End of the Third World* that the discourses of populism and internationalism in mainstream nationalism were responses to the socioeconomic necessities of new nation-states. Leaders of the Non-Alignment Movement such as Nehru could legitimately claim, in the aftermath of independence, that they represented the united voice of working and poor masses of the world who had been robbed by the rich, imperialist countries. But their "vision of an independent state and of the creation of a national power" had "much appeal for those likely to inherit what the foreigners left behind—whether land, business or official positions" (Harris 177).

6. This aside from Khushwant Singh's obvious nationalism as expressed in his essays and work outside of fiction.

7. See Menon and Bhasin.

8. Bhatnagar approvingly reads all of Sahgal's texts, in fact, as being Gandhian, considering her cosmopolitan proclivities and her emphasis on women's equality to be simply an internal critique of it (e.g., *Political* 107–18). But Sahgal's secularism and acceptance of nontraditional cultural practices is more in line with Nehru's departure from Gandhian traditionalism and religiosity.

9. Such reclamation of lost space is central to my reading of *The God of Small Things* in chapter 5. See Sinha on the centrality of such clubs to British rule in terms of fashioning ideals of racial and national identity. George Orwell's *Burmese Days* (1936) portrays debates among the British about the exclusiveness of the clubs after the Jallianwala Bagh massacre in 1919.

10. Less central than Harish and Girish but memorable nonetheless is the businessman Sir Harilal Mathur, who was knighted in 1942 for donating 6 lakhs of rupees (Rs. 600,000) to the war effort. At one point, this "black Englishman," as the English call him, donates a large sum to the Sharanpur Club for the building of a swimming pool—one that Indians could not use. "No doubt," our narrator adds, "it pleased him to contribute to a cause that excluded [Indians], even though it excluded him too" (*A Time* 159).

11. Compare with my discussion in chapter 4 of Sonali and the Beggar in Sahgal's 1985 novel, *Rich Like Us*.

12. Compare with Brennan's discussion of the "imperial-universal" in relation to Salman Rushdie's writing (*Salman Rushdie* 56).

13. Bhattacharya's *Shadow* directly addresses the conflict between steel towns and rural India. For a historical perspective on Nehruvian steel towns, see S. Roy, chapter 4.

14. Cohn employs these terms to study the British use of South Asian languages in consolidating power.

15. See Trotsky, *History of the Russian Revolution:* "The privilege of historic backwardness [*sic*]—and such a privilege exists—permits, or rather compels, the adoption of whatever is ready in advance of a specified date, skipping a whole set of intermediary stages" (26–27).

Chapter 3

1. Indira Gandhi herself was assassinated by one of her Sikh bodyguards in 1984, a victim of the communalism that she had helped invoke.

2. For accounts of this period I have relied primarily on Bose and Jalal, R. Gopal, Jalal, and Vanaik.

3. The economic success of the Green Revolution—due to a combination of high-yield seeds, fertilizers, and irrigation methods based on tube-wells and widespread electrification—vastly increased grain production and staved off the severity of 1960s food shortages. But the Green Revolution also "exacerbated social tensions everywhere in the subcontinent" since only wealthy farmers could keep affording new crops, poorer peasants were drawn into wage labor, and high crop yields were offset by crop instability (Stein 387). See Vandana Shiva, *The Violence of the Green Revolution.*

4. By "state capitalism" I mean the direct use of the state in capitalist accumulation, not only the protection of capitalist interests through laws, police, foreign policy, and so on. "State capitalism" is often mistaken for "socialism." In fact, given the weakness of the Indian bourgeoisie after independence, it was "the industrialists themselves [who]

favored a larger, direct role for the State in many of their activities" in the early years of Indian planning (Vaidyanathan 16).

5. See both Tarlo and Perry on Emergency violence and resistance. From a different angle, B. Chandra in *In the Name of Democracy* does not exonerate the Emergency and the excesses carried out "in the name of democracy," but also points to the right-wing tendencies of the JP movement. M. Keith Booker goes much further, defending the Emergency and criticizing Rushdie's negative representation of it in *Midnight's Children* (305–7).

6. Like many texts critical of the Emergency, Sahgal's could be published only after it ended. Upon returning to power in 1980, Indira Gandhi immediately revoked Sahgal's status as ambassador to Italy.

7. Highlights include the Naxalist uprising in rural Bengal (1967); the Shahada movement of landless laborers in Maharashtra (1972–73); the Chipko movement against deforestation in Uttar Pradesh (1973); the student-based Nav Nirman movement in Gujarat (1972–74); the massive, twenty-day, all-India Railways strike (1974); and the Bihar movement for "Total Revolution," headed by J. P. Narayan (1974–75).

8. See Jayawardena and West for nuanced studies of the relationship between women's movements and nationalist movements. P. Bose also demonstrates the usefulness of the category of "feminist-nationalism."

9. This was not unique in and of itself, as women built the feminist movement of the 1920s and participated in the nationalist and radical struggles leading up to independence. See R. Kumar, *History of Doing*, Kannabiran and Lalitha, and Stree Shakti Sanghatana. The leadership of women often shifted the ideological orientation of specific struggles from traditional to radical approaches (R. Kumar, *History* 101–2).

10. See Forbes, pp. 226–29.

11. In 1977–78 a vigorous campaign centered in Delhi won important legal reforms against dowry deaths. In 1979–80 mass anger against the Supreme Court's acquittal of three policemen who had raped a teenage girl in their custody in Mathura made rape a public issue. It forced the Supreme Court to reverse its decision and support the passage of antirape laws. In the 1980s and 1990s, feminists took up a variety of issues including denial of inheritance, misuse of contraceptives and sex-determination tests, sati, forced prostitution, undernourishment and excessive childbearing, inadequate divorce rights, and child marriage.

12. The nationalist movement had similarly provided women writers in the regional languages a larger arena for their practice (Natarajan 12).

13. It is worth emphasizing that while all but the wealthiest women bore the unequal burden of housework, child-rearing, and family obligations, it is mainly elite, middle-class women who experienced the severe cloistering in the home that many novels portray. See Agarwal; R. Kumar, "Family and Factory"; and Mukul Mukherjee.

14. See readings of *The Day in Shadow* in Bhatnagar (both works), Iyengar, and Jain (both works), and analyses of *Clear Light of Day* in Afzal-Khan, Banerjee, and Dhawan.

15. See Phelan on the ethics of character narration.

16. Following Abbott, I distinguish between free indirect style and interior monologue on the basis of how long it is sustained. Like Abbott, I realize that the terms may overlap at some point (70–72, 192).

17. "Reporting, interpreting, evaluating" is Phelan's more readable gloss of classical narrative theory's categories of "reporting, reading, regarding" (50).

18. *Relationship* is a published collection of love letters that Sahgal exchanged with E. N. Mangat Rai in the aftermath of *her* divorce from Gautam Sahgal, apparently an irrepressible Panjabi businessman very much like Som. See Harish and S. Narayan.

19. Divorce under the Hindu Code Bill ostensibly existed to give equal rights to women, but the restrictions imposed by both the law and societal custom actually made a husband's divorce of his wife far more common (Parashar 115–19). Indeed, women had not even received absolute property and inheritance rights by the 1950s, which exacerbated their economic dependence (118).

20. Ignoring this "Christian" element, Khair misreads Raj's discourse about national emasculation as a sign of the text's affiliation with Hindu-fundamentalist paradigms (190).

21. Nehru held progressive views on women's equality, but the nationalist movement as a whole could be quite reactionary. While women's equality was official Congress policy, women themselves were treated as separate and inferior, which even led to a (failed) call for a separate women's Congress (Forbes 142–43). Gandhi's own position on women's equality was quite problematic, as he called on women to emulate Sita, the mythic, ideal wife (Forbes 129) and claimed that women were more suited for nonviolence because of their spirit of self-sacrifice (Jayawardena 97).

22. Afzal-Khan consistently takes this position.

23. Compare with Parekh's reading of Bim and Tara.

24. The NRI is the "Non-Resident Indian," an official designation for those who are Indian by race, ethnicity, or birth but who live abroad. It has a negative cultural reference ("Not Really Indian," "Not Reliable Indian") that I'm ironically accessing here (since I am myself an NRI).

25. The intensity of feeling on this topic recalls the relationship between Little Chandler and Ignatius Gallagher in "A Little Cloud," a short story from James Joyce's *Dubliners* (1901).

26. Amitav Ghosh's *The Shadow Lines,* similarly, divides the novel into two parts—"Going Away" and "Coming Home"—in order to employ this powerful rubric for investigating cosmopolitanism and nationalism.

27. There are undoubtedly instances in the context of Western prejudice and racism in which a member of a non-Western diaspora might emphasize the positives as opposed to the negatives of his or her country. But the sort of representation that Bakul offers is not only a poor response to Orientalism (which also cites the *Bhagavad-Gita* and Taj Mahal) but also the mark of someone who has little to say about day-to-day Indian life in the first place.

28. I thank the graduate students in my spring 2008 seminar on postcolonial women's writing for providing a rich intellectual forum for my thoughts on the conclusion of *Clear Light of Day.*

29. Later articles such as "The Virtuous Woman" (*The Tribune,* 24 December 1988) are a bit more inventive, speaking of "re-writing" the myths of passive heroines such as Sita and Savitri in the "search for identity and emancipation" (*Point of View* 33).

30. The left/progressive discourse that marks Indira Gandhi's speeches gives a sense of the ideological complexity of the times.

Chapter 4

1. In terms of plot, the Emergency is referred to only toward the end of *Midnight's Children*. But its impact on the first-person narrator, retelling the story after the Emergency, makes it central to the text on multiple levels.

2. See Brennan, *Salman Rushdie and the Third World*.

3. See Jani, review article on *Mapping Subaltern Studies and the Postcolonial*.

4. See Lazarus, *Nationalism,* pp. 117–19, for a discussion of Guha and Spivak.

5. See Guha, "Nationalism."

6. See S. Sarkar, "The Decline of the Subaltern in *Subaltern Studies.*"

7. Some readers, like Robbins, have mistakenly read this novel as a cosmopolitan critique of nationalism because of its unrelenting opposition to the specific form of Hindu-communalist nationalism that emerged in the Bengali Swadeshi movement of the early twentieth century (*Feeling Global* 161–63). But Said, whose model of cosmopolitanism Robbins finds attractive, places Tagore first on his list of cosmopolitan-elites who supported national liberation while being critical of existing nationalist formations (Lazarus, *Nationalism* 141).

8. See Eagleton, "Nationalism: Irony and Commitment."

9. Contrast this model with Kincaid's lines about tourism from *A Small Place.* The first line of the passage I am considering sounds like an idealist vision of borders—"Every native of every place is a potential tourist, and every tourist is a native of somewhere" (18)—but is actually about situating border-crossing within specific spaces. This dimension is furthered by the end of the passage: "But some natives—most natives in the world—cannot go anywhere. They are too poor [. . .] They are too poor to escape the reality of their lives" (19).

10. This trajectory also parallels the changing fortunes of the "Third World" as a political idea. See Prashad and Harris.

11. Contrast my view of Rushdie's turn away from the nation with Hogan's discussion of Rushdie and Gandhism in "*Midnight's Children.*" Also see Rege, who argues that this novel gave Indian writers "the courage to tell their own stories as Indian stories" and to "be ironic and ambivalent about their relationship to the nation state" (274).

12. See P. Chatterjee's implicit critique of universalism itself in "Community in the East."

13. The U.S. war on Afghanistan in 2001, for instance, was launched by George W. Bush and backed by liberal groups such as the Feminist Majority.

14. Thanks to Leo Coleman for his comments on my reading of Padma.

15. While the Sanskrit word *pankaj,* a synonym for *padma* ("lotus"), etymologically means "born in the mud," neither *padma* nor *lakshmi* has such a meaning.

16. Compare the resolutions of scenes of communalist violence in Manto; Devi; A. Ghosh, *The Shadow Lines;* Rushdie, *The Moor's Last Sigh;* and Mistry, *Such a Long Journey.*

17. See Tharoor, *India: From Midnight to Millennium* and *The Elephant, the Tiger, and the Cell Phone.*

18. This is a reference to the shadowy production of the Maruti car by Sanjay Gandhi, Indira Gandhi's son. According to the report of the Maruti Commission (31 May 1979), every transaction having to do with the car was influenced by governmental pressure (R. Gopal 83–86).

19. See B. Chandra, *In the Name of Democracy,* chapter 9.

20. S. Sarkar, *Modern India,* is the classic text here; compare with B. Chandra, *Nationalism and Colonialism.*

21. There is more than a little romanticization of the British working class here, particularly in relation to the World War II bombing of London. Compare with the similar representation of the London bombing in A. Ghosh, *The Shadow Lines.*

22. The larger context is important, as Marxism itself (in this period, in which the Soviet Union supported Indira Gandhi) is represented as little more than book knowledge. Ravi, Sonali's ex-boyfriend, was a great reader of *The Communist Manifesto* while in

school in England but, for most of the novel, becomes merely a tool for the Emergency when in India.

23. Sita was married to the god-king Ram, which is also the name of Rose's husband. Sita provides the Hindu-scriptural model for the "good woman" that is often championed by conservative Hindus and critiqued by feminists.

24. See A. Roy, "Land and Freedom."

25. The Indian Communists' position, which Lenin opposed, can be characterized by the following letter they sent to the British Communists on August 9, 1920—just two days after the Second Congress (July 19–Aug. 7)—requesting that they send organizers and agitators to "take the leadership of the masses away from the nationalist politicians and passive resisters and [. . .] organize the Indian workers on class lines for political freedom and economic and social liberation" (Persits 174). The massive Non Co-Operation movement led by those "passive resisters" exploded in September, launching a new era of rebellion in the anticolonial struggle.

26. In *Inhuman Conditions,* Cheah cites *The Communist Manifesto* against Lenin's theses defending anti-imperialist national liberation struggles in order to oppose Marx and Lenin on the national question (26–29). See Lewis for an opposing view. In "Karl Marx, Eurocentrism, and the 1857 Revolt in British India," I contend that the Revolt started to shift Marx's ideas about anticolonial struggle, a movement that led him to theoretically and practically rally around Irish national self-determination in the late 1860s.

Chapter 5

1. Cited in "EMS Attacks Literary Content of Arundhati Roy's Novel." The Rediff piece reports on, and presumably translates, an article that E. M. S. published in *Deshabhimani,* the CPI(M)'s Malayali newspaper. The audience for the article, in other words, would be a CPI(M)-friendly one that 1) has a direct interest in Roy's portrayals (*The God of Small Things* is set in a town in Kerala), and 2) is susceptible to cultural-nationalist critiques of "the West" and English-language texts given the politics of language and location in postcolonial India.

2. I call *Frontline* CPI(M)-friendly not only because it has regularly featured articles and columns by CPI(M) leaders and intellectuals but also because even its journalistic articles—usually very thorough—rarely interrogate CPI(M) policies and positions.

3. See the Web page of the Narmada Bachao Andolan (Save the Narmada Movement) at http://www.narmada.org.

4. *Frontline* favorably covered Roy's work with Dalit literacy and writing workshops in the late 1990s and has continued to publish articles by and about Roy. For instance, see R. M. Nair on Roy's support of Dalit literary programs, and "A Novel Gesture."

5. See N. Rao, "Politics of Genre," on the popularity of *The God of Small Things* as a "safe" text in the Western academy versus the virtual avoidance of Roy's hard-hitting essays.

6. A. Ahmad seeks to differentiate between his critique of the novel's political ideology and his reading of the novel as fiction, but the distinction between the two is lost throughout.

7. See my discussion in the conclusion of Charlie Rose's interview with Rushdie and Roy on 14 August 1997.

8. Head's metaphor for the effects of postcolonial development is exceedingly poi-

gnant to me, as my seventeen-year-old cousin, Tapan Malay Dave, was crushed to death by a rampaging truck on a highway in India in June 2001.

9. A. Ghosh's *The Glass Palace* (2000) provides an intriguing comparison, for it too aims to chart out spaces for survival, resilience, and rebellion in the midst of cataloguing the atrocities of colonialism and failed anticolonial struggles.

10. Wilson's article appears in *Liberation,* a publication of CPI (Marxist-Leninist) Liberation, a party that is critical of the CPI(M). While this political context is important to consider, the paper is so deeply engaged with the novel on a textual level that it deserves consideration on literary-critical grounds.

11. "Dalit," meaning "the oppressed," is how politically conscious members of the group often known as "untouchables" and "harijans" have referred to themselves since the 1960s and 1970s.

12. This is not to minimize the impact of Sophie Mol's death on the children; we are told that "The Loss of Sophie Mol grew robust and alive. Like a fruit in season. Every season" (*The God of Small Things* 17).

13. Rahel's feelings of loss and confusion at Sophie Mol's funeral can be reread in this light, for it is only after Estha sees Velutha's broken body 300 pages later ("blood spilled from his skull like a secret" [*The God of Small Things* 303]) that we understand what Rahel saw when her fantasy painter fell ("dark blood spilling from his skull like a secret" [8]).

14. The twins are born during the India–China war of 1962—which some historians regard as the beginning of the demise of Nehruvian India.

15. Paravans are the specific Dalit caste group identified in the novel.

16. "The Greater Common Good," similarly, reports that it is difficult to find facts and figures about how many were displaced in past development projects, but its function is to invert the truths that it finds: "where there's no press, no NBA, no court case, there are no records. The displaced leave no trail at all" (52).

17. E. M. S. Namboodiripad claims that "the two most effective means" in literature for diverting people from "surging forward against capitalism" are the valorization of sexual deviance and anti-Communist politics, and Roy's text contains both ("EMS Attacks"). There is little to distinguish E. M. S.'s concern for the rise of "literature that in recent years has been tickling the senses and exerted a bad influence on the younger generation" ("EMS Attacks") from the position of Sabu Thomas, the conservative Syrian Christian lawyer who tried to sue Roy because "the sexual deeds described in the book will corrupt readers' minds" (qtd. in Sreedharan).

18. Herman's essay, written in spring 2008 for my graduate seminar, is unpublished. I reference the essay when citing Herman, but refer to quotations from Nixon's and Said's original work directly.

19. A. Ahmad remarks that "Naxalite" becomes "somewhat of an all-purpose term in Roy's fiction," the mark of the "truly revolutionary" ("Reading" 104). The fleeting references to Naxalites are significant in that they signify a *Left* voice that challenged the CPI(M) in the 1960s and 1970s.

20. Omvedt also misreads Roy's work as an expression of the postmodernist rejection of development: from "an Enlightenment faith in progress and rational human planning, we have come to a post-modernist questioning of development itself" ("Dams and Bombs-I"). But Omvedt's leftist championing of development is not sufficiently critical of it as *capitalist* development.

21. See A. Roy, "Tide? Or Ivory Snow?," and A. Roy, "Land and Freedom."

22. See the debate between Patnaik and S. Sarkar/T. Sarkar.

23. See A. Roy, "It's Outright War."

24. See especially chapter 1, "Rebellious Aesthetic Acts," which aims to specify the change that "magical realism" can and cannot effect in the real world.

Conclusion

1. Said reads Karl Marx's writings on India to show that nineteenth-century European writers on Asia were Orientalist despite differences in ideology (*Orientalism* 153–57). See A. Ahmad, *In Theory*, chapter 6, and Jani, "Karl Marx," for alternative views on Marx's India articles.

2. The entire interview can be viewed at http://www.youtube.com.

3. See chapter 3.

4. In "When the Negro Was in Vogue," Hughes reflects back on the 1920s and the phenomenon of whites enjoying the work of Black jazz musicians—in segregated Harlem clubs.

works cited

Abbas, Khwaja Ahmad. *Inquilab*. Delhi: Jaico Publishing House, 1958.

Abbott, H. Porter. *The Cambridge Introduction to Narrative*. Cambridge: Cambridge University Press, 2002.

Achebe, Chinua. *Things Fall Apart*. 1958. London: Heinemann, 1989.

Adiga, Aravind. *The White Tiger*. New York: Free Press, 2008.

Afzal-Khan, Fawzia. *Cultural Imperialism and the Indo-English Novel: Genre and Ideology in R. K. Narayan, Anita Desai, Kamala Markandaya, and Salman Rushdie*. University Park: Pennsylvania State University Press, 1993.

Agarwal, Bina. *A Field of One's Own: Gender and Land Rights in South Asia*. Cambridge: Cambridge University Press, 1994.

Ahmad, Aijaz. *In Theory: Nations, Classes, Literatures*. London: Verso, 1992.

———. *Lineages of the Present: Political Essays*. 1996. London: Verso, 2000.

———. "Reading Arundhati Roy *Politically*." Review of *The God of Small Things*, by Arundhati Roy. *Frontline* 14.15 (26 July–8 Aug. 1997): 103–8.

Ahmad, Dohra. "This fundo stuff is really something new": Fundamentalism and Hybridity in *The Moor's Last Sigh*." *The Yale Journal of Criticism* 18.1 (2005): 1–20.

Aidoo, Ama Ata. "For Whom Things Did Not Change." *No Sweetness Here*. 1970. Garden City, NY: Doubleday, 1972. 8–29.

Akhmatova, Anna. "Lot's Wife." 1922–24. Trans. Tanya Karshtedt. http://www.poetry-loverspage.com/poets/akhmatova/lots_wife.html.

Aldama, Frederick Luis. *Postethnic Narrative Criticism*. Austin: University of Texas Press, 2003.

Ali, Tariq. *The Clash of Fundamentalisms*. London: Verso, 2002.

———. *An Indian Dynasty: The Story of the Nehru-Gandhi Family*. New York: G. P. Putnam's Sons, 1985.

Anand, Divya. "Inhabiting the Space of Literature: An Ecocritical Study of Arundhati Roy's *God of Small Things* and O. V. Vijayan's *The Legends of Khasak*." *Isle: Interdisciplinary Studies in Literature and Environment* 12.2 (2005): 95–108.

Anand, Mulk Raj. *Coolie*. 1936. New Delhi: Penguin, 1993.

———. *Untouchable*. 1935. London: Bodley Head, 1970.

Anderson, Benedict. *Imagined Communities: Reflections on the Origins and Spread of Nationalism*. 1983. Second edition. London: Verso, 1991.

Appadurai, Arjun. *Modernity at Large: Cultural Dimensions of Globalization.* Minneapolis: University of Minnesota Press, 1996.

Appiah, Kwame Anthony. *Cosmopolitanism: Ethics in a World of Strangers.* New York: W. W. Norton, 2006.

———. "Is the Post- in Postmodernism the Post- in Post-Colonial?" *Critical Inquiry* 17 (Winter 1991): 336–57.

Armah, Ayi Kweh. *The Beautyful Ones Are Not Yet Born.* 1968. Oxford: Heinemann International, 1969.

Arnove, Anthony, Peter Binns, Tony Cliff, Chris Harman, and Ahmed Shawki. *Russia: From Workers' State to State Capitalism.* Chicago: Haymarket Books, 2003.

Balfour, Edward. *The Cyclopaedia of India and of Eastern and Southern Asia.* Vol. 3. London: Bernard Quaritch, 1885.

Banerjee, Laksmisree. "Indian Women's Voices: The Postcolonial and Post-Modernist Era." *Postcolonial Discourse: A Study of Contemporary Literature.* Ed. R. K. Dhawan. Delhi: Prestige, 1997. 127–38.

Batty, Nancy E. "The Art of Suspense: Rushdie's 1001 (Mid-) Nights." *Reading Rushdie: Perspectives on the Fiction of Salman Rushdie.* Ed. M. D. Fletcher. Amsterdam: Rodopi, 1994. 69–82.

Bhabha, Homi. *The Location of Culture.* London: Routledge, 1994.

Bhatnagar, M. K. *The Fiction of Nayantara Sahgal.* New Delhi: Creative Books, 1996.

———. *Political Consciousness in Indian English Writing: A Study of Manohar Malgonkar, Nayantara Sahgal, and Bhabani Bhattacharya.* Delhi: Bahri Publications, 1991.

Bhattacharya, Bhabani. *He Who Rides a Tiger.* New York: Crown Press, 1954.

———. *Shadow From Ladakh.* New York: Crown Publishers, 1966.

———. *So Many Hungers!* Bombay: Hind Kitabs, 1947.

The Bible. New International Version. http://www.biblegateway.com.

Booker, M. Keith. "*Midnight's Children,* History, and Complexity: Reading Rushdie after the Cold War." *Critical Essays on Salman Rushdie.* Ed. M. Keith Booker. New York: G. K. Hall and Co., 1999. 283–313.

Bose, Brinda. "In Desire and Death: Eroticism as Politics in Arundhati Roy's *The God of Small Things.*" *ariel* 29.2 (Apr. 1998): 59–72.

Bose, Purnima. *Organizing Empire: Individualism, Collective Agency, and India.* Durham: Duke University Press, 2003.

Bose, Sugata and Ayesha Jalal. *Modern South Asia: History, Culture, Political Economy.* London: Routledge, 1998.

Brass, Paul. *The Politics of India Since Independence.* Second edition. Cambridge: Cambridge University Press, 1994.

Breckenridge, Carol A., Dipesh Chakrabarty, Homi Bhabha, and Sheldon Pollock, eds. *Cosmopolitanism.* Durham: Duke University Press, 2002.

Brennan, Timothy. "Cosmopolitanism and Internationalism." *Debating Cosmopolitics.* Ed. Danielle Arghibugi. London: Verso, 2003. 40–50.

———. *At Home in the World: Cosmopolitanism Now.* Cambridge: Harvard University Press, 1997.

———. *Salman Rushdie and the Third World: Myths of the Nation.* New York: St. Martin's Press, 1989.

Brown, Judith M. *Modern India: The Origins of an Asian Democracy.* Delhi: Oxford University Press, 1985.

Chakrabarty, Dipesh. *Provincializing Europe: Postcolonial Thought and Historical Difference.* Princeton: Princeton University Press, 2000.

Chandra, Bipan. *In the Name of Democracy: JP Movement and the Emergency.* Delhi: Penguin, 2003.

———. *Nationalism and Colonialism in Modern India.* Hyderabad: Orient Longman, 1979.

———, Mridula Mukherjee, and Aditya Mukherjee. *India After Independence, 1947–2000.* New Delhi: Penguin, 1999.

Chandra, Vikram. *Red Earth and Pouring Rain.* Boston: Little, Brown and Co., 1995.

Chatterjee, Partha. "Beyond the Nation? Or Within?" *Social Text* 56 (Autumn 1998): 57–69.

———. "Community in the East." *Economic and Political Weekly* (Feb. 7, 1998): 277–82.

———. "The Nationalist Resolution of the Women's Question." *Recasting Women: Essays in Indian Colonial History.* Ed. Kumkum Sangari and Sudesh Vaid. New Brunswick: Rutgers University Press, 1990. 233–53.

———. *Nationalist Thought and the Colonial World: A Derivative Discourse.* Minneapolis: University of Minnesota Press, 1993.

Chatterjee, Upamanyu. *English, August.* London: Faber and Faber, 1988.

Cheah, Pheng. *Inhuman Conditions: On Cosmopolitanism and Human Rights.* Cambridge: Harvard University Press, 2006.

———. *Spectral Nationality: Passages of Freedom from Kant to Postcolonial Literatures of Liberation.* New York: Columbia University Press, 2003.

——— and Bruce Robbins, eds. *Cosmopolitics: Thinking and Feeling Beyond the Nation.* Minneapolis: University of Minnesota Press, 1996.

Chrisman, Laura. "Nationalism and Postcolonial Studies." *The Cambridge Companion to Postcolonial Literary Studies.* Ed. Neil Lazarus. Cambridge: Cambridge University Press, 2005. 183–98.

Cohn, Bernard S. *Colonialism and Its Forms of Knowledge.* Princeton: Princeton University Press, 1996.

Conrad, Joseph. *Heart of Darkness.* New York: Dover, 1990 (1902).

Crane, Ralph J. *Inventing India: A History of India in English-Language Fiction.* London: Macmillan, 1992.

Dabashi, Hamid. *Iran: A People Interrupted.* New York: New Press, 2007.

Danticat, Edwidge. *The Dew Breaker.* New York: Random House, 2004.

Davidson, Basil. *The Black Man's Burden: Africa and the Curse of the Nation-State.* New York: Times Books, 1992.

Derrida, Jacques. *Of Grammatology.* Trans. Gayatri C. Spivak. Baltimore: Johns Hopkins University Press, 1976.

Desai, Anita. *Clear Light of Day.* 1980. London: Penguin Books, 1982.

———. Interview with Feroza Jussawalla. *Interviews with Writers of the Post-Colonial World.* Ed. Feroza Jussawalla and Reed Way Dasenbrock. Jackson: University Press of Mississippi, 1992. 156–79.

Deshpande, Shashi. *The Dark Holds No Terrors.* Ghaziabad: Vikas Publishing House, 1980.

Devi, Jyotirmoyee. *The River Churning.* Trans. Meenakshi Chatterjee. New Delhi: Kali for Women, 1995.

Devji, Faisal. "Apologetic Modernity." *Modern Intellectual History* 4.1 (2007): 61–76.

Dharwadker, Vinay. "Indian Writing Today: A View from 1994." *World Literature Today* 68.2 (Spring 1994): 237–41.

Dhawan, R. K. "Introduction." *Indian Women Novelists.* Ed. R. K. Dhawan. New Delhi: Prestige Publishers, 1991.

Dingwaney, Anuradha. "Salman Rushdie." *A History of Indian Literature in English.* Ed. Arvind K. Mehrotra. New York: Columbia University Press, 2003. 308–17.

Eagleton, Terry. "Nationalism: Irony and Commitment." *Nationalism, Colonialism, and Literature.* Ed. S. Deane. Minneapolis: Minnesota University Press, 1990.

Ellison, Ralph. *Invisible Man.* 1952. New York: Vintage International, 1995.

Emecheta, Buchi. *The Joys of Motherhood.* Oxford: Heinemann, 1979.

"EMS Attacks Literary Content of Arundhati Roy's Novel." *Rediff On The Net.* 29 Nov. 1997. 25 Aug. 2008. http://www.rediff.com/news/nov/29roy.htm.

Faiz, Faiz Ahmad. "Dawn of Freedom" (*Subh-e Azadi*). Trans. Agha Shahid Ali. *Eqbal Ahmad: Confronting Empire.* Interviews with David Barsamian. Boston: South End Press, 2000. viii.

Fanon, Frantz. *The Wretched of the Earth.* New York: Grove Press, 1963.

Forbes, Geraldine. *Women in Modern India.* Cambridge: Cambridge University Press, 1998.

Gandhi, Indira. *Indira Gandhi on Herself and Her Time.* Interview with N. S. Bose. Calcutta: Anand Publishers, 1987.

———. *Indira Gandhi Speaks: On Democracy, Socialism, and Third World Non-Alignment.* Ed. Henry M. Christman. New York: Taplinger, 1975.

Gandhi, Leela. "Novelists of the 1930s and 1940s." *A History of Indian Literature in English.* Ed. Arvind K. Mehrotra. New York: Columbia University Press, 2003. 168–92.

Gandhi, Mohandas K. *The Story of My Experiments with Truth* (Satya-na Prayogo). Trans. Mahadev Desai. New York: Dover, 1983.

Genoways, Ted. "'Let Them Snuff Out the Moon': Faiz Ahmad Faiz's Prison Lyrics in *Dast-e Saba.*" *The Annual of Urdu Studies* 19 (2004): 94–119.

Ghosh, Amitav. *The Calcutta Chromosome.* New Delhi: Ravi Dayal, 1996.

———. "The Ghosts of Mrs. Gandhi." *The Imam and the Indian.* New Delhi: Ravi Dayal, 2002.

———. *The Glass Palace.* New York: Random House, 2000.

———. *The Shadow Lines.* Delhi: Ravi Dayal, 1988.

Ghosh, Bishnupriya. *When Borne Across: Literary Cosmopolitics in the Contemporary Indian Novel.* New Brunswick: Rutgers University Press, 2004.

Gopal, Priyamvada. "'Curious Ironies': Matter and Meaning in Bhabani Bhattacharya's Novel of the 1943 Bengal Famine." *ariel* 32.2 (July 2001): 61–88.

———. *Literary Radicalism in India: Gender, Nation, and the Transition to Independence.* London: Routledge, 2005.

——— and Neil Lazarus. Editorial. *After Iraq: Reframing Postcolonial Studies.* Ed. Priyamvada Gopal and Neil Lazarus. Special issue of *New Formations* 59 (August 2006): 7–9.

Gopal, Ram. *India Under Indira.* New Delhi: Criterion Publishers, 1986.

Gopinath, Gayatri. *Impossible Desires.* Durham: Duke University Press, 2005.

Gordimer, Nadine. *Burger's Daughter.* New York: Penguin, 1979.

Guha, Ranajit. *Elementary Aspects of Peasant Insurgency in Colonial India.* Durham: Duke University Press (New Delhi: Oxford University Press), 1983.

———. "Nationalism Reduced to 'Official Nationalism.'" *Asian Studies Association of Australia* 9.1 (1985): 103–8.

———. "On Some Aspects of the Historiography of Colonial India." *Subaltern Studies I: Writings on South Asian History and Society.* Ed. Ranajit Guha. Durham: Duke University Press (New Delhi: Oxford University Press), 1982. 1–8.

————— and Gayatri C. Spivak, eds. *Selected Subaltern Studies.* Introd. Gayatri C. Spivak. Durham: Duke University Press (New Delhi: Oxford University Press), 1988.

Gupta, R. K. "Trends in Modern Indian Fiction." *World Literature Today* 68.2 (Spring 1994): 299–307.

Habib, Irfan. "Civil Disobedience 1930–31." *Social Scientist* 25.9–10 (Sept.–Oct. 1997): 43–66.

Hagedorn, Jessica. *Dogeaters.* New York: Penguin, 1991.

Hall, Stuart. "Gramsci's Relevance for the Study of Race and Ethnicity." *Critical Dialogues in Cultural Studies.* Ed. David Morley and Kuan-Hsing Chen. London: Routledge, 1996. 411–40.

Hammad, Suheir. "First Writing Since." *Middle East Report* 221 (Winter 2001): 2–3.

Hardiman, David. *Gandhi in His Time and Ours.* London: C. Hurst and Co., 2003.

—————. *Peasant Nationalists of Gujarat.* Delhi: Oxford University Press, 1981.

Harish, Ranjana. "Evading a Self." *Nayantara Sahgal's India: Passion, Politics, and History.* Ed. Ralph J. Crane. New Delhi: Sterling Publishers, 1998. 165–73.

Harris, Nigel. *The End of the Third World.* London: I. B. Tauris and Co., 1986.

Head, Bessie. "The Wind and a Boy." *The Collector of Treasures and Other Botswana Village Tales.* Oxford: Heinemann, 1977. 69–75.

Herman, Jennifer. "The Postcolonial Pastoral in Arundhati Roy's *The God of Small Things:* Toward Politicized Representation or Silencing of a Romanticized Subaltern?" Unpublished paper, The Ohio State University, 2008.

Hogan, Patrick. *Colonialism and Cultural Identity: Crises of Tradition in the Anglophone Literatures of India, Africa, and the Caribbean.* Albany: SUNY Press, 2000.

—————. *Empire and Poetic Voice.* Albany: SUNY Press, 2003.

Hosain, Atia. *Sunlight on a Broken Column.* London: Chatto and Windus, 1961.

Hughes, Langston. "The Negro Artist and the Racial Mountain." *The Nation.* June 23, 1926. http://www.thenation.com/doc/19260623/hughes.

—————. "When the Negro Was in Vogue" *Empire City: A Treasury of New York.* Ed. Alexander Klein. New York: Ayer Publishing, 1990. 265–69.

Ibrahim, Huma. "The Troubled Past." *Between The Lines: South Asians and Postcoloniality.* Ed. Deepika Bahri and Mary Vasudeva. Philadelphia: Temple University Press, 1996. 298–312.

Ismail, Qadri. *Abiding by Sri Lanka: On Peace, Place, and Postcoloniality.* Minneapolis: University of Minnesota Press, 2005.

Iyengar, K. R. S. *Indian Writing in English.* Fifth edition. New Delhi: Sterling, 1985.

Jaggi, Maya. "An Unsuitable Girl." Review of *The God of Small Things,* by Arundhati Roy. *Electronic Mail and Guardian: Review of Books.* 13 Aug. 1997. 30 Aug. 2000. http://mg.co.za/mg/books/aug97/13aug-roy.html.

Jain, Jasbir. "The Emperor's New Clothes." *The New Indian Novel in English: A Study of the 1980s.* Ed. Viney Kirpal. New Delhi: Allied Publishers, 1990. 27–35.

—————. *Nayantara Sahgal.* New Delhi: Arnold-Heinemann, 1978.

Jalal, Ayesha. *Democracy and Authoritarianism in South Asia: A Comparative and Historical Perspective.* New Delhi: Cambridge University Press, 1995.

Jameson, Fredric. "Third World Literature in the Era of Multinational Capitalism." *Social Text* 15 (1986): 65–88.

Jani, Pranav. "Beyond 'Anticommunism': The Progressive Politics of *The God of Small Things.*" *Globalizing Dissent.* Ed. Ranjan Ghosh and Antonia Navarro. London: Routledge, 2009. 47–70.

—————. "Karl Marx, Eurocentrism, and the 1857 Revolt in British India." *Marxism,*

Modernity, and Postcolonial Studies. Ed. Crystal Bartolovich and Neil Lazarus. Cambridge: Cambridge University Press, 2002. 81–97.

———. Review. *Mapping Subaltern Studies and the Postcolonial.* Ed. Vinayak Chaturvedi. *Historical Materialism* 11.3 (2003): 271–88.

——— and Mytheli Sreenivas. "Anti-Colonialism and Resistance: South Asia." *A Historical Companion to Postcolonial Literatures in English.* Ed. Prem Poddar and David Johnson. Edinburgh: Edinburgh University Press, 2005. 20–28.

Jayawardena, Kumari. *Feminism and Nationalism in the Third World.* London: Zed Books, 1986.

Jose, D. "Now, It Is EMS's Turn to Slam Arundhati Roy!" *Rediff On The Net.* 30 Aug. 1997. 25 Aug. 2008. http://www.rediff.com/news/aug/30ems.htm.

Joyce, James. *Dubliners.* 1914. New York: Oxford University Press, 2001.

Kannabiran, Vasantha and K. Lalitha. "That Magic Time: Women in the Telangana People's Struggle." *Recasting Women: Essays in Indian Colonial History.* Ed. Kumkum Sangari and Sudesh Vaid. New Brunswick: Rutgers University Press, 1990. 180–203.

Katrak, Ketu. "Post-Colonial Women Writers and Feminisms." *New National and Post-Colonial Literatures: An Introduction.* Ed. Bruce King. Oxford: Clarendon Press, 1996.

Khair, Tabish. *Babu Fictions: Alienation in Contemporary Indian English Novels.* New Delhi: Oxford University Press, 2001.

Khan, Sayyid Ahmad. "The Causes of the Indian Revolt." Trans. Ed. Frances W. Pritchett. 2005 [1858]. http://www.columbia.edu/itc/mealac/pritchett/001itlinks/txt_sir_sayyid_asbab1873_basic.html.

Kincaid, Jamaica. *A Small Place.* New York: Farrar, Straus, Girroux, 1988.

Krishnaswamy, Revathi. "Globalization and Its Postcolonial (Dis)Contents: Reading Dalit Writing." *Journal of Postcolonial Writing* 41.1 (May 2005): 69–82.

———. "Mythologies of Migrancy: Postcolonialism, Post-Modernism and the Politics of (Dis)location." *ariel* 26.1 (Jan. 1995): 125–46.

Kumar, Gajendra and Kuldeep Kumar. "The Native Voices: A Case for the Second Tradition of the Post-Colonial Theory." *Studies in Commonwealth Literature.* Ed. Mohit Ray. New Delhi: Atlantic, 2003. 154–61.

Kumar, Radha. "Family and Factory: Women in the Bombay Cotton Textile Industry, 1919–1939." *Indian Economic and Social History Review* 20.1 (1983): 81–110.

———. *The History of Doing: An Illustrated Account of Movements for Women's Rights and Feminism in India, 1800–1990.* London: Verso, 1993.

Kuransky, Mark. *Salt: A World History.* New York: Penguin, 2003.

Lazarus, Neil. "The Global Dispensation Since 1945." *The Cambridge Companion to Postcolonial Literary Studies.* Ed. Neil Lazarus. Cambridge: Cambridge University Press, 2005. 19–40.

———. *Nationalism and Cultural Practice in the Postcolonial World.* Cambridge: Cambridge University Press, 1999.

———. "The Politics of Postcolonial Modernism." *Postcolonial Studies and Beyond.* Ranikhet: Permanent Black, 2005. 423–38.

———. *Resistance in Postcolonial African Fiction.* New Haven: Yale University Press, 1990.

Lelyveld, David. "Of Mixed Loyalties: Sayyid Ahmad Khan's Accounts of the Uprising in Bijnor." *Biblio* 12.3–4 (Mar.–Apr. 2007). http://www.biblio-india.org/archives/07/MA07/tocMA07.asp?mp=MA07.

Lenin, V. I. "The Discussion on Self Determination Summed Up." 1916. *The National*

Liberation Movement in the East. Third revised edition. Moscow: Progress Publishers, 1969. 184–93.

Lewis, Tom. "Marxism and Nationalism—Part II." *International Socialist Review* 14. Oct.–Nov. 2000. July 20, 2009. http://www.isreview.org/issues/14/marxism_nationalism_part2.shtml.

The Life of Swami Vivekananda by his Eastern and Western Disciples. Fifth edition. Calcutta: Advaita Ashram, 1981.

Livett, Jennifer. "When Less Is More." *Nayantara Sahgal's India: Passion, Politics, and History.* Ed. Ralph J. Crane. New Delhi: Sterling Publishers, 1998. 51–62.

Macaulay, Thomas Babington. "Minute on Education." 1835. *Project South Asia.* http://www.mssu.edu/projectsouthasia/history/primarydocs/education/Macaulay001.htm. July 29, 2008.

Maira, Sunaina. "Youth Culture, Citizenship, and Globalization." *Comparative Studies of South Asia, Africa, and the Middle East* 24.1 (2004): 219–31.

Mallick, Ross. *Indian Communism: Opposition, Collaboration, and Institutionalization.* Delhi: Oxford University Press, 1994.

Manto, Saadat Hasan. "Black Margins." 1948. *Inventing Boundaries.* Ed. Mushirul Hasan. New York: Oxford University Press, 2000. 287–99.

Maramkal, M. B. and Radha Rajadhyaksha. "Submerged Subcontinent." *Times of India.* July 13, 1997. *Center for the Study of Culture and Society* Archives. July 29, 2008 http://www.cscsarchive.org:8081/MediaArchive/clippings.nsf/(docid)/A8C205A5EA2713BD65256942003139B4.

Markandaya, Kamala. *The Coffer Dams.* New York: John Day, 1969.

———. *A Handful of Rice.* New York: John Day, 1966.

———. *Nectar in a Sieve.* New York: John Day, 1954.

Markels, Julian. *The Marxian Imagination: Representing Class in Literature.* New York: Monthly Review Press, 2003.

Marx, Karl. *The Eighteenth Brumaire of Louis Bonaparte.* 1852. *The Marx-Engels Reader.* Ed. Robert C. Tucker. New York: W. W. Norton, 1978. 594–617.

Mee, John. "After Midnight: The Novel in the 1980s and 1990s." *A History of Indian Literature in English.* Ed. Arvind K. Mehrotra. New York: Columbia University Press, 2003. 318–36.

Mehrotra, Arvind Krishna. Introduction. *A History of Indian Literature in English.* Ed. Arvind K. Mehrotra. New York: Columbia University Press, 2003. 1–26.

Mehta, Rama. *Inside the Haveli.* 1977. New Delhi: Penguin, 1996.

Menon, Ritu and Kamla Bhasin. *Borders and Boundaries: How Women Experienced the Partition of India.* Delhi: Kali for Women, 1998.Mishra, Vijay. "Rushdie and Bollywood Cinema." *The Cambridge Companion to Salman Rushdie.* Ed. Abdulrazak Gurnah. Cambridge: Cambridge University Press, 2007. 11–28.

Mistry, Rohinton. *A Fine Balance.* 1995. New York: Vintage, 1997.

———. *Such a Long Journey.* New York: Knopf, 1991.

Morrison, Toni. *Sula.* New York: Knopf, 1974.

Mother India. Dir. Mehboob Khan. Perf. Nargis, Sunil Dutt, and Rajendra Kumar. Mehboob Productions, 1957.

Mukherjee, Meenakshi. "Interrogating Post-Colonialism." *Interrogating Post-Colonialism: Theory, Text, and Context.* Ed. Harish Trivedi and Meenakshi Mukherjee. Shimla: Indian Institute of Advanced Study, 1996. 3–11.

———. *The Perishable Empire: Essays on Indian Writing in English.* New York: Oxford University Press, 2000.

———. *The Twice-Born Fiction: Themes and Techniques of the Indian Novel in English.* Second edition. New Delhi: Arnold-Heinemann, 1974.

Mukherjee, Mukul. "Women's Work in Bengal, 1880–1930: A Historical Analysis." *From the Seams of History: Essays on Women.* Ed. Bharati Ray. Delhi: Oxford University Press, 1997.

Naik, M. N. *A History of Indian English Literature.* New Delhi: Sahitya Akademi, 1982.

Nair, R. Madhavan. "In Solidarity: Novelist Arundhati Roy Expresses Solidarity With the Cause of Dalits and Dalit Literature." *Frontline* 16.3 (30 Jan.–12 Feb. 1999). 30 Apr. 2000. http//:www.the-hindu.com/fline/f11603/16030810.htm.

Naison, Mark. *Communists in Harlem During the Depression.* Champaign: University of Illinois Press, 2004.

Namak-Halaal. Dir. Prakash Mehra. Perf. Amitabh Bachchan, Waheeda Rahman, Shashi Kapoor, and Smita Patil. Full Moon Entertainment, 1982.

Namak-Haraam. Dir. Hrishikesh Mukherjee. Perf. Rajesh Khanna, Rekha, Amitabh Bachchan. British Screen Productions, 1973.

Narayan, R. K. *The Guide.* 1958. London: Penguin, 1992.

———. *Waiting for the Mahatma.* 1955. Mysore: Indian Thought Publications, 1997.

Narayan, Shyamala A. "The Autobiographical Element in Nayantara Sahgal's Fiction." *Nayantara Sahgal's India: Passion, Politics, and History.* Ed. Ralph J. Crane. New Delhi: Sterling Publishers, 1998. 16–27.

——— and John Mee. "Novelists of the 1950s and the 1960s." *A History of Indian Literature in English.* Ed. Arvind K. Mehrotra. New York: Columbia University Press, 2003. 219–31.

Natarajan, Nalini. "Regional Literatures of India—Paradigms and Contexts." Introduction. *Handbook of Twentieth-Century Literatures of India.* Ed. Nalini Natarajan. Westport, CT: Greenwood Press, 1996. 1–20.

"Nayanar Pours Scorn on *God of Small Things.*" *Rediff On The Net.* 3 Nov. 1997. 25 Aug. 2008. http://www.rediff.com/news/nov/03booker.htm.

Ndebele, Njabulo S. *The Rediscovery of the Ordinary: Essays on South African Literature and Culture.* Johannesburg: Congress of South African Writers, 1991.

Needham, Anuradha D. and Rajeshwari Sunder Rajan, eds. *The Crisis of Secularism in India.* Durham: Duke University Press, 2007.

Nehru, Jawaharlal. *The Discovery of India.* 1946. Delhi: Oxford University Press, 1989.

———. "Tryst With Destiny." 1947. *Mirrorwork: 50 Years of Indian Writing, 1947–1997.* Ed. Salman Rushdie and Elizabeth West. New York: Vintage, 1997. 3–4.

Ngugi wa Thiong'o. *Devil on the Cross.* 1977. Trans. Ngugi wa Thiong'o. London: Heinemann. 1982.

———. *A Grain of Wheat.* 1967. London: Heinemann, 1994.

Nixon, Rob. "Environmentalism and Postcolonialism." *Postcolonial Studies and Beyond.* Ed. Ania Loomba. Durham: Duke University Press. 233–51.

"'No Alternative to Capitalism.'" *The Hindu.* 4 Jan. 2008. 25 Aug. 2008. http://www.hinduonnet.com/2008/01/04/stories/2008010460781100.htm.

"A Novel Gesture." *Frontline* 16.14 (3–16 July 1999). 30 Apr. 2000. http://www.indiaserver.com/frontline/1999/07/03/16140360.htm.

Nussbaum, Martha. *For Love of Country: Debating the Limits of Patriotism.* Ed. Joshua Cohen. Boston: Beacon Press, 2002.

Omvedt, Gail. "Dams and Bombs-I." *The Hindu.* 4 Aug. 1999. 30 Apr. 2000. http://www.indiaserver.com/thehindu/1999/08/04/stories/05042524.htm.

———. "Dams and Bombs-II." *The Hindu.* 5 Aug. 1999. 30 Apr. 2000. http://www.indiaserver.com/thehindu/1999/08/04/stories/05052524.htm.

Orwell, George. *Animal Farm.* 1945. New York: Penguin, 1996.

———. *Burmese Days.* 1934. New York: Harcourt, Brace, Jovanovich, 1962.

Paranjape, Makarand. "The Crisis of Contemporary India and Nayantara Sahgal's Fiction." *World Literature Today* 68.2 (Spring 1994): 291–98.

———. "Inside and Outside the Whale." *The New Indian Novel in English: A Study of the 1980s.* Ed. Viney Kirpal. New Delhi: Allied Publishers, 1990. 213–26.

Parashar, Archana. *Women and Family Law Reform in India: Uniform Civil Code and Gender Equality.* New Delhi: Sage, 1992.

Parekh, Pushpa Naidu. "Redefining the Postcolonial Female Self." *Between The Lines: South Asians and Postcoloniality.* Ed. Deepika Bahri and Mary Vasudeva. Philadelphia: Temple University Press, 1996. 270–83.

Parry, Benita. *Postcolonial Studies: A Materialist Critique.* London: Routledge, 2004.

Patnaik, Prabhat. "The Left and Its 'Intellectual Detractors.'" *Macroscan.* 12 Dec. 2007. 25 Aug. 2008. http://www.macroscan.org/cur/dec07/cur121207Detractors.htm.

Pearmain, Andrew. "England, the English, and the 'National-Popular." *Soundings: A Journal of Politics and Culture.* 2007. 5 Aug. 2008. http://www.lwbooks.co.uk/journals/articles/pearmain07.html.

Perry, John Oliver, ed. *Voices of Emergency: An All-India Anthology of Protest Poetry of the 1975–77 Emergency.* Bombay: Popular Prakashan, 1983.

Persits, M. A. *Revolutionaries of India in Soviet Russia.* 1973. Trans. Lev Bobrov. Moscow: Progress Publishers, 1983.

Phelan, James. *Living to Tell About It.* Ithaca: Cornell University Press, 2005.

Pliny, the Elder. "The Various Properties of Salt." *Natural History.* http://www.perseus.tufts.edu/cgi-bin/ptext?doc=Perseus%3Atext%3A1999.02.0137&query=head%3D%232254.

Prabhu, Anjali. *Hybridity: Limits, Transformations, Prospects.* Albany: SUNY Press, 2007.

Prashad, Vijay. *The Darker Nations: A People's History of the Third World.* New York: New Press, 2007.

Ranasinha, Ruvani. *South Asian Writers in Twentieth-Century Britain.* Oxford: Oxford University Press, 2007.

Rao, Mukunda. *The Death of an Activist.* Hyderabad: Orient Longman, 1997.

Rao, Nagesh. "Cosmopolitanism, Class, and Gender in *The Shadow Lines.*" *South Asian Review* 24.1 (2003): 95–114.

———. Introduction. *Exile: Conversations with Pramoedya Ananta Toer.* Interviews by André Vitchek and Rossie Indira. Ed. Nagesh Rao. Chicago: Haymarket Books, 2006. 17–38.

———. "The Politics of Genre and the Rhetoric of Radical Cosmopolitanism; or, Who's Afraid of Arundhati Roy?" *Prose Studies* 30.2 (Aug. 2008). 159–76.

Rao, Raja. *Kanthapura.* 1938. Westport, CT: Greenwood Press, 1977.

Rege, Josna E. "Victim Into Protagonist? *Midnight's Children* and the Post-Rushdie National Narratives of the Eighties." *Critical Essays on Salman Rushdie.* Ed. M. Keith Booker. New York: G. K. Hall and Co., 1999. 250–82.

Robbins, Bruce. *Feeling Global: Internationalism in Distress.* New York: New York University Press, 1999.

Roy, Arundhati. *The Cost of Living.* Includes "The Greater Common Good" and "The End of Imagination." New York: Modern Library, 1999.

———. *The God of Small Things.* New York: Random House, 1997.

———. "It's Outright War and Both Sides Are Choosing Their Weapons." Interview with

Shoma Chaudhury. 31 Mar. 2007. *Tehelka*. 3 Sept. 2008. http://www.tehelka.com. Path: Arundhati Roy Outright.

———. "Land and Freedom." *The Guardian*. 22 Aug. 2008. 24 Aug. 2008. http://www.guardian.co.uk/world/2008/aug/22/kashmir.india.

———. "Success Devastated My Life." Interview with Shoma Chaudhury. 8 March 2008. *Tehelka*. 10Sept. 2008. http://tehelka.com. Path: Arundhati Roy Success.

———. "Tide? Or Ivory Snow? Public Power in the Age of Empire." Speech. 16 Aug. 2004. San Francisco, CA. *ZNet*. 4 Sept. 2008. http://www.zmag.org/znet/viewArticle/7996.

Roy, Srirupa. *Beyond Belief: India and the Politics of Postcolonial Nationalism*. Durham: Duke University Press, 2007.

Rushdie, Salman. "'Commonwealth Literature' Does Not Exist." 1983. *Imaginary Homelands: Essays and Criticism, 1981–1991*. London: Viking, 1991. 61–70.

———. "Günter Grass" *Imaginary Homeland: Essays and Criticism, 1981–1991*. London: Viking, 1991. 275–81.

———. *Haroun and the Sea of Stories*. London: Granta, 1990.

———. "Imaginary Homelands." 1982. *Imaginary Homelands: Essays and Criticism, 1981–1991*. London: Viking, 1991. 9–21.

———. "In Good Faith." *Imaginary Homelands: Essays and Criticism, 1981–1991*. London: Viking, 1991. 393–414.

———. Interview with Bill O'Reilly. *The O'Reilly Factor*. Fox. 22 Sept. 2005. Aug. 30, 2008. http://www.youtube.com. Path: Bill O'Reilly; Salman Rushdie.

———. Introduction. *Mirrorwork: 50 Years of Indian Writing, 1947–1997*. Ed. Salman Rushdie and Elizabeth West. New York: Vintage, 1997. vii–xx.

———. *Midnight's Children*. New York: Knopf, 1980.

———. *The Moor's Last Sigh*. 1995. New York: Vintage, 1996.

———. "Outside the Whale." *Granta* (Fall 1984): 125–38.

———. *The Satanic Verses*. 1988. New York: Viking, 1989.

———. *Step Across This Line: Collected Non-Fiction from 1992 to 2002*. New York: Random House, 2002.

———, Arundhati Roy, and Barbara Crossette. Interview with Charlie Rose. *The Charlie Rose Show*. PBS. 14 Aug. 1997. 30 Aug. 2008. http://www.youtube.com. Path: Salman Rushdie; Arundhati Roy; Charlie Rose.

Russell, Jane. *Communal Politics Under the Donoughmore Constitution, 1931–1947*. Dehiwala: Tisara Prakasakayo, 1982.

Sahgal, Nayantara. *The Day in Shadow*. Delhi: Vikas Publishing House, 1971.

———. *From Fear Set Free*. London: Victor Gollancz, 1962.

———. *Indira Gandhi's Emergence and Style*. New Delhi: Vikas Publishing House, 1978.

———. *Lesser Breeds*. Delhi: HarperCollins India, 2003.

———. *Mistaken Identity*. London: Heinemann, 1988.

———. *Point of View: A Personal Response to Life, Literature, Politics*. New Delhi: Prestige, 1997.

———. *Prison and Chocolate Cake*. 1954. New Delhi: HarperCollins India, [1965].

———. *Rich Like Us*. New York: New Directions, 1985.

———. *This Time of Morning*. New York: W. W. Norton and Co., 1965.

———. *A Time to Be Happy*. 1958. Mumbai: Jaico Publishing House, 2002.

——— and E. N. Mangat Rai. *Relationship: Extracts From a Correspondence*. New Delhi: Kali for Women, 1994.

Said, Edward W. *Culture and Imperialism*. New York: Vintage, 1994.

———. *Orientalism*. New York: Vintage, 1978.

————. "Reflections on Exile." *Reflections on Exile and Other Essays*. Cambridge: Harvard University Press, 2000. 173–86.

————. *Representations of the Intellectual: The 1993 Reich Lectures*. New York: Pantheon Books, 1994.

————. *The World, the Text, and the Critic*. Cambridge: Harvard University Press, 1983.

————. "Yeats and Decolonization." *Nationalism, Colonialism, and Literature*. Ed. Terry Eagleton, Fredric Jameson, and Edward Said. Minneapolis: University of Minnesota Press, 1990. 220–38.

Sangari, Kumkum. "The Politics of the Possible." *Cultural Critique* (Fall 1987): 157–86.

Sarkar, Sumit. "The Decline of the Subaltern in *Subaltern Studies*." *Mapping Subaltern Studies and the Postcolonial*. Ed. Vinayak Chaturvedi. London: Verso, 2000. 300–323.

————. *Modern India: 1885–1947*. Madras: Macmillan, 1983.

———— and Tanika Sarkar. "Who Is the Left?" *Hardnews*. Dec. 2007. 25 Aug. 2008 http://www.hardnewsmedia.com/2007/12/1860.

Sarkar, Tanika. *Hindu Wife, Hindu Nation: Community, Religion, and Cultural Nationalism*. Bloomington: Indiana University Press, 2001.

Scott, Helen. *Caribbean Women Writers and Globalization: Fictions of Independence*. Hampshire: Ashgate, 2006.

Shamsie, Kamila. *Kartography*. Orlando: Harcourt, 2002.

Shiva, Vandana. "In Praise of Cow Dung." *ZNet*. 20 Nov. 2002. 4 Sept. 2008. http://www.zmag.org/znet/viewArticle/11378.

————. *The Violence of the Green Revolution: Third World Agriculture, Ecology, and Politics*. Penang: Third World Network, 1991.

Singh, Anita. "Margin at the Center: Reading of *The God of Small Things*." *The Fictional World of Arundhati Roy*. Ed. R. S. Pathak. New Delhi: Creative Books, 2001: 132–36.

Singh, Khushwant. *Train to Pakistan*. New York: Grove Press, 1956.

Sinha, Mrinalini. "Britishness, Clubbability, and the Colonial Public Sphere: The Genealogy of an Imperial Institution in Colonial India." *Journal of British Studies* 40.4 (Oct. 2001): 489–521.

Sivanandan, Tamara. "Anticolonialism, National Liberation, and Postcolonial Nation Formation." *The Cambridge Companion to Postcolonial Literary Studies*. Ed. Neil Lazarus. Cambridge: Cambridge University Press, 2005. 41–65.

Spivak, Gayatri C. "Can the Subaltern Speak?" *Marxism and the Interpretation of Culture*. Ed. Cary Nelson and Lawrence Grossberg. Urbana: University of Illinois Press, 1988. 271–313.

————. *A Critique of Postcolonial Reason: Toward a History of the Vanishing Present*. Cambridge: Harvard University Press, 1999.

————. *Death of a Discipline*. New York: Columbia University Press, 2003.

————. "Subaltern Studies: Deconstructing Historiography." *Subaltern Studies IV: Writings on South Asian History and Society*. Ed. Ranajit Guha. Delhi: Oxford University Press, 1985. 330–63.

Sreedharan, Chindu. "Booker or Not, Arundhati's Still in the Dock." *Rediff On The Net*. 15 Oct. 2007. 25 Aug. 2008. http://www.rediff.com/news/oct/15case.htm.

Sreenivas, Mytheli. *Wives, Widows, and Concubines: The Conjugal Family Ideal in Colonial India*. Bloomington: Indiana University Press, 2008.

Sri, P. S. "Twentieth-Century Tamil Literature." *Handbook of Twentieth-Century Literatures of India*. Ed. Nalini Natarajan. Westport, CT: Greenwood Press, 1996. 289–305.

Stein, Burton. *A History of India*. Oxford: Blackwell, 1998.

Steingass, Francis J. *A Comprehensive Persian-English Dictionary, Including the Arabic Words and Phrases to Be Met With in Persian literature*. London: Routledge & K. Paul, 1892.

Stree Shakti Sanghatana, ed. *"We Were Making History": Women and the Telangana Uprising*. London: Zed Books, 1989.

Subbarayudu, G. K. and C. Vijayasree. "Twentieth-Century Telugu Literature." *Handbook of Twentieth-Century Literatures of India*. Ed. Nalini Natarajan. Westport, CT: Greenwood Press, 1996. 306–29.

Tagore, Rabindranath. *The Home and the World*. 1919. Trans. Surendranath Tagore. London: Penguin, 1985.

Tarlo, Emma. *Unsettling Memories: Narratives of the Emergency in Delhi*. Berkeley: University of California Press, 2003.

Tharoor, Shashi. "1947, First-Hand." *The Hindu* (online). 15 Aug. 2004. 4 Aug. 2008. http://www.shashitharoor.com/articles/hindu/1947-first.php.

———. *The Elephant, The Tiger, and the Cell Phone: The Emerging 21st Century Power*. New York: Arcade Publishing, 2007.

———. *The Great Indian Novel*. 1989. New York: Arcade, 1991.

———. *India: From Midnight to Millennium*. New York: HarperPerennial, 1997.

Tharu, Susie and K. Lalitha, eds. *Women Writing in India: 600 B.C. to the Present*. 2 vols. Delhi: Oxford University Press, 1993.

Trivedi, Harish. "India and Post-Colonial Discourse." *Interrogating Post-colonialism*. Ed. Harish Trivedi and Meenakshi Mukherjee. Shimla: Indian Institute of Advanced Study, 1996. 231–47.

Trotsky, Leon. *History of the Russian Revolution*. 1932–33. Trans. Max Eastman. New York: Pathfinder Press, 1980.

———. *Literature and Revolution*. 1923. London: RedWords, 1991.

Truax, Alice. "A Silver Thimble in Her Fist." Review of *The God of Small Things*, by Arundhati Roy. *New York Times on the Web*. 25 May 1997. 25 Aug. 2008. http://www.nytimes.com/books/97/05/25/reviews/970525.25truaxt.html.

Vaidyanathan, A. *The Indian Economy: Crisis, Response, and Prospects*. New Delhi: Orient Longman, 1995.

Vanaik, Achin. *The Painful Transition: Bourgeois Democracy in India*. London: Verso, 1990.

Varma, Rashmi. "Provincializing the Global City: From Bombay to Mumbai." *Social Text* 22.4 (Winter 2004): 65–89.

Viswanathan, Gauri. *Masks of Conquest: Literary Study and British Rule in India*. New York: Columbia University Press, 1989.

West, Lori A., ed. *Feminist Nationalism*. London: Routledge, 1997.

Wilson, A. Jeyaratnam. *Sri Lankan Tamil Nationalism: Its Origins and Development in the Nineteenth and Twentieth Centuries*. Vancouver: University of British Columbia Press, 1999.

Wilson, Kalpana. "Arundhati Roy and the Left: For Reclaiming 'Small Things.'" Review of *The God of Small Things*, by Arundhati Roy. *Liberation*. Jan. 1998. 25 Aug. 2008. http://www.cpiml.org/liberation/year_1998/january/books.htm.

Wilson, Keith. "*Midnight's Children* and Reader Responsibility." *Reading Rushdie*. Ed. M. D. Fletcher. Amsterdam: Editions Rodopi B. V., 1994. 55–68.

Xala. Dir. Ousmane Sembene. Perf. Thierno Leye, Seun Samb, Younouss Seye, Myriam Niamg. 1975. Videorecording. New Yorker Films, 2005.

index

Abbott, H. Porter, 250n16
Achebe, Chinua, *Things Fall Apart,* 18, 207
Adiga, Aravind, *The White Tiger,* 24, 243
Africa: and the postcolonial world, 32, 93, 99, 150, 173, 188; and Anglophone novels, 7, 31, 43, 172. *See also individual artists and theorists*
African-American writers. *See* Ellison, Ralph; Hughes, Langston; Morrison, Toni
Ahmad, Aijaz: on *The God of Small Things,* 191–92, 209–11, 220–32 *passim,* 254n19; on Indian literature, 247n7; Marx and India, 255n1; modernism and postmodernism, 75, 148; nationalism, 188–90, 247n14. *See also* Communism; Marxism
Aidoo, Ama Ata, "For Whom Things Did Not Change," 184, 195
Akhmatova, Anna, "Lot's Wife," 245n1
Ali, Tariq, 179, 183, 243, 247n6
Anand, Mulk Raj, 59; and M. K. Gandhi, 42; and Progressive Writers' Association, 34–35, 41–42, 247n13; *Untouchable,* 42, 73
Anderson, Benedict, *Imagined Communities,* 15, 34–35, 55, 246n2
Appadurai, Arjun, 157–58, 247n14
Appiah, K. Anthony, 8, 27, 33, 44
Armah, Ayi Kweh, *The Beautyful Ones Are Not Yet Born,* 171, 195, 214–15

Bhabha, Homi, 86–87, 169, 234, 247n14. *See also* hybridity; identity
Bhattacharya, Bhabani, *He Who Rides a Tiger,* 60–61; *Shadow from Ladakh,* 40, 59, 249n13
Bose, Brinda, 210–13, 227
Bose, Purnima, 103, 250n8
Brennan, Timothy, *At Home in the World,* 3, 37, 44, 146–47, 245n2, 247n14; *Salman Rushdie and the Third World,* 27, 245n5, 249n12, 251n2

capitalist modernity: and cosmopolitanism, 26–27, 37–38, 43, 74–81, 245n9; and the environment, 215–20; and the postcolonial world, 30–37, 57, 98–101; as state capitalism, 30–31, 35, 235, 247n10, 249n4, 252n4. *See also* cosmopolitanism; postcolonial development, representations of
Chandra, Bipan, 32, 247n14, 248n1, 250n5, 252n19
Chandra, Vikram, *Red Earth and Pouring Rain,* 50, 194, 235
Chatterjee, Partha, "The Nationalist Resolution to the Women's Question," 103–4, 246n13; critique of postnationalism, 158, 247n14, 252n12
Cheah, Pheng, 44, 247n18, 248n23, 253n26

Chughtai, Ismat, 34, 41.

Clear Light of Day (Desai), 6, 10, 98, 101–2, 108–11, 121–40, 194–95, 240, 250n14, 251n28; contexts of, 104–8; family/nation, violence of, 127–33; feminist narrative strategies of, 108–11; NRI nationalism, critique of, 121–27; as political novel, 101–2; and tradition, return to, 137–40. *See also* Desai, Anita

Coffer Dams, The (Markandaya), 6, 10, 54, 59, 61, 63–66, 81–97, 194; contexts of, 59–63; "hybridity," alternatives to, 86–94; *The God of Small Things,* comparison, 215; narrative strategies of, 63–65; postcolonial modernity, critique of, 81–86, 87–93, 94–97; sexual violence, 86, 93–94, 95; subalternity and knowledge, 86–92. *See also* Markandaya, Kamala

Cohn, Bernard, 249n14

Communism: and anticolonial struggle, 189, 253n25; contemporary intellectuals and, 220, 224, 228–32 *passim;* and the Emergency, 140, 252n22, 254n19; *The God of Small Things,* CPI(M)'s critique of, 191–94, 209, 254n17; *Midnight's Children* and, 153; and post-Emergency movements, 223–24; Roy on, 202–4, 220–23, 225–26, 229; Sahgal on, 117, 135, 145–46, 252n22. *See also* Marxism

cosmopolitanism, 37–52: "cosmopolitics," 39, 246n14; gendered, 121–27; and hybridity, 81–94; in Indian (English) writing, 37–44; nationalism, as antagonistic to, 21, 44, 57–58; 252n7; and middle-class subjectivity, 26–27, 37–38, 43, 74–81; multiplicity of, 5–11, 38. *See also* capitalist modernity; *namak-halaal* cosmopolitanism; nationalism

Davidson, Basil, 32, 74

Das, Veena, 35

Day in Shadow, The (Sahgal), 6, 10, 98, 101–2, 108–21, 133–40, 175, 195, 250n14; contexts of, 104–8; feminist narrative strategies of, 108–13;

nationalism in, 117–21, 133–35, 175; political consciousness, representations of, 113–17; as political novel, 101–2; tradition, return to, 135–37. *See also* Sahgal, Nayantara

Desai, Anita, 6, 10, 105, 134, 140, 194, 236; *Clear Light of Day,* 108–11, 121–40. See also *Clear Light of Day*

Deshpande, Shashi, *The Dark Holds No Terrors,* 106

Ellison, Ralph, *Invisible Man,* 206–7

Emecheta, Buchi, *The Joys of Motherhood,* 102, 171

Emergency, the, 35–36, 43–44, 98–99, 141–42, 151, 183, 247n22, 250n5, 250n6, 252n19, 252n22; Ghosh on, 170–71; Indian English novel, shifts in, 7–11, 20–21, 25, 36, 235–37; in *Midnight's Children,* 153, 156–57, 166–74, 251n1; in *Rich Like Us,* 174–75, 178–85; Sahgal and Rushdie on, 141–43; Sahgal and, 100, 108, 117–20, 136; and postnational turn, 50–52; and shifts in the Indian English novel, and women's movements, 104–6. *See also* Gandhi, Indira

English, writing in. *See under* Indian literatures

Faiz, Faiz Ahmad, 33; "Dawn of Freedom," 60, 62–63, 101

Fanon, Frantz, 15; on colonized intellectual, 75–77; on nationalism/internationalism, 189

feminist nationalism. *See* postcolonial women's writing; women

film, 2, 27, 34, 150, 157, 227, 245n4; *Mother India,* 1–5; *Namak-Halaal,* 45, 248n30; *Namak-Haraam,* 248n30; *Xala,* 150

Forbes, Geraldine, 105, 250n10, 251n21

free indirect style, 68–69, 85, 89–91, 109–110, 113, 115, 123, 180, 215, 246n12

Gandhi, Indira, 7, 20, 35–36, 98–101, 150, 249n1, 250n6, 251n30, 252n18,

252n22; in *Midnight's Children,* 153, 72, 175, 178; in *Rich Like Us,* 183; in Sahgal's nonfiction, 100, 108, 150. *See also* Emergency, the

Gandhi, Leela, 37, 39, 42, 59, 61

Gandhi, M. K.: as cosmopolitan, 58, 67; and Anand, 42; as ideological influence on writers, 60–61, 142, 195; 249n8, 252n11 (*see also* Sahgal, Nayantara); in "Tryst with Destiny," 55, 141, 238; Roy, alternatives to, 201, 238; and Salt Satyagraha, 48–49; and women, 251n21. *See also* Nehru, Jawaharlal; nationalism

Ghosh, Amitav, "The Ghosts of Mrs. Gandhi," 148, 170–71; *The Glass Palace,* 186–87, 243, 254n9; *The Shadow Lines,* 35–36, 50, 141, 145, 186, 199, 235, 251n26, 252n16

God of Small Things, The (Roy), 6, 11, 63, 92, 191–232 *passim;* Aijaz Ahmad on, 191–92, 209–11, 220–32 *passim,* 254n19; big things/small things, paradigm of, 197–204; class politics of, 220–27; CPI(M)'s critique of, 191–94, 209, 254n17; "dialectic of suffering and redemption" in, 171, 204–9; as a leftist, *namak-halaal* text, 196, 229–32; narrative structure of, 197–201, 213–15; as "postcolonial pastoral," 215–20; postmodernist historiography, rejection of, 205–6, 229; subaltern, representations of, 144–45, 206–9; resistance, 92, 215; sexuality and power in, 209–15. *See also* Roy, Arundhati

Ghosh, Bishnupriya, 36, 246n14, 247n18

globalization. *See* capitalist modernity; postcolonial development, representations of

Gopal, Priyamvada, 248n25; "'Curious Ironies,'" 58–61; *Literary Radicalism in India,* 23, 33–35, 41, 247n8, 247n13; Postcolonial Studies after Iraq, 158

Gramsci, Antonio: "national-popular" 56–57; "imperial-universal," 76; "pessimism of the intellect, optimism of the will," 214–15

Guha, Ranajit, 15, 143–44, 246n2; bourgeois nationalism, critique of, 150, 187, 248n1; Benedict Anderson, critique of, 34–35, 252n5; subaltern narratives, recovering, 185, 197, 252n4; subalternity and anticolonial nationalism in early *Subaltern Studies,* 143–44. *See also* subalternity

Habib, Irfan, 48

Hall, Stuart, 56, 248n2

Hammad, Suheir, "First Writing Since," 241–42

Hardiman, David, 48

Head, Bessie, "The Wind and a Boy," 191, 195–96, 253n8

history: historicist criticism (*see* Marxism: aesthetics); "history from below," 143–45, 205–6; literary representations of, 88–89, 157, 164–65, 235–36; 243; *namak-halaal* cosmopolitanism, contexts of, 39–44, 54–59; 98–102, 104–8; postcolonial world, contexts, 30–37; postmodern turn and, 19–20, 103–4

Hogan, Patrick, *Colonialism and Cultural Identity,* 247n13, 247n20; *Empire and Poetic Voice,* 66, 89, 245n9, 247n17

Hughes, Langston, "The Negro Artist and the Racial Mountain," 33; "When the Negro Was in Vogue," 243, 255n4

hybridity: as celebrated category, 2–3, 19, 50–51; *The Coffer Dams,* alternatives to, 86–94; and elite contexts, 35–36; and totality, 245n9

identity, 5, 9–11; and "competence," 89–91, 247n17; constructions of colonial, 249n9; cosmopolitanism, class, and, 20–27 *passim,* 37–44 *passim; namak-halaal* orientation and, 8, 49; and subjectivity, 245n9; voice and regaining, 86–94, 110–16, 120–27, 127–33, 206–8, 230–31, 251n9. *See also* interiority; narrative strategies; subalternity ideology, 8–11, 20–1, 136–37, 174, 193, 196; and orientation, 40, 46. *See also* Marxism: aesthetics

imperialism, 12–13, 14–15, 35, 232; and language, 16–17, 24–25; and literature, 40–41, 243; and nationalisms, 44, 46–49, 145–46, 186–90

implied audience, 8, 40, 51, 238, 241–42, 246n12; and pre-Emergency narratives, 78–79, 89, 106, 108–10, 113, 119, 122, 131–32, 138; and post-Emergency narratives, 141–42, 146, 152–54, 159–68 *passim,* 174–76, 180, 183, 186; and real audience, 2, 142, 242; and subalternity, 196, 199–201, 207–8, 219, 231

implied author, 113, 120, 128, 236, 246n12; implied author and post-Emergency narratives, 146–47, 154–57, 160–69, 186, 195, 207, 223, 229, 236; and real author, 156, 222, 228

India, anticolonial struggle in. *See* Gandhi, M. K.; Guha, Ranajit; nationalism

Indian literatures: and "bilingualism," 41–43; colonialism's influence on, 40–41; Indian writing in English, dominance of, 23–25, 35–36; diversity of, 3, 21, 53; cosmopolitan-elite production of, 5–6, 27–28, 42–44; elites and Englishness, 37–38, 57–58, 70–71, 74–79, 233–34, 249n10; and *namak-halaal* cosmopolitanism, 40; Progressive Writers' Association and, 33–34, 58–59; Rushdie's changing perspectives on, 14, 16–18, 23–24; and women's writing, 105–7

intellectuals, 233–44. *See also* cosmopolitanism

interiority, 10–11, 68, 154, 236; free indirect style and, 109; politics of, 85, 101–2, 106–7, 176, 207; and women's voices, 110–16; 121–27, 138, 198–201. *See also* narrative strategies

internationalism, 38; and anticolonial nationalism, 54–57, 186–90, 248n5; liberal versions of, 76, 146, 149–50. *See also* Marxism; nationalism

Iraq, 11, 158, 188–89, 202–3, 228, 233, 243

Jain, Jasbir, 177, 179, 250n14
Jalal, Ayesha, 249n2
Jayawardena, Kumari, 121, 250n8, 251n21
Joyce, James, "A Little Cloud," 251n25
Jussawala, Adil, 42–44

Katrak, Ketu, 107–8
Khair, Tabish, 28, 159, 246n14, 251n20
Khan, Sayyid Ahmad, 45, 248n25
Krishnaswamy, Revathi, 23, 31, 245n7, 247n8
Kumar, Radha, 105, 107, 250n9, 250n13
Kuransky, Michael, 46–49

Lahiri, Jhumpa, 243
Lazarus, Neil, 247n14; "The Global Dispensation Since 1945," 30–31; *Nationalism and Cultural Practice,* 144, 244, 248n3, 252n4, 252n7; Postcolonial Studies after Iraq, 158; *Resistance in Postcolonial African Fiction,* 7, 214–15; "The Politics of Postcolonial Modernism," 19. *See also* Postcolonial Studies

Lelyveld, David, 248n25
Lenin, V. I.: on anti-imperialism, 189; and Indian Communists, 189–90, 253n25; and Marx on anticolonial nationalism, 253n26

Macaulay, Lord Thomas Babbington, "Minute on Indian Education," 52, 76–77
magical realism. *See under* realism
Maira, Sunaina, 173
Manto, Saadat Hasan, 34, 252n16
Markandaya, Kamala, 6, 10, 43, 60–61; *The Coffer Dams,* 81–97; *A Handful of Rice,* 81; *Nectar in a Sieve,* 59, 61. See also *Coffer Dams, The*
Marx, Karl, 29–30, 253n26, 255n1
Marxism: and aesthetics, 9–11, 21–20, 25–29, 193–96, 220–32 *passim (see also* narrative strategies, realism), and middle-class subjectivity, 42–44,

245n9; and subalternity, 143–45, 251n3

Midnight's Children (Rushdie), 6, 10–11, 36, 52, 100–101, 151–74, 186–87, 246n10; and Booker victory,14–15, 20–21, 50, 59, 235–36; compared with *The God of Small Things*, 193–95; as elite-centered, 141–44, 151, 171–74, 179, 186–87; gender and narrative in, 159–66; nation as palimpsest in, 100–101, 142, 184, 252n11; postnational narrative strategies in, 151–59, 169–74; subaltern agency in, 166–69. *See also* Rushdie, Salman

Mehta, Rama, *Inside the Haveli*, 106

migrancy, 1–2, 7, 37–38, 123–27, 149, 159, 173, 240–41. *See also* cosmopolitanism

Mistry, Rohinton: *A Fine Balance*, 36, 50, 235; *Such a Long Journey*, 252n16

modernity. *See under* capitalist modernity; postcolonial development, representations of

Morrison, Toni, *Sula*, 213

Mother India (Khan), 1–3, 5

Mukherjee, Meenakshi: "Interrogating Postcolonialism," 246n3, 247n9; *Perishable Empire*, 51, 194; *Twice-born Fiction*, 68

namak-halaal cosmopolitanism, 7, 20–21, 39–40, 45–50, 57–66; from *namak-halaal* to postnational, 36–37, 99–102; *namak-halaal* versus postnational, 7–8, 49–52, 80, 142–44, 145–50, 151–59, 235–38, 241–44. *See also* cosmopolitanism

Narayan, R. K., 59, 61

narrative strategies, 113, 246n12, 250n17; concordant/discordant, 8, 146, 236, 246n12. *See also* free indirect style; implied audience; implied author

nationalism: cosmopolitanism, as antagonistic to, 21, 44, 57–58, 252n7; as reactionary, 21, 55, 57–58, 143; and radical possibilities, 32–35; and sub-

altern agency, 34–35, 143–44; feminist nationalism and women's writing, 102–10; as heterogeneous, 34–35, 186–90; as imagined community, 15, 55; and internationalism, 186–90; and *namak-halaal* orientation, 60–63, 194–95, 233, 241; and nation-statism, 32, 74; and "national-popular," 56–57; as site of cross-class alliance, 31, 48–49, 58–60; "NRI nationalism," 51, 123–25, 239–40, 251n24; Rushdie and, 1–5, 17–18, 155–56, 173–74, 238–41; in postnational writing, 51–2, 100–101, 151–59, 238–41; postnational turn and failures of, 31–32, 35–37, 235–36

Ndebele, Njabulo: "The Rediscovery of the Ordinary," 116, 196, 204–5, 209, 241. *See also* subalternity

Nehru, Jawaharlal, 2, 54–57; and cosmopolitanism, 37–38, 42, 57–58, 120–21, 145–46; India after, 7, 35, 61, 99, 107–9, 141, 179, 235, 248n32; influence on Nayantara Sahgal (niece), 22, 74, 120, 135, 145, 149–51, 178, 249n8; policies of, 35–36, 99, 248n5, 249n13; representations of, 60–63, 79–81, 129–31; in Rushdie, 152, 159, 172; and tradition, 134–35; "Tryst with Destiny," 54–57; and "unity in diversity," 51, 248n31; and women's education, 120–21. *See also* nationalism; postcolonial development, representations of; "Tryst with Destiny"

Ngugi wa Thiong'o, *Devil on the Cross*, 171, 195

9/11: and Postcolonial Studies, 12, 158; and Rushdie, 22, 247fn6

Nixon, Rob, 216–20; 254n18

Nussbaum, Martha, 44

Omvedt, Gail, 254n20

Orwell, George: *Animal Farm*, 52–53; *Burmese Days*, 249n9; Rushdie and, 53

Palestine, 217, 233–34, 241

Paranjape, Marakand, 14, 42–44, 115, 117, 140, 247n22

Partition: and *Clear Light of Day*, 101, 110, 121, 129–31; in "Dawn of Freedom" (Faiz), 62–63; as failure of nationalism, 33, 56, 139, 150, 185; imagining the end of, 239; in *Midnight's Children*, 153; portrayals of refugees from, 79–80, 129–30; in *Train to Pakistan* (Singh), 61–62; in "Tryst with Destiny" (Nehru), 55–56.

Phelan, Jim, 154, 250n15, 250n17

postcolonial cultural production: restoring diversity of 1–5, 19–22, 53. *See also* Indian literature; Postcolonial Studies

postcolonial development, representations of, 195–96; and Nehruvian modernity, 60–61, 63–67, 78–84, 94–99; and 1970s, 99–101, 117–21, 129–30; and neoliberal phase, 191–96, 201–4, 229–30, 238–40, 253n8, 254n16, 254n20. *See also* capitalist modernity; subalternity

postcolonial pastoral. See under *God of Small Things, The*

Postcolonial Studies: cosmopolitanism and postcoloniality as limited concepts, 3, 6, 8, 11, 13, 44; historicism and "postcoloniality," 20–22, 26, 140, 194–95, 235, 240–44; "hybridity" in, 86–87; postmodern theory and, 15–16, 19, 24, 235–36; migrancy in, 37–38; nationalism and, 21, 55, 57–58, 187–88; Said and, 233–35; "subalternity" in, 143–45; women and nation in, 102–4. *See also* postcolonial development, representations of

postcolonial women's writing, 6, 102–10, 139–40, 237–38; cosmopolitanism and gender, 121–27; the family in, 111–15, 127–33, 197–98; gender and class in, 198–201; in India, 101–2, 105–8; and interiority, 101–2, 106–7, 110–16, 121–27, 138; narrating public/private spheres, 108–10; and "political novel," genre of, 101–2, 253n5; representations of rape and

sexual violence, 61, 86, 93–95, 182, 197–98, 200, 212, 225; and tradition, 107–8, 133–40. *See also* sexuality, representations of

postmodernism: aesthetics versus epistemology, 11, 193–96, 202–4, 205–7, 228–30, 254n20; and *Midnight's Children*, 153–55, 159–60; and modernism, 4–5, 75; and oppositional politics, 10, 188, 212; the postcolonial and, 3, 4, 7, 15–16, 87, 143, 157–59, 235–36; the *telos* of, 51, 154, 171, 186

postnational cosmopolitanism. *See* cosmopolitanism; *namak-halaal* cosmopolitanism

Prabhu, Anjali, 245n9

Prashad, Vijay, 35, 252n10

Progressive Writers' Association (PWA): and anticolonial nationalism, 7, 34–35, 58, 62; Communist influence in, 247n13; cosmopolitan origins of, 41

Rao, Raja, *Kanthapura*, 41, 59, 73

Rao, Mukunda, 24

Rao, Nagesh, 35, 247n10, 253n5

realism: contemporary critique of, 31, 160, 165–66; and irony, 96; magical realism and *namak-halaal* orientation, 193–96 *passim*, 255n24; magical realism and "Rushdie", 2, 6–8; multiple forms of postcolonial, 6–7, 52–53; new forms of, 243; and psychology, 8, 10, 43, 101, 106–7, 110; as sign of the political, 210; shifts in modes of, 8–10, 24, 31, 33; social-realism, complexity of, 5, 85, 113, 131; "socialist" realism, 28–29, 247n13. *See also* interiority; Marxism: aesthetics, narrative strategies

Rich Like Us (Sahgal), 6, 10, 36, 174–185, 186–87; compared with *The God of Small Things*, 230–31; compared with *A Time to Be Happy*, 120, 249n11; cosmopolitanism and poverty, 183–85; as *namak-halaal* but elite-centered, 141–44, 172, 174–75,

186–87; narrative strategies and sub-altern resistance in, 175–79; subaltern voices, spectrum of, 179–85. *See also* Emergency, the; Sahgal, Nayantara

Robbins, Bruce, 44, 247n18, 252n7

Roy, Arundhati, 6, 11, 63, 236, 253n5; *The God of Small Things*, 191–232; "The Greater Common Good," 201–2, 219–20, 228, 254n20; on Iraqi resistance, 188–89; on Maoist insurgencies, 202–4; as public intel-lectual, 191–96, 206, 228–30, 233, 253n4; roundtable with Rushdie and Charlie Rose, 238–41. See also *God of Small Things, The*

Roy, M. N., 189

Roy, Ram Mohun, 37

Roy, Srirupa, 245n4, 248n31, 249n13

Rushdie, Salman, 1–5, 6, 11–13, 14–15, 19–20, 22; autobiographical, 25, 246n1, 147–51; "Commonwealth Literature Does Not Exist," 16–18, 23–24, 41, 247n21; comparison with Sahgal, 9, 145–50, 242–43; "Imaginary Homelands," 1, 2–5, 159, 246n2; knighthood (2007), 12; *Midnight's Children*, 14–15, 20–21, 100–101, 151–74; *Mirrorwork* introduction, 14, 18, 23–25, 173; and 9/11, 22, 247fn6; "Outside the Whale," 53, 150; roundtable with Roy and Charlie Rose, 238–41; ver-sus "Rushdie," 6–7, 9, 11–13. See also *Midnight's Children*

Sahgal, Nayantara, 6, 9–10, 22, 33, 105, 116, 140, 236–37; *The Day in Shadow*, 108–21, 133–40; *From Fear Set Free*, 151; Gandhian/Nehruvian influences on, 64–69, 74–75, 78–81, 117–21, 146–49, 174, 178–79, 183, 242–43; 249n8; *Indira Gandhi's Emergency and Style*, 100, 250n6; as *namak-halaal* and nationalist, 59–63; *Point of View*, 134; *Prison and Choc-olate Cake*, 145–49, 150–51; *Rela-tionship*, 116, 250n18; *Rich Like Us*, 174–85; *A Time to Be Happy*, 66–81.

See also *Day in Shadow, The; Rich Like Us; Time to Be Happy, A*

Said, Edward, 15, 233–35, 246n2, 247n14, 252n7; *Culture and Impe-rialism*, 18; *Orientalism*, 15, 235, 255n1; "Reflections on Exile," 247n19; *Representations of the Intel-lectual*, 233–43 *passim*; *The World, the Text, and the Critic*, 39; "Yeats and Decolonization," 216–17, 220

Salih, Tayeb: *Season of Migration to the North*, 33, 41

salt: history and symbolism of, 46–49; in language, 45, 47–48; pillars of, 1, 4–5, 245n1; redefining loyalties, 45–46, Salt Satyagraha, 48–49

Sangari, Kumkum, 188

Sarkar, Tanika, 104, 248n1, 254n22

Sarkar, Sumit, 248n1, 252n6, 252n20, 254n22

Scott, Helen, 21, 25–26, 31–32

Sembene, Ousmane, *Xala*, 150

sexuality, representations of: as "bour-geois decadence," 191, 254n17; as emancipatory space, 92, 210; as contradictory sign of modernity, 211–15; as site of modern violence, 61, 86, 93–95, 113–15, 127–33, 182, 197–98, 200, 212, 225; and "trysts," 54–57, 61, 62. *See also* postcolonial women's writing

Shiva, Vandana, 164, 249n3

Singh, Khushwant, *Train to Pakistan*, 40, 60–62, 237, 248n6

Sivanandan, Tamara, 33, 41, 247n14

Spanish Civil War, 42, 145–47

Spivak, Gayatri, 15; and the postnational: 157, 234, 247n14; and the subaltern: 143–44, 204, 234, 252n4

Sreenivas, Mytheli, 103–4, 247n11

subalternity: and early *Subaltern Stud-ies*, 143–45, 251n3; and anticolonial nationalism, presence in, 34–35, 54–57, 252n5; and bourgeois nation-alism, critique of, 150, 187, 248n1; and "rediscovery of the ordinary," 116, 196, 204–5, 209, 236, 241; and sexuality (*see* sexuality, representa-tions of); and Spivak, 143–44, 204,

234; subaltern narratives, recovery of (Markandaya, Roy, and early Sahgal), 71–73, 81–84, 86–94, 185, 197, 199–201, 207–8, 219, 228–32, 252n4; subaltern voices, representations of (Rushdie and later Sahgal), 144–45, 166–73, 175–85

Tagore, Rabindranath, *The Home and the World,* 2, 145, 245n1; 252n7; references to, 3, 103, 145–46
Tarlo, Emma, 35, 99, 247n15; 247n16; 250n5
Tharoor, Shashi: *The Great Indian Novel,* 36, 50, 235; and India: 56, 173–74, 252n17
"Third World," 35, 248n5, 252 n10. *See also* postcolonial development, representations of
Tharu, Susie, 41, 106
Time to Be Happy, A (Sahgal), 6, 10, 33, 54, 59, 60–63, 66–81, 100; comparisons with: *The Coffer Dams,* 63–66, 94–97; *The Day in Shadow,* 119–20; *The God of Small Things,* 208; *Rich Like Us,* 177; colonialism and racism, critique of, 69–71; cosmopolitanism and poverty, 71–73; early postcolonial contexts of, 59–63; narrative strategies of, 66–73; Nehruvian resolutions in, 73–81. *See also* Sahgal, Nayantara
Trivedi, Harish, 3
Trotsky, Leon, 28–29, 90, 249n15. *See also* Marxism: aesthetics
"Tryst with Destiny" (Nehru), 54–57, 69, 14, 238; comparison with "Dawn of Freedom" (Faiz), 60–62; contrast with Indian realities, 99, 101. *See also* Nehru, Jawaharlal

Vanaik, Achin, 105, 224, 249n3
Viswanathan, Gauri, 37, 77

women: gender and narrative, 93–95, 110–16, 121–27, 159–66, 198–201; and *namak-halaal* writing, 6, 139–40, 237–38; and nation, 10, 102–10, 117–21, 250n8, 251n2; Nehru, Gandhi, and, 120–21, 251n21; and 1970s movements, 104–8. *See also* postcolonial women's writing
Williams, Raymond, 10, 26

Zinn, Howard, 206